THE LOCUST EFFECT

THE LOCUST EFFECT

WHY THE END OF POVERTY REQUIRES THE END OF VIOLENCE

BY
GARY A. HAUGEN AND VICTOR BOUTROS

OXFORD
UNIVERSITY PRESS

OXFORD
UNIVERSITY PRESS

Oxford University Press is a department of the University of Oxford.
It furthers the University's objective of excellence in research, scholarship,
and education by publishing worldwide.

Oxford   New York
Auckland   Cape Town   Dar es Salaam   Hong Kong   Karachi
Kuala Lumpur   Madrid   Melbourne   Mexico City   Nairobi
New Delhi   Shanghai   Taipei   Toronto

With offices in
Argentina   Austria   Brazil   Chile   Czech Republic   France   Greece
Guatemala   Hungary   Italy   Japan   Poland   Portugal   Singapore
South Korea   Switzerland   Thailand   Turkey   Ukraine   Vietnam

Oxford is a registered trademark of Oxford University Press
in the UK and certain other countries.

Published in the United States of America by
Oxford University Press
198 Madison Avenue, New York, NY 10016

Library of Congress Cataloging-in-Publication Data
Haugen, Gary A.
The locust effect : why the end of poverty requires the end of violence /
by Gary A. Haugen and Victor Boutros.
pages cm
ISBN 978–0–19–993787–5 (hardback : alk. paper)   1. Violence—Developing countries.
2. Poor—Violence against—Developing countries.   3. Poverty—Developing countries.
4. Human rights—Developing countries.   5. Law enforcement—Developing countries.
I. Boutros, Victor.   II. Title.
HN981.V5H39 2013
305.5′69091724—dc23
2013013401

9 8 7 6 5 4 3 2 1
Printed in the United States of America
on acid-free paper

For Jan
with gratitude for your sheltering tree of grace

CONTENTS

INTRODUCTION

It was my first massacre site. Today the skulls are all neatly stacked on shelves, but when I first encountered them, they definitely were not. They were attached to bodies—mostly skeletal remains—in a massive mess of rotting human corpses in a small brick church in Rwanda. As the director of the tiny United Nations "Special Investigations Unit" in Rwanda immediately following the genocide in 1994, I was given a list of 100 mass graves and massacre sites across an impoverished, mountainous country where nearly a million people had been slaughtered—mostly by machete—in a span of about 10 weeks. When I stepped off the military transport plane to join the small international team of criminal investigators and prosecutors that were assembling in the Rwandan capital in the early weeks after the genocide, the country carried an eerie, post-apocalyptic emptiness. I didn't even realize, until I was loading into a van outside the airport, that I had entered Rwanda without passing through customs and immigration—because there was no customs and immigration. The usual and powerfully subconscious markers of order and civilization—and security—had been utterly swept away in an engulfing orgy of genocidal war. And it didn't feel good.

In those early days, my task was to help the UN's Commission of Experts make a gross accounting of what had taken place and to begin gathering evidence against the leaders of the genocide (it would be more than a year before any international tribunal would be set up). But with hundreds of thousands of murders, where were we to start?

We ended up starting in Ntarama, a small town south of Kigali, in a small church compound where all the bodies remained just as their killers had left them—strewn wall to wall in a knee-high mass of corpses, rotting clothes and the desperate personal effects of very poor people hoping to survive a siege.

But they did not survive.

And now four Spanish forensic experts were working with me in picking through the remains and lifting out each skull for a simple accounting: "Woman—machete. Woman—machete. Child—machete. Woman—machete. Child—machete. Child—blunt trauma. Man—machete. Woman—machete..." On and on it went for hours.

Our task was to assemble from survivor testimony and the horrible mess of physical evidence a very precise picture of how mass murder actually happens. And over time, the question began to take a fierce hold on me. I couldn't stop trying to picture it in my mind. What is it like, exactly, to be pressed up against the back wall of this church with panic on every side from your terrified family as the steel, blood-soaked machetes hack their way to you through your screaming and slaughtered neighbors?

What eventually emerged for me, and changed me, was a point of simple clarity about the nature of violence and the poor. What was so clear to me was the way these very impoverished Rwandans at their point of most desperate need, huddled against those advancing machetes in that church, did not need someone to bring them a sermon, or food, or a doctor, or a teacher, or a micro-loan. They needed someone to restrain the hand with the machete—and nothing else would do.

None of the other things that people of good will had sought to share with these impoverished Rwandans over the years was going to matter if those good people could not stop the machetes from hacking them to death. Moreover, none of those good things (the food, the medicine, the education, the shelter, the fresh water, the micro-loan) was going to stop the hacking machetes. The locusts of predatory violence had descended—and they would lay waste to all that the vulnerable poor had otherwise struggled to scrape together to secure their lives. Indeed, not only would the locusts be undeterred by the poor's efforts to make a living, they would be fattened and empowered by the plunder.

* * *

Just as shocking to me, however, was what I found following the Rwanda genocide as I spent the next two decades in and out of the poorest communities in the developing world: a silent catastrophe of violence quietly destroying the lives of billions of poor people, well beyond the headlines of episodic mass atrocities and genocide in our world.

Without the world noticing, the locusts of common, criminal violence are right now ravaging the lives and dreams of billions of our poorest neighbors. We have come to call the unique pestilence of violence and the punishing impact it has on efforts to lift the global poor out of poverty *the locust effect*. This plague of predatory violence is different from other problems facing the poor; and so, the remedy to the locust effect must also be different. In the lives of the poor, violence has the power to destroy everything—and is unstopped by our other responses to their poverty. This makes sense because it can also be said of other acute needs of the poor. Severe hunger and disease can also destroy everything for a poor person—and the things that stop hunger don't necessarily stop disease, and the things that stop disease don't necessarily address hunger. The difference is that the world *knows* that poor people suffer from hunger and disease—and the world gets busy trying to meet those needs.

But, the world overwhelmingly does not know that endemic to being poor is a vulnerability to violence, or the way violence is, right now, catastrophically crushing the global poor. As a result, the world is not getting busy trying to stop it. And, in a perfect tragedy, the failure to address that violence is actually devastating much of the other things good people are seeking to do to assist them.

For reasons that are fairly obvious, if you are reading this book, I'm pretty sure you are not among the very poorest in our world—the billions of people who are trying to live off a few dollars a day. As a result, I also know that you are probably not chronically hungry, you are not likely to die of a perfectly treatable disease, you have reasonable access to fresh water, you are literate, and you have reasonable shelter over your head. But there is something else I know about you. I bet you pass your days in reasonable safety from violence. You are probably not regularly being threatened with being enslaved, imprisoned, beaten, raped, or robbed.

But if you were among the world's poorest billions, you would be. That is what the world does not understand about the global poor—and that is what this book is about. Together, we will make the difficult journey into the vast, hidden underworld of violence where the common poor pass their days out of sight from the rest of us. My colleagues at International Justice Mission (IJM) spend all their days walking through this subterranean reality with the poorest neighbors in their own communities in the developing world; in this volume, their intimate stories allow the data and statistical reality to take on flesh and a human heart that matters to us.

IJM is an international human rights agency that supports the world's largest corps of local, indigenous advocates providing direct service to impoverished victims of violent abuse and oppression in the developing world. In poor communities in Africa, Latin America, South Asia, and Southeast Asia, IJM supports teams of local lawyers, investigators, social workers, and community activists who work full-time to help poor neighbors who have been enslaved, imprisoned, beaten, sexually assaulted, or thrown off their land. These teams work with local authorities to rescue the victims from the abuse and to bring the perpetrators to justice—and then they work with local social service partners to walk with the survivors on the long road to healing, restoration, and resilience for the long haul. And after thousands of individual cases, their stories have brought a different reality of poverty to the surface.

When we think of global poverty we readily think of hunger, disease, homelessness, illiteracy, dirty water, and a lack of education, but very few of us immediately think of the global poor's chronic vulnerability to violence—the massive epidemic of sexual violence, forced labor, illegal detention, land theft, assault, police abuse, and oppression that lies hidden underneath the more visible deprivations of the poor.

Indeed, I am not even speaking of the large-scale spasmodic events of violence like the Rwandan genocide, or wars and civil conflicts which occasionally engulf the poor and generate headlines. Rather, I am speaking of the reality my IJM colleagues introduced to me in the years that followed my time in Rwanda—the reality of common, criminal violence in otherwise stable developing countries that afflicts far more of the global poor on a much larger and more persistent scale—and consistently frustrates and blocks their climb out of poverty.

But we simply do not think of poverty this way—even among the experts. Perhaps the highest profile statement of the world's most fundamental priorities for addressing global poverty were set forth by the UN in its Millennium Development Goals—eight economic development goals endorsed by 193 nations at the UN's Millennium Summit in 2000 as *the* framework for galvanizing the world to attack global poverty. And yet, in that monumental document, addressing the problem of violence against the poor is not even mentioned.

This is particularly tragic because, as we shall see, the data is now emerging to confirm the common-sense understanding that violence has a devastating impact on a poor person's struggle out of poverty, seriously undermines economic development in poor countries, and directly reduces the effectiveness of poverty alleviation efforts. It turns out that you can provide all manner of goods and services to the poor, as good people have been doing for decades, but if you are not restraining the bullies in the community from violence and theft—as we have been failing to do for decades—then we are going to find the outcomes of our efforts quite disappointing.

This is not to say, of course, that poverty alleviation efforts haven't met with some impressive results—especially in reducing the most extreme forms of poverty, i.e. those who live off $1.25 a day. But as we shall see, the number of people forced to live off $2.00 a day (more than 2 billion) has barely budged in thirty years, and the studies are now accumulating to make a nexus to common violence undeniable. No one will find in this volume any argument for reducing our traditional efforts to fight poverty. On the contrary, the billions still mired in fierce poverty cry out for us to redouble our best efforts. But one will find in these pages an urgent call to make sure that we are safeguarding the fruits of those efforts from being laid waste by the locusts of predatory violence.

In fact, as you encounter these intimate stories of how common poor people are relentlessly ambushed by violence in the developing world, have an eye for the brutal real-life implications of these terrifying events for the individuals who endure them—the productive capabilities lost, the earning potential stolen, the confidence and well-being devastated by trauma, the resources ripped away from those on the edge of survival and poured instead into the pockets of predators. Then, as you consider the statistical data that multiplies these devastating individual tragedies by the millions across the developing world, you will sense the scandalous implications of this failure to address the massive sinkhole of violence that is swallowing up the hope of the poor.

But perhaps even more surprising than the failure to prioritize the problem of violence against the poor is the way that those who do appreciate the problem ignore the most basic solution—and the solution they rely upon most in their own communities: law enforcement. As we shall see together, the poor in the developing world endure such extraordinary levels of violence because they live in a state of de facto lawlessness. That is to say, basic law enforcement systems in the developing world are so broken that global studies now confirm that most poor people live outside the protection of law. Indeed, the justice systems in the developing world make the poor poorer and less secure. It's as if the world woke up to find that hospitals in the developing world actually made poor people sicker—or the water systems actually contaminated the drinking water of the poor.

One would hope that if the world woke up to such a reality, it would swiftly acknowledge and respond to the disaster—but tragically, the world has neither woken up to the reality nor responded in a way that offers meaningful hope for the poor. It has mostly said and done nothing. And as we shall see, the failure to respond to such a basic need—to prioritize criminal justice systems that can protect poor people from common violence—has had a devastating impact on two great struggles that made heroic progress in the last century but have stalled out for the poorest in the twenty-first century: namely, the struggle to end severe poverty and the fight to secure the most basic human rights.

Indeed, for the global poor in this century, there is no higher-priority need with deeper and broader implications than the provision of basic justice systems that can protect them from the devastating ruin of common violence. Because as anyone who has tasted it knows, if you are *not safe*, nothing else matters.

The Locust Effect then is the surprising story of how a plague of lawless violence is destroying two dreams that the world deeply cherishes: the dream to end global poverty and to secure the most fundamental human rights for the poor. But the book also reveals several surprising stories about why basic justice systems in the developing world came to be so dysfunctional. It turns out that when the colonial powers left the developing world a half a century ago, many of the laws changed but the law *enforcement* systems did not—systems that were never designed to protect the common people from violence but to protect the regime from the common people. These systems, it turns out, were never re-engineered.

Secondly, given the brokenness of the *public* justice system, forces of wealth and power in the developing world have carried out one of the most fundamental and unremarked social revolutions of the modern era in building a completely parallel system of *private* justice, with private security forces and alternative dispute resolution systems that leave the poor stuck with useless *public* systems that are only getting worse.

Finally, for surprising historical reasons (and to tragic effect), the great agencies of poverty alleviation, economic development, and human rights have purposely avoided participating in the strengthening of law enforcement systems in the developing world.

From a realistic confrontation with the challenge, *The Locust Effect* pivots toward the great hope for change that comes from history and current projects of transformation quietly going forth in the world. It turns out that just about every reasonably functioning public justice system in the world today was, at one time in history, utterly dysfunctional, corrupt, and abusive. *The Locust Effect* seeks to recover the lost and inspiring story of how, in relatively recent history, justice systems were transformed to provide reasonable protection for even their weakest citizens. Moreover, great signs of hope are profiled in a variety of demonstration projects being carried out by IJM and other agencies around the world that demonstrate it is possible to transform broken public justice systems in the developing world so they effectively protect the poor from violence.

To secure meaningful hope, however, we must be standing on the solid rock of reality. A breezy wishful thinking that has not seriously confronted the depth of the problem will not do. Before the world could begin to turn the corner on the AIDS epidemic, as it has now begun to do, millions of perfectly healthy people around the world had to stomach an honest look at what was happening to millions of other people in the world who were dying in horrific ways on an apocalyptic scale. From that brave refusal to look away—a decision made by millions of common people around the globe who could have turned the page, changed the channel, or clicked away—a hope grounded on hard reality was found, and a steady march out of the darkness has begun.

Likewise, a better day for the poorest in our world will only come as we are willing to walk with them into the secret terror that lies beneath the surface of their poverty. Accordingly, we would ask you to *decide* to persevere through these first chapters as they take you, with some authentic trauma, through that darkness—because there is real hope on the other side. Later, not only will we discover together a fresh and tangible reminder from history of how diverse developing societies reversed spirals of chaotic violence and established levels of safety and order once considered unimaginable, but we will also explore a number of concrete examples of real hope emerging today, including projects from IJM, other non-governmental organizations and government agencies, that have measurably reduced the poor's vulnerability to some of the worst forms of violence—including sex trafficking, slavery, sexual abuse, torture, and illegal detention.

Before jumping in, however, a few clarifying notes seem critical.

This volume is not meant to be the last word on anything. It is meant primarily as a conversation-starter about an immense problem that is not being addressed with anything like the urgency, thoughtfulness, and resources it deserves. The book introduces a number of massive topics of tremendous complexity: levels and categories of criminal violence against the poor; the impact of violence on economic development, poverty alleviation, and the modern human rights struggle; the legacy of colonial justice systems in the developing world; the privatization of justice systems; the story of justice systems in aid programs; the political economy of criminal justice systems in the developing world; the history of law enforcement development; current experiments in justice system reform; and more. Each of these topics touches on a vast field of intellectual endeavor that features diverse experts, scholarly literature, treatises, and the latest academic article just posted to the Internet. What follows, therefore, is not exhaustive in any area but is hopefully a coherent and provocative weaving of credible arguments that makes the case for urgent and energetic engagement with the woefully neglected global crisis of violence against the poor.

It is also critical to note at the outset that while my co-author and I think access to law enforcement that protects the poor from common criminal violence is critical to their advancement and well-being, we emphatically do *not* think law enforcement is the only thing that protects people from violence. Criminal violence is a highly complex social phenomenon with many contributing factors that have to be addressed. Our simple argument is that if one tries to stop criminal violence by addressing these other contributing factors *in the absence of a credible law enforcement deterrent*, such an approach will fail (and *is* failing in the developing world). Secondly, while we appreciate and hope to learn from the successes of Western forms of law enforcement, as civil rights lawyers, we are deeply familiar with the failings of our own criminal justice systems. Having spent our early careers addressing systematic law enforcement abuses in the United States, we can affirm that there are no acts of abuse, brutality, or corruption occurring overseas that we have not seen within systems in our own country. Nor do we believe that Western systems of criminal justice offer cookie-cutter solutions for other countries. The best solution will come from a combination of home-grown, highly-contextualized remedies with the best of what might fit from external sources. What we want is for the poorest in our world to have whatever criminal justice systems will work best in their context to protect them from violence—whatever that might be.

This volume is simply the story of that long journey of terrible discovery from the piled carnage inside the church in Ntarama to the deeply hidden plague of everyday violence that is the terror of global poverty in our day. In either case, the challenge is to see violence for what it is and to end the impunity that allows it to happen again. In Ntarama, the remains we pulled out in 1994 are all neatly stacked on shelves in a genocide memorial now constructed at the site. If the stark reminder of what we are capable of doing *to* each other, and what we are capable of failing to do *for* each other provokes to action the better—and more courageous—angels of our nature, that would be a worthy memorial.

In the following pages, some of the names have been changed and some images have been obscured to protect the identities of those involved.

The views expressed by Victor Boutros are his own and do not purport to represent the views of the U.S. Department of Justice.

THE LOCUST EFFECT

WHAT ARE WE MISSING?

In many ways it makes perfect sense that the world cannot see what is happening in the Peruvian town of La Unión.

Even if I try to use the miraculous geography tool of Google Earth to simply find La Unión, I cannot see the town at all. From the eye altitude of 60,000 feet provided by Google Earth, the whole town completely disappears into the craggy topography of the Andean mountains. By contrast, if I use Google Earth to swoop down into my own neighborhood, I can not only find my town, my townhouse, and my parked car—I can also read the words on the marquee of the local art house theater. But the entire Andean town of La Unión—with its cathedral, courthouse, hospital, Inca ruins, stadium, schools, central market, town square, and thousands of residents—cannot be seen at all.

I don't think Google is to blame for this. The resolution of its images for any particular spot on the globe has depended upon "points of interest and popularity," and most of the world is perfectly happy to view La Unión from 12 miles in the air—that is, not at all. This muted global demand for high-resolution images of anything in La Unión is largely a matter of market economics. Somebody has to pay for those satellites and imaging technology, and it's not likely to come from the purchasing power of La Unión's indigenous Quechan townspeople.

But there's another reason that you and I can't see this little town: there is nothing terribly wrong happening there—or so it seems.

Google Earth, to its credit, actually has a special layer of images that allows us to see more clearly places of noteworthy catastrophe, like genocide, deforestation, conflict, or severe need that would otherwise be lost in global remoteness—places like the Eastern Congo, where, in 2011, armed conflict in the region reportedly gave rise to an epidemic of sexual assaults against women at the stunning rate of 48 rapes *every hour.*[1]

In comparison to that kind of horror, what is there to see in the Huánuco region where La Unión sits?

What about a prevalence rate of rape that appears comparable to that of the war-torn Congo?*

The first time I visited Huánuco, the regional capital city with about 200,000 people in the surrounding area, the local newspaper reported that the medical examiner had seen 50 rape victims walk into his office in just 5 days.[2] Moreover, the medical examiner who had personally examined each of the 50 victims told me that each of the girls were between the ages of 10 and 13. Worse, perhaps, no one I spoke with—lawyers, local leaders, victim advocates—could remember *anyone* being sent to prison for one of these or any other sexual assaults.

Apparently there was *something* going on in these Andean mountain towns—something horribly wrong.

To the rest of the world, the Huánuco region might look like another unremarkable outpost of remote and routine developing-world poverty; and in many ways it is. But two local Peruvian lawyers were eager to take me deeper. The ugliness beneath the surface of a town like La Unión had bubbled up and left a corpse in the streets—the brutalized body of an 8-year-old girl.

The little girl's name was Yuri, and one early morning somebody had dumped her crumpled body in a small pool of blood and gravel in the main street—her skull crushed, her legs still wrapped in wire cables, and her panties bunched around her ankles. The perpetrators hadn't even bothered to

---

* Distributed over the Congo's 70 million people, the reported rate of 48 rapes every hour suggests a rate of 16 rapes per 200,000 people every 5 days. In Huánuco, one medical clinic recorded 50 rapes over a population of 200,000 in 5 days. This is not, of course, a systematic comparison of sexual assault prevalence, but simply illustrative of the way outrageous levels of everyday sexual violence against the poor in the developing world can take place deep below the radar of the headlines.

dump her body a few feet away in the river that rushed with mountain speed through the center of town.

A girl so young, so openly and horribly murdered, so casually left to be taken out with the city's morning trash—maybe this one grotesque assault in La Unión would tell the world something about the hidden violence rolling with quiet devastation through the lives of Peru's weakest and most vulnerable.

Entering into the depth of this one terrible story would not be easy, however, and would take me into the surreal intimacy, cruelty, and in-your-face corruption of murder in a small town—where everybody knows everybody, where everybody knows exactly what they've done to whom, where guilt and innocence pass one another in the street, and where the strong mock the weak, over generations.

This is why I found myself curled into the fetal position, fighting waves of nausea in a late-model Toyota winding its way to La Unión—up 7,000 vertical feet of nonstop, hairpin turns on the green-carpeted and terraced pyramids of the Andes mountains. In the front seats were José and Richard, two Peruvian lawyers, who wanted the world to know what was happening there.

Richard and José are both lawyers for one of Peru's most respected human rights agencies, Paz y Esperanza. As the sheer mountain cliffs and hairpin turns of our bumpy journey left me commending my soul to God, they happily chatted, laughed, made jokes at one another's expense, and celebrated the way the newly paved road to La Unión had cut the drive in half, down to four hours.

Richard was born in Huánuco, the first in his family to get any substantial education while his father drove trucks on these same dangerous roads. Richard is generous to a fault: He works too hard, gives too much, and promises his wife every year to take better care of himself. He's a deeply kind and earnest man, with ebullience, a massive smile, easy laughter, and a touch of mischievousness. After all, Richard says he became class president of his law school in Huánuco by exposing the corrupt dean who was selling coveted job placements to the highest bidders. Today, I doubt there is another lawyer in Peru who has worked harder and longer than Richard to send child rapists to prison.

José, paradoxically, began his legal career getting people *out* of prison. During the ugly, bloody years of vicious conflict between Peru's Fujimori regime and the terrorists of the Shining Path in the 1990s, thousands of innocent Peruvians disappeared into prison through secret trials held by the government's terrorist courts. José and his colleagues at Paz y Esperanza came to the defense of impoverished Peruvians accused of crimes, risking being snatched up by the very same system of abusive detention they were fighting. José survived those years and, with his activist wife, went on to help launch Paz y Esperanza's work addressing sexual violence against the poor. For them, that work began in 2003—the same year Yuri's little body had turned up bound and broken in the streets of La Unión.

YURI'S STORY

José and Richard wanted to show me what outsiders almost never see. Not a remote and picturesque Quechan town; hearty tourists see these little communities all the time. Not Third World poverty; everybody going to the developing world or "emerging market" countries sees the shacks, the raggedy kids, the garbage heaps, the outhouses, the dirty water.

Rather, Richard and José wanted to take me beneath this familiar surface to see the vast, subterranean world of violence where the poor move and have their being—and to lay bare the <u>forces that work very hard to keep the poorest submerged in this suffocating</u> underworld of physical brutality and <u>humiliating abuse.</u>

Nobody, for instance, actually saw what was being done to Yuri that dark night in La Unión in 2003—except for Yuri and the perpetrators, and they are not talking. The aftermath of this violence is also usually not dumped out like Yuri was on the main street for everyone to see—rather, it is thrown in the river, locked in a room, held behind bars, covered up with a blouse, buried in the ground. It's no wonder there can be communities in Peru with rates of sexual violence like that of the rate of rape in one of the worst war zones in Africa—and you and I wouldn't hear a peep.

What else are we missing?

* * *

Horribly, Yuri's 11-year-old brother Jhon was among those who first found Yuri's body in the streets that cold December morning. "I remember the morning I left my house," Jhon told me. "Someone was banging on the door of our house—and I heard someone say someone killed my sister."

It was before 5:00 in the morning on December 19, 2003, and Jhon and his uncles and aunts hurried down the gravelly main street of adobe and cinderblock storefronts from their small home to the sidewalk where a small crowd had begun to gather. They knew the spot because it had been the place of celebration the very night before.

Despite the struggles of fierce poverty, Jhon's mother and extended family had made it possible for Jhon to go to primary school—and to graduate. The night before, Jhon's teacher and graduating class of 30 sixth graders gathered with their families and sponsors at a rented party hall to celebrate this significant milestone in the life of the community. Jhon had been looking forward to his school party for weeks. His mother, Lucila, who had been forced to look for work hundreds of miles away, couldn't come, but she had scrimped and saved to send him his first suit for the occasion.

Jhon tells me that for a month in advance of the graduation, he had secretly been pulling the dark suit from its package, trying it on, and carefully putting it back in its place. In the old photo he hands me, I can see him inside the party hall, posing stiffly between his grandmother and his uncle, looking very well-behaved in his slightly oversized, double-breasted, dark blue suit and tie, holding his graduation certificate. It's a very nice photo of a very big day in the life of a very poor family.

But behind Jhon in the photo, I can also see the staircase leading up to the living quarters of the locally powerful family that owns the party hall—the staircase where the blood stains would be found the next day, and the staircase where Yuri was last seen alive.

Yuri lived with her brother and relatives just a few blocks from the party hall. A spunky little 8-year-old with big dark eyes and broad, smiling Quechan cheeks, Yuri made the family laugh even when there wasn't a lot to laugh about. She had followed her big brother to the celebration with her pack of friends, all bundled in layers against the chilly Andean air. The hall was filled with kids and music and a traditional feast of roast pig. Yuri and her friends were busy playing and exploring, occasionally climbing the stairs to the upper level, where Jhon told us the owners were selling cheap toys to parents looking for Christmas gifts for their new graduates. As the evening went on and the children filtered out, the well-worn party hall filled with adults, and the older crowd began to drink away the night from the landlords' makeshift bar.

Pedro Ayala and his wife Kelly owned the party hall and lived in the residence above with their 19-year-old son, Gary, and an 11-year-old boy we'll call Jerardo—a runaway from a sexually abusive home who had been working for food and shelter there. By Richard and José's description, the Ayalas seemed like familiar stock characters for a small, impoverished town like La Unión: those who are aggressive and clever enough to know how to make money in a poor community. The Ayalas turned their party hall into a disco-theque at night, sold beer and food, operated the neighborhood pay phone, sold clothes, and hawked plastic toys at Christmas or anything else that might be within reach of those with meager means. In a community of per-vasive poverty, deferential modesty, and fragile day-to-day existence, there are those who seem to manage their days with an uncommon and force-ful self-assertion that comes to take on its own momentum of power and gain. Against a landscape of dreary squalor, they are the ones with the large painted house, the satellite dish on the roof, the teenagers in trendy clothes, and plastic covers on their furniture. The common poor will point to them as the ones who have money, the powerful ones, the important ones, the "somebodies." This is how Yuri's family described the Ayalas—and by com-parison, their family and the rest of the poor people in La Unión were, in their words, "little people," and "nobodies."

*   *   *

It was a small crowd of these "nobodies" who had gathered around Yuri's lifeless body in the street below the Ayala's second floor balcony the morn-ing after the graduation celebration. Eleven-year-old Jhon found his sister with wire cables binding her hands and legs, and her panties rolled down to her ankles. "She had scrapes and bruises everywhere," he told me, "They broke her legs at the knees, and her head was smashed in."

"She looked like a lamb split open," Aunt Carmen added.

The last time they had all seen Yuri was inside the Ayala's party hall. Gathered around the body, the aunts, uncles and young Jhon were hit with the sickening realization that they had inadvertently left Yuri there the night before, everyone thinking someone else had taken the little girl home. One of the children who had been at the party said that he had seen Yuri go up the stairs to Ayala's second-floor residence, and that, although he remained by the stairs, he never saw her come back down.

Eventually, Pedro Ayala emerged from the house. He saw the little corpse lying in the street and the neighbors huddled outside his home—but strangely, he manifested no curiosity or concern and headed down the main street without a second glance.

Two police officers and a prosecutor were called to the scene and col-lected Yuri's body to take it to the morgue. But when the police and prosecu-tor departed without asking the Ayalas any questions or even entering their home, Yuri's relatives and neighbors grew agitated. What was happening? Feeling desperate, they hurriedly made their way into the party hall.

Upstairs, they found a dirty mattress on the floor, soaked with blood and other stains. Next to it were Yuri's little boots, her hat, and several layers of her clothes. Pedro's wife, Kelly Ayala, tried to claim that the clothing was hers, but the items were clearly those of a small child, and the relatives readily identified them as Yuri's. Then, next to the rooftop sink where the Ayalas did their laundry, Yuri's relatives found more of her clothing (soaking wet) and a bloody shirt, later identified as Gary's—the Ayala's 19-year-old son.

A little later that morning, Jerardo, the Ayala's 11-year-old "house servant," was taken by the police to the hospital to meet with a psychologist to debrief about what, if anything, he had seen. According to the boy's statement, he had fallen asleep in the party hall, but was awakened in the middle of the night by a little girl crying out, "Mommy, mommy, mommy!" and Gary and Pedro's voices. Jerardo said he tried to go upstairs to see what was going on, but was stopped by Gary, who told him that it was just kids playing in the street and not to worry about it. Jerardo went back to sleep, but when he woke up in the early morning and went upstairs, he found a little girl covered in a blanket next to Pedro, who was drunk. Jerardo nudged the little girl, he said, but there was no response. Jerardo recounted how Pedro had yelled at him to keep quiet, threatened to take him back to his violent stepfather, and ordered him to go clean up the party hall. When Jerardo returned upstairs, the little girl's body was gone.

Eventually, the police returned to the Ayalas' house that morning and carted away the mattress, Yuri's boots and clothes, and the bloody half-washed shirt from the rooftop laundry. Yuri's relatives then made their way to the hospital, where they were told the little girl's body had been taken for an autopsy. And now, dreadfully, they had to decide who was going to tell Yuri's mom the unspeakable news.

*   *   *

Lucila was hundreds of miles away doing what she had been doing all her life—working hard to scratch out a life for herself and her family. Lucila carries the features of a traditional Quechan woman—dark eyes, high cheek bones, and a low center of gravity—but she is of the generation that has transitioned out of the traditional dress of wool skirt, knit shawl, and black fedora. On my visit to La Unión, she was dressed in jeans and a warm brown pull-over, with her dark hair up. As we walked through her town, she brought me by the tiny hovel of stone, adobe, and corrugated tin where she grew up, only a few hundred yards from where Yuri's body was found in the street.

As a child, Lucila was able to attend school when there was enough family stability and income to support it, but like so many Andean children, she mostly remembers spending endless hours miles from home, alone in the mountains, tending the family's pigs, goats, and sheep. Eventually she had to leave school altogether when her family crumbled under the strain of her father's drunkenness and violence. Years later, when Lucila was married and raising Jhon and Yuri, her home would be shattered again. They had found work north of Lima, but her husband grew abusive and violent, and Lucila felt like she and Yuri (Jhon was back in school in La Unión, staying with his grandmother) were no longer safe. Lucila separated from her husband, scrambled for work on her own, and sent Yuri to live with her mom and relatives back in La Unión.

This is how Lucila found herself hundreds of miles away on that dark morning. It was now up to Lucila's brothers and sister to find a way to let her know what had happened to her little girl. There are lots of mobile phones in the developing world for sure, but the poorest like Lucila and her family still depend upon a friend, a relative, or shopkeeper in the neighborhood who has a phone.

"A neighbor came banging on the door early in the morning," Lucila said. "The neighbor was yelling, 'There's someone on the phone for you.' So I got dressed and went down the street to the public phone."

Lucila's sister Carmen was supposed to make the call—but she found she couldn't talk and had to hand the phone to her brother's wife.

"Someone on the phone said, 'Yuri has been murdered at the party hall,'" Lucila told me, her dark eyes now beginning to swim with tears. "That's all they said. I collapsed. I couldn't talk. I thought, 'What enemies do I have? People don't even know us. Why was Yuri at the party hall? Who did this?'"

Hanging up the phone, Lucila realized she couldn't afford to take any of the daytime buses to La Unión ($15), so she would have to wait for the cheaper all-night bus. On the winding unpaved roads up the mountains, it was going to take 12 hours to get to La Unión—12 hours to turn over and over in her mind those horrible, strange words: "Yuri has been murdered at the party hall."

* * *

Lucila may come from a world of dirt floors, contaminated water, illiteracy, and a relentless trail of quiet humiliations that come with desperate need, but there are hints of familiar dreams. I got a glimpse of them from Lucila's treasured photographs of Yuri in cherished moments of abundance—a birthday party, a trip to the beach, a school pageant, a parade—each a monumental effort by Lucila to give her girl a special occasion like the kind she might see a child have in the middle-class houses she cleaned. My favorite photo (below) shows 4-year-old Yuri standing proudly on a chair, hands behind her back, with a wide smile in front of a massive birthday cake. There are mounds of food on a neat white tablecloth, decorations, plastic party cups, and, in the far corner, Lucila, trying unsuccessfully to lean out of the picture. Like any suburban mom, she is beaming with pride over what she's put together for her little girl.

Over the years, I have sat with many very poor mothers and fathers as they have shared their stories of surviving genocide, slavery, murder, torture, humiliating rapes, and abuse. The pain they describe is unfathomable—and

Figure 1.1

the mental temptation is to imagine that the people who endure it are some-how fundamentally different from me. Maybe, somehow, they just don't feel things like I do. Maybe they expect less, care less, hope for less, want less, or need less. But painfully, over time, I have seen that they are *exactly* like me—and what Yuri endured on that mattress or what Lucila endured in her 12-hour bus climb up the Andean mountains was in no way easier for them because they are poor. Like any parent, Lucila just wanted to know what happened to her daughter. She wanted people to do the right thing, and she wanted to see the sick people who murdered her daughter brought to justice.

But sadly, as Lucila stepped off that bus in La Unión, she would have no idea of the forces already arrayed against her—and by the time she knew what she was up against, it would be too late.

*   *   *

It's true that most acts of "common" violence take place beyond our view, but rape and homicide are particularly messy crimes. And in Yuri's case, the perpetrators left behind a shameful mess. With a tortured and murdered little girl on the sidewalk right *outside* their home, and a bloody mattress and the victim's clothing *inside* their home, the Ayalas would have a lot of work to do to find alternate explanations for the crime that didn't involve them. Shortly after the police removed Yuri's body and the physical evidence from the home, Kelly Ayala slipped out of the house and headed a few blocks across town to purchase the services of the man who would know what to do: a local lawyer named Estacio Flores.

This is the typical moment, José and Richard explained to me, when the struggle for justice ceases to be a fair fight for the poor in the developing world. In rural Peru, they explained, if you are a victim of a crime and you want the law enforcement system to seek justice on your behalf, you have to pay for it. Period. José and Richard acknowledge this can sound strange for people from the developed world, where relatively well-financed public justice systems pay for police investigators, prosecutors and examining mag-istrates to seek justice on behalf of the victims of violent crime—indeed, in developed countries these violent offenses are considered a crime against the state.

But in Peru—and much of the developing world—these services must be purchased. While wealthy and powerful perpetrators will definitely pay to defend themselves (legitimately and illegitimately), poor people, living off $1.00 to $2.50 dollars a day, simply cannot. So their cases do not move forward, there is no justice for those who abuse them, and there is no meaningful deterrent to stop it from happening again.

When a mother like Lucila goes to see the public prosecutor, Richard explained, "The first thing the prosecutor is going to ask is: 'Do you have money?'—either to pay for the operating expenses for the prosecutor to work on the case, or to pay for a private lawyer who will do the work for the prosecutor." Lucila did not have the money for a $15 bus ride to recover the body of her slain daughter, let alone the resources to hire a lawyer to take up her case.

"But here is a case of obvious rape and murder," I asked Richard. "What's going to happen if the mother cannot pay?"

Richard just looked at me for a moment with his kind eyes and a slightly pained expression—pained because I didn't understand something so obvious, or pained because he was embarrassed for his country, or pained because of what this meant for mothers like Lucila. Probably all three.

"If she doesn't have money," Richard said, "*nothing* is going to happen."

I would later meet a half-dozen other mothers from the Huánuco region who had joined together to represent hundreds of mothers whose daughters had been raped. They told me the same thing: "They just dismiss us and say, 'I can't help you,' when they see we do not have money. We don't get justice," they said simply and painfully, "because we are poor."

*   *   *

The consequence of their inability to pay for someone to safeguard the investigation of Yuri's death became quickly apparent to Lucila's family. Under Peruvian law, the victim's family is entitled to have a representative present for the autopsy, but according to Yuri's family the prosecutor in the case, Rosario Fretell, refused to allow anyone from their family in. She did, however, allow Estacio Flores, the Ayala's lawyer, to be present, which was especially odd because his clients (Pedro and Gary Ayala) had not yet been accused of any crime.

During the autopsy, a vaginal sample was taken from the victim and the presence of sperm was identified.[3] But mysteriously, these samples—which would have established the identity of Yuri's assailant—were thrown out and never recovered. The doctor who took them later testified that the director of the hospital told him that the samples had been thrown out but could give no reason for doing so.[4] Likewise, Yuri's underwear was still on her body when she arrived at the morgue, but Fretell—the official responsible for evidence-gathering—never secured this critical source of biological evidence.

Later the same day, the doctor who took the first vaginal samples was given a very strange order from the director of the hospital. He was ordered to go to the house of Yuri's relatives where the family and friends were grieving, and to take new vaginal samples from the child's body—at the wake. Such a procedure actually required authorization from the court and the presence of the prosecutor, but the director had neither. Also, strangely, present with the director of the hospital in giving these directions was the lawyer the doctor recognized from the autopsy—Flores—who now, when asked, lied and said he was the lawyer for *Yuri's* family.

Amazingly, Yuri's relatives say Flores used the same lie when he arrived later that night with two police officers and two medical staff at their little one-room hovel. According to Yuri's family, Flores ordered all of the gathered family and friends out of their own home, and over their confused and distressed objections, he shamelessly put the mortified hospital staff to work collecting samples again, telling the family, "Don't worry. Nothing will happen. I am your lawyer. In life she was my niece, too. I am your lawyer."

There was one more thing Flores needed: the clothing that was taken off Yuri's body. While waiting outside the hospital during the autopsy, Aunt Carmen had quickly gone to buy a clean white dress for Yuri. After washing Yuri's body and wrapping her in the new lace dress, the family had brought home her old clothes—and with them, all the forensic traces they contained. At the home, Flores insisted that the family hand over the clothes. Reluctantly, Yuri's Uncle Obed complied, thinking that the man claiming to be "their lawyer" was trying to help them. The clothes would disappear with the original bio samples—never to be seen again—and the new bio samples would "mysteriously" show no sperm.

But what about the bloody mattress and the clothes found that morning in the Ayala's home? They had been transferred from the police to the prosecutor's office, where they were never examined or entered into evidence. In fact it wasn't until many months *after* the trial that acquitted Pedro and Gary Ayala, when Richard and his colleagues were finally brought in on the case, that the mattress was found locked away in the prosecutor's closet. The whole mattress had been completely washed and scrubbed clean.

Most stunning of all, the blood stained portion of the mattress had been cut off, and the mattress re-sown back together as if nothing happened. This seemed so absurd to me when Richard first told me about it that I had trouble picturing it in my mind—but then I looked at the pictures myself. There is the photo taken in the Ayala's house the morning Yuri's body was found: I can see the off-white mattress with seven blue and green stripes running length-wise, with blood stains on the left portion of the mattress. Then there is the picture of the mattress from the prosecutor's office: same off-white mattress with the distinctive blue and green stripes running length-wise. But now, there are only four stripes—not seven. The left third of the mattress has been sliced off, and sown back up on the side—as if no one would notice, or, more accurately, as if it would never matter even if someone did notice.

Figure 1.2

Figure 1.3

Within a very short time, and in an absurdly obvious fashion, the Ayala's lawyer, the director of the hospital, the police captain, and the town prosecutor had managed to get rid of the biological evidence from the autopsy, the victim's clothing, and the bloody portions of the mattress where the little girl was so brutally raped. But a little girl had still clearly been raped and murdered—so someone had to be responsible. It just needed to be someone other than the Ayala men.

*   *   *

In his first statement to the hospital psychiatrist the morning Yuri's body was found, Jerardo—the 11-year-old street kid who'd been staying at the Ayala's home in exchange for work—had already implicated Pedro and Gary Ayala.

But the police and prosecutor's office had picked up an elderly, well-known alcoholic and beggar named Shesha off the street to charge him with Yuri's rape and murder, so young Jerardo was brought to the police station and pressured to corroborate this new story.

With zero evidence apart from Jerardo's coerced accusation, Shesha was formally charged with rape and murder. But the authorities had miscalculated. When the townspeople heard about the charges, a crowd showed up at the police station protesting the arrest. It was just too absurd: Too many people knew that Shesha wasn't at the party hall, and the townspeople considered him a harmless drunk. They demanded to know why the powerful and wealthy Ayala men were not being investigated. Quickly, the authorities reversed course, and as swiftly as they had arrested Shesha for rape and murder, they released him without explanation.

It was time to try another version of events. Estacio Flores, the Ayalas' lawyer, had a sister who rented out a few places on the floor for poor laborers to sleep when they came in and out of the city. One of these impoverished workers was a round-faced boy of nineteen named José, whom locals suspected, not unkindly, of being simple-minded. When he could, José worked collecting coins for the driver on a mini bus that ran between La Unión and Pachas.

José was picked up off the street, taken to the police station and charged with raping and murdering Yuri—a crime that took place when José was three hours away at home in Pillcocancha. According to José's testimony, the La Unión police stripped him naked, beat him, choked him, and violated him—torturing him for two days until he complied.

José's "confession," however, needed some corroboration—so young Jerardo was again swept up into the nightmare. Like José, Jerardo would later describe how the police beat, abused, and tortured him until he agreed to sign a statement (written out by the police) saying that *both* he and José had raped and murdered the girl. In addition to the torture, both later said that Kelly Ayala promised to pay them with money and food for taking the blame, and that Jerardo, as a minor, would never have to go to jail.

Three days later, when they finally appeared before a magistrate, they both protested that the confessions were false and coerced, and Jerardo gave an even clearer eye-witness account accusing Gary of the rape and murder. But it was all too late. The train had left the station and was now on iron tracks. The "somebodys" of La Unión had thrown the switch and locked the rails on course. The physical evidence that might positively identify the per-petrators was thrown off the train, and a "nobody" named José was loaded into its locked cargo container.

Lucila and her family tried to hire a lawyer to fight for a course correc-tion in the proceedings, but in a cruel joke that I've seen played out in poor communities all around the world, they only managed to drive themselves even more desperately into poverty. To pay for a lawyer, Lucila sold her one hard-earned piece of capital—a small plot of land—at a fraction of the pur-chase price, devastating years of work and savings, worked extra jobs and even took up selling fried donuts in the streets just to try and pay the lawyer. Her relatives took on extra work, and her dad sold all his livestock. They felt compelled to throw ever more money into an endless black hole that they could neither understand nor, out of love for Yuri, refuse. And in an utterly predictable ending to the story, successive lawyers simply took the money, did nothing, and then abandoned the case.

Figure 1.4
Gary Haugen, left, visits Yuri's grave with her family

On the other hand, Gary and Pedro Ayala applied their wealth and status to secure aggressive and unscrupulous legal counsel from the first minutes of the struggle, and in the end were acquitted of all wrongdoing. Instead, the full weight of the grotesque crime was thrust upon the shoulders of José, who, without ever having *any legal representation* for any portion of the proceedings, was sent away for 30 years to a harsh and dangerous Peruvian prison, where he sits and rots today.

THE HIDDEN TERROR OF POVERTY

This is the terror of poverty—the violent part that you and I and the rest of the world are unlikely to know much about. We may know, for example, that there are a massive number of Peruvians living in poverty—but how much do we know of the violent nightmare that lies underneath that poverty? We might know that a majority of rural women in Peru struggle below the poverty line to meet their daily needs for food and shelter, but do we know that 50 to 70 percent of Peruvian women struggle against sexual assault and other forms of violence[5]—the way Lucila, her mom, and her daughter all did? Would we know about the research that says about 47 percent of Peruvian women have been victims of attempted or completed rape?[6]

When we think of the global poor, we easily think of hunger, disease, homelessness, contaminated water, illiteracy, and joblessness. But José and Richard think of another reality that keeps the poor in poverty, and that is violence. This reality is very hard for outsiders to see—even for frequent and sophisticated visitors to the developing world—because most acts of violence against the poor are intentionally hidden. It's hard not to see the squalor, the shanties, the sewage, the begging, and the trash. But behind the walls of poverty, few ever see with their own eyes the swift strike across the face, the ugly struggle of rape, the iron blow to the head, the hands throttled against the throat.

It would be too easy to imagine that Yuri and Lucila's stories are singular tragedies of spectacular and rare brutality. Sadly, they are not. Their stories are microscopic sampling of the massive wave of "common" violence silently crashing over hundreds of millions of poor people in the developing world.

Indeed, the world has not even begun to fathom the devastating implications of a simple, straightforward statement buried in a little-known but thorough report by the United Nations which simply states:

> most poor people do not live under the shelter of the law, but far from the law's protection.[7]

Given that there are at least 2.5 billion very poor people in the world,[8] any condition that affects "most poor people" affects *a lot* of people. And if the condition affecting most of those 2.5 billion people is that they are outside the protection of law, then a lot of people are in big trouble—and a depth of trouble that the rest of us can scarcely imagine. To put it simply: They are not safe. They are—by the hundreds of millions—threatened every day with being enslaved, imprisoned, beaten, raped, and robbed.

But maybe this nightmare of hidden violence is isolated in these small forgotten pockets of intractable poverty in places like Huánuco that are so obscure that even Google Earth can't see them?

That might be comforting if true—but it's not. This raging epidemic of violence against the poor takes place right under our noses in many of the most celebrated and visible places in the developing world.

India is perhaps the most stunning example—a nation whose explosive rate of growth makes it the subject of breathless excitement in global economic circles. And perhaps no city in India receives more attention for seemingly miraculous economic development and modernization than the booming high-tech metropolis of Bangalore. The "Silicon Valley of India" is the nation's third largest city, with over 9 million people. It enjoys an economic growth rate of 10.3 percent,[9] has at least 10 billionaires,[10] over 10,000 millionaires,[11] and is the place where Thomas Friedman famously reached his epiphany about global competition—that *The World Is Flat*. Unlike the invisible city of La Unión in Peru, you and I can ride Google Earth's high resolution satellite photos to swoop down into Bangalore's every street, boulevard, and alleyway. We can count the jumbo jets parked at Bangalore's shiny new international airport, or fly over the manicured lawns and glass buildings that caught Friedman's attention on the sprawling campuses of Bangalore's technology giants.

But Sashmeeta Mulmi, a young Bangalore lawyer, wanted to show me something else in her city. Sashmeeta is a striking young woman from an elite high-caste family who made her way to Bangalore to attend law school. A star student, Sashmeeta was quickly snatched up by one of the city's prosperous commercial firms and found herself on the fast track because she excelled in her firm's core work which, to her surprise, turned out to be negotiating bribes. Any large and complex economy must continually resolve a massive volume of disputes, transactions, and regulatory matters—and in India, these are frequently resolved through an intricate system of corruption and bribery. Of course, any intricate system of this sort needs a professional corps of sophisticated practitioners and fixers, and in India, it is lawyers who frequently provide these services.

As a new lawyer, Sashmeeta went with the flow, but after a number of years, she said, the work felt increasingly empty and wrong. So she followed the advice of some mentors in her life and answered an ad to work with my colleagues at IJM in Bangalore.

Before taking on this new job, Sashmeeta—like just about everyone else—knew there was poverty in India. There are about 410 million Indians trying to stay alive on about $1.25 per day—that's about 100 million more people than the entire population of the United States. Forty-six percent of Indian children are malnourished,[12] and about 78 million Indians are homeless.[13] This is what people picture when they think of poverty: slums, malnutrition, beggars, dirty water, and disease. But Sashmeeta wanted to show me what her new career had revealed: an entire subterranean economy of abduction, forced labor, and torture engulfing millions, hidden in plain sight in the rice compounds, brick kilns, rock quarries, and plantations of South Asia.

The word *slavery* is so powerful that, to me, there is something obscene and sensationalizing to lightly suggest that such a grotesque atrocity is taking place on any meaningful scale today. But the shocking truth is this: There are more slaves in the world today (best estimate—27 million) than were extracted from Africa during 400 years of the transatlantic slave trade. And there are more slaves in India today than in any other country in the world.[14] For Sashmeeta, slavery is not a statistical matter—it is an urgent, personal matter. She and her colleagues have rescued thousands of their fellow Indians from slavery in factories, farms, and facilities around Bangalore and the neighboring state of Tamil Nadu.

Sashmeeta takes me a short ride across town, arriving just off the southwest corner of Bangalore's Outer Ring Road, where she points through the tall grasses and spreading trees to a collection of small, white cement structures and low-sloping red tile roofs under which thousands of handmade bricks are stacked and stored.

All was quiet on this cool late February afternoon, but in this compound, set back in the fields just beyond earshot, about a dozen slaves had been locked in a nightmare of abduction, beatings, starvation, sadistic torture, forced labor, and gang rapes.

Of course, such slavery is clearly against the law in India. So, how is it that millions of people can be held in slavery, and why does virtually no one *ever* go to jail for these crimes?

For answers, Sashmeeta would take me to meet with the former slaves released from the brick factory, to hear their stories, and to learn how it could be that, seven years later, the man who allegedly abducted, enslaved, raped, and tortured them continues to walk the streets of Bangalore utterly free and unafraid.

To get at the source of the story, Sashmeeta would have to drive me about an hour outside of Bangalore and into the villages that are scattered across the vast rural countryside that surrounds the "Silicon Valley of India." It seemed odd to stop at a McDonald's on the way out of town to meet people who were about to explain what it is like to be owned and enslaved by another person—but there it was: a brand new McCafé off the main highway, complete with stylized golden arches, a massive ceramic Ronald McDonald sitting out front, and the latest espresso drinks, all within an hour's drive of people working as slaves making bricks the way people did thousands of years ago.

Paved roads give way to dirt ones, and—frothy McDonald's cappuccinos in hand—we drive through the countryside of grassy fields, plowed dirt, palm tree groves and roadside hamlets. We disembark a few hundred yards from a small village and walk across a furrowed field to join a dozen adults and assorted children who have gathered on straw mats under the shade of an enormous tamarind tree. Sashmeeta and her IJM colleagues have been walking alongside these men and women for seven years—first in their struggle for freedom and then for justice. Over those years, children had been born, two of their number have died, some sweet encouragements had been celebrated, and many bitter losses have been endured.

I am a stranger to these villagers, but on the strength of Sashmeeta's deep companionship with them, I am greeted with trusting kindness and gentle smiles. With long black hair neatly pulled back to accentuate their sharp cheek bones, the women wear beautiful saris of flowing and folded red, green, and orange—each wife adorned with small gold piercings of the nose and ears, with bangles on the wrists and rings on the toes. For the occasion, their husbands are wearing cleaned and pressed collared shirts, in long pants or *lungis*, the traditional plaid cotton wrap-around skirt. These men and women are in their twenties and thirties, but they carry a weariness that would suggest forties and fifties. Sashmeeta holds no illusions that they are bearers of any special perfections of virtue—they are regular, messy people just like the rest of us. But unlike the rest of us, they have persevered through hardships and terrors from an unspeakable world of darkness, and the resilience of their humanity, openness, and dignity is striking and humbling.

MARIAMMA'S STORY

At one time, these men and women had worked together as free laborers in a brick factory about 60 kilometers from Bangalore. It was hard but good work, they seem to agree. Living inside the brick compound, they worked as a team from 6:00 in the morning until 6:00 at night making several thousand bricks a day in a manufacturing process that has not fundamentally changed in thousands of years.

The bulk of the work is done by stooping or squatting within six inches of the ground to mold the bricks and lay them in rows, or by trudging under loads of heavy bricks stacked on the head. I have seen Indian women and children of less than 100 pounds carrying brick loads of 50, 60, 70 pounds on their heads, across stretches of 30, 50, 100 yards—for hours, non-stop. Experimenting with any part of the process for more than 10 or 15 minutes has always sent my muscles and joints into knots of aching pain, to say nothing of the mind-numbing monotony of living every day as a human cog in a medieval brickmaking machine, but these friends considered the work an acceptable means for feeding their families and staying alive.

Low caste, too poor to be able to go to school as kids, illiterate, married as teenagers, landless (or dividing an increasingly smaller garden plot among siblings), the work in the brick facility allowed these laborers to eat, to feed their children, to shelter their families, and to go to a doctor if needed. They had the freedom to explore other opportunities, to scheme toward something better, to visit their relatives, to go to festivals and to allow their kids to go to school.

Mariamma, a tiny woman in an orange and gold sari sitting next to me, explained that Sunday was their day of rest. When I asked her what they did, she smiled at the thought of it and told me, "We get to take a good bath—and we beautify ourselves. It's the one day the women get to feel beautiful."

Mariamma had been the first to greet me when we gathered under the shade tree that afternoon. I should have recognized her from the pictures I had reviewed in advance from her IJM case file, but the face of a slave and the face of a free human can be shockingly different. In those file photos, Mariamma's face was utterly drained with numb exhaustion and her whole being seemed resigned to absorb whatever crushing pain or humiliation would inevitably come next. But today, sitting gently and confidently next to me in her home village, there is light, passion, intensity and intelligence in her face. Like the other wives, Mariamma sat patiently as the men tried to narrate the story and answer questions, but inevitably, this feather-weight woman emerged as the bold, clear, tell-it-like-it-is spokesperson for the group.

Figure 1.5 Mariamma on the mat

She described their fateful decision to work in a different brick factory. At the old compound, they were paid about $6.00 for every 1,000 bricks they made, but they were running out of room to lay out the bricks for drying and needed a larger facility to maximize their output and earnings. One day, a friend of the factory owner—a man we will call Mr. V. because of an ongoing judicial process—visited them and offered jobs at his brick facility, providing the group with a cash advance of about $333—just over $40 per person—to pay for the costs of moving themselves and their families to the new facility and to meet some very basic financial needs.

Once Mariamma and the other families moved into the new facility, however, the darkness of slavery fell quickly. Conditions within the brick factory were nothing like what they had imagined. Mr. V. and his older son were abusive and brutal. The bizarre lie and brutality of bonded labor worked this way: Mr. V. insisted that Mariamma and the others owed him money and therefore were required to work for him until they paid him back—a requirement which he felt entitled to enforce with violence. They could not leave to work anywhere else, and any payment of wages was utterly at Mr. V.'s discretion, and so he would pay them only enough money to eat (and would require that they buy the food from him). He might choose to pay them nothing at all. Sometimes, he would not even provide the materials for making bricks—and so he would neither pay them, nor feed them, nor allow them to leave. Mariamma and the others told me that they would be left starving for as long as seven days with no food at all.

And according to the laborers, Mr. V. made sure they knew there was no way out: He would bring in a jeep-load of thugs armed with chains, sticks, and knives, drag a laborer into a room and viciously beat the captive through the night. Later, dragging out the beaten victim, Mr. V. would tell the rest of the laborers, "If you run away, this is what will happen to you."

Trapped, Mariamma and her husband Shushil could not visit their two young children, whom they had left back at their village under the care of Mariamma's parents. Once, when Mariamma got word that the children were critically ill, she and Shushil slipped out of the brick factory to try and help the children. Mr. V., however, chased them down in their village with his thugs. Twisting a small napkin in her hands, Mariamma described to me how Mr. V. brought her and Shushil to his home in Bangalore, tied Shushil to a banana tree and, with his son and a hired thug, beat him all over his body with their hands, fists and a wooden stick as thick as a man's arm.

Mariamma said she had to watch as her husband wept and cried out to them, "Don't beat me! Don't beat me!" As she begged them to stop, "Mr. V. grabbed my arm and pulled me into the next room," Mariamma told me. "When I protested, his son grabbed the back of my head and pushed me into the room. They both pushed my head against the wall. I collapsed, and then they both raped me. When I screamed out, Mr. V. yelled at me, 'If you dare open your mouth, I will kill you.' "

In the end, the laborers told me it would be these vicious sexual assaults that would most painfully terrorize the families. Mariamma and Mayukhi (another of the laborers) explained that Mr. V. would come at night to the brick factory, tie up their husbands, load the women (including a 12-year-girl) into his jeep, and drive them to the construction site where he was building a temple next to his central Bangalore home, and he and his son would rape them there. Soon, the women told me, Mr. V. would be joined by several thugs for regular gang rapes at the temple construction site.

The women said they came to fear the darkness every night, never knowing when Mr. V. was going to come for them. Some felt like committing suicide—but they didn't want to desert their families. Eventually they decided to take their lives in their hands and run away and hide. "We were living with great fear," Mariamma said. "We didn't even eat—we were afraid they would kill us. So we took a risk. If we stay we die. If we go we may die."

*   *   *

And so they fled the brick factory—and waited to see what would happen. Unable to find his slaves, they said Mr. V. simply loaded up his friends in the jeep, headed toward the village and kidnapped three men who were tenuously connected to the laborers, sending word that he was holding them as hostages until his slaves returned.

Back under the tamarind tree in the waning hours of my afternoon visit, I got to hear from these three men—Namdev, Mallesh, and Maruti—on how they survived their ordeal.

Mr. V. and his entourage took their hostages to his home in central Bangalore, where they were stripped naked, their heads shaved, their clothes burned, and beaten at intervals. On the fourth day of this torture, they were all driven out to the brick factory and put to work. The *goondas* came again at intervals and beat them with field hockey sticks and thick wooden rods all over their bodies and joints. On the seventh day, Maruti was put through a bizarre test of fire before one of the house idols and was selected to return to the village to make one last plea for the laborers' return—or else, they were told, Mallesh and Namdev would be killed.

We must step back for a moment and observe that it became Maruti's job to return to his village and *publicly* announce that Mr. V. was holding hostages and would murder them if the runaway laborers did not return. Mr.

V. *wanted* the whole countryside to know it. That was his plan. He clearly had zero fear of law enforcement while committing these brazen crimes— all right in the middle of India's most celebrated and advanced metropolitan center.

For the runaway slaves and the three hostages, on the other hand, it was *all* fear. Locked inside a concrete cell at the brick factory, bleeding from the head, and too crippled to stand or sit by the tenth day of torture, Mallesh looked over at Namdev on the floor and whispered to him, "I think this is the last day of my life."

"At that moment," Mallesh told me, "I curled up in the corner of the room to die." "I also thought I was going to die there," Namdev agreed, softly. "I thought I will never see my family again."

*   *   *

Fortunately, at that very moment, Sashmeeta's IJM colleagues—who had uncovered what was going on—had arrived at Mr. V.'s brick factory with a district magistrate. When confronted, Mr. V. vigorously denied mistreating any laborers or holding hostages. But the IJM team managed to locate the hostages with the magistrate, brought them from their locked cell, and had them tell their entire story of terror before the magistrate—with a video camera rolling. Needless to say, things were not looking good for Mr. V., and for the first time, he looked worried.

But, it turns out, he need not have been concerned. Under Indian law, Mr. V. had committed at least 35 very serious criminal offenses against these victims—everything from bonded labor and labor imprisonment to assault, abduction, rape, extortion, theft, wrongful confinement, and on and on. But just like sexual assault in Peru, these offenses are not, in fact, *as a practical matter* prohibited by law when committed against very poor people— because the laws are not enforced by the justice system.

Sashmeeta explained to me that the Bangalore law enforcement authorities had multiple corroborating eye-witness accounts for each of Mr. V.'s crimes from nearly a dozen victims. The authorities had a magistrate who had, with his own eyes, caught the perpetrator red-handed with hostages locked in a cell and traumatized from beatings—and had the discovery of the hostages and their immediate description of their abduction and torture on video tape. And if that were not enough, the authorities had Sashmeeta and her team of public service lawyers, investigators, and social workers standing by to render any assistance the authorities or the victims might need to secure justice.

So, I asked Sashmeeta, what happened?

First, she said, the local police refused to even file charges against Mr. V. or his accomplices for *two years*. But why, I asked?

When the police deigned to give a reason for failing to file charges, here is what they told Sashmeeta and her colleagues:

- Because *one* of the victims was arguably from another police jurisdiction. (But under Indian law, it is a "dereliction of duty" for the police to fail to investigate on such a basis.)
- Because the rape victims had not obtained a medical exam on their own. (But under Indian law, such an exam is not necessary, and would be absurd when the victims were held prisoner by the rapist for the period of time in which such an exam would have been of helpful evidentiary value.)
- Because the police had (secretly) filed a report with the court dismissing the victims' claims as false and unworthy of investigation. (But they did so without any investigation of the crime and without stating any basis for their finding.)
- Because the victims had not produced themselves at the police station. (But, in fact, the police had repeatedly refused to receive the victims at the police station despite *endless offers to come*. After more than a year, the police eventually agreed to take the victims' testimony—and the victims provided all necessary corroborating testimony of the crimes.)
- Because they could not find the victims. (But IJM told the police exactly where they were, and they *never* went to see them—and IJM always offered to bring them to the police).
- Because the victims did not testify to their wounds or produce medical certificates. (But they did, in fact, testify to their wounds and, under Indian law, no such certificates were required—especially now that it was a year and half after the wounding.)
- Because they did not have jurisdiction over the bonded labor offenses. (But they did.)
- Because IJM had not provided the police with explanations of the relevant law. (But it is not IJM's responsibility to do so, even though they had actually done so repeatedly.)

- Because the rapes could not have happened with other people around, and because a father and son would never do such a thing. (But of course they could and did—according to multiple eye-witnesses.)
- Because the Public Prosecutor had not specifically written to urge the police to file the charges. (But this is never required—moreover, the Public Prosecutor refused to provide such unnecessary correspondence unless the police specifically wrote to request it.)
- Because they felt they had to impound the perpetrator's jeep as evidence but couldn't do so because the tires were now missing. (But this is no reason for not filing charges and, honestly, too silly for words.)

Finally, after *two years* and after the victims had provided corroborating eye-witness statements about all the criminal offenses to the police on *three separate occasions*—the police finally responded to the relentless pressure from Sashmeeta and her colleagues and filed proper charges against Mr. V. and his son for assault, wrongful confinement, criminal intimidation, rape, criminal conspiracy, and bonded labor.

What happened then, I asked?

Again, Sashmeeta ran through the highlights:

The court released Mr. V. and his son on bail, despite the seriousness of the violent offenses with which they were charged. Bail was granted by the court because the defense attorney claimed that his clients (the accused slave owners, rapists, kidnappers, and violent assailants) were "not doing well."

Then, the government lost the weapons that the perpetrators had used to torture the victims and other physical evidence that had been collected on the day of the raid. Also lost were the copies of photos and videos of the discovery of the hostages and their stories of what they endured. In addition, the police did not even file the videos and the photos given to them by IJM as a part of the charge sheet before the court. The prosecutor failed to get this evidence marked during the government officer's testimony, then the court failed to take any action to remedy the situation despite knowing about the photos and the videos.

Nevertheless, at the trial, the magistrate gave clear testimony to the trial judge of what he had seen of the accused perpetrators' crimes, and multiple victims gave corroborating testimony of all the relevant offenses. But, amazingly, even though Mr. V.'s elder son was the one charged with the crimes, the police arrested and produced the wrong son at trial—which meant that the witnesses could not affirm that the accused *present at trial* had committed the offenses. Not wanting to embarrass the police, the public prosecutor refused to make proper arguments to ensure the real accused would be produced before the court. This deliberate fraud by the perpetrators and their defense counsel and the screw-up by the police and prosecutor required a series of appeals to the state's highest authorities that delayed final re-trial of the proper accused by another *three years*.

Finally, six and a half years after the victims were rescued from the brick factory and had first made their complaint to the authorities, a full trial was held, and the victims provided, yet again, corroborating testimony about the relevant crimes. However, the judge who heard the case was given notice of reassignment; although he had ample time to reach a verdict and did so in other cases completed after notice of his reassignment, he refused to issue a judgment in this case. The case was reassigned to a new judge who, without listening to any of the witnesses and without taking evidence, proceeded to acquit Mr. V. and his son of all charges.

After taking this all in from Sashmeeta and her colleagues, I sat stunned for a bit. "The worst part," Sashmeeta concluded, "is that there is nothing special or exotic about the outcome in this case. There will be no outrage, no scandal—nothing in the media about it. Not a single police officer, prosecutor, magistrate, clerk, or judicial official will be reprimanded, exposed, or held accountable in any way for the failure. We have worked hundreds of these cases, and this is *normal.*"

In fact, the only thing special about the case was the extraordinary assistance that Sashmeeta and her IJM colleagues gave the Bangalore law enforcement authorities in order to help them succeed. In this one case, Sashmeeta and her team traveled to meet with police 26 times. They made 53 visits to other relevant government officials. Over 7 years, they made 73 trips to the courthouse (for proceedings including a dozen unexplained adjournments) and met 79 times with 10 different prosecutors.

If the Indian authorities could not enforce the laws against abduction, forced labor, gang rape, and assault for these kinds of citizens with this kind of over-the-top assistance, what is the likelihood of poor people getting enforcement of the law against abusive violence *without* such assistance?

Outsiders will see laws on the books, police officers in uniform, and judges in black robes and may assume that those police officers and court officials are enforcing the laws with reasonable regularity for India's poor citizens. But Mariamma, Sashmeeta, and—most importantly—Mr. V. all know this is not true.

And Mariamma knows why the laws aren't enforced for her. It's the same answer Lucila and all those Peruvian mothers gave: Because they are poor.

"The injustice [is] inflicted on us, [and] we have to somehow accept it," Mariamma told me. "I don't know anything about the law. The cruelty—we have to take it—because we don't have money or power. The police will believe Mr. V. and not us because we are slaves to Mr. V. What he says, the police will believe."

When it comes to the authorities, Mariamma said, "We don't look good in their eyes—if we give money, they look—otherwise no."

THE ALARM SYSTEM IS OFF

In Yuri's and Mariamma's stories we see the way wealthy and powerful people in poor communities in the developing world aggressively use the broken and corrupt criminal justice system to protect their violent abuse of the poor—either by affirmatively using the authorities as their instruments of abuse, or by proactively purchasing official protection of their abuses through bribes. But in many settings in the developing world, the working parts of the criminal justice systems are so corroded and frayed that violent abusers of the poor don't need to worry about the justice system *at all*.

In these settings, perpetrators don't need to *make* the justice system fail; it fails all by itself. It's like the burglar who sees the exterior sign indicating that there is an alarm system but then finds that no one has bothered to turn the system on. He doesn't have to do anything to overcome the alarm system—it's already going to fail.

For a picture of this kind of utter brokenness, imagine a metropolitan center with about 3 million people (about the population of Montreal, San Francisco, or Rome). Next, imagine the city has a very high rate of rape (say, about 10 percent)—meaning there are about 150,000 women and girls who become rape victims each year.

Now to successfully prosecute the assailants in almost all the rape cases, the victims will need to be examined by a doctor to gather physical and forensic evidence. However, imagine there is only *one* police doctor in the whole city responsible for completing examinations and testifying for *every assault case* on behalf of the government in the entire city of 3 million.

If you are a victim of a violent assault, you have to get in line with approximately 600 other rape victims who need to see this lone doctor on a single day—in addition to the hundreds of other *non*-sexual assault victims who also need the doctor's attention. Of course, because the good doctor probably did not get through all 600 to 1,000 assault victims who needed his examination the day before, the backlogged cases from yesterday (and all the proceeding days) are in line as well. Realistically, if you get assaulted halfway through the year, you can expect a backlog of 149,000 rape victims in line ahead of you—a line of people about 56 miles long.*

Sounds insane, doesn't it? But this is *exactly* the reality in the largest city in East Africa. Moreover, odds are you would *never* know about the insanity—unless you were deep in the weeds of the city's public justice system.

But if you are a young girl like Laura, it is not just insane—it means that even though you are only 10 years old, and you have been raped by three different men in your neighborhood, you have zero hope of seeing your rapists brought to justice.

LAURA'S STORY

To understand something of Laura's world, Google Earth will pluck us from the lush green fields of Mariamma's village outside Bangalore, and transport us over the blue Indian Ocean, swoop over into East Africa, and place us hovering right over Laura's home in Nairobi, Kenya. Millions will remember these slums from the movie *The Constant Gardner*—the checkerboard mass of rusty corrugated iron roofs, the narrow slippery pathways channeling trickling streams of filth between the shanties; the patches of color from hanging laundry, plastic buckets, and peeling paper posters, all scattered across a massive, hard, brown sponge of terrain absorbing generations of human refuse and debris.

---

* But for the rape examination to be very useful it must be done within the first 72 hours of the assault—96 hours at the outside limit.

Laura—who has big, dark almond eyes and a toothy smile that bursts easily across her face—lives with her father, her 9-year-old brother Seth, and her 4-year-old sister Cantai—in a 10 foot by 10 foot room they rent among the rows of shanties. Laura's mother recently went home to her village about four hours away—but she never came back, slipping away forever as part of that long night that is HIV/AIDS in Africa.

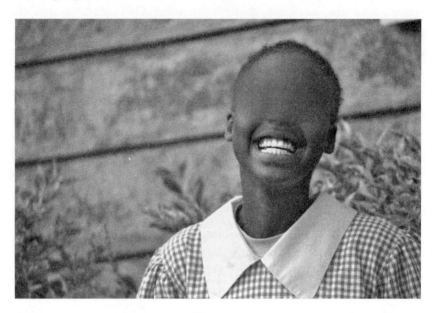

Figure 1.6

In the developing world, about 1 out of 3 urban dwellers lives in a slum—which means there are nearly a billion people who, like Laura, live in squalid, overcrowded ghettos without secure tenure on the land (about 828 million according to United Nations estimates). In sub-Saharan Africa, about 62 percent of urban dwellers live in slums. That's a lot of people, about 200 million.[15] The slum where Laura lives—called Korogocho—squeezes a population the size of Montgomery, Alabama into just a little more than half a square mile. Laura's neighbors—about 120,000[16] of them—make on average about half the monthly income of La Unión's residents.

This is the familiar picture of developing world poverty: massive slums with their unemployment, bad sanitation, hunger, and substandard housing. To outsiders, these slums can feel vaguely scary, but most outsiders have no idea how scary these slums feel to the insiders—the people who actually live there. Recent UN reports on slums suggest that residents' biggest fear

Figure 1.7

is not being evicted, or hungry, or sick, but being hurt by violence. In fact, "violence and security issues can be regarded by poor people as considerably more important than housing or income issues."[17]

When a study was done of slums like Laura's in Nairobi, residents overwhelmingly identified violence as the "main problem" in their community.[18] Indeed, the vast majority of households in the Nairobi slums reported that they do not feel safe.[19] This is especially true for women and girls. An often-cited global report on slums found, not surprisingly, that living conditions in the massive ghettos were "alarming," but "equally disturbing, if not more so, is the fact that violence against women in the slums is rampant. It is this single issue which emerged as perhaps the *strongest cross-cutting theme* in [the] study."[20]

Of course for ten-year-old Laura, this rampant violence against women and girls is not a "crosscutting theme" in a study—it's the nightmare of life that she was born into. The sexual violence against Laura began, as it does for many,[21] in the rickety box of wood scraps and rusted corrugated iron she called home. After her mother's death, when night would fall and the old, blue kerosene lantern had been extinguished, Laura's father would pick her up, put her on the bed, cover her mouth and force himself upon her. Neighbors later said they could hear her muffled screams in the night, begging her father to stop. But they did nothing. It was a "family matter," they said, and it felt risky to report the matter to authorities since it probably wouldn't do any good. Over time, Laura stopped crying because, she said, "I got used to it."

* * *

For women and girls in these slums, the threat of violence is everywhere. Going to the bathroom, for instance, is not safe. Seventy-five percent of slum households do not have their own toilets,[22] so hundreds of thousands of women and girls must walk hundreds of yards through the slums to use communal pit latrines and bathing stations that lack privacy, sanitation, or lighting at night. According to a systemic study of the slums in Laura's city:

> Inadequate and inaccessible toilets and bathrooms, as well as the general lack of effective policing and insecurity, make women even more vulnerable to rape and other forms of gender-based violence. Violence against women is endemic in Nairobi's slums and settlements, goes widely unpunished and significantly contributes to making and keeping women poor.[23]

Laura, terribly, has a more basic understanding of this reality. One day, while she walked to a kiosk to buy a bathing sponge, a neighborhood man named Joseph Irungu grabbed her, dragged her struggling, 70-pound body into one of these community bathrooms in Korogocho and raped her. He threw her 50 cents and told her not to tell anyone what he had done.

At this point, I wish could tell you about a magical space of safety in this nightmare. But in the land of impunity where Laura and millions of the world's poorest girls live, the home is not safe, the bathroom is not safe—and even schools are not safe. A powerful and inspiring movement of advocates has worked to demonstrate over the past decade that almost nothing has a greater positive impact on the life of a girl and her community than education. But for Laura's sake, and for millions like her, we should be crystal clear about something: *In the absence of effective law enforcement*, schools will not protect girls from violence.

Indeed, studies in the developing world now show that violence is one of the most important reasons girls do not go to school in the first place. As a recent UN study concluded, a "significant, though rarely mentioned factor behind low school enrolment in poor urban neighborhoods is a perceived lack of safety, especially for girls."[24]

Horribly, Laura knows all about this, too. One morning, as she was walking to her fourth grade class, another neighbor, Antony Mutokia, grabbed her, pulled her into his little shanty room and raped her. Afterwards, Mutokia tossed 75 cents at Laura and told her keep quiet. In Laura's neighborhood, it was the only price a rapist was expected to pay.

* * *

Of course, it's impossible to see any of this ugliness in Nairobi's slums from an eye altitude of 6,000 feet on Google Earth. The ocean of rusty, steel roofs jammed into rectangle formations looks rather orderly in its own way. Even visitors who come right into the streets and narrow alleys of Korogocho are unlikely to ever see what is happening to Laura inside the corrugated walls of her home when the lantern goes out, or in the terrible darkness of the communal bathroom, or Mutokia's shack on the way to school.

And given the shame, the fear, and the hopelessness, Laura is unlikely to tell anyone what is happening either. From La Unión, to Bangalore, to Nairobi, this is the most deeply hidden layer of what it means to be poor: the dark humiliation and debasement of being assaulted and hurt by other people. Relentlessly, every day, from every side, Laura knows that she is not safe—and the predators all around her know it, too.

But the rest of us do not. We will look upon her vast slum and see shacks and filth, and a pang of vague dread will come upon us if we think of a 10-year-old girl living in such a place, but we will not *see* with our own eyes the most terrifying parts.

Fortunately for Laura, however, there is someone very loving and brave in her neighborhood who *does* see. From the outside, Naomi Wanjiru's Korogocho home—a rented room in a long row of rusty shacks—is utterly indistinguishable from Laura's or anyone else's in the slum, surrounded by the same muddy alleys, wash bins and brown rust chewing through everything. Stepping inside to meet Naomi in her home, however, is to step into another world. Naomi's eyes greet you with life and joy. She is a woman of royal proportions, with her hair wrapped up inside a turban of pure white. In the custom of her neighborhood, the rough iron and wood scrap walls of her home are covered with hanging white fabric, and a pine-colored, floor-to-ceiling china cabinet serves as entertainment center, photo gallery, stuffed animal storage and tea station. Naomi is a volunteer social worker in Korogocho, and many terrified and humiliated girls have found their only shelter in this tiny protectorate where Naomi reigns with love and hope for the undefended.

When Laura finally arrived at school the morning after she was raped by Mutokia, she was in so much pain that she allowed the truth to spill out to her teacher, who immediately knew what to do—and brought Laura to Naomi. Over time, Naomi won Laura's trust and put together the full picture of sexual violence that Laura had endured. She took Laura to the hospital for care, and the treating physician documented the clear physical evidence of rape.

Naomi knew from experience that the assailants—especially the father—would vociferously deny the allegations and go on the offensive against the credibility of this scared and confused little girl. Naomi also knew that there would be no other witnesses to testify about the abuse. Neighbors—even those who had heard Laura's screams at night inside her home—knew that defendants would often pay local gangs to threaten would-be witnesses and were struck with paralyzing fear. Even Laura's teacher would feel too intimidated to testify. And so, accordingly, Naomi knew that the medical documentation in her hands was going to be indispensable for Laura to receive justice.

But here is where the utter brokenness of the system makes justice for Laura virtually impossible.

In Nairobi, the medical evidence that Naomi has obtained—although recorded on the correct government issued form—isn't enough.

And why is that? Is the doctor unqualified? Was the evidence improperly taken? Is there some law or regulation that prohibits using this evidence? No, it's because all police in the city insist that medical evidence be documented on a form completed by *one* specific doctor—the Police Doctor whom we will call Dr. K.—and the police will not present the form in court or provide it to the prosecutors otherwise.

In fact, the only way they'll be willing to present this piece of evidence is if it is "verified" through a re-examination of the victim completed and documented by Dr. K.

That's correct. Nairobi is a city of 3 million people where, according to studies, one can expect about a half million victims of physical assault in a given year, including about a 150,000 victims of rape.[25] In that context, the Nairobi police require that *all* victims of *any* assault be examined by Dr. K.—and *only* Dr. K.—if they wish medical evidence of their assault to be submitted to the court.[26] This, of course, ensures an impossible backlog of cases stacking up outside Dr. K.'s dilapidated one-room office (below)— and produces a perfect choke point for addressing the epidemic of sexual violence in Nairobi.

Needless to say, it can take months for an assault victim to see Dr. K.— who is, in any case, rather famous with patients and social workers for being frequently absent from his office. One social worker told me, "It's a very traumatizing experience for a young girl. There is no comprehensive medical exam or report. He doesn't have more than ten minutes to do the exam."

Figure 1.8
Exam table in Dr. K's office

Laura's experience was much the same. And after all the waiting and mortifying humiliation of the perfunctory exam, Dr. K. simply issued a summary document denying that there was any evidence manifesting sexual assault, and concluded that Laura had not been raped.

It didn't matter that Laura had documentary evidence consistent with rape from a qualified physician. It didn't matter that such evidence was perfectly admissible in a Kenyan court. It didn't matter that there are hundreds of doctors in Nairobi who could perform these exams and provide such evidence. It didn't matter, because the Nairobi police have insisted for years that any medical evidence of assault submitted to the court must come on the government form completed by Dr. K.

And worse, perhaps: No one knows why. After years of inquiries from IJM Nairobi lawyers and clear Kenyan case law that holds to the contrary, the police still insist that Dr. K. must be the one to complete the form. The only explanation that the police officials could assert was that "this is the way it is done here."

So girls like Laura return to their slums with rapists on the loose who don't even need to bribe the justice system to leave them alone. Their defenders like Naomi return to those same narrow alleyways of Korogocho utterly defeated by the absurdity, and with no story to tell to the next young rape victim about why she should come forward and fight for justice.

Laura's story is a stunning example not only of the violent, lawless chaos that millions of the world's common poor must contend with every day, but also of the appalling neglect of the basic criminal justice system that is supposed to protect them—a level of neglect so profound that, in the largest city in East Africa, the system can be rendered virtually inoperable by an absurd practice that no one bothers to know about or even attempt to justify. The most fundamental systems of law and order (which communities in affluent countries consider *the* most basic public service) have been so useless for so long in much of the developing world that violent criminals preying upon the poor don't have to give it a second thought—and tragically, much of the world has ceased to give a second thought to fixing or even understanding the breakdown.

And the implications are as profound as they are underappreciated. Laura, Mariamma, Yuri, and Lucila not only represent the billions of people in the developing world who are struggling to escape severe poverty, but they also represent the way that struggle is fundamentally undermined by forces of common violence that run rampant in the developing world in the absence of functioning criminal justice systems. Various movements over the last half-century have rallied vast international support for combatting poverty in the developing world, but as we shall see, there has been very little attention paid to the devastating way that violence continually pulls the rug out from underneath the global poor just as they are struggling to get to their feet. It's time, therefore, to get a clear understanding of four massive undercurrents of violence that continuously undermine the poor's scramble to escape the squalor.

THE HIDDEN CRISIS AT HISTORY'S INFLECTION POINT

The year is 1981. Ronald Reagan has just become the new president of the United States, Lady Diana Spencer and Prince Charles are wed, Anwar Sadat of Egypt is assassinated, Bill Gates releases his MS-DOS operating system on IBM's first personal computer, MTV is launched, scientists identify a virus they call HIV, *Raiders of the Lost Ark* is in theaters, and interest rates in the United States are at 15.75 percent (and I am graduating from high school). Around the globe, in the developing world, one out of two people (52 percent) are living in extreme poverty—meaning they are trying to survive off less than $1.25 a day.

Now, fast forward to 2010, when the percentage of people in the developing world living in extreme poverty has been slashed to one out of every five (21 percent)—and experts expect extreme poverty to continue declining to 15 percent in 2015.[1] This is amazing and unexpected progress—but the *bad* news is impressive as well: Even if the good news continues, there will still be almost a *billion* people (883 million) in *extreme* poverty in 2015—and living off $1.25 a day is brutal poverty, affording nothing for critical things like medical care or schooling.[2] What's more, the number of people living between $1.25 and $2.00 a day *doubled* from 648 million to 1.18 billion between 1981 and 2008.

Looking at poverty alleviation trends, the question is: Are you a glass-half-empty person or a glass-half-full person?

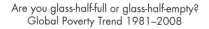

Are you glass-half-full or glass-half-empty?
Global Poverty Trend 1981–2008

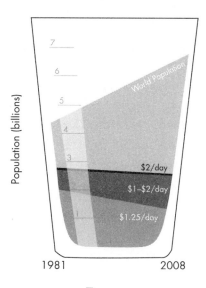

Figure 2.1

Poverty rates: The absolute number of people living on $2.00 a day, which is *very* tough poverty, barely budged from 2.59 billion in 1981 to 2.47 billion in 2008—and there will still be 2 billion in 2015. On the other hand, a whopping 70 percent of people in the developing world in 1981 lived on less than $2.00 a day, which came down to 43 percent in 2008.

Health: 7.6 million children under 5 years of age die from preventable and treatable causes (mostly lack of food and medical care) each year—but that is half (15 million) the child mortality rate of 30 years ago.[3]

Water: 780 million people do not have access to the most basic building block of life—clean water—but since 1990, 2 billion people who used to only have water that sickened and killed them now have gained access to clean water.[4]

Hunger. Almost a billion people in the world go hungry (925 million), and 16 percent of the people in developing world are undernourished, but in 1981, a full quarter were undernourished.[5]

Education. Around the world, 67.5 million children do not get to go to school at all, and 775 million adults cannot read or write.[6] But from 1999 to 2008, 52 million children who previously had no chance to go to school could get a get a primary education.

Housing. There are 1.6 billion people in substandard housing, with 100 million homeless,[7] but the percentage of people living in slums has decreased from 46 percent to 32 percent.[8]

Stepping back even further, the epic struggle against severe poverty and deprivation seems to be reaching a critical inflection point for the first time in human history. Two hundred years ago, 75 percent of human beings lived in the harshest poverty (the modern equivalent of under a $1.00 a day), and now, stunningly, only about 12 percent do.[9] This is good news. But, painfully, with today's population growth, that 12 percent is still around 800 million people—which is about exactly the same absolute number of people living on the equivalent of a $1.00 a day two hundred years ago.[10]

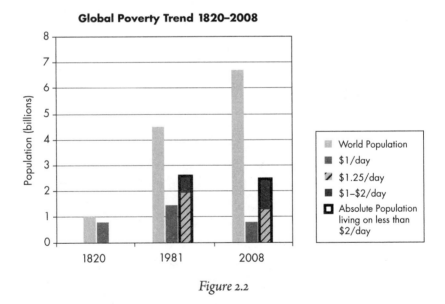

Global Poverty Trend 1820–2008

Figure 2.2

Dramatically, history's grand struggle against the brutality of poverty seems to be accelerating to a point of extraordinary possibility in our era. Billions of people, for the first time in human history, seem poised to find that escape velocity that catapults them out of the gravitational pull of severe poverty that previously crushed their forbearers back to earth. On the other hand, there are also signs that the momentum of progress is stalling out, as those escaping a life at $1 a day find themselves simply filling up the expanding crater where people are stuck living off $2 a day.[11]

So which way is this going to go?

Understanding What We Are Up Against

One thing we know for sure: The world is up against a formidable foe. Acute poverty is obvious and hidden, simple and complex. The problem of the hungry child, for example, is obvious and simple. She will even plainly say to you: "I am hungry," and clearly, what she needs is food. What is hidden are all the ways her hunger is affecting her, and what is complex are all the reasons why she doesn't have enough food. The history of the world's effort to fight severe poverty is largely a story of seeing what's obvious and simple and trying to do something about it, and in the process, discovering the hidden and complex realities of that poverty, and then trying to re-engineer solutions that better fit those realities.

If you were caring for the poor in Mexico and India in the 1950s, people seemed to be hungry because they couldn't grow enough wheat and rice. But then it turns out that perhaps they were just growing the *wrong kind* of wheat and rice. Agronomists like Norman Borlaug introduced high-yield variations of these crops in the developing world, launched a Green Revolution, made Mexico and India net exporters of these grains, and saved a billion poor people from starvation. But the agronomists couldn't save 3 million people from dying of starvation in Bangladesh when it had a plentiful supply of food, because as the economist Amartya Sen teaches the world, the problem is not the *supply* of food, but the *inequities in the distribution system* that rob the poor of the capacity to access the food.

Access to that food solves the hunger problem, and improved nutrition even reduces a poor person's vulnerability to disease, but public health experts know that *the food* is not going to stop epidemic levels of infectious diseases like polio, dysentery, malaria, or HIV. To meet these needs, the poor will need access to medical care, vaccinations, hygiene, and sanitation programs. But people in low-income countries may not be able to access these services if their national governments are saddled with excessive debt payments that crowd out budgets for basic public health services, or if corrupt authorities steal funds intended to provide those services.

An otherwise impoverished mom in that low-income country might be able to pay for mosquito nets and improved sanitation for her family on her own if she could have a micro-loan to buy that sewing machine for the tailoring business she runs out of her home. Of course, she may not bother to set up such a business or improve the sanitation in her home if she is afraid the local council is going to shut down her business or throw her off her land because neither is properly "licensed," or because wealthy friends of a local politician are preparing to steal her property. And even if she isn't paralyzed by those fears, it turns out the reason she can't get the licenses is because she is illiterate, has never been to school, and has no idea how to access the process or fill out the forms. She didn't go to school because in her family, school was for boys, they were too poor to pay school fees, and she was married off to an older man and started having children when she was 15. She can't work as a maid outside the home anymore because she has a sick child at home who is ill from drinking the local water that has been polluted by the unregulated mining operation in her town. The local officials in her town have accepted bribes from the international company running the mining operation to look the other way, and her husband lost his job with the mine because they hired cheaper laborers who are refugees from the civil war in the neighboring country.

This is just a taste of the complexity of poverty, and in such a composite poverty scenario, one can see the way each aspect of poverty is clearly connected to other problems. But each problem is also distinct—which simply means that it does not get addressed by solving the related problems if the core problem itself is not addressed. For example, diarrhea from bad sanitation clearly exacerbates the problem of hunger because it prevents the body from absorbing nutrients, but, obviously, if you solve the sanitation and diarrhea problem, but you don't have food, you still have no hope of solving your hunger problem. It's true that each aspect of poverty is exacerbated by other factors, but it does no good to solve those related factors in the absence of the direct solution. Sometimes the exacerbating factor is so acute that it can render the direct solution nearly useless—but solving the exacerbating factor is *always inadequate* in the absence of the direct solution.

That is why, at this critical inflection point in the fight against global poverty, we must clearly elevate an aspect of poverty in our world that is both underappreciated and very distinct. In other words, people do not commonly see it as intrinsic to the problem of poverty—and if they do, they commonly try to address it by solving the exacerbating factors without first prioritizing the direct solution.

That aspect of poverty is *violence*—common, everyday, predatory violence. The way our world works, poor people—*by virtue of their poverty*—are not only vulnerable to hunger, disease, homelessness, illiteracy, and a lack of opportunity; they are also vulnerable to violence.[12] Violence is as much a part of what it means to be poor as being hungry, sick, homeless, or jobless. In fact, as we shall see, violence is frequently the problem that poor people are most concerned about. It is one of the core reasons they are poor in the first place, and one of the primary reasons they stay poor. Indeed, we will simply never be able to win the battle against extreme poverty unless we address it.

Violence from war or conflict, which affects many of the world's poorest and has been identified by some, especially Paul Collier in *The Bottom Billion*, as a major source of poverty or development trap, may occasionally enter our global conversation about the plight of the global poor. But that is not what we are speaking of here. Rather, we are directing attention to the billions of additional poor people who are impacted by "common," everyday violence in their otherwise relatively stable country. For these billions of people at the inflection point in the struggle against poverty, forward progress will depend on whether the world is ready to finally address the epidemic of ordinary terror that swallows up many of our well-intentioned attempts to assist them in sustainably improving their lives.

Poverty's Hidden Terror

The most insidious problems are the ones we cannot see—and when it comes to fighting poverty in the developing world, there is a terror beneath the surface that most of us are missing. Violence in the developing world is like grief in the developed world—it's everywhere, but we just don't see it.

As a young, oblivious summer associate in a large corporate law firm, I remember the day I found out that one of the senior partners, who seemed to me to stride through every day with master-of-the-universe brilliance and omni-competence, had watched helplessly as his son slipped away forever from illness in a hospital intensive care unit just a few days before. And yet, there he was in front of me—in the office at 9:40 AM, showered, shaved, in a crisp suit, breathing in and out, sorting out a complex matter of environmental tort law, wanting no cream in his coffee, all the pictures of his son right there in their dark wood frames. If someone had not told me what had happened, I would have had *no idea.*

It was like a thin curtain had been pulled back on another horrible world just behind the surface of the reality I was walking through. From then on I became mesmerized by two realities in my affluent, white-collar, professional world: first, the massive amount of grief that is all around us all the time in our work-a-day reality (from death, cancer, suicide, dementia, infidelity, failure, addiction, etc.), and secondly, the way we almost never see it. We readily see other more external struggles. But grief? We would have to go very deep to see that.

It is likewise with violence among poor people in the developing world. The relentless threat of violence is part of the core subtext of their lives, but we are unlikely to see it and they are unlikely to tell us about it. We would be wise, however, to not be fooled—because like grief, the thing we cannot see may be the deepest part of their day.

It's true that, for external observers, almost all of the suffering of the poor is hard to see—because it is remote and physically segregated from the affluent, because it's frequently microscopic, because the poor smile and scrub up, and because we ignorantly assume so much without looking or asking carefully. The hidden nature of violence, however, is special for three reasons. First, violence has behind it an intelligent, willful perpetrator who is working hard—frequently *very* hard—to hide it. Indeed, the actual *act* of violence is almost never seen by outsiders. Second, violence is an aspect of life that poor people—like all people—find exceptionally hard to talk about because it is uniquely traumatic. For the human being who has been intentionally humiliated, violated, dominated, defiled, and degraded by violence, the experience is shameful. Paradoxically, the perpetrator and the victim end up sharing a powerful, reflexive inclination: They *both* want to hide it. Finally, for many poor people, the threat of violence has become such a part of the air they breathe that they rarely speak of it as a distinct phenomenon. They simply absorb it.

Surprisingly perhaps, one of the most massive and successful efforts to listen to poor people was sponsored by the World Bank in 1999 in a study released in three volumes titled *Voices of the Poor*. There had never been anything like it. In tens of thousands of detailed personal accounts, very poor people speak for themselves, answering the questions: How do you view poverty and well-being? What are your problems and priorities?

And what did the world learn from listening directly to the poor? Without a doubt, one of the most powerful revelations came from allowing poor people to finally pull back the curtain on the relentless forces of violence that they must contend with on a daily basis—violence that is not the result of war or geopolitical conflict, but simply the result of stronger neighbors harming weaker. The study provided many insights about poverty, but when it came time for the World Bank to announce their massive work, the press release headlined two overarching realities: powerlessness and violence, especially violence against women and girls.[13]

The report confirms that even people with a sophisticated understanding of global poverty can easily miss the reality of violence in everyday, non-conflict settings because "the world over, fear of repercussions cast[s] a silence around the subject of violence" and combines with deep shame to make it very difficult for poor people to be forthcoming about the violence and threats they endure.[14]

Secondly, the report confirms the ubiquitous, global nature of the problem for poor people. It doesn't matter whether they live in the poorest countries or (increasingly) in middle-income countries; on every continent, if they are poor, they are victims of violence.[15]

- In Malawi: "in every community visited, poor men and women reported theft, robbery, burglary, murders, and other acts that pose physical threats to people's lives."[16]
- In Brazil: "people living in Brazil's favelas report an extraordinary prevalence of violence and crime in their everyday lives."[17]
- In Thailand: "poor people reported feeling unsafe and insecure."[18]
- In Nigeria: "poor people in both rural and urban areas fear crime; armed robbery and food theft are frequently mentioned."[19]
- In Ecuador: "poor people face an array of physical dangers . . . of muggings, robberies, rapes and murders."[20]

On and on it goes. These findings from *Voices of the Poor* simply confirm the growing body of evidence documenting that poor people in otherwise stable developing and middle-income countries experience much higher rates of everyday violence than the rest of us,[21] that people who live in impoverished urban areas increasingly fear violence more than anything else,[22] and that the poor frequently name violence as their "greatest fear" or "main problem."[23] When the poor speak for themselves, the plague of violence laying waste to their lives and communities is unmistakably clear.

Understanding the Problem, But Misunderstanding the Solution

Interestingly, even when people with a sophisticated understanding of global poverty *do* understand the massively undermining effect of violence in the lives of poor people in the developing world, they overwhelmingly try to solve violence by addressing the exacerbating factors rather than prioritizing the direct solution *first*, and then addressing the exacerbating factors.

And what is the direct solution to violence? In modern societies, it is *law enforcement*. That is to say, acts of violence are declared to be "against the law" and then the state (the entity holding a monopoly on the legitimate use of coercive force) is authorized to use coercive power to *enforce the law* by restraining and punishing those who commit illegal violent acts.

Law enforcement is not the only answer to violence; indeed, there is a huge range of activities that modern societies properly pursue to reduce violence (everything from broad economic opportunity, education, cultural attitudes, community mediation, street lights, midnight basketball, etc.) because these interventions address the factors that can exacerbate levels of violence (joblessness, lack of opportunity, economic inequality, bigotry, misogyny, poor lighting, young people with nothing to do). But no modern society that thrives tries to address violence by addressing these exacerbating factors *in the absence* of a functioning law enforcement capacity to provide an effective restraint and credible deterrent to acts of violence.

Strangely, however, to the extent people have come to appreciate the problem of violence in the lives of common poor people in the developing world, they have sought to address the problem by primarily addressing the exacerbating factors (like ignorance, cultural attitudes, lack of economic opportunity or education) *in the absence* of a functioning criminal justice system that effectively protects the poor from violence through enforcement of the law. It is proper to address all of the exacerbating factors as vigorously as possible, but it's a losing game to do so without a very focused and rigorous effort to establish a functioning law enforcement capacity—and it's a game the poor cannot afford to lose.

Inputs and Protections

The indispensable need of poor people for protection from violence through basic law enforcement becomes obvious when we pause for a moment to consider the nature of poverty and the human condition. Human beings enter and remain in the world in a severely fragile state because we are utterly dependent upon inputs and protections from *outside of ourselves*. We are not self-contained units. We do not hold within our being the elements we require to survive and thrive; rather, we must go outside ourselves and obtain a continuous flow of resources to meet our needs and to protect ourselves from threats.

We have a set of metabolic needs that must be met because our bodies are in relentless search for calories, nutrients, oxygen, water, and other elements that are beyond us but necessary to simply stay alive. We not only need these *inputs* from outside ourselves to survive and grow, but we also need *protections*, because we lack the capacity on our own to defend ourselves from threats. We need, for example, shelter and (usually) some clothing to protect us from the elements; we need antibiotics and medicine to defend us from bacteria and disease. Accordingly, we say a person is in poverty when she is too poor to obtain all the inputs and protections she needs to survive, develop, and flourish as a human being.

All of this is quite mainstream and common sense thinking about the nature of poverty: People need *external inputs* of good food, good water, and good education to thrive as human beings, and they need *external protections* against bad germs, bad water, and bad weather in order to secure their well-being against threats. What must be added to this framework, however, is a very conscious appreciation of an additional external protection that human beings must obtain from outside themselves—and that is protection against *other people*. They need protection from forces of human violence. Moreover, individual human beings cannot protect themselves from violence alone—they must go outside themselves to secure protection—and such protection is *expensive*.

Protection from Violence

If you are reading this book in a state of reasonable security and peace without fear of being enslaved, imprisoned, beaten, raped, or robbed, it is either the case that you are in a place of isolation far away from human beings, or you are the beneficiary of a system that is protecting you from the violent impulses of the human beings that are around you. There will always be someone stronger, more aggressive, more cunning, or better equipped, and protection costs money.

So if you are feeling safe, it is because you have paid for protective services, either directly through private security or (more likely) indirectly through taxes supporting a system of law enforcement and public safety. If these protective services are working well, you almost never think of them, and you usually forget that the human population in your city is actually capable of tremendous predatory violence in the absence of a coercive system of law and order. It is likely that the forces protecting you from violence are operating like a nice vaccine that you paid a reasonable price for, which you have forgotten about within an hour of swallowing (even though it is continually prepared to do battle on your behalf), and which is so successful that you have become quite unconscious of the fact that you are mortally vulnerable to an aggressive, microscopic organism that is held at bay every minute by that invisible, forgotten vaccine.

What happens, however, if you are living in a community that is too poor (or unwilling) to pay for effective public law enforcement services? And what if you don't have enough money to pay for private security services? Then you are left vulnerable to forces of violence, and it is only a matter of time before you are victimized. Like germs in the air, harsh weather, and invisible contaminants—violence is endemic to the human social condition, and if you do not have the resources (public or private) to secure protection against forces of violence, you are not safe, and your well-being is not secure. In fact, your *ill-being* is quite assured.

But most of us in affluent societies have grown so accustomed to the peace and security that is purchased through massive and expensive law enforcement systems (that are largely out of sight and out of mind) that we have forgotten about the germ of violence that is always in the air. We are no longer mindful of the forces of violence ever pressing at the borders of human nature, and so we do not enter into poor communities urgently asking: How are these people going to be protected from violence? We haven't been trained to ask the question, and so we are unlikely to probe beneath the surface. If we want to understand the violent reality in which the poor actually live, we will have to look very hard because, of all the conditions that afflict the poor, violence is simply the hardest to see.

Sexual Violence

If you want to learn something more of poverty's quiet terror beneath the surface of the developing world, you might come along as my IJM colleague Delmi Ramirez takes me to visit with some of the girls she cares for in her community in Guatemala City. Delmi is a petite social worker in her 40s who exudes all the gentle warmth, old wisdom and buoyant joy you would ever want in someone who seeks to love back to wholeness girls who have suffered the devastation of sexual violence.

Delmi has worked with hundreds of impoverished girls in her city who have been victims of sexual assault. When she recounts their individual stories with a gentle whisper, she lifts the back of her hand to cover her mouth and fresh tears still come easily to her eyes. But when she is with them, she laughs, hugs, and teases these girls with an auntie's ease and embraces them for the regular kids that they are.

Delmi has arranged for me to visit with a number of these children in a group home, and I eventually find myself sitting at a fold-out table with craft supplies, holding a chubby 1-year-old boy on my lap, with a half dozen giggling girls between 8 and 15 working on their projects around the table. The scene feels surreal in all its delightful childhood innocence because Delmi has provided me with the back story of these girls in advance—and in their stories all the violence in the global experts' reports comes horribly to life.

The baby boy I am holding is actually the son of the 11-year-old girl sitting next to me. This "mom" is a tiny not-yet-a teenager in blue jeans and a soft white t-shirt with colorful cartoon characters on the front. She has curly dark hair pulled back with a blue flower pin on the side, and a firecracker grin that explodes over her normal shy smile when she decides to unleash it. I'll call her Gloria. She comes from one of those poor households that experts refer to as living off less than $2.00 a day.

When Gloria was 10 years old, she was raped by her mother's boyfriend while her mother was at work; as a result, she gave birth to this sweet little boy on my lap. The boyfriend had actually been sexually assaulting Gloria and her *younger* sister for some time, and both girls had fallen badly behind in school. They had been forced to live with the boyfriend because their own father had been murdered some years earlier; then, when Gloria and her sister had moved in with her grandparents, her grandparents were murdered as well. None of these murders were ever solved or brought to justice, but that was the world of torrential violence into which Gloria was born. When her rapist said he'd kill her if she ever spoke of the abuse, one can imagine how easy it would be for Gloria to believe the threats.

There it was all around me: the shocking and disorienting levels of extreme violence in the everyday lives of the poor; the extraordinary vulnerability and victimization of children (especially girls); and the unconscious confluence of silence and shame that, ordinarily, would never permit you to see the terror behind the veil.

But go behind the veil we must if we want to really understand the plight of the global poor and mobilize the interventions that are most helpful. And we must begin with sexual violence—one of the most pervasive and devastating sources of violence against the poor. It is worth taking the time and effort to do this because, despite its massive cruelty and unrivaled number of casualties, there is something about the problem that keeps falling off our radar screen. Why is that?

Perhaps it's because the disasters that occur every day aren't considered real news. The Pulitzer-Prize-winning human rights journalist Nick Kristof and his fellow-journalist wife, Cheryl WuDunn, wondered about this:

> as many infant girls die unnecessarily *every week* in China [from discriminatory neglect] as protesters died in the one incident at Tiananmen [Square]. Those Chinese girls never received a column inch of news coverage, and we began to wonder if our own journalistic priorities were skewed.... When a prominent dissident was arrested in China, we would write a front page article; when 100,000 girls were routinely kidnapped and trafficked into brothels, we didn't even consider it news.[24]

Kristof and WuDunn have now done more than anyone to put the global problem of sexual violence on the public's radar screen with their bestseller,

Half the Sky—but their own journey illustrates how difficult it is to secure focus on this massive man-made disaster. But let's see if we can't at least get a grip on the basics—because for masses of the global poor, few things are more threatening to their health and well-being.

So what do we need to know about sexual violence and the global poor? Perhaps we need to know just two big, horrible things: that sexual violence is both a virulent epidemic and a profitable business.

The Epidemic of Sexual Violence

First, because of its vast scale and lethal power, sexual violence is best spoken of as a global epidemic. For the poor, its threatening presence seems to be everywhere, all the time, showing no mercy. Over and over again, the most knowledgeable international leaders speak of sexual violence in terms of a contagious disease that quietly spreads its devastation across the globe and, one by one, shatters hundreds of millions of lives in its wake. Like some dread plague, sexual violence has seeped into every nook and cranny of the developing world—the homes, schools, alleys, workplaces, orphanages and places of worship, commerce, and care.*

And what do the experts tell us about this epidemic from a global altitude? To begin with, they can see that sexual violence flows out of an even larger plague ravaging its way through the global poor—and that is *gender violence* more broadly, which combines sexual violence, domestic abuse, and other forms of coercive abuse that females endure from males. While impoverished men and (especially) boys are also victims of sexual violence in poor communities, it is overwhelmingly women and girls who are the victims of a daily onslaught of violence *simply because they are female.*

All across the poor communities that were studied in *Voices of the Poor's* review of 60 countries, "physical violence against women appears to be widespread and considered part of everyday life."[25] From Pakistan to Ethiopia to Ghana to Argentina to Bangladesh—women and girls spoke about sexual assaults, beatings, domestic violence, and abuse.

---

* Sexual violence plagues the developed world as well, but for the poorest of the poor in the developing world there is no hope of recourse for injustice as systems are structurally designed to work against them.

And the numbers are huge. One out of three women around the world has been beaten, forced into sex, or otherwise abused in her lifetime.[26] The rates of violence against women and girls are even higher among poor women.[27] Studies suggest that 49 percent of Ethiopian women will be assaulted, 48 percent of Ugandan women, 62 percent of Peruvian women, 35 percent of Indian women, and 34 percent of Brazilian women.[28] We could travel across the globe gathering up similar statistics of abuse throughout the developing world. One can see why the World Bank has estimated that the epidemic of gender violence kills and disables more women and girls between the ages of 15 and 44 than cancer, traffic accidents, malaria, and war *combined*.[29]

These mind-numbing statistics start to ring true when you get deep into the details of the individual lives of women and girls in the developing world. In Peru, not only was Lucila's daughter Yuri raped and murdered—but Lucila herself had to leave her home because of domestic violence, and her mother before her fled *her* home because of domestic violence. In Guatemala City, Gloria has been raped, her sister raped, her mother assaulted, and her grandmother murdered.

In the developing world, gender discrimination takes on horrifyingly violent and lethal forms.[30]

- Globally, 5,000 women and girls are murdered every year in so-called "honor killings" by family members who feel disgraced because a sister or daughter has seemed to act immodestly, or because they have fallen in love with the wrong guy, or because (most cruelly) they have been "defiled" by rape.[31]
- An estimated 15,000 women and girls are murdered each year in India in family disputes over dowry—the payment of cash or goods made by the bride's family to the groom's family.[32]
- Every year, millions of girls in the developing world (about one in seven) are forced into marriage before the age of 15, a situation in which incidents of violence are high and sexual initiation is accompanied by force, fear, and pain.[33]
- *Every day*, about 6,000 girls around the world are faced with enduring female genital mutilation (FGM), which is the cutting away of all or part of the external female genitalia—generally done without anesthetic.

It is especially worth noting that all of this violence against women and girls in the developing world—all the wife beatings, the dowry murders, honor killings, the acid burnings, the coercive child marriages and the genital mutilation—is *against the law* in nearly all the countries where it occurs. These laws, however, are simply not enforced—and it becomes "open season" against women and girls. As Amnesty International has affirmed after years of global experience with gender violence:

> Most acts of violence against women are never investigated, and perpetrators commit their crimes safe in the knowledge that they will never face arrest, prosecution or punishment. Impunity for violence against women contributes to a climate where such acts are seen as normal and acceptable rather than criminal, where women do not seek justice because they know they will not gain it, where the original pain and suffering are prolonged and aggravated by the denial that a serious violation of human rights has been committed.[34]

It is out of this context of massive and generalized violence against women and girls that the epidemic levels of *sexual* violence emerge in the developing world. As the epidemiologists at the Centers for Disease Control tell us, sexual violence "is a global human rights injustice of vast proportions with severe health and social consequences."[35] Moreover, like most epidemics, it is the poor who are left undefended and endure the worst. A massive study on violence around the world conducted by the World Health Organization found that poor women and girls are disproportionately vulnerable to sexual violence, and that while all social classes experience sexual violence, research consistently shows that people with the lowest socioeconomic status are at greatest risk.[36] It is famously difficult to establish a definitive quantitative assessment of sexual violence, but from across every region of the developing world, data trickle in in a variety of forms to create a composite picture of what the poor are experiencing. When the WHO surveyed 22,656 students from five African countries, nearly one out of every four children (and over one out of every four girls) reported having been forced to have sex. Across Africa, similar figures pour in: In one Ethiopian study, 59 percent of women report being victimized by sexual violence, and in another,[37] 68.5 percent of Ethiopian *girls* said they had been sexually abused.[38] Thirty-eight percent of girls in Malawi said they were "not willing at all" when they first had sex, and 30 percent of girls said the same in Ghana.[39] In South Africa, the most prevalent crime reported against children appears to be rape, with 40 percent of rapes or attempted rapes reported to the police coming from girls under age 18.[40] And among sexually experienced Kenyan girls ages 10 to 19, 45 percent reported that they been forced into non-consensual sex at least once. Of course, the sexual violence pandemic rages outside of Africa as well—and with fury. In Bangladesh, 36 percent of provincial women who first had intercourse before age 15 said they were coerced. In Lima, Peru, 45 percent of such women said the same thing. In Thailand, 30 percent of women reported that they were victims of rape or attempted rape. In parts of Mexico, it was 42 percent. A review of sexual violence studies in Latin America found that "sexual violence is a serious and pervasive problem in the region" with the lifetime prevalence of forced sex by an intimate partner ranging from 5 percent to 47 percent.[41]

The scattered data on sexual violence against the poor are beginning to get the world's attention, but as the experts are careful to explain, the relationship between the data they have and the actual "global magnitude of the

Sexual Violence and the Tip of the Iceberg

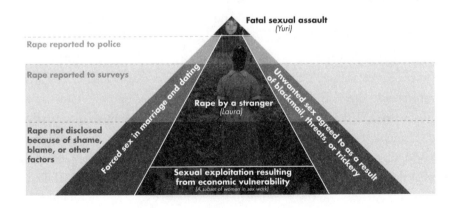

Figure 2.3

Adapted and published with permission of the World Health Organization. "World Report on Violence and Health." Ed. Krug, Dahlberg, Mercy, Zwi and Lozano. Geneva: World Health Organization. 2002. 150.

problem" should be thought of as "an iceberg floating in water."[42] That is, *most* of the sexual violence against the poor is hidden beneath the surface.

Thousands of women and girls in the developing world tell my colleagues that they simply don't feel safe—and that sexual violence can feel like a threat everywhere, all the time. For instance, sexual violence is in the place that is supposed to be safest: the home—with high rates of sexual assault by relatives (and the friends and sexual partners of those relatives) in the often cramped quarters of the poor. Laura was inside the four walls of her little slum home when her father raped her—and Gloria was inside her own home when her mother's boyfriend repeatedly violated her. The home can be a place of silent, lawless brutality for the poorest women and girls.

Sexual violence also lurks as an ever present specter in the surrounding neighborhood as well. In Korogocho, Laura was dragged into a neighbor's house and into the neighborhood latrine when she was assaulted by two other men. And sadly, this is a common narrative around the world. Doctors Without Borders (MSF) is one of those global agencies for whom the epidemic of sexual violence among the poor is not a hidden phenomenon. They live and serve in the midst of it and they have declared it a global "medical emergency."[43] This declaration extends not only to difficult zones of war or conflict, but as MSF is careful to emphasize: "sexual violence also affects millions of people living in stable contexts."[44] Formal studies in the developing world confirm this terrifying way in which the plague of sexual violence seeps into all the places a girl in poverty would hope to find familiarity and safety. Indeed, in the world's poorest communities, "non-consensual sexual events are most likely to occur in familiar settings (such as the neighborhood, home or school), in the course of routine activities, and are largely perpetrated by those with whom the young person is acquainted."[45]

Particularly tragic is the way sexual violence in and on the way to *school* is stealing away the promising prospects of what development experts call "The Girl Effect"—that is, the disproportionately positive impact that occurs when girls in the world's poorest communities have a chance to go to school and get educated. Just as experts are beginning to appreciate the incredible promise of education for girls—other experts are coming to understand that one of the primary reasons girls *don't* go to school in the developing world is sexual violence. In fact, according to the WHO, studies indicate that, for large populations of girls in the developing world, school is the *most* common place where sexual violence occurs.[46] Horribly, studies in the developing world show that both teachers and peers are perpetrators of sexual violence in schools.[47] And parents in the developing world are no different from you and me: They want to protect their daughters from rape. It's a tragically common reason cited by parents for withdrawing their daughters from school—and, as this legitimate fear reverberates throughout the communities of the developing world, its impact is seen with particular clarity in South Asia and sub-Saharan Africa, where the enrollment of girls in school declines sharply as they hit adolescence.[48]

In order for The Girl Effect to have its intended and glorious effect, the girl must be safe to go to school, and right now, in the absence of credible enforcement of the laws against sexual violence—those schools are *not safe*. Moreover, the broader impact of this particular brand of violence is devastating to the girl child, causing physical and psychological trauma, increasing her risk for a sexual and reproductive health problems—and even causing her death, as the experts at the WHO clinically note: "Mortality associated with sexual violence may occur through suicide, HIV infection, and murder, either during the attack or subsequently in 'honour killings.'"[49]

Women and girls, everywhere, are vulnerable to sexual violence, just as all women and girls are vulnerable to germs. Indeed, anthropologists have identified rape as a "human universal"—a behavioral tendency common to all human societies with no known exception.[50] Just like germs in the air. The difference is, some women and girls get protected from germs through medicine and sanitation—and some women and girls do not (the poorest). Likewise, some women and girls get an earnest and, though imperfect, generally effective enforcement of local laws against sexual violence—and some women and girls do not (the poorest). In the midst of a raging epidemic, the poorest and most vulnerable of our sisters, daughters, and mothers around the world are left undefended.

Sexual Violence as a Business

The second thing we ought to understand about sexual violence is that it is not only an epidemic—but it is also a *business*. That is to say, there is actually money to be made off of rape and sexual assault—*a lot* of money. And this is very bad news for impoverished women and girls in the developing world. It's bad enough when violence emerges out of personal disputes, social pathology, or bigotry, but when it becomes clear that a form of violence is a way to make a lot of money, then you have strapped an economic engine onto the epidemic and provided a vast number of people with a powerful incentive to spread the "disease" as vigorously as possible. There are not a lot of people who think they can get rich off more malaria, more dirty water, or more dysentery—but there are a lot of people who *know* they can make a lot of money off of sexual violence, and they are pursuing the opportunity against the vulnerable poor with a brutal zeal.

It is a very untidy thought to realize that there is actually a vast business of rape for profit in the world—but such is the messiness of human nature and the world as it actually is. *Every day* in the world, there are millions of rapes and acts of sexual molestation that take place for money—as a commercial transaction. *Every day* there are millions of people (mostly women and girls, and some boys) who are raped or sexually molested (i.e., compelled by force or the threat of force to endure a sexual act to which they would not otherwise have consented) as part of a commercial transaction. *Every day*, there are many more millions who pay for these rapes and sexual assaults, and hundreds of thousands of people who facilitate it and profit from it.

This can sound all rather sensational and hysterical, so it is worth breaking the numbers down.

First, every day there are millions of people who are raped or sexually molested as part of a commercial transaction.

Credible and conservative estimates of global sex trafficking indicate that there are between 4.2 million and 11.6 million people held in forced commercial sexual exploitation—people who are compelled by force and coercion to endure sexual acts that customers pay for.[51] Conservatively, Kristof and WuDunn have looked at the numbers and found that there are at least "3 million women and girls (and a very small number of boys) worldwide who can be fairly termed enslaved in the sex trade." Moreover, they are quick to add:

> That is a conservative estimate that does not include many others who are manipulated and intimidated into prostitution. Nor does it include millions more who are under eighteen and cannot meaningfully consent to work in brothels. We are talking about 3 million people who in effect are the property of another person and in many cases could be killed by their owner with impunity.

Deriving a precise estimate of the number of victims of an illicit activity is difficult, but a number of smart and thorough efforts have begun to help us with a sense of scale. The sober and rigorous British medical journal *The Lancet* looked at just the *children* and found that there were at least 1 million children forced into prostitution *every year* and perhaps a total of 10 million prostituted children in the world.[52] UNICEF tells us that there are 2 million *children* coerced to endure sexual violence in the commercial sex trade.[53] The ILO has estimated that there are about 2.3 million women and girls held in forced prostitution against their will in India alone.[54]

Next, every day there are millions more who pay for these sexual acts coerced by violent force.

It is safe to say that many of the 4 to 11 million people held in forced prostitution will be compelled to endure sex acts with multiple customers in a single day. This makes sense because the commercial sex operator who has secured the victim wants to make as much money off his or her investment as possible, and that investment is maximized by generating as many trans-actions as possible. In our experience around the world, it is common for victims of forced prostitution to service three to 10 customers in a day; and if this was the experience of even half, then *every day* somewhere between 6 and 50 million people (men, really) pay money for sexual intercourse that has been compelled by violence (rape) or some other sex act that has been compelled by violence (sexual molestation).

To be sure, the vast majority of these customers do not actually desire that the sex act per se be compelled by violence. They just want the sex act. Indeed, the customers generally prefer to imagine that the victim is a willing and even eager participant, and so the commercial sex opera-tor will actually use violence or threats to compel the victims to appear happy and willing, and will punish them if they do not. The custom-ers' posture is similar to those who buy pirated DVDs. They don't actu-ally want a "stolen" movie per se—they just want their movie at a cheap price. Likewise, it is a relatively small group of customers in the com-mercial sex trade who actually are seeking to have sex that they *know* is compelled by violence. The vast majority of customers just want the sex, and they are very willing to ignore and deny the coercion that makes it possible for them to purchase the cheap sex (even when they see it or are told about it).

Finally, every year in the world there are hundreds of thousands of people who are knowingly facilitating and profiting from rape and sexual molesta-tion as a commercial transaction.

Behind each victim of forced prostitution there are generally at least three people making money and making it all possible. They are 1) the recruiter who wins the victim's trust, 2) the middleman or trafficker who bridges the connection to 3) the commercial sex operator, who in turn provides the connection to the customer pool. In fact, there are generally a good deal more than three people participating in and profiting from the forced prostitution conspiracy. As a result, the global business of forced prostitution that victimizes 4 to 11 million people a year surely involves hundreds of thousands (if not millions) of people profiting every year.

It is a hard but authentic reality that sexual violence is a very significant *business* in our world. Indeed, the conservative estimates suggest that the global business of forced prostitution generates revenues of $18.5 billion in developing world countries.[55]

But why focus so much attention on this problem of forced prostitution? In the number of people affected, it is not the biggest problem facing the global poor—and because it is about sex, it's subject to exaggeration and can divert attention away from larger more pressing needs. But commercial sexual exploitation is worthy of our focused attention for a few reasons: First, it's a form of violence that actively and overwhelmingly *targets* the poor. Secondly, it is against the law everywhere in the developing world and requires the commission of multiple felonies, but like other forms of violence against the poor, it carries on day after day *on a vast scale*. These multiple felonies of forced prostitution are committed millions of times a day against millions of poor people with impunity *because the victims are poor*. And finally, forced prostitution has been hidden. One would think that a large global business of rape for profit would be well known. But it has not been. It certainly raged all the way through the twentieth century with almost no attention from the international development community until the 1990s when Human Rights Watch,[56] ECPAT, and a few other small advocacy organizations began to bring the horror to light. When IJM began to bring survivors from the developing world up to Capitol Hill to speak for themselves about the problem in 1998 (to support what became the Trafficking Victims Protection Act of 2000) the problem was received as if it were new. Awareness was new (indeed, it was new to us at IJM), but the problem was not, and its "sudden" appearance upon the global scene manifested the way the massive problems of violence against the poor can remain utterly below the radar—even among the otherwise well-informed.

Understanding sexual violence as a business comes from understanding the motivations and calculations of the perpetrators—because it is their will, their intentionality, their thinking, their calculation, incentives, and disincentives that drive the dynamics of the business. Unfortunately, however, insight into the business from the perpetrator's perspective is exceedingly rare. As pointed out at one of the highest level United Nations forums convened to address trafficking: "For a universally condemned, but globally evident issue, surprisingly little is known about human traffickers—those who enable or partake in the trade and exploitation of individual human beings."[57]

Since 1997, IJM has spent hundreds of thousands of hours infiltrating commercial sex operations in the developing world and investigating thousands of individual perpetrators. We even conducted a rare study of convicted forced prostitution perpetrators through systematic interviews with about 60 brothel keepers and traffickers who were serving their sentences in prison.[57] Forced prostitution is a highly complex crime, human behavior, and socio-economic phenomenon, and we do not presume to know more than a fraction of what there is to know, but we do feel like we have learned a lot from spending a great deal of time with the criminals who are the driving force behind the business.

From what we have seen and what studies of the victims have shown,[59] perpetrators of forced prostitution learn to turn their focus on women and girls *in poverty*. But why?

Overwhelmingly, it seems that perpetrators view them as *easier to coerce*—because they seem easier *to deceive*. Physically compelling someone into a brothel or commercial sex operation where they are going to be raped or molested is difficult, so perpetrators use various deceptions to induce cooperation and reduce resistance.

Among the thousands of forced prostitution cases that IJM has worked from around the world, I doubt there is a single one that did not at some stage involve deceiving the victim.

- Nilaya, a teenage girl from a village in Nepal, was told that she would have a job as a maid for a wealthy woman in Kathmandu—instead she was trafficked into a brothel in Kolkata.
- Lien, a Vietnamese teenage girl, was told that she could get a job in a coffee shop in Poipet and was trafficked instead into a massage parlor that operated as a brothel.

- Sangrawee, Son-Kiln, and Prang, three Thai teenagers, were each offered different jobs in Malaysia as a waitress, a bartender, and a clerk in a clothing store as part of their abduction into a brothel in Johor Bahru, Malaysia.
- Maleah in the Philippines needed money for her mother's medical care and was offered a job as a singer in Malaysia that turned out to be confinement in a bar that functioned as a brothel.
- Nabilah and other teenage girls from Nigeria thought they were going to get jobs as typists in the Ivory Coast and eventually in Europe before they found themselves forced to submit to rapes in a sex trafficking operation in the Ivory Coast's largest city of Abidjan.

The poor are especially susceptible to these schemes of deception because the desperation of their economic situation makes them (and their parents or caretakers) more willing to suspend their disbelief, set aside their suspicions, and take greater risks. Their poverty frequently also means they are more likely to be less educated, more naïve, less sophisticated, deferential to people of higher status, and less accustomed to asserting themselves—and therefore easier for confident schemers to deceive. For reasons one can readily anticipate, all of these vulnerabilities are vastly multiplied if the female in poverty is a child.

For all these reasons, perpetrators of forced prostitution target *poor* women and girls because they are easier to deceive. But here we have to pause so as not to draw the wrong conclusion. Deception is such a major part of forced prostitution that many lose sight of the violent force that *always* lies at the critical core of *forced* prostitution. So to be clear: Eventually *every* deceptive trafficking scheme is exposed, and the victim is presented with the customer who has paid money to have sex with the victim. In that moment, if the victim is unwilling (as almost all are) the perpetrator must use force or the threat of force to compel compliance, and the transaction has become a commercial rape—and a serious violent crime. All of the work on the deceptive scheme is completely wasted if the perpetrator cannot compel compliance with violence—and so violence becomes the final, defining feature of the transaction.

This bit of clarity then leads to the second reason why perpetrators intentionally target the poor: namely, once the deception is over and it is time for violence, the poor are undefended.

The perpetrators of forced prostitution know that there will always be the coercive moment at the end of all their schemes of deception; therefore, they are looking for *soft* targets. They are prowling for people who are likely to offer less resistance at the moment of violence (because they are physically weaker or less assertive). But more importantly, the perpetrators are targeting people who will have fewer resources coming to their defense. Perpetrators engaged in forced prostitution are, to be blunt, selfish cowards—and they have zero interest in a fair fight. They want to exert as little effort as possible and take as few risks as possible—and therefore they do not want to take on any additional people coming to the defense of their victims. The perpetrator wants to assemble as many thugs and co-conspirators as possible on his side and take on, if possible, an utterly isolated victim.

For the average person there are, in theory, four lines of defense against violent abuse—the family, the community, private security, and the government. If a girl is threatened with violence, her vulnerability is generally reduced by the watchful eye of the family, neighborhood, community, tribe, or clan. For additional levels of defense, those with more wealth pay other people to watch over them, to defend them, and to go and secure additional help when threats arise. Finally the last line of defense is the government— the law enforcement authorities who are given coercive power for the precise purpose of defending citizens against violent threats.

For a person living in poverty in the developing world, however, while the protections of the family and community may be quite strong, the third and fourth lines of defense are almost non-existent. The common poor person in the developing world cannot afford to hire private security the way wealthier people in the developing world can—and, as we have seen and shall see further, poor people do not get the protections of law enforcement.[60]

Therefore, the perpetrator of forced prostitution knows that he must simply get past the first two lines of defense (the family and the community)— and then he is home free. The sex trafficker knows that if he can simply separate the victim from the potential defenses of the family and the community, there will be no one else (no private security guard or government police officer) coming to the victim's aid, and no one imposing a penalty upon him for his abuse. So the focused task becomes separating the woman or girl from the family and community—and this where all the deception comes into play.

Indeed, if you look at all the deceptive schemes of the sex trafficker, almost all of them are intended to separate the woman or the girl from her family and community (where she might know who to turn to and how to turn for help). And for the poor, the most compelling reason to leave your family and your community is the promise of economic opportunity somewhere else. Moreover, if that job opportunity outside the community might potentially benefit the family with increased shared income (which is the way any single family member's job prospects are generally viewed)—then the family is actually recruited to the task of encouraging the targeted victim to leave the family and the community.

Of course the sex trafficker's job is made all the easier if the victim's protections within the family or community are weak; here again, there is good reason for the trafficker to target the poorest families in the developing world. The harshness, desperation, and pressure of poverty in the developing world leave many with weaker protections in the family and community. People living in poverty are often separated from the protections of both the family unit and the community by long hours of distance, and unsteady or migratory work. Protections of community can be further eroded when someone's gender, ethnicity, religion, status, or caste is marginalized. Family protections may be splintered by gender violence or by domestic or substance abuse.

And, even if a girl or woman benefits from reasonably strong protections of family or community, in communities of great poverty where many people are desperately seeking to scrape together food, water, and shelter to survive the day, it can be easy to find someone who, for a little money, is willing to help participate (knowingly or not) in a scheme that separates a woman or girl from whatever protections she does have in the her family and community.

One can readily see two powerful and dangerous implications from all this. First, in the cruel logic of criminal violence, the poor person's extra vulnerability to violence actually makes them a more attractive target for violence and draws more violence their way. The poor are the hemophiliacs in the shark infested waters—everybody is in danger, but they bleed more when they get cut and they attract more sharks when they do.

Secondly, unlike others who may have money to hire private security or may live in communities with functioning law enforcement systems, once the woman or girl in poverty is separated from the protections of family and community, there will be no one left to respond when the victim sees the moment of violence advancing toward her and lifts her voice for help. For the poor in the developing world, those cries go nowhere.

And when it comes to the reality of the "coercive moment" of forced prostitution, I would have few concrete images to understand what that means if the survivors had not personally described what that meant for them: the way they were beaten with sticks, clubs, electrical cords, and metal rods; how they had to clean up the blood of other girls beaten, tortured, and even killed in front of their eyes; how they were forcibly injected with narcotics that left them powerless and nauseous; that they were forced to watch their children burned with cigarettes until they submitted to rape.

Figure 2.4
"The coercive moment": Footage from an IJM investigation shows an accused pimp brandishing the club he used to beat girls in his brothel

Their stories are worth paying attention to if we can endure them because they help secure a sense of urgency about the millions of others whose voices would otherwise dissolve into the vast ocean of muffled violence that remains deep beneath the visible surface of poverty.

We would never come to know what was happening to Maya, for instance, when she encountered the coercive moment at the end of her trafficking deception. While traveling from her brother's home in one rural village of West Bengal, India, to her parents' in another, she met a familiar older couple who asked her to accompany them on a short errand. She agreed to what was to be a brief excursion, and when they kept traveling much farther than she had anticipated, she didn't want to be rude and ask about it—these were her elders, and she trusted them. Eventually, the couple gave Maya food and tea. She quickly fell asleep, and awoke later in a hotel, with no idea how much time had passed.

Maya's anxiety began to roll from uneasiness in her stomach to tightness in her chest when she found herself ushered alone into a room and then found the door locked behind her—from the outside. Sitting alone, she heard a girl's scream below. Eventually a woman came and opened Maya's door. Maya stepped out and immediately noticed a stream of young girls dressed in very revealing clothes. "Why are they dressed like that?" Maya asked her escort.

"All the girls dress like this nowadays," the woman said.

"They took me to another room and left me alone," Maya later remembered. "That's when I began to realize that they had sold me there and left me. I was crying the whole time. Three girls brought food up for me to my room. They were from the same area as me. I asked them how I could get help, and they said they couldn't help me, because if they tried they would be killed. Then one of the helpers came into my room and left a bottle of whiskey, two metal pipes and two wooden bars. I got very scared seeing that."

Maya had found herself right in the middle of sexual violence as a business—in a brothel on the outskirts of Kolkata, India, run by a man named Nakul Bera.

"Nakul came up to the room and was drinking alcohol," Maya remembered. He was a thin, wiry man in his forties with a sharp jaw and a rough beard. "He was using very bad language and told his friends to go and call up a girl named Madhuri. They brought her in, dragging her by the hair. Nakul poured all the alcohol into a glass and made her drink it all. Then he started beating this girl. He stripped her and started beating her over and over with the stick and pipe. When she went unconscious, he would throw water on her to wake her up. I learned that he did all of this because she tried to run away," Maya said.

For Maya, the horror of her first night was just beginning. With Madhuri beaten unconscious and bleeding on the floor, Nakul turned to Maya, pressed in on her and began forcing alcohol down her throat. He grabbed her, dragged her downstairs, and violently raped her. "I passed out," Maya says. When she woke up again she was in such pain she couldn't walk.

Later that same night, this young woman, who 12 hours before had simply agreed to accompany trusted neighbors on quick errand, became a tiny data point lost amidst the mind-numbing statistics of forced prostitution in the developing world. Maya was taken down to the bottom level of the brothel, dressed in skimpy western clothes, and offered up to the crush of men who had come to give Nakul their money in exchange for sex with the girls in his brothel.

For almost a year inside the brothel, Maya endured a reality we wrap up in the phrase "forced prostitution."

Eventually, my colleague Melita Fernandes and other local Indian staff with IJM would lead an operation with the Indian authorities that rescued Maya and other girls from this hell. Melita as well as Maya's IJM social worker would both comment on Maya's extraordinary determination to see Nakul prosecuted and her insistence that the world understand what happens to a girl like her in a place like that. Maya wanted us to know what happened when an older girl in a brothel got caught helping a younger girl try to escape. And she explained it to us in details I find hard to forget.

"Nakul brought all of us in the brothel into one room," Maya said. "We all knew something bad was going to happen. They brought in a lot of alcohol, sticks, and pipes. I asked the other girls what was going to happen and they replied, 'Be quiet. Don't shout, don't cry, and don't say anything—just watch.'"

"The pimps dragged the girl into the room. She was the older girl who had tried to help the younger girl. They made her drink a lot of alcohol. Nakul was telling her, 'You know what kind of man I am: If I forgive someone I forgive them; if I don't, I kill them.' He stripped her naked and began beating her. He wouldn't stop, even after he had broken her arms. The whole area was full of blood."

"She was half-dead and was asking for someone to please give her some water. Nakul said that no one could get up or they would be next. He took her to her room and she died that night. They say he put her body in a sack in the back of his car," Maya finished, "and threw her into a river."

It would take seven unsuccessful rescue operations for Melita and the IJM team to reach Maya and finally bring rescue with a trusted unit of the

Indian police. With an IJM-assisted manhunt, Nakul was eventually arrested by the Indian authorities.

As I write, Maya has been testifying in an Indian court about what happened to her and the other girls in Nakul's brothel.[60] It's a frightening task for a young woman to face down a violent criminal like Nakul—especially in a system where so very few are ever brought to justice. But Maya seems to know what she is doing.

"If you have seen so much abuse and torture in front of your eyes, don't you want the person who did all this to get justice?" Maya asks. "If you don't protest against what he did, he will never be stopped. I have to be brave. If I want to live, I have to fight. I am using all the strength I have inside my heart. I will make sure he gets punished."

Reflecting on all of this, Melita told me, "Blaming 'poverty' for crimes like this is convenient—it seems to make trafficking a problem 'beyond our control.' But I strongly believe that poverty is just one of the factors that makes people vulnerable to being trafficked—and that trafficking still exists because an effective public justice system doesn't in my country. Maya's story and the stories of all my clients affirm my faith in this."

FORCED LABOR

A second category of massive violence afflicting the poor in the developing world is forced labor. But unlike sexual violence, in which only a portion of the violence is a money-making business—forced labor is a category of violence that is driven *entirely* by money and the willingness to put violence to work as an economic enterprise.

There is nothing new about using violence to steal from people: This is the most classic concept of crime and the most primal reality of the strong preying upon the weak. But the poor don't have much in the way of money or possessions to steal—so it turns out that the most profitable thing to steal is the whole person.

This is the essence of forced labor—the use of violence to steal the poor person's whole body and put it to work in ways that will make money for the perpetrator[†]—to make bricks, scrub floors, rake rice, roll cigarettes, shovel

[†] This is the nature of forced prostitution, which is both a subcategory of sexual violence and a subcategory of forced labor—where the form of labor that is compelled is the provision of a sexual act.

charcoal, break rocks, plant crops, cut wood, build buildings, make matches, dig ditches, sew garments, weave carpets, herd cattle. On and on it goes. All the perpetrator has to do is feed and water that body a little bit, give it a bit of shelter, and he can extract from that body hours and hours of work, seven days a week, month after month, for years on end. And all that work will generate an enormous amount of money. Even in the lower-income economies of the developing world, forced labor outside the business of forced prostitution will gush forth another $7 billion per year in profits.[62]

This helps explain why experts believe that there are actually more slaves in the world *today* than ever before in human history. It's true that a smaller *proportion* of humanity is held in slavery than ever before,[63] and a smaller *proportion* of the world's economy is generated by slavery than ever before[64]—but, in absolute numbers, the world has never seen so many people in slavery at one time.[65]

In fact, historians tell us that about 11 million slaves were extracted from Africa during *four hundred years* of the trans-Atlantic slave trade[66]— which is as little as half of the number of people held in slavery in our world *this year.*

Figure 2.5
Millions are still held in slavery: More than 500 children, women and men seen on the day of their 2011 rescue from a life of slavery in a brick factory outside Chennai, India

So in an era of unprecedented global economic prosperity, freedom, and opportunity, who are these people who live in *slavery* by the millions?

Not surprisingly, they are the poor. By every conceivable measure, the victims of modern-day slavery tend to be the poorest people—and low-income countries tend to have the highest levels of slavery.[67] As we have seen, the desperate poverty of the poor leaves them especially vulnerable to fraudulent job offers and trafficking schemes that separate them from family and community—but at the end of the day, the reason they can be kept as slaves is because they are the people on our globe left undefended against the forces of violence. The world's foremost scholar on modern-day slavery, Kevin Bales, explains the way slavery targets the poor:

> The government has little time or attention to give to these poor and dis-enfranchised people, relegating them to second class status. This pattern is repeated across the developing world, and the result, whether in Rio, New Delhi, Manila, or Bangkok is extreme vulnerability. The police do not protect you, the law is not your shield, you can't buy your way out of problems, and any weapon you have is no match for those of the gangs and the police.[68]

Indeed, if we listen to voices from the developing world, the vast reality of modern slavery begins to surface. In Pakistan, Jawad Aslam, with the Society for the Protection of the Rights of the Child, will explain that landlords in his country hold nearly 7 million of Pakistan's poorest citizens in forced labor on plantations and private homes—while others are held in bondage in carpet weaving, mining, glass, and fishing industries—with about one million slaves held in Pakistan's brick factories alone.[69] In Mauritania, Boubacar Messaoud and Abdel Nasser Ould Ethmane, a former slave and former slave holder, have established an agency called S.O.S. to help slaves in their country. If their government allowed them to speak openly, they could explain how hundreds of thousands of their countrymen—between 10 percent and 20 percent of the population—still live as slaves.[70] Local Haitian spokespersons from the Restavek Foundation can explain how 250,000 to 300,000 impoverished children in Haiti are sent from their homes at a young age to work as live-in domestic slaves (called *restaveks*) in the households of the country's wealthier families, where they are forced to work around the clock without pay, are generally not permitted to go to school, and are frequently subject to violent abuse and sexual assault.[71] Local Ghanaian advocates have taken my colleagues to the banks of Lake Volta in Ghana to meet scores of boys sold into forced labor on small fishing boats, working 12 to 16 hours a day under dangerous circumstances where many drown each year. Experts estimate that there are more than 200,000 children held in various forms of forced labor in West and Central Africa.[72‡] Xavier Plassat, from the Pastoral Land Commission of Episcopal Conference of Brazil, will explain the way 25,000 Brazilian rural laborers are lured into slavery every year[73] by middlemen or employers with false promises of good jobs and money. These landless, frequently illiterate, and desperately poor workers are taken to work in remote areas in Northeastern Brazil and compelled to work in forestry, charcoal production, the ranching industry, and on sugar, cotton, and soybean plantations.[74]

Perhaps the most confusing aspect of modern-day slavery is the way notions of *debt* are used to obscure reality. Remember how Mariamma's slavery began after she and her fellow workers accepted a small advance payment from Mr. V to move to his facility? When you get close to it, it's obvious that the relationship between the laborer and the person who loaned the money has nothing to do with debt (in fact, the lender doesn't even want the debt paid off); rather, it's a just a trick (like the fake job offer in forced prostitution) used to lure a poor person into a place where the lender can control the laborer with violent force—a place where the lender becomes a slaveholder and the debtor becomes a slave.

It's important to pause over this for two reasons. First, relationships of "debt bondage" or "bonded labor" are by far the largest category of forced labor,[75] and the vast majority of slave conditions in the world today use some kind of deceptive concept of debt or an advance of money to hide or disguise the slavery. Secondly, there are so many thoughtful people who suddenly feel a sense of relief when the concept of "debt" is introduced into a discussion of modern slavery. "Oh. Ok," we say to ourselves. "It's not *real* slavery—it's just some substandard and exploitive labor situation that's probably sad and unfair, but it's not the kind of slavery where you lose all your freedom and are forced through violence to work for another person."

Well, unfortunately it is. Slavery is about the total coercive control of another human being; in bonded labor, nothing could make that control

---

‡ In sub-Saharan Africa, the ILO estimates that there are at least 660,000 victims of forced labor.

more clear than the owner's power to beat his laborers to death with impunity. When Pranitha Timothy, a social worker for IJM Chennai who has helped lead more than 50 rescue operations that have freed thousands of slaves, takes me through her files of bonded labor cases, the murders are shocking: Madur, a 12-year-old boy held as a bonded laborer in the Mohan Reddy Brick Factory, says he watched while the overseers tied his dad to a post in the middle of the brick yard and beat him to death because Madur had run away from the facility. Lahari, a bonded laborer in the YBI Brick Factory, had to watch as her teenage son died of his wounds from a severe beating received from the owner when he was already struggling with illness and was late returning to the facility. Another mother, Chahna, held as a bonded laborer with her family in the SLN Brick Factory, likewise could not save her teenage son, Adit, from dying after a vicious beating from his overseer.

In all of these cases, the victims were lured into the facility with an advance payment of money for their work in the factory. Then once inside the facility, they could not leave and remained under the owner's complete violent control. In each of these cases, the police failed to conduct any meaningful investigation of the murders and the perpetrators were never brought to justice.

I sense the enormous self-control that Pranitha must exercise when government officials or other educated people speak dismissively of forced labor conditions involving debts. It brings to mind the way Lincoln felt about the flippancy of slavery apologists in his era. "Whenever I hear anyone arguing for slavery," Lincoln said, "I feel a strong impulse to see it tried on him personally."

I don't ever hear anyone arguing for slavery, but I do hear people belittling forced labor conditions that involve indebtedness as "not really slavery." And in such moments, I likewise feel a strong impulse to see it tried on them personally to see if it alters their view at all. I am absolutely sure that if the skeptic should personally find himself in circumstances of bonded labor, he would find two things: 1) he would never be able to extricate himself from his bondage without outside intervention, and 2) he would no longer be a skeptic that bonded labor was slavery.

Indeed, the fundamentals of bonded slavery are exceedingly simple. You use a loan to lure someone to work for you under conditions in which 1) they cannot leave until they repay the debt, and 2) they have no say in how much they get paid for their work. Under such conditions, it's *impossible* for them to pay off the debt because the lender simply never pays them enough to pay them back—and they can't go anywhere else to earn money to pay it off. And, *if they can't leave*, they have to "buy" food and shelter from the lender to stay alive—at whatever price the lender sets and as part of a debt that accumulates in perpetuity. There is just one essential ingredient to the whole scheme: the over-arching threat of force to keep them from leaving—which is legitimated because they have "taken the lender's money," and he is just restraining them from "stealing."

Such insanity doesn't happen to you or to me for one simple reason—we live in communities where people are not permitted to collect on a debt by the personal use of violent force. In communities throughout the developing world, however, where hundreds of millions of the poorest live, the private use of coercion and intimidation is actually the prevailing system for dealing with indebtedness.[76] And without outside intervention, the bonded slave can never set himself free. Such is the nature of slavery.

I've read thousands of pages of reports on forced labor and attended hundreds of hours of meetings, seminars, and forums on bonded labor and human trafficking—but none of it comes close to the education I get when Pranitha takes me into the world of a real human being who has had to live through it.

Gopinath is one of those real human beings—a young man in Tamil Nadu whose descent into slavery began with borrowing $10 for some food. Under the insanity of bonded labor, this loan granted his owner a license to use force to hold him in a rock quarry for 15 years. When Pranitha introduced me to Gopinath at IJM's Freedom Training in Chennai, he was on his third week as a free human being. His skin stretched like thin, dark rice paper over his cheek bones, and his cheerful, crinkled eyes were bloodshot and cloudy from fifteen years of catching granite and iron sparks in his unprotected face. In the many hours we spent together, his wiry arms never let go of his tiny, exhausted son sleeping on his shoulder.

Fifteen years ago, Gopinath had been hungry. His work as a laborer digging wells had entered a slow season, so he accepted an offer of a $10 advance on wages from the owner of the Alamelu Blue Metals, where he would start new work breaking rocks in a quarry with a hammer and chisel. Under a searing hot sun, Gopinath and his wife worked feverishly all day swinging sledgehammers and cranking crowbars to break boulders into gravel sufficient to meet their required daily quota. They soon realized, however, that it was impossible to meet the daily quota (filling an entire flatbed truck). Despite previous promises, the owner paid them only $1 or $2 *every three or four weeks*, and would abuse them if they objected. Indeed they had to return their wages to the owner for food. It became painfully clear that they had no way to ever pay off their meager $10 debt, and that if they tried to leave they would be chased down and beaten.

The only food they could obtain was a thin rice porridge which they had to purchase from the owner—the "price" of which over the years ballooned the $10 debt to $325. Even when Gopinath asked to go into the forest in the night and cut wood as a way to raise extra money to pay off the debt, the owner only mocked him and said: "You can leave the quarry to go any-where—as soon as you pay back the money you took from me"—which was, of course, impossible.

For a poor family like Gopinath's, there was a subsidized school for his children to attend—but, like millions of other children in bonded slavery, they were never released from the quarry to go to school. Likewise, there was a hospital nearby to treat the many ailments and dis-eases from which his malnourished family was suffering—but they were never permitted to go to the hospital and they only got slapped when asked. Vital social services aimed at breaking the cycles of poverty for Gopinath and his family were rendered useless through the violence of forced labor. Outsiders could easily look out upon the Indian landscape and see poor people steadily at work—yet they would have no idea why the work was only digging them deeper into a hole, and never moving them forward.

Of course, all of this grotesque violence in the bonded labor system is illegal and only possible because it is legitimized by the complicity of local authorities. On numerous occasions Pranitha's colleagues conducting undercover operations in bonded slavery facilities have caught owners brag-ging about their capacity to pay the local police to come and beat their labor-ers or to track them down if they run away.

This is how the owner of a brick kiln in Southern India coached another less experienced brick factory owner on how to deal with laborers who might try to escape:

OWNER: All of the laborers have taken good beatings from me.
IJM [POSING AS AN INEXPERIENCED OWNER]: Have all?

OWNER: Yes, all.

IJM: Are you the one?

OWNER: Yes and also the watchman. I just have to tell the watchman and he will beat them nicely. Then I will practically have to stop him from beating them. That is how much he beats them.

You beat them and they will be fine. If not, they will not work and will also run away. After you track them back you have to give them beatings and then they will not leave your factory because they'll be scared that you will track them back from wherever they are.... Initially I was also scared of beating them. They would say they would complain in the labor office if I hit them. But later on I gained courage and started asking, "Has the labor officer told you to take an advance and escape without repaying?"

I get the police to beat my laborers.

IJM: The police here are your friends, but how can we manage to do the same thing?

OWNER: Why? Don't you have police there?

IJM: Yes, we have.

OWNER: So just give 100 rupees to a policeman and ask him to come and beat your laborers and he will come and beat them.

IJM: Is the police station nearby for you?

OWNER: Yes, if I just give them a call, they will immediately come here.

Once I asked a bonded slave who was held illegally in a rock quarry why he didn't go to the local police and get help. His answer clarified things for me. "We don't have to go to the police," he said, "the owner pays the police to come to us—to beat us."

This is the hidden world of terror and lawless violence where the poorest live beyond our view. Outsiders would see a busy brick factory, respectable businessmen, laborers gainfully employed, schools and clinics nearby, and the economic miracle of India. Such outsiders would have no clue about the reality: that the laborers are slaves, that the businessmen are violent criminals, that the schools and clinics are a cruel and inaccessible taunt for those held in slavery, and that the miracle of economic progress is simply not available to the poor living under violence.

Violent Land Seizures

The terror of poverty lies in the poor person's vulnerability to violence. The poor are anxious about food and how they will feed their children. They dread the weakness and waste of disease. They feel overwhelmed and demoralized by the lack of jobs or education or opportunity. But they feel *terror* in the face of violence—when someone stronger is coming in rage to hurt them. And to be poor means you are never safe from the terror. You are not safe at the bus station, in the market, on the way to school, at the well, in the fields, in the factory, in the alleyways. Most terribly, you are not safe in your own home; not just because the bully may be *in* your home—but because the bullies may come to *take your home,* at any time, day or night.

For Susan, the abstract phenomenon of "property grabbing" crystalized into a nightmarish reality of violence and homelessness on what was supposed to be a day of celebration. Susan had left her village for the day on foot to attend a relative's wedding many miles away; when the darkness of the rural Ugandan night descended, her three young grandchildren quickly fell asleep in the stillness of their grandmother's tiny brick house that sat sturdily on a plot of red dirt amidst leafy coffee and cassava trees. Suddenly, a loud crack jolted the children out of their slumber. They sat up. A second crack sounded, and the whole house shook. They looked up and felt bits of hard mortar and dust raining down on their faces. The front of the one-room house was cracking and crumbling from the blows. Jagged holes in the house exposed pieces of the dark sky as the glint of a terrifying steel edge came crashing repeatedly through the brick and mortar wall. They heard an enraged voice beyond the blows: "Let me kill this lousy woman!"

The children recognized the voice as coming from the furious neighbor who had been filling their home with terror ever since he began threatening to kill their grandmother because she refused to give up her land and property. Now he had finally come and was crashing his way into the house with a pick ax. Quickly, the children crawled on hands and knees across the dirt floor. They exited out the back door and fled towards their blind uncle's home nearby, stumbling into the night.

Figure 2.6
Susan's small home, destroyed by the more powerful neighbor who stole her land

The next day when Susan received word of the attack from her neighbors, her first thought was for her grandchildren. She was relieved to hear that they were safe, but when she learned that her house was destroyed and her little plot of land occupied, her second nauseating thought was: "Now what?"

She was now homeless. Her garden patch of land had been her only means for growing food, for sheltering her orphaned grandkids, for keeping her pig, and selling vegetables for her grandkids' school fees. Now the little brick shelter she called home was in rubble (Fig 2.6), her garden was occupied, her pig was dead, all her possessions were stolen or destroyed, and her violent neighbor was still breathing threats and publicly declaring his occupation of her land. For an elderly woman already bearing the heavy burdens of trying to scratch out survival for herself and her grandkids, what was she supposed to do now?

This is the terrifying question for millions of poor people in the world who at one time or another find themselves thrown out of their homes and off their land by violence and threats. Personally, I learned about "property

Figure 2.7
Susan pictured with two of her grandchildren

grabbing" from the most extraordinary African army colonel I have ever met—and I've met a few. In an era when so many in the world associate African colonels with *making* widows and orphans, this Zambian colonel spent a career *protecting* widows and orphans. Violent land theft began to make sense to me one afternoon when he shared the story of his own childhood nightmare of being thrown into destitution when his widowed mother and all his siblings were thrown out of their house and robbed of all their possessions.

"They even took the little Bible that I earned in my Sunday school class," Colonel Mudenda remembered. Clement Mudenda was just 9 years old in 1964 when his father died; as was customary in his community in southern Zambia, after the funeral, his father's relatives came to claim all the property back for "the family"—casting his mother and siblings out onto the street and into destitution. Like so many dispossessed and landless families, they made their way to the capitol city of Lusaka, where Mudenda's mother fought a daily battle of survival on behalf of her eight children. A Catholic school provided a subsidized education for Mudenda, and for a time, he thought he might be a priest but instead accepted the offer of a career in the military. Exceptionally bright, mature, and well-spoken, Mudenda rose quickly through the ranks, and was sent by the Zambian Army to law school, and then around the world to represent the Army in various United Nations deployments.

"But when I looked around back home," Mudenda told me, "there was always something in my heart for these vulnerable mothers and their children—because I could look at them and see me and my own mother." Letting go of a well-connected career and elite opportunities as one of his country's finest and most respected lawyers, Mudenda spent the next decade defending the rights of penniless widows and orphans, first with Zambia's National Legal Aid Clinic for Women, and then as the Director of the IJM office in Lusaka.

All of us at IJM felt a little bit in awe of the Colonel. He was smart for sure—but he was also wise. He was so calm and articulate, so gentle with the poorest elderly widow and so energetic with the most powerful government official. And with his thin mustache, crooner's singing voice, and smooth backhand on the tennis court, he was just cooler than everybody else. He was an extraordinary leader, but tragically, the Colonel died quite suddenly from an infection in the brain. In truth, he probably died because the nation of Zambia did not have a single working CAT scan machine at the time. We rushed him to South Africa for the best care on the continent—but it would prove to be too late.

At his funeral, there would be hundreds of widows, orphans, and other survivors of violent abuse who would come to sing their grief over the Colonel who fought for them.

One of them sure to be in the crowd would be the widow Venus Soko. The Colonel had introduced me to Venus several years before at an outdoor market in one of Lusaka's slums where Venus served us *n'shima* in her little cafe stall made of grey cinder blocks. She greeted the Colonel like a brother. Venus and her husband had worked the stall together for years selling food in the market and had managed to keep their family fed, clothed and sheltered. When her husband was swept away with disease, however, more powerful forces in the slum noticed a widow without a defender. A bully manhandled her, occupied her store, and stole her property. Without her market stall, Venus had no way to feed her family.

A year later she heard of IJM and the Colonel, and she walked all day to the office where she appeared in the single garment she owned—a black T-shirt and *chitenga* that she had been wearing every day for several months.

Mudenda and the IJM team took on her case, and after a struggle, they restored Venus to her property. But sitting with her in the market that day, she explained to me what it had meant to lose her property for a year. It meant she had lost her son. I listened rather dazed as Venus explained that without income from the stall, she had to watch her children grow weak with malnutrition, and to watch the youngest one, Peter, slip away and die. I met one of Venus' surviving sons later that afternoon at her home. He shyly indicated he wanted to stand to greet me, but his year without regular food had taken the strength of his limbs away, for good. After my day with Venus, her children and the Colonel, I found myself reading about "property grabbing" differently.

"Property grabbing" is a starkly straightforward phrase used in Africa and other parts of the developing world to describe the phenomenon of violent land seizures in the poorest communities. The big picture globally is this: Most of the world's poorest people live in circumstances in which they can be summarily thrown out of their homes and off their land because there is no reliable record keeping system for accurately demonstrating who owns the land and the property—and even if there were, there is little willingness or no capacity to actually enforce those rights on behalf of the poor.

The idea that there would be no formal paper trail clarifying who owns what is so unfathomable to people from the developed world that very smart people from the West pretty well missed this plain fact until Hernando De Soto, a Peruvian economist, and others woke the world up to its amazingly mistaken assumption that formal property ownership in the developing world is the norm. Our certainty that we can walk down to the local government records office and find the title or deed to document who or what owns every square inch of land simply does not apply where most poor people live in the developing world. Venus could not produce a proper title for her land, nor could any of her neighbors. Indeed 90 percent of rural sub-Saharan Africans (of whom 370 million are considered poor) live and work on land that has no formal or secure title. The same is true for 40 million Indonesians, 40 million South Americans, 40 million Indians, and about 350 million impoverished indigenous people around the globe. Indeed, around 1.5 billion of the globe's urban poor live in informal settlements and slums without any secure right to their property.[77]

Of course this chaos without property rights is a vicious invitation for the strong to prey upon the weak. As the US Agency for International

Development has come to recognize about this "hidden dimension of poverty" throughout the developing world, poor people "with insecure tenure rights are often indiscriminately or forcibly removed from their land."[78] Indeed, every year millions of the world's poorest people are forcibly thrown out of their homes and off their land—with an estimated five million victimized by forced evictions and millions more simply run off their property and kicked out of their homes by more powerful neighbors.[79] As Dr. Hamid Rashid, the senior Bangladeshi economist and a leader of the UNDP's Legal Empowerment of the Poor program, has flatly stated: "With limited and insecure land rights, it is difficult, if not impossible, for the poor to overcome poverty."[80]

And once again, it is the women in the developing world who are most devastated by the lawless chaos of insecure property rights. In the absence of clear and documented legal rights to property, there are two other social forces that step into the vacuum and settle who gets what: 1) brute force, and 2) traditional cultural norms. And under both influences women generally lose—and brutally so. In much of the developing world, traditional cultural norms frequently view women as less valuable, subordinate, and even as property. In sub-Saharan Africa, for example, it has only been in the last 20 years that women have won the right to inherit property; however, a woman is still not viewed as a legitimate owner or possessor of the property that is left behind when the man departs the family by death or abandonment—and immediately, other forces step in to grab the property to forcibly dispossess the female-headed household.

This is succession-related property grabbing. It is devastating and even deadly for its victims. Without a defender, widows and orphans are stripped of their sole source of livelihood and cast on the street. They have little hope against their stronger perpetrators and little chance of survival.

This sounds bad, but what is the scale of the problem?

First, it's worth noting that in sub-Saharan Africa, 80 percent of the food production is performed by women, but almost none of the land upon which it is cultivated is *owned* by women. Indeed, women own only about 1 percent of the arable land.[81] Consequently, there are desperate implications for basic food production when the primary producers face chronic insecurity on their land.

Secondly, with HIV-AIDS and other sources of high mortality, the number of widows in the developing world is massive. Recent studies indicate that there are more than 115 million widows living in extreme poverty around the world. Even more arresting is the fact that there are *half a billion children* who depend upon the care and support of these widows.[82] Indeed there are some countries where a majority of the nation's children are in the care of widows—as much as 70 percent in Rwanda, 60 percent in Mozambique, and 35 percent in Cambodia.[83] Therefore, in the absence of enforceable property rights to defend themselves against violent seizure of their land and property—over a hundred million widows and half a billion dependent children are threatened with being thrown out of their houses and off their land.[84]

And help seems nowhere to be found. As the World Bank observed, in Africa, it is often the widow's *relatives* who are the perpetrators—and who strip her of everything from cows to cooking utensils, bank savings to farming equipment, homes to clothing, leaving her and her children destitute and vulnerable to exploitation, abuse and violence.[85] All around the world, in the absence of enforceable property rights to repel the violence, millions of widows find that "'property grabbing' and 'chasing-off' are part of the common experience of widows whether animist, Christian, Hindu or Muslim—regardless of their ethnic group, caste or culture."[86] And all this violent dispossession of the weakest and most vulnerable is met by "indifference" by the police, "hostility" from the courts, and almost no one ever being arrested for the violence.[87] What's more, many of the widows being chased from their own homes suffer from the same HIV that killed their husbands: In many IJM cases, after being violently chased from her property, a widow is forced to resettle in a location that makes it virtually impossible for her to access the critical health care she needs to combat her own HIV. What initially looked like "just" a property crime can quickly spiral into a death sentence.

In addition to the common communal and inter-family displacement of the widows and orphans from their land, the absence of enforceable property rights also means that, when demand for land increases, or the value of the land where they've made their home happens to rise, the poor are subject to forcible eviction from abusive corporations, unscrupulous developers and criminal gangs. Such forces are often supported by corrupt government authorities, or it may be the government itself that is initiating the forced displacement. Around the world, families who've built their lives in informal settlements face the takeover of their homes and businesses through mass evictions by outside forces, generally their very own local or national governments.[88] These forced evictions are frequently performed illegally, violently, and secretly—and with devastating consequences for the poorest and most vulnerable.[89]

The best efforts of the struggling poor and their allies can be swept away in an instance through violent land seizures. Oxfam, a global leader in exposing the violent dispossession of the poor in the developing world, has been working to elevate awareness of the threat. "Many of the world's poorest people are being left worse off by the unprecedented pace of land deals and the frenetic competition for land," concludes Dame Barbara Stocking, chief executive of Oxfam, issuing a report that studied violence and forced removals of the poor flowing from dubious land deals in Indonesia, Guatemala, South Sudan, Uganda, and Honduras.[90]

For the global poor, forced removals and land grabbing joins forced labor and forced prostitution as another massive category of violence that is driven by powerful economic incentives—and against which the poorest have no defender. What makes matters even worse—indeed, the factor that drives the poor over the cliff—is the way the institutions that are supposed to deter the violence (i.e., law enforcement) are actually a source of predatory violence *adding* to the poor's vulnerability. Rather than being a primary part of the solution to violence through protection and deterrence, law enforcement in the developing world is a primary *source* of violence and loss for the poor—and of *protection for the bullies.* This bizarre and devastating reality is what we must come to grips with next.

Abusive Police and Arbitrary Detention

Facts are hard things—and either we deal with the facts, or the facts will deal with us. Here then is another brutal fact about global poverty that the world has yet to seriously confront: The institutions of law enforcement in the developing world that are meant to be the primary solution to violence are actually *adding* to the violence.

And this is no small thing. Imagine if the world found out that the hospitals in the developing world made poor people *sicker,* or the new water wells actually *contaminated* the water, if the schools *punished* kids for learning, and the antibiotics *spread* infection. One imagines the world would respond with outrage and urgent determination to address the problem. And indeed, this is

precisely what the poor have been trying to tell the world about law enforcement in their communities: It is making things worse. This was the powerful
conclusion of the landmark study by the World Bank, *Voices of the Poor:*

> Perhaps one of the most striking revelations of the study is the extent
> to which the police and official justice systems side with the rich, perse-
> cute poor people and make poor people *more insecure, fearful and poorer.*
> Particularly in urban areas, poor people perceive the police not as uphold-
> ing justice, peace and fairness, but as *threats and sources of insecurity.*[91]

Repeatedly, all around the world, the theme is the same from the developing
world: The most pervasive criminal and predatory presence for the global
poor is frequently their own police force. As the authors of *Voices of the
Poor* drew their report to a close, they concluded this way: "Poor people
regard the police as agents of oppression, not protection. Over and over
again poor people said that justice and police protection are only for rich
businesses, rich people and those with connections."[92]

I get a much more vivid sense of these realities when my IJM colleague,
Benson, introduces me to Bruno and Caleb from his hometown of Nairobi,
Kenya. Bruno is a husband and father in his late forties. He is neatly dressed
in shirt and trousers that mostly sag on his wiry frame, and he carries the
marks of poverty on his cleanly shaven face—nicks and scars, rough teeth,
and weary eyes. Bruno wakes up around 6:00 AM each morning in his
cramped little home in Nairobi's second largest slum. Bruno lives and works
in the city, sending money back home every month to his wife and three kids
who live in their rural community outside of Nairobi.

On a morning like so many others, Bruno washes up as the sun rises and
grabs his hand-beaded belts, all crafted from strips of raw leather, so that he
can sell them at the local street market. As he walks to work, anxious to claim
a good spot in the market, a Land Cruiser pulls up beside him. It's a police
Land Cruiser. Suddenly, Bruno feels someone grabbing him from behind.
Bruno remembers: "When I asked him what was wrong, he just pushed me
and put me into the car." His wife and children, mother and siblings will not
know for weeks where he is or what has happened to him.

A few miles away, in another crowded Nairobi slum, Caleb is just getting home from his job as a night watchman at an open air market where
he makes sure no one steals the tomatoes. Caleb is a tall, slender man in

his thirties with big gentle eyes and a wide, toothy smile. He wears the blue plaid shirt that his wife, Adelina, has cleaned and pressed out for him, and he likes his black baseball cap with its unlikely penguin logo. Adelina has just left their matchbox-sized home in the slum for her job selling shoes and doing part-time tailoring, so Caleb helps his little boy, Gerry, get ready for kindergarten. Caleb and his wife work hard so their three kids can get a good education. Their oldest daughter has just finished high school and is dreaming of college. They are clearly very proud of her. Neither one of them had the chance to graduate from high school, but they have been saving for years so she can make her dream a reality and go to the nearby community college.

Today, Caleb and Gerry leave a little bit later for school than usual. As Caleb is enjoying the very ordinary routine of walking his 5-year-old son to school, police officers armed with assault rifles suddenly confront Caleb on the street. A voice spits at him: "We hear you are making trouble." Caleb doesn't know what they are talking about. He hasn't been making trouble; he has been helping his son get ready for school. The armed officers order Caleb, along with several other men off the street, into the police SUV.

The police jerk Caleb away from his 5-year-old son. Gerry is just left standing alone on the street. Raw panic and helplessness descend over Caleb. Gerry screams for his daddy. A local woman on the street recognizes little Gerry's school uniform and ushers him to school. But it will be days before Gerry knows what has happened to his father.

The police drive back to Caleb's home. While he looks on helplessly, the police officers rummage through his family's meager belongings, stealing two sewing machines his wife uses for part-time tailoring and the cash they've been saving to pay for their daughter's college fees. After the officers finish helping themselves to Caleb's belongings and life savings, they throw Caleb into the SUV with about seven other men, a few more still to be rounded up along the way.

Now, in the back of the SUV, Caleb and Bruno meet for the first time. They and the other men all share similar stories: They were just leaving for work, boarding a bus, or going to the market when the police arrested them, cuffed them, and threw them into the vehicle. Men cycle in and out of the vehicle all morning. Release comes that morning only to those who pay the bribes demanded by police—2000 shillings (about $23)—half of Caleb's monthly income. Caleb and Bruno do not have enough money and cannot pay for their release.

After several hours, Caleb and Bruno remain stuck in the vehicle with two other bewildered men. The police take Caleb and Bruno to a local police station, where they are punched and kicked and beaten mercilessly with metal rods. The police then drive Caleb and Bruno to some woods on the outskirts of Nairobi, and to a clearing where there sits a TV set and several metal rods. Caleb and Bruno are terrified.

The officers are shouting at the men now, insisting that Caleb and Bruno conspired to steal the TV from a hotel and demanding to know where they've hidden the other stolen items. The TV sitting in the clearing on that May afternoon had indeed been stolen from a hotel several weeks earlier, and the police must find someone, anyone, to hold responsible to quell the pressure. The officers force them face down on the ground. Trembling, with their mouths in the dirt, the violence escalates. "It got to a point," recalls Caleb, "where I told the officers, 'If you want to kill me, just go ahead, because I don't know anything about that robbery. Just shoot me instead of torturing me like this.'" Eventually, the men are taken from the woods to jail. Finally, after two weeks of confinement, the police haul the broken and tired men to court and confidently tell the judge that they are guilty of robbery with violence, a capital offense.

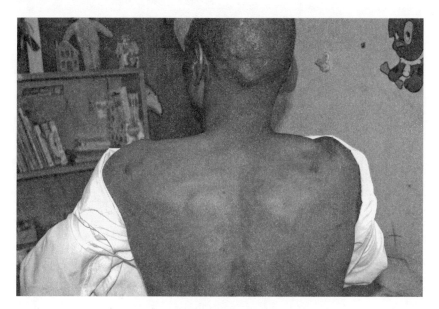

Figure 2.8
Bruno shows how the Kenyan police beat him so badly the wounds turned to scars

The judge does not require that the police present *any* evidence to support their case. Caleb and Bruno have no lawyer, because they can't afford one and none is provided. Relying solely on the officers' baseless accusations, the judge imprisons them indefinitely while they await trial on an unspecified date. After about a year, Bruno learns in prison that his wife has reached a breaking point. The family is failing without his help, and she has to move on without him, and has taken the children with her. Caleb's family remains behind him, but they are struggling just to survive. The family has had to move out of their home in the slum to an even cheaper home. Worse, his dreams for his eldest daughter have evaporated; she's dropped out of school to work a cut-rate, part-time job as a shop assistant to help the family. All the while, Caleb is trapped, rotting indefinitely in a filthy pre-trial detention center and feeling deeply his powerlessness to help his family as they spiral down into the abyss of destitution.

Figure 2.9
Caleb walks outside his home in a Nairobi slum.

Bruno and Caleb's story is just one story in one city in the developing world, but in it we can vividly see all the elements of the law enforcement violence that threatens hundreds of millions of the poorest people in our world every day: 1) police as marauding predators; 2) abusive pre-trial detention; and 3) torture.

Police as Marauding Predators

The authors of the *Voices of the Poor* summed it up most powerfully when they observed that for many of the poor in the developing world, "the police are just another gang."[93] The poor are familiar with violent criminal gangs in their neighborhoods and have to navigate their assaults, intimidation, robbery, and extortion. And for many common poor people in the developing world, the police are just another armed, predatory gang in the community that steals, rapes, extorts from, and assaults them. In fact, it is likely that the local police extort and rob money from the poor on a more regular basis than any other criminal presence in their community.

Voices of the Poor made clear that predatory policing is a reality that dominates the developing world:

- "When the police come here, it is to rob us…to humiliate everybody."—*Brazil*[94]
- The police are just "illegal toll collectors."—*Bangladesh*[95]
- "We're more afraid of the police than we are of the criminals."—*Argentina*[96]
- "For a majority of police officers, the police uniform is a tool for generating income. They make money by extorting law-abiding citizens."—*Nigeria*[97]
- "The poor lambasted the police service for its inefficiency, corruption and disruptive role in society.…It is common practice for the police to engage in harassment, extortion, and blackmailing, and their threats prevent the poor from leading a peaceful life."—*India*[98]

Throughout the developing world, poorly paid police use their coercive powers to continuously extort money from those who are most vulnerable. There are even well-established systems by which the money extorted by low-level officers makes it way up the chain of command to high-ranking officers overseeing a vast syndicate of extortion across the entire city or jurisdiction. My colleagues have had numerous transparent conversations with officers throughout the police ranks in Cambodia, India, Philippines, Guatemala, Thailand, Kenya, Zambia, Bolivia, Malaysia, Honduras, Uganda, and many other countries in which the system of bribes and extortion payments up the chain of command is described.

Police in the developing world not only prey upon the poor by relentlessly stealing from them through a system of extortion; they are also frequently a force of predatory sexual assault against women and girls in the community. While the men in the poor communities fear being picked up by the police and being beaten or detained as a way of extorting money, surveys among the poor reveal that women and girls fear being raped and sexually assaulted by the police.[99]

And in a terrible irony, throughout the developing world, it seems the more vulnerable to violence you are—the more you *need* the police protection— the more you have to *fear* from them. Street children and sex workers, who regularly find themselves assaulted by and the victims of theft at the hands of marauding officers will look at you with sad disbelief in their eyes when you ask why they don't report crimes to the police. In so many communities in the developing world poor people do not run *to* the police when they are in trouble; rather, they run *away* from the police to stay out of trouble.

Abusive Detention

The second element of law enforcement violence that wreaks havoc upon the poor around the developing world is abusive detention. As one can immediately appreciate from Bruno and Caleb's nightmare, the detention power can become a dreadful weapon of simple extortion. Indeed, the *Voices of the Poor* study revealed a great fear among poor people all around the developing world of being picked up and thrown in jail by the police on false charges as a way of extorting money, sex acts, property and other goods and services.

In fact, the police only need to abusively detain a small fraction of the citizenry to establish a pervasive and terrifying threat that will move everyone to cough up the suggested bribe immediately—as most men picked up that morning with Bruno and Caleb did. The most severe losers therefore are those too poor to afford whatever the prevailing price is for staying out of prison.

Once again this all sounds like a bad thing, but in a world full of unfortunate things, what is the real scale of the problem for the poor in the developing world and what are the depths of its implications?

If you go into the prisons and jails in the developing world, you frequently find that the vast majority of the people being held there have never been convicted or even charged with a crime. Many are held without any status at all—that is to say, they have no file at all to explain why they are being held in

Rates of Pre-trial Detention

Liberia	97%
Mali	89%
Bolivia	84%
Benin	80%
Nigeria	78%
Niger	76%
Congo-Brazzaville	70%
Pakistan	70%
Philippines	66%
Venezuela	66%
India	65%
Peru	58%
Guatemala	54%
Argentina	53%

Figure 2.10

Statistics from: "Entire world—Pre-trial detainees/remand prisoners
(percentage the prison population)." International Centre for Prison Studies. n.d. Web. Available online
at: http://www.prisonstudies.org/info/worldbrief/wpb_stats.php?area=all&category=wb_pretrial

detention, or they are being held clandestinely, with no explanation and no accountability whatsoever. Most of the prisoners in the developing world, however, are not held in this classic status of illegal detention; rather they are detained under a different status that turns out for most to be just as bad, called "pre-trial detention." In fact, in any given year, there are about 10 million people held in pre-trial detention in the world's prisons and jails.[100] In many of the poorest countries, over three quarters of the prisoners are in pre-trial detention. This means that in many low income countries and middle income countries with large populations of the very poor people, *the majority* of the people in the prisons and jails have not been convicted of anything—they are being held in advance of a proceeding that will determine if they are guilty or innocent.

One must remember, as in Caleb and Bruno's case, that in many communities in the developing world, the police need *zero* evidence to detain you, because they are given great discretion over the basis for detention. The question then becomes, how long can they detain you before they must show some evidence to a judicial authority, and how much evidence do they have to show to sustain the detention? If they can go a long time without showing any evidence, or if they must show very little evidence to sustain your detention, then you are in big trouble.

Herein lies the problem for these millions of people held in pre-trial detention in the developing world. First, if you live in a "developed" country and are arrested, the police or detaining authority would be required to produce you before a judicial authority to demonstrate the legal legitimacy of your detention within a time frame generally measured *in hours.* In much of the developing world, prisoners like Caleb and Bruno will not make their first appearance before a judge for *months or years.*[101] The average length of pre-trial detention in Nigeria, for example, is 3.7 years. That means, if an innocent man is arrested and thrown in detention in Nigeria the same day my kid starts high school, that innocent prisoner will spend roughly the same amount of time in prison waiting to be acquitted that my kid will spend in high school.

My IJM colleagues have worked countless cases on behalf of utterly innocent, falsely accused, poor prisoners like Caleb and Bruno in Kenya, and we generally find that, without intervention, they will languish forgotten in a prison for about a year and a half before there is any meaningful examination of the evidence in their case. Other advocacy organizations have seen Kenyan prisoners detained up to 17 years before they got a trial.[102] In India, there are 30 million cases pending in the clogged court system, and the average pendency of cases is 15 years.[103] In these circumstances, it is not uncommon for an innocent poor person to be held in prison waiting for trial longer than he would have if he had been found guilty and served his sentence.

It will only rub salt into the wound to know that—after you are released from your nightmare—the detaining authority will pay no penalty at all for having stolen your life and well-being away.

And the theft of time can be a fierce thing. Recently, my IJM colleagues in Kenya secured the release of an innocent man after more than a year of pre-trial detention, at which point he learned that his wife had passed away and he had no chance to say goodbye. Having studied the plight of prisoners held in pretrial detention in the developing world like no one else, the advocates with Open Society Justice Initiative have summed it all up so clearly and simply: "Pretrial detention is one of the worst things that can happen to a person." What makes the pre-trial detention power so terrifying is not only the way it is unlimited and not meaningfully supervised by the judiciary, but *the conditions* of the detention.

Once you have personally entered into one of these detention centers and allowed the stench of disease, filth, violence, and degradation to waft over you—you do not need long lectures on the point. But few of us have taken such a visit, so a little context is important. First of all, the facilities used for pre-trial detention were never designed to house masses of people for years and years at a time, and so they have devolved into the worst and nastiest of places.[104] My IJM colleagues and I have been in many pre-trial detention facilities where detainees were so overcrowded that they had no room to lay down, had to sit in each other's laps "egg-carton" style, and had to take turns sleeping to allow some to lay down. In many of these circumstances, the food and water you get depends on what your family or friends can deliver and what your fellow detainees will allow you to keep or share. Indeed, the International Committee of the Red Cross (ICRC) tells us that detention centers in the developing world have crude mortality rates—that is deaths per 10,000 people per month—that are comparable to or worse than those encountered by the ICRC in war zones or rapid onset disasters.[105]

Figure 2.11
An overcrowded prison cell in Manila, Philippines

So, who are these millions of people who, by mere accusation, must endure these horrific and lethal conditions inside these detention centers each year in the developing world? Overwhelmingly they are Caleb and Bruno; that is, they are the common poor. A global study of the problem summed it up plainly: "Pretrial detention centers are populated almost entirely by poor people."[106] As the Open Society Justice Initiative found, "The ability to put cash in the right hands often makes the difference between freedom and detention."[107]

Kenya's former commissioner of prisons said he thought one out of five prisoners in the nation's detention centers would be released if they simply had a lawyer.[108] A review of pretrial detention in Bangladesh found that 1) almost all of the people detained in the prisons were poor; 2) 73 percent had never been tried for a crime; 3) many had been in prison awaiting trial longer than the maximum sentence for the crime with which they are charged; 4) most never had any legal counsel; and 4) most detainees who are entitled to release on bail simply never get it.[109]

The psychological impact of arbitrary confinement, isolation, abuse, chronic uncertainty, powerlessness, violence, abandonment, and trauma are incalculable. My IJM colleagues and I have sat hundreds of times in cramped, dilapidated, and stuffy developing world courts as a mangy clump of pre-trial detainees are shuffled into court for yet another charade of Kafkaesque insanity where they will sit through some intermittent non-event that they don't understand and in which nothing meaningful or comprehensible will happen before they are shuffled back to their detention cell. The exhaustion, numbness, death, and debasement in their eyes form a deep and glassy abyss. They slump for a while and then are shuffled back out—hearing adjourned (judge not here today), proceeding postponed (file misplaced, prosecutor not available), judgment delayed (no explanation given). It always strikes me as impossibly hard to try and stay human through such a hell.

On the other hand, my IJM colleagues get to celebrate the release of their (non-paying) clients from these circumstances on nearly a weekly basis—as we eventually did with Caleb and Bruno. But these experiences also usher us into the deeper pain of pre-trial detention's typical *aftermath*. Consider: You have left prison sick and diseased (maybe with HIV) and your family can't afford medical care. You have lost your job because you didn't show up for work for a year and a half (and who will hire someone who has been in prison for all that time?). Your children have had to quit school because you couldn't afford to send them, are now way behind, and you can afford it even less. You have been evicted from your home because you could not pay for it or hold it, and it has been sold and occupied by someone else. What now?

The list of devastating realities *after* you get out of abusive pre-trial detention go on and on[110]—and I raise them here not to depress us further, but to make sure we are making a realistic calculation of the costs that poor people, their families, and their communities pay as a result of this nasty bit of hiddenness called abusive pre-trial detention. Again, the global experts at Open Society Justice Initiative nail it on the head, pointing out that the 10 million people held in pretrial detention every year—some of the poorest, most marginalized people in the world—"are the tip of the iceberg: There are hundreds of millions of family and community members affected by those 10 million pretrial detentions."[111]

Torture

A Zambian lawyer put it this way: "A prison sentence is a harsh punishment even for someone who has been proven guilty of an offence, but when the state subjects people to such treatment, who are merely suspected of having done something wrong, the state itself becomes the worst of all criminals."[112]

To some, such a statement can sound like another angry human rights lawyer demonizing law enforcement and governmental authorities as the paramount evil in the world. "Worst of all criminals"? Really? The point can sound overblown until we move to the third subcategory of law enforcement violence against the poor—which is closely related to pre-trial detention—and that is *torture*.

When we think of torture we typically think of a brutal dictator or repressive regime using its security apparatus to arrest and torture dissidents, political prisoners and opposition leaders as a way of maintaining political power and control. As a human rights lawyer who came of age during the Cold War era, when I think of torture, I immediately think of personal friends who were tortured by the Special Branch of the South African Police during the apartheid regime, of friends who survived torture by the Marcos military forces in the Philippines, of photographs of those who did not survive the torture factories of the Pol Pot regime in Cambodia, of Latin American university students disappearing into military torture chambers and never seen by their mothers again. With great embarrassment and shame, I also think of the U.S. government's use of "enhanced interrogation techniques" against suspected terrorists to extract critical information, which crossed previously accepted lines for what constituted torture.

But this kind of political and state security torture actually represents only the tiniest fraction of the very large amount of torture that takes place every day around the globe. Indeed, the vast majority of torture victims in our world today are common, everyday poor people in the developing world—and most of the torture takes place in pre-trial detention.[113] "Many people think that torture is primarily the fate of political and other 'high-ranking' prisoners," observed Manfred Nowak, the UN Special Rapporteur on Torture after his global review of torture conditions in the world. "In reality, most of the victims of arbitrary detention, torture, and inhuman conditions are usually ordinary people who belong to the poorest and most disadvantaged sectors of society."[114]

Careful experts document that "in many countries around the world torture remains a routine part of police work to extract confessions or other information from suspects who refuse to 'cooperate.'"[115] Developing world police are generally very poorly trained in the basic investigative techniques that would actually empower them to solve a crime—and when pressure for conviction is combined with endemic corruption within the police culture, the result is a prevailing sense that a confession coerced by torture is the easiest and perhaps only way of convicting a suspect.[116] As Nowak, the UN Special Rapporteur on Torture, observed during six years of visits investigating pre-trial detention torture around the world, "Unfortunately, in many countries, torture of criminal suspects who are in police custody is practiced in such a widespread or systematic manner that every other 'new arrival' at pre-trial detention centres shows clear marks of beatings and similar forms of torture."[117]

Around the globe, billions of the poorest people live in contexts where law enforcement not only fails to protect them from epidemics of sexual violence, forced labor, and violent land seizures—but affirmatively ravages its way through the community as a source of devastating and rapacious violence among the poor. Increasingly, the brutal facts about violence in the lives of the global poor are forcing their way to the surface. It's time then for the deeper reckoning—namely, what is the impact of all this runaway violence on dreams for economic development that might lift the poor out of poverty and earnest international efforts to make poverty history among the poorest? This is the urgent and critical question we turn to next.

THE LOCUST EFFECT

It would prove to be one of the saddest and most truly tragic tales of rural poverty in the American Midwest in the nineteenth century. For a family of six in St. Clair County, Missouri in 1875, it would end with a simple wooden tombstone that read, "Starved to Death." Like so many of the anonymous poor, historical accounts from the era don't identify their names but only that the "six died within six days of each other from the want of food to keep body and soul together."[1]

Like most families of the Midwest in their era, that forgotten family was accustomed to great hardship. There weren't enough trees on the Great Plains of the United States for proper houses, so many families began by living in holes in the ground and shelters made of sod. They scraped at the earth, first with a human- and then with a horse-drawn plow to grow enough food so they and their livestock wouldn't starve during the harsh winter. If they lasted five years, the government would give them some land, and they could bet it all on putting the land up as collateral to buy more horses for plowing, some seeds for planting, and some lumber for a house.

And lo and behold, with non-stop struggle, some government help, some neighborly cooperation, and fierce perseverance, by April of 1875, things had been looking up for families across the rugged homesteads of Missouri.

The rains had been good, the wheat fields were bursting with promise, the vegetable gardens were abundant, and the livestock ready to be off their winter rations. With a strong harvest, the massive gamble could pay off, and the teetering weight of debt could be thrown off. At long last, they might provide a future beyond poverty for their children.

But, in a matter of hours, it was all swept away. An enormous dark cloud rolled into St. Clair County, blocked out the sun, descended upon the land, and destroyed every last square inch of crops and vegetation. As farm families crouched helplessly behind their shelters, the greatest plague of locusts in human history laid waste to all they had toiled so hard to build. "Every spear of wheat, oats, flax, and corn were eaten close to the ground. Potatoes and all vegetables received the same treatment, and on the line of their march, ruin stared the farmer in the face, and starvation knocked loudly at his door."[2]

In 1875, trillions of locusts weighing 27 million tons swarmed over nearly 200,000 square miles across the American Midwest (an area greater than California) and ate everything— *every day* consuming the equivalent of what 2.5 million men would eat. Lush gardens and massive fields of bumper crops were reduced to barren deserts within a matter of hours. Crops needed to sustain families and their farm animals were destroyed, leaving no means of support during the coming winter. The locusts ate fence posts and the paint and siding from houses. They ate the wool off the backs of live sheep and the clothes left outside on clothes lines. When families hurriedly threw blankets over their gardens, the locusts devoured the blankets and then gorged themselves on the plants.[3] Settlers watched their cows and other livestock die without grain or feed to provide them, and were forced to subsist on bread and water alone. A contemporary newspaper reported: "The owners having paid out all their money...now are left with nothing to eat, their stock has starved to death, and they have no money."[4]

The locusts had come and destroyed it all. All the hard work, sacrifice and effort of these impoverished families didn't matter. All the government grants of free land didn't matter. The assistance of neighbors and well-wishers from the other side of the country didn't matter. Indeed, to those who saw "the labor and loving of years gone within ten days" through the onslaught of the devouring locusts, talk of assistance from outsiders "seemed but a mocking."[5]

Waking Up to the Locusts

Likewise in our era, efforts to spur economic development and to alleviate poverty among the poor in the developing world without addressing the forces of violence that destroy and rob them can "seem like a mocking." To provide Laura and Yuri with the promise of schools without addressing the forces of sexual violence that make it too dangerous to walk to or attend school seems like a mocking. To give Caleb job training or Bruno a micro-loan for his belt business without protecting them from being arbitrarily thrown into prison where Caleb loses his job and Bruno loses his business seems like a mocking. To provide Susan with tools, seeds, and training to multiply crop yields on her land without protecting her from being violently thrown off that land seems like a mocking. To provide Laura and Mariamma with AIDS education and training on making safe sexual choices without addressing the violence in the slums and brick factories where women don't get to *make* choices seems like a mocking. To establish a rural medical clinic in the area where Gopinath is held as a slave without addressing the violent forces that refuse to allow him to leave the quarry and take his dying kid to a doctor seems like a mocking.

Indeed, for the rural poor of the American Midwest in the 1870s, it just didn't matter what they did for themselves or what others contributed in terms of land, or seeds, or plows, or training, or education, or irrigation, or livestock, or capital. If the locusts were coming to swarm and lay waste to it all, then the impoverished and vulnerable farmers on those Plains were not going to thrive—ever. All the other efforts were important, life-giving, and vital, but the usefulness of those efforts just could not withstand the devastating impact of the devouring locusts—*and* those other efforts could not stop the locusts.

Likewise, it seems that we are approaching a pivotal moment in history where agreement is beginning to emerge that if we do not decisively address the plague of everyday violence that swarms over the common poor in the developing world, the poor will not be able to thrive and achieve their dreams—ever. Indeed, the Harvard scholar Christopher Stone, now the head of the Open Society Foundations, summed it all up in his report to the World Bank: "In terms of social and economic development, high levels of crime and violence threaten to undermine the best-laid plans to reduce poverty, improve governance, and relieve human misery."[6]

For those who care about poverty alleviation and economic development for the global poor, the facts and data will no longer allow us to carry on as if the locusts of violence are not laying waste to our efforts. Slowly but surely, deep experience and significant data is accumulating to clarify the way common lawless violence is devastating the efforts of the poor to carve out a better future in the developing world.

While the broader world is still paying attention to other things in the fight against poverty, experts are coalescing to confirm the devastating reality of "the locust effect"—the crushing impact of the plague of violence on the poor—and that addressing violence against the poor is a "precondition" for achieving economic development that is actually meaningful for the poor in the developing world.[7] It is not a precondition in the sense that other poverty alleviation and development efforts must wait until the violence has stopped. Rather, it is just a recognition of the simple fact that as hard you should work on the plowing, and the planting and the fertilizing, if you don't deal with the locusts of violence you are still in big trouble—and you may have wasted a lot of effort.

Indeed, for nearly a decade, the World Bank has been reiterating its finding that "crime and violence have emerged in recent years as major obstacles to the realization of development objectives."[8] The Bank has stated flatly, "In many developing countries, high levels of crime and violence not only undermine people's safety on an everyday level, they also undermine broader development efforts to improve governance and reduce poverty."[9] Multiple studies by the United Nations Office on Drugs and Crime (UNODC) have concluded that restraining violence is a precondition to poverty alleviation and economic development, plainly stating that "a foundational level of order must be established before development objectives can be realized."[10] Leaders of the United Kingdom's Department for International Development (DFID) have concluded, "Poor people want to feel safe and secure just as much as they need food to eat, clean water to drink and a job to give them an income. Without security there cannot be development."[11] When it comes to violence, researchers are increasingly concerned that development experts are missing Amartya Sen's insight that "development [is] a process of expanding the real freedoms people enjoy," and are failing to appreciate the idea "that freedom from crime and violence are key components of development. Freedom from fear is as important as freedom from want. It is impossible to truly enjoy one of these rights without the other."[12]

Of course, this is what poor people tell us when they speak for themselves—that all their hard work and hopeful progress can be utterly devoured by violence. They know the locust effect all too well.

Siddhi in South India weeps when she recalls how hard her father worked to try and give her a good life out of poverty and the way that was all stolen away once she was abducted into the brothel and forcibly infected with HIV. Shanthi is proud that her country has put schools in her rural area but it also wounds her to know that those schools are useless to her three children who are held as slaves in a rice mill every day. Likewise, Venus was proud of her capacity to provide for her family at the market stall until bullies stole her property away and malnutrition began to devour her children.

In the end, outsiders can seek to provide all kinds of assistance to the poor in the developing world—to the tune of more than $3 trillion over the last half century—but if there is no restraint of the bullies who are prepared to steal every sprig of prosperity away from those who are weak, then the outcome of our assistance is going to be disappointing (as in many ways it has already proven to be).

As we shall see, the economists and social scientists are beginning to measure and count the costs of the complex ways violence undermines economic development and poverty alleviation efforts in the developing world, but simply listening to poor people gets you much of what you need to know about the locust effect. As one African villager summed it up for interviewers in the World Bank's landmark study, *Voices of the Poor*: "Where there is no security, there is no life."[13] Of course this makes perfect common sense if we pause to think about it. If you were part of a poor family in the developing world trying to increase your standard of living through higher income and better education and health services—how could it *not* make things more difficult if you were enslaved, imprisoned, beaten, raped, or robbed? Indeed, one would be hard-pressed to find any credible authority to argue that a poor person's struggle out of poverty is not undermined by these categories of massive predatory violence that poor people tell us about. Every credible development economist from Amartya Sen to William Easterly readily appreciates the way market-driven economic development depends upon people being protected in their person and property.[14] Likewise, in *Why Nations Fail*, Daron Acemoglu and James Robinson emphasize the importance of legal institutions (and other state institutions) that are "inclusive" through rights and incentives equally available to all people rather than "extractive" (that is, designed to extract resources from the many for the few) if countries are to experience sustained economic growth.[15] Soros and Abed warn that recent gains in poverty alleviation may "come undone if we fail to strengthen the rule of law in developing countries."[16] But as we shall see in subsequent chapters, just because it is intuitively and experientially obvious doesn't mean that it is widely discussed or appreciated.

Perhaps if the locusts of violence laid waste to everything all at once like they did in the Midwest in 1875 it would get the world's attention—but all the daily slavery, rape, extortion, and dispossession gnaws its way through hundreds of millions of poor people one assault at a time, and the cumulative disaster of the locust effect is hard to see. Slowly but surely, however, the experts are starting to add it up, and the price tag is staggering.

Counting the Cost

In 2011, the World Bank devoted its annual World Development Report to examining the impact of violence on development. The report was primarily focused on the impact of war and conflict violence, but it could not ignore the facts emerging about the impact of common criminal violence as well. The truth is, very high rates of common criminal violence can have the same devastating impact on economic development as a civil war, economic shocks, or the worst natural disasters. Very high levels of criminal violence reduce a nation's economic productivity by 2 to 3 full percentage points of GDP—and as the Report noted, "These estimates are conservative: other studies estimate the costs of crime to range from 3.1% to 7.8% of GDP."[17]

In 2005, surveying the human and economic destruction wrought by Hurricane Stan's torrential rains and mudslides, Guatemala's vice president described the damage as "colossal"[18]—but a subsequent report found that common criminal violence in Guatemala cost an estimated US$2.4 billion, or 7.3 percent of GDP, *more than twice* the damage of Hurricane Stan that year.[19] But there would be no headline as the locusts of violence gradually did their worst—and no headline as crime and violence reduced economic growth by 25 percent in El Salvador, 25 percent in Columbia, or 11 percent in Brazil.[20]

Admittedly, these attempts to estimate the "overall costs" of criminal violence on developing countries as a percentage of GDP are still quite crude, but another World Bank study put it this way: If other countries in the region could match Costa Rica's reduced level of criminal violence, then they could boost their rate of annual economic growth by between 1.7 and 5.4 percentage points of GDP—and that would mean billions of dollars in desperately needed economic growth.[21] Globally, another study estimated that the aggregate costs of crime and violence in low-income countries equal 14 percent of their GDPs.[22] As economists have sought to explain:

> Violence generates a number of significant multiplier effects on the economy such as lower accumulation of human capital, a lower rate of participation in the labor market, lower on-the-job productivity, higher rates of absenteeism from work, lower incomes and an impact on the future productivity of children, as well as—at the macroeconomic level—lower rates of savings and investment.[23]

To make it more concrete, one of the ways economists measure the costs of violence is by counting the aggregate years of productive life that violence takes away through disability. They call this measure the Disability Adjusted Life Years (DALY). Now, try to fathom the fact that *9 million years* of disability adjusted life years are lost *each year* worldwide as a result of rape and domestic violence against women.[24] Now think about food production in Africa and the fact that women do almost all the work (80 percent). Imagine the impact on food production and on the tenuous economy of the poor as millions of Disability Adjusted Life Years are lost every year by women in Africa because of violence. Likewise, in India, a survey of women in Nagpur found that 13 percent of women had missed paid work because they were being beaten and abused in the home—that, on average, they had to miss a week and a half of work per incident.[25] In Nicaragua, researchers found that women who were abused earned *about half* of what other women earned in wages.[26]

In these ways, economists are beginning to calculate the impact of violence on *human capital*—that is the productive wealth embodied in a man's or woman's labor, skills, and knowledge. Experts have found that violence "is a major source of un-freedom in developing societies that directly inhibits the efforts of individuals to better themselves."[27] In fact, researchers found that the "net accumulation of human capital" over a 15-year period in Latin America and the Caribbean was cut *in half* because of violence and crime.[28] Similarly, research in Africa found that violence and crime was eroding human capital and impeding employment, discouraging the accumulation of assets, and hindering entrepreneurial activity.[29]

Economists have also found that violence devastates the *development* of human capital in poor communities—which is the process by which people actually grow the level of skill and knowledge they are able to bring to their struggle out of poverty. I have met grown adult slaves who not only were never allowed to learn to read, write, or do arithmetic, but in the 21st century, did not know what an ocean was, or what another country was, or what an airplane was because their minds were never permitted an introduction to such ideas. Likewise, girls across the developing world cannot access the empowering miracle of education because of sexual violence. As Erika George of Human Rights Watch put it, "Girls are learning that sexual violence and abuse are an inescapable part of going to school every day—so they don't go."[30] Sometimes, as a World Bank study found in Zambia, it is the teachers who are afraid to go to school because they are scared of the violence in their poor communities.[31]

And what happens when you add up the costs of all this crushed human capital and reverberating fear in the lives of millions of poor people? As one might imagine, it has massive social costs, which economists refer to as the destruction of *social capital*—the social norms and networks that enable people to work and interact together. Violence destroys the social fabric of communities and has a disruptive impact on community and intra-familial relationships; it erodes social relationships through the trauma of loss but also in restricting physical mobility and increasing levels of tension.[32] Why should Bruno take risks in re-starting his leather belt business if the police are going to just come back, steal the money, and abuse him? Mariamma has long since given up on the idea of her children going to school since they are just going to be bonded slaves anyway. Gopinath stops asking for wages because he just gets abused when he does.

In studying the impact of violence on economic development in Africa and Latin America, UNODC researchers found that even the *fear* of violence had the capacity to "paralyze development at the grassroots. If development is the process of building societies that work," they concluded, then "crime acts as a kind of 'anti-development,' destroying the trust relations on which society is based."[33] There is evidence that people living in fear of violence unproductively divert resources to security measures, and the payment of bribes and protection money; are risk-averse, less entrepreneurial, and prone to short-term economic decision-making; and are discouraged from accumulating assets or opening a business.[34]

These are the day-to-day distortions that undermine the productive economic activity of people who live in a world where, any minute, the locusts of violence may swarm and lay waste to all their hard work and effort.

The locusts of violence have a punishing impact on every family and every community they touch—both in the direct monetary losses, and the destruction of human and social capital. But think about those Midwestern families living on the American Great Plains in 1875: All of them were affected by the locusts, but not all of them ended up in shallow graves of starvation. For some families, the locusts were a temporary setback; for others, the locusts were the end of the line, and there would be no coming back.

Likewise, violence is hurtful and costly wherever it strikes, but for the global poor, violence packs a uniquely devastating one-two punch. First of all, unlike the locusts of the Great Plains, who were equal-opportunity destroyers, the locusts of violence in the developing world actually *seek out* the poor—they are easy prey and attractive targets for violence and exploitation. Secondly, because the poor live on a very thin margin of survival, violence hits them and their households with much more devastating effect.

I recall the way an old history professor of mine defined poverty: He said the poor are the ones who can never afford to have any bad luck. They can't get an infection because they don't have access to any medicine. They can't get sick or miss their bus or get injured because they will lose their menial labor job if they don't show up for work. They can't misplace their pocket change because it's actually the only money they have left for food. They can't have their goats get sick because it's the only source of milk they have. On and on it goes. Of course the bad news is, everybody has bad luck. It's just that most of us have margins of resources and access to support that allow us to weather the storm, because we're not trying to live off $2.00 a day.

Physical injury, disease, and disability from violence are all the more devastating to the poor who lack access to health care and weakened systems of immunity and healing from malnutrition.[35] Even relatively small losses of property through violent theft or extortion can be debilitating to poor households—especially if it is one of their few productive assets like a tool, vehicle, or livestock.[36] They don't have extras. If a breadwinner is victimized by violence—locked up, enslaved, assaulted—and can't work, the ripple effect is deep and wide. Among the poor, more people are likely to be dependent upon that breadwinner and more desperately affected by his or her victimization. The loss of livestock, or land, or healthy labor capacity can be utterly devastating in a way that those with greater resource margins could scarcely comprehend.[37]

The Hidden Cost of Trauma

In addition to the massive direct and indirect financial costs of violence, experts are also beginning to count the more profound and personal *non-monetary* costs of violence—the way violence can change a person's life forever. Violence significantly raises levels of depression, suicides, panic disorders, alcohol and substance abuse/dependence, and post-traumatic stress disorders[38]—to a point that the poor endure levels of psychological damage comparable to living in a war zone.[39] The locusts of violence do not simply destroy your financial prospects—they destroy your life.

This is perhaps the greatest catastrophe of all, for the greatest devastation of violence is *invisible*—it is the destruction of the person *inside*. For victims of slavery, forced prostitution, sexual assault, and other intensely violent forms of oppression, the psychological wounds of trauma are invisible; they receive almost no treatment in poor communities;* and they do *not* simply "heal with time."

My colleagues Benson, Delmi, and Pranitha, or the on-the-ground medical teams of groups like Doctors Without Borders, or anyone else who works directly for and with survivors of prolonged, repeated trauma in the developing world, recognize the way these victims of violence can develop an "insidious, progressive form of post-traumatic stress disorder that invades and erodes the personality."[40] Social workers and therapists working in the developing world see how trauma victims are forced to live in a debilitating psychological state of denial, disavowal, or fragmentation as they suppress or avoid the memories of their victimization. Victims frequently continue to experience "intrusive memories of the past [that] are intense and clear," keeping them disengaged from the present and unable to take initiative.[41]

---

* People in poor communities do have their own traditional sources of support, comfort and recovery from trauma that should be appreciated. These should not be regarded, however, as anywhere adequate to meet the serious psychological damage of trauma—it simply is untreated, and no human beings are immune to the mental health implications of trauma.

"These staggering psychological losses," writes psychiatrist Judith Herman in her groundbreaking *Trauma and Recovery*, "can result in a tenacious state of depression" infused with deep rage.[42]

Again, if we have dreams of providing meaningful assistance to the hundreds of millions of the world's poorest citizens in their struggle against poverty, we must also have our eyes wide open to the countless millions of the world's poorest suffering under conditions of such acute traumatic stress—with access to virtually none of the mental health resources we would consider indispensable for recovery and return to a healthy, productive life. If they were in our affluent communities they would be hospitalized or otherwise under very earnest psychological care, just so they could be reasonably healthy and functional. This is important to understand not for purposes of setting unrealistic expectations for providing high-end psychological services in communities that barely have enough to eat. Rather, it is important to understand so we are more realistic about the effectiveness of our efforts to help poor people develop and thrive economically if we do not address the violence. We may seek to provide all manner of programs of personal and community empowerment—but if violence is unrestrained in the community, it will be generating levels of personal trauma that may severely undermine the capacities of community members to make meaningful use of the assistance we seek to provide.

We Know Enough to Sound the Alarm

For those who care about the struggle against global poverty, the time of reckoning has come. We must be willing to speak openly and honestly about the locust effect—the way lawless violence uniquely lays waste to economic development and the human and social capital upon which increased standards of living are built. It is bracing, for example, to inventory what diverse experts actually now know about the way specific forms of violence directly thrust vulnerable populations into poverty or keep them there.

For example, we now know that gender violence and land grabbing throw women and girls out of stable homes and communities and force them into urban slums where they are even more insecure and find it even more difficult to overcome poverty. Studies show that many women migrate to the urban slums "not so much in search of something as to escape from something which threatens to harm them."[43] We now know that education for girls in the developing world has a spectacular rate of return in helping girls and their communities escape from poverty. But we also now know— but rarely discuss—that violence against girls in the developing world has a devastating impact on their school attendance, their educational performance, their achievement levels, their self-esteem, and their physical and psychological health.[44] We now know that sexual violence is one of the most powerful drivers of the HIV/AIDS epidemic and its devastatingly disproportionate assault upon women and girls in the developing world (especially in Africa) and the epidemic's unparalleled economic destruction in poor communities.[45]

We now know from sophisticated studies from the developing world that forced labor directly causes poverty and extreme poverty—locking poor people "in a cycle of poverty from which they cannot extricate themselves."[46] In economic terms, experts find that forced labor adversely impacts "efficiency and equity" and undermines economic development through low or no wages, withholding of wages, lack of cash wages, denying children access to education, and denying laborers the very means to invest in their livelihoods, their human capital, or in their children's future.[47]

We now know from recent, ground-breaking research that abusive detention practices in the developing world have a devastating economic impact on the poor through lost income (billions lost to the poor), lost employment, lost education, lost harvest, lost market space; devastating costs for fees, bribes, travel visits; and increased risks of bankruptcy, property theft, family disintegration, and destitution for poor families living on the edge of survival.[48]

We certainly know that lawless violence undermines economic development and makes it harder for poor people to improve their standard of living through increased income, medical services, and education. But the algorithms of economic growth and development are exceedingly complex and our capacity to isolate and measure the precise impact that lawless violence has on rates of economic growth, or income generation, or poverty alleviation, can prove elusive. So, even as we sound the alarm about the locust effect, we don't need to pretend like we know *everything* yet.

To begin with, securing highly accurate data on incidents, rates, and levels of violence and crime is very difficult because violence and crime are intentionally hidden. Researchers are forced to use official statistics of reported crime, or victim surveys, or proxy measures (like homicide as a proxy for violence in general) or other data sources that are notoriously unreliable and imprecise. The scholarly disquisitions on the difficulties of measuring violence and crime (especially across different countries and communities) could, and do, fill vast social science libraries.

And even if you could get great data on the amount of violence, isolating the causal link of that particular violence from all the other factors impacting economic growth or poverty in a given community or nation is extremely challenging. Moreover, some of the very specific causal connections between violence and poverty that seem intuitively obvious fail to be validated under the microscope of intense empirical study. For example, the idea that violence against poor women in the home reduces their capacity to get productive work outside the home has not been validated by careful studies that examined the proposition.[49] So sometimes the causal links between violence and poverty that make sense simply have not been proven or are too complicated for experts to clearly isolate.

Finally, we also do not have nearly enough data on the impact lawless violence has on specific poverty alleviation programs in the developing world. As we've seen, we have a good bit of empirical data, for example, on the way sexual violence undermines education programs and health programs among poor girls in the developing world. But what exactly is the impact of land grabbing on programs to increase the food production of women in Africa? What is the impact of bonded slavery on rural health programs targeting the poor in South Asia? What is the impact of gender violence on access to the new clean water sources? What is the impact on child sponsorship programs of child sexual violence? What is the impact on micro-loan programs of police extortion against families in poor communities?

Practitioners who run these various programs in the field will tell us candidly that lawless violence has a painful impact on their work and on the poor communities where they work; but outside the high-profile contexts of war and civil conflict, they rarely see systematic studies that calculate the true cost of the violence on their poverty alleviation efforts in the more stable settings where *the vast majority* of the world's poor live. Since few traditional poverty alleviation programs in the developing world claim to include a component that measurably reduces the poor's vulnerability to violence, some practitioners say there is little incentive to study and discuss a phenomenon that is undermining the usefulness of their programs, but for which they have no effective response.

But, for the sake of the larger fight against global poverty, denial is never the answer. Nor is the difficulty with data and empirical complexity a reason to turn away in silence from what we *do* know—namely, that the locusts of lawless violence have been allowed to swarm unabated in the developing world and they are laying waste to the hope of the poor. The gaps in data and knowledge are reasons to prioritize and fund research that will help us understand the reality as rigorously as possible, but they are not a reason to falter in sounding the alarm. There remain enormously complex data questions about issues like global warming, the AIDS epidemic, unsustainable entitlement programs, obesity, and other crises of public affairs—but it is only the foolish deniers and irresponsible contrarians who allow data complexity to push these crises off the agenda of urgent public discourse.

In a comfortable, western intellectual culture that can value an easy and clever complexity over the risks of responsible action, this can be a real danger. The truth is, human and social reality is so complex, and our tools of analysis so exquisite that demonstrating unequivocal relationship of cause and effect in human affairs that meet our highly specialized standards for empirical truth has become nearly impossible—in ways that can't help but seem funny to people of common sense.

The latest headline appears above the fold, stating that a rigorous study has established a link between obesity and portion size or sedentary lifestyles. Experts celebrate because demonstrating such linkages to the satisfaction of modern empirical standards is amazingly difficult—indeed, measuring precisely the relationship between weight gain and how much you eat and how much you exercise is full of misunderstandings, falsehoods, rumors, fad theories, and bogus correlations. But the common person probably got the core idea a long time ago.

Likewise, when it comes to lawless violence and the struggle against the worst poverty in the developing world, while we're not done learning, we know enough. Recognized as one of today's most careful scholars, Christopher Stone of Harvard has said after reviewing the state of knowledge in the field:

> Whether the aim of development assistance is the growth of national economies, the effective administration of national and local governments, or

simply the relief of those conditions that people in poverty identify as their greatest concerns, reducing crime and violence is important.[50]

Indeed for the millions of poor men, women, and children in the developing world who find that they cannot go to school, or go to the medical clinic, or keep their wages, or keep their land, or keep their job, or start a business, or walk to the water well, or stay in their house, or stay healthy because they are enslaved, imprisoned, beaten, raped, or robbed, "violence is important." In the same way, the problem of the locusts was "important" to those six family members in the shallow grave in Missouri in 1875.

Fortunately for the hardy survivors of the 1875 plague, the Rocky Mountain grasshoppers never swarmed in such a devastating way again. In fact, mysteriously, they were extinct as a species by the turn of the century. Unfortunately for the vulnerable poor in the developing world, the forces of predatory violence will not simply go away like the locusts of the Great Plains. On the contrary, if the forces of violence are not restrained, it is the hope of the poor that will just keep going away—generation after generation—and there is nothing that our programs for feeding, teaching, housing, employing, and empowering the poor will be able to do about it. If we can't overcome the locust effect, nothing else good people do to help the poor will be truly sustainable.

So How Do We Make the Violence Stop?

To consider that question, we will need to back up and ask some other questions first—namely, why do the poor suffer such massive and disproportionate levels of violence in the developing world? Why are forces of such brutal violence allowed to swarm and wreak such relentless and brutal havoc among the global poor? These are the questions we turn to next.

"NO ONE'S DRIVEN THAT TRUCK IN DECADES"

I think if you haven't seen it yourself, you might find it hard to believe. And I think that is a huge part of the problem. Vast numbers of intellectuals, policy-makers, opinion leaders, and thoughtful people would say that every society must have a justice system to restrain violence, but few have ever seen with their own eyes how that system actually operates for a poor person in the developing world. I think you have to see, for example, what is about to happen to Dan, and to do that, you have to go sit in the Kenyan courtroom where he is about to appear. It is safe to say that what is about to transpire would leave you confused and disbelieving, and would leave any Western legal professional dumbfounded in the face of the impending absurdity. It is equally safe to say that what is about to happen would seem utterly routine and unexceptional to a poor person in the developing world.

To show me what outsiders rarely ever see, Joseph Kibugu, my IJM colleague and a local Kenyan lawyer, has offered to escort me into his world— the world of the Nairobi criminal courts. Joseph is a deeply earnest but cheerful young lawyer who was rescued as a boy from a harsh future of dead-end rural poverty by being one of the fortunate few to receive a free ticket to a private education. He has never forgotten where he came from and where he'd be if others had not been generous, and so he has spent his entire legal career serving those in his country who cannot afford a lawyer, which is just about everybody.

I've always found something very moving about the warmth and gentleness with which Joseph would lean in to get close to those with the faintest voices—the whispers of a young rape victim, the scared inquiries of a lost prisoner, or shy thanks of a widow who has nothing to give Joseph in exchange for his help.

Now Joseph was ushering me into the arena where being heard becomes a matter of life and death—the arena where guilt or innocence is placed before the coercive power of the state, where a judge decides if you live or die, if you are released to freedom or confined to an iron cell. Joseph wants me to see firsthand what "going to court" means for a poor person in his country—because he suspects that an outsider like me is likely to have something different in mind.

On this chilly Nairobi morning, Joseph in his dark suit has taken me to the outskirts of the massive Kibera slums and to a low row of brick buildings that look a bit like an elementary school but which is marked by a sign that reads Kibera Law Courts. I follow him to scrunch into a seat in the second row bench of a plain courtroom about the size of an elementary school classroom, where indeed the public seating in front of the bar is packed with common Kenyans looking mostly tired.

After we'd been sitting for a half an hour, the boy that Joseph points out as Dan is finally led into the courtroom from a side door and onto a bench in the prisoner's box. Dan is a slight boy of 17, with a shaved head, sad almond eyes, and a teenage boy's rough complexion. He looks exhausted and sick as he slumps down on the dark wood bench in the dock, eyes cast down and staring. He is wearing old pale jeans and a t-shirt stretched out of shape at the collar and sagging over his slight shoulders. The faded shirt looks like a probable discard from a game park souvenir shop, with a map of Kenya, illustrations of lions and elephants, and lettering on the front in safari font that really does say *Hakuna Matata*—Swahili for "no worries." In fact, few 17-year-old boys in the world have more to worry about than Dan, given that he is being accused of a capital crime.

Dan has been languishing in prison for the past eight months. Dan's nightmare began when he and two other boys were given the task of guarding the hose that provides scarce fresh water for his slum community. When an older man from outside the community appeared to siphon off some of the water, an altercation ensued. Infuriated, the older man fetched a police officer friend and had the boys arrested for "robbery with violence."

Three things are important to know about what's at stake for Dan in this small, whitewashed courtroom. First, at the time of Dan's arrest, "robbery with violence" was a non-bailable offense, which simply means that no matter how absurd the charge, once you have been arrested and detained, you will sit in the Kenyan prison for months or years until the indescribably slow court system has reached a full disposition on the merits of the case. Second, robbery with violence is a capital crime that carries the harshest of penalties. Thirdly, these two facts combine to make this offense one of the most powerful tools by which abusive police extract bribes from the poor.[1] If they can afford it, families will pay almost any price to keep their loved ones out of the Kafkaesque nightmare of third-world incarceration into which they can descend on the mere naked accusation by the police—police who are consistently rated in public surveys as the most corrupt segment of all Kenyan society.

So Dan has had a rough eight months awaiting his first opportunity to respond to the charges against him. But now here he is on trial for his life. Dan is too poor to pay for legal representation, so he gets what most of the poor in the developing world get when they come to trial—not incompetent, sleepy, or second-rate counsel, but *no* legal representation at all.

Indeed, Dan and any other poor person accused of a crime (even one with a life sentence) will just have to do the best he can to defend himself. But this will be hard because Dan's entire proceeding in the Kibera Law Courts (like every other court in Kenya at the time) is being conducted in English. Dan does not speak or understand English. His language is Swahili. So Dan faces a life sentence at the end of a legal proceeding in which he has no legal representation and cannot even understand what the prosecutor and the judge are saying.

But again, Dan's circumstance is not an exotic anomaly or a quirky story from the Nairobi newspapers. The fact is, Dan's story will never make the newspapers because there is nothing interesting about it. Dan's experience is routine. It *is* the system.

Because Joseph said we were going to court, I had assumed we were going to watch a proceeding where the accused would have a lawyer—or at least a proceeding conducted in a language the accused could understand. I had also assumed that the prosecutor would be a lawyer, but here again I would be wrong. Most prosecutors in Kenya are actually police officers with little to no legal education at all—which, with a little practice in court, turns out to be good enough for prosecuting a poor person like Dan who has no lawyer to defend him and doesn't understand English. But it is usually not good enough for prosecuting a wealthy criminal who can hire a lawyer who has been to law school and can argue circles around the police prosecutor.[2] This helps explain why, according to auditors, perpetrators of high-level theft and corruption "invariably walk away scot free," and 87 percent of murder suspects are released back on the streets.[3]

But with so much violent crime in Nairobi, the police prosecutors are under pressure to show some convictions, so a 17-year-old boy from the slums with no lawyer and no ability to understand the proceedings will probably give the police prosecutors a win. Moreover, should it eventually be discovered that Dan's conviction is a grotesque mistake, there will be no transcript of the court proceeding that could form the basis of an appeal, because the only record of the trial are the notes the magistrate makes *by hand*, and magistrates rarely take detailed notes of the obvious errors and absurdities that they permit in their court. But this is the way the criminal justice "system" works in East Africa's largest city and wealthiest nation.

That "system" works a little differently for Maria in Peru. Maria is 14 years old and has been raped three times in the last month by the same taxi driver in her town. You won't really understand how the system works for her unless you see it, so my Peruvian lawyer friends, Richard and José, will perhaps let you go with Maria to the police station when she finally musters enough courage to report the assaults. If you were not there to see it yourself, you might not imagine all the ways the police find to humiliate her. "What did you do to entice him?" they yell at her. "Why are you bothering this man?" "Why do you want to bring shame to your family?" In the end, they simply refuse to investigate the complaint or arrest the rapist. The truth is, none of the police in Maria's town have ever actually been trained on how to conduct a rape investigation or how to interview a child victim of a sex crime. They have never heard of a "rape kit."

Or you could go with Sashmeeta (the Bangalore anti-slavery lawyer who was fighting for Mariamma in court) to the office of the local official responsible for enforcement of the Bonded Labour Abolition Act of 1976, and listen as she presents compelling evidence—complete with video footage—of a case of slavery. And then you could listen to the litany of reasons this particular official gives *not* to take action: Perhaps the magistrate is not familiar with the Bonded Labour Abolition Act of 1976 (let alone read it), or his schedule is too full, or he'll respond if they come back "next week," or he thinks the laborers are probably lying, or he needs "more evidence," or it's a government holiday, or it's election season, or he doesn't have the funds for the required restitution payments, or he thinks the slave owners are too powerful, or, again, "next week" would probably be a better time.

One could also ask my lawyer friend about the way the criminal justice "system" works in his country in Southeast Asia—for his protection, I'll keep the location vague. He would generously take you along on his visit to a provincial police station armed with a detailed report describing the plight of three teenage girls who, having been trafficked into a bar that doubles as a brothel, face being serially raped to pay off their "debts." On the ride to the police station, you peruse the report that features pictures of the girls in the bar, the operators of the bar, the address of the bar, and a map with a diagram of the rooms where the girls are being held. Before disembarking from your vehicle to enter the police station, the lawyer asks: "If you provided such information to your police back home about such crimes taking place in your neighborhood, what do you think they would do?"

You think: photos and a map of kids being serially raped for money? And you imagine your local police gearing up and getting busy very quickly.

By contrast, you get to watch this local Southeast Asian lawyer be stonewalled at the police station for hours. Finally, he succeeds in convincing the police that they should go with him to try and get the girls out, but they only agree to do so *in a few days*—which is, of course, plenty of time for a tip-off. Indeed, when the local lawyer and the police arrive at the brothel to conduct the operation it is shut down for the night and empty. No girls anywhere. Later my friend would confirm to you that the brothel was just one of five owned by the same man—who had been collecting $500 a month from his floor managers to pay for police protection and tip-offs.

To visualize the way public justice systems in the developing world "work" for hundreds of millions of the world's poorest people, I find myself thinking about the old broken-down truck that always sat rusting and decomposing amidst the weeds in the back corner of my grandfather's raspberry farm when I was a kid. If you asked him if he had a truck, he'd say, "Sure." And he could point to things on the truck called an "engine," and "tires" and a "steering wheel"—but if you asked him if it worked, he'd smile slightly over the absurdity and say, "Oh, no. No one had driven it in decades. No raspberries have been hauled, no supplies have been moved. In fact, I best not go near it," he would advise, "It's just a hide-out for snakes and spiders now."

Likewise for the great mass of poor people in the developing world, if asked about the public justice system, they could probably point to things in their country called "police" or "courts" or "laws" or "lawyers." But these things are useful to them in the same way the "truck" was to grandpa—and that is, not at all. Just as my family had no experience of anyone ever making use of grandpa's truck for trucking, the poor in the developing world have no life experience of the justice system being a useful source of justice for them. In fact, police, courts, laws and lawyers have become, like the rusty truck in the weeds, mysterious at best and dangerous at worst. Something they'd best stay away from.

These brief snapshots of public justice "systems" in the developing world help us begin to uncover a surprisingly straightforward answer to the urgent question that Yuri, Mariamma, and Laura placed before us: Namely, *why* do the poor suffer such devastating and disproportionately high levels of violence in the developing world—violence that so relentlessly steals away their chance for a better life? *Why* does the locust effect destroy their hopes and futures with such brutal routineness?

The most obvious—and most neglected—answer is that the poor do not get the most basic protections of law enforcement that the rest of us depend upon and unconsciously presume are there every minute of every day. The basic capacities of the law enforcement systems in the developing world are so broken that, as the UN's global study concluded, most poor people live outside the protection of law. The functional plumbing of the criminal justice system is so busted, leaking, clogged, and corrupt that the wonderful protections promised in the law books do not actually get delivered for the poor. Consequently, they literally live in a state of de facto lawlessness.

It is critical for the world to understand with clarity this very specific source of the poor's vulnerability to violence, or else we risk rolling up the problem of violence into the massive, vague ball of insoluble problems we generically call poverty. If we do so, we will miss both the precise source of the problem and the targeted solution.

By analogy, one could make a similar mistake by looking at global malaria, which kills up to about a million people a year, mostly kids under the age of five.[4] About 90 percent of global malaria deaths occur among the very poor, so one might think that poverty causes malaria deaths. But, of course, poverty does not cause malaria—mosquitoes and the malaria parasite cause malaria. The difference is the poor don't get something that the rest of the world does get: mosquito abatement and prophylaxis protection from the malaria parasite. As a result, the poor die from malaria and the non-poor do not. Likewise, poverty does not cause violence against the poor; violent people do. But if you are poor and living in the developing world, you don't get what everyone else in the world gets—namely, basic law enforcement to protect you from violent people.

The failure to differentiate discrete problems facing poor people can lead us to miss opportunities. It turns out for instance, that the world does not need to wait to solve poverty before it can substantially reduce (and even eradicate) malaria deaths among the poor. Rather, the world simply needs to help protect the poorest children from the mosquitoes and the plasmodium parasite with treated bed nets, indoor insecticides, and drug treatments.[5] Of course, in the process of trying to provide these protections to the poor, one discovers the ways interconnected problems of poverty complicate the picture and make even the delivery of protection more difficult, but these challenges don't suggest we stop protecting poor children from mosquitoes and the malaria parasite—they just suggest we be smarter and more innovative about it.

Likewise, we do not need to wait for poverty to be solved before we meaningfully reduce the horrific and gratuitous violence that hundreds of millions of the world's poorest are currently forced to endure. Rather, we must help protect the poor from the violent people who seek to abuse them by providing basic law enforcement systems that bring the perpetrators to justice, end the culture of impunity, and deter acts of violence against the poor. In the process, we will certainly discover the way other issues of poverty make the delivery of these law enforcement protections more difficult—but again, this will not be a reason for giving up on law enforcement for the poor, but a reason to be smarter, more innovative, and more deeply committed to the fight.

Indeed, my colleagues from the Philippines demonstrated this point quite dramatically. They showed the world that communities don't have to wait to eradicate poverty before effectively protecting the poor from violence through their own justice systems. In 2007, the Bill and Melinda

Gates Foundation provided funding for a project to address an epidemic of violent commercial sexual exploitation of minors in the city of Cebu, the Philippines' second largest city. Project Lantern, as it came to be called, mobilized a corps of Filipino lawyers, criminal investigators, social workers, and community activists to lead a coalition of forces in the city that would train, equip, and support the local police, prosecutors, courts, and social services in an effort to enforce existing laws against forced child prostitution. After four years of effort, the rescue of hundreds of children, and the arrest and prosecution of about a hundred sex traffickers, outside auditors were able to document a 79 percent reduction in the victimization of girls in the commercial sex trade throughout Cebu—during a time period in which there was *no significant reduction in the poverty indices in their city.*

Through law enforcement, children were safer—not only safer from a violence of grotesque brutality, but from a violence that further imprisoned poor girls in a cycle of abuse, disease, trauma, ignorance, indignity, substance abuse, and squalor.

Do the Poor Really Need Law Enforcement?

There is much encouragement to be found in stories like this dramatic transformation in Cebu, and other recent experiments in building law enforcement capacity in the developing world to protect the poor from violence, which we'll discuss later. But the sober truth we must face now is this: Building effective public justice systems in the developing world is costly, difficult, dangerous, and unlikely. As we shall see later, a few ill-fated (and largely ill-conceived, half-hearted, and poorly executed) efforts to do so over the last fifty years have dashed many hopes—and the notion of strengthening law enforcement capacities (the institutions of the state's coercive power) in the frequently corrupt and abusive context of the developing world is enough to send a quick shiver down the spine of any experienced advocate for the global poor. So to make the necessary commitment to such an effort, we have to be convinced that it's worth the effort and the risk. That is to say, we have to believe that basic, functioning law enforcement capacities are *indispensable* for stopping the violence. Secondly, we will need to understand that, for the vast majority of the poor in the developing world, such systems *do not actually exist.*

Depending on your background, the idea that law enforcement is indispensable for stopping violence will either strike you as an obvious no-brainer, something you've not thought much about, or as seriously doubtful.

For most people, the idea that the poor need basic law enforcement systems will seem obvious and non-controversial. When José and Richard in Peru, Sashmeeta in India, and Joseph in Kenya explain that the most urgent need for addressing violence against the poor in their country is a functioning criminal justice system, common people in the world's more affluent societies will readily appreciate the need. When they feel threatened by a rash of carjackings, muggings or rapes in their own neighborhoods, their thoughts and conversations turn immediately to the police—and they demand a response. They eventually may also want to talk to leaders in the community about youth unemployment, self-defense classes for women, or better street lighting—but they will never imagine that these steps will be successful in the absence of police who are patrolling the streets, investigating the crimes, catching the offenders, and making sure violent criminals are brought to justice. When it comes time to vote for public services, they understand that law and order provide the foundation for everything else and that being safe from predatory violence in their neighborhood is priority number one. Accordingly, when it becomes clear to them that poor people in the developing world must navigate life *without* basic law enforcement, such a state of affairs will seem to them intolerable.

For others, however, the systems of law enforcement are so out of sight and out of mind that the urgent need for them will feel more remote. Violence occasionally appears on the evening news or the metro section of the newspaper, but for the most part these incidents feel like exotic, unpleasant events that are somehow being taken care of by responsible parties and don't require much attention. Violence has not yet stepped in to fiercely rearrange their sense of personal reality. In the streets where they live, walk their dogs, and watch their children play, the human capacity for predatory violence is not a present threat nor is it a problem they have ever desperately sought to solve. Consequently the subculture of people and institutions that do work the problem of predatory violence (i.e., the world of law enforcement, policing, criminal courts, incarceration facilities, etc.) will seem to occupy a distant planet that occasionally shows up only on TV dramas or odd cable-news documentaries. From this perspective, when Delmi in Guatemala or Pranitha in India explains that the global poor desperately need functioning law enforcement, the idea is going to sound reasonable in the moment it is being explained, but is unlikely to grip the imagination and the gut the way other more familiar issues of global poverty do—like hunger, disease, homelessness, illiteracy, and unemployment.

Finally, there is a third set of people who are going to have the hardest time believing Joseph from Kenya and Richard from Peru when they argue that law enforcement is the urgent, priority solution to violence against the poor in their countries. This third group of skeptics is already too painfully aware of the way law enforcement in the developing world is the *source* of so much violence against the poor. It's going to sound farfetched to suggest that the current cause of the problem is likely to be the primary solution. The criminal justice system has never been seen to actually serve the interests of poor people in these communities before, and the idea of training, resourcing, and empowering law enforcement in the developing world will sound quixotic at best and dangerous at worst. Moreover, they will tend to see law enforcement advocates as zealots with hammers who see every problem as a nail. For these skeptics, enthusiasm for law and order neglects the "deeper roots" of violence found in cultural attitudes, economic desperation, migratory dislocation, communal conflict, gender bias, neglect of traditional dispute resolution systems, disruption of indigenous cultures, political marginalization, etc.

There will be other skeptics as well. Many Western policy experts working in systems of highly developed and resourced law enforcement capacities have been fighting an onslaught of simplistic, election-year policies that seek to achieve the next marginal unit of crime prevention with ever more cops, stiffer penalties, more intrusive security measures, and more people in prison longer—all at the expense of addressing the profound social problems that generate violent crime. When these experts turn their attention to violence in the developing world, this hard-earned skepticism about the efficacy of more "law and order" is likely to go with them. Some American criminal justice experts, in particular, are likely to have grave fears that attempts to strengthen law enforcement systems in the developing world will result in the mindless exportation of criminal justice practices from the United States that they criticize for producing massive and counter-productive incarceration rates in their country.

Similarly, other experts familiar with the extraordinary complexity of proving (by modern quantitative methods) a causal relationship between any given law enforcement intervention and a specific quantitative reduction in violent crime are going to doubt that significant investments in law enforcement will produce the kind of measurable outcomes that should undergird any costly programs that seek to improve the lives of the poor. In the developed world, there is a massive and complex social science debate about the efficacy of law enforcement in reducing violence—a debate which ranges from iconoclastic experts like David H. Bayley, who declares flatly that "police do not prevent crime," to sociologist Carl B. Klockers who concludes with equal confidence that the police capacity to successfully prevent crime is "virtually irrefutable."[6] When sophisticated experts cannot seem to agree on the effectiveness of law enforcement, many are likely to be dissuaded from taking on all the risks, complexity, and cost of building criminal justice systems in the developing world.

Facing the Fundamentals of Deterrence

So, to move forward in seeking to protect the poor from violence through effective law enforcement, we must be convinced that law enforcement is an *indispensable* part of the solution to violence against the poor—and here the case is much easier to make than it might initially appear. First, even the experts don't really disagree on the fundamental realities. While there are clever contrarian moments when experts will want to burst some bubble of conventional wisdom in criminology or development economics, there is virtually no credible social science evidence to support the idea that violence in societies can be effectively addressed in the absence of the state exercising its monopoly on the legitimate use of coercive force through law enforcement. As one scholar observed:

> The real issue here is not whether police prevent crime but the extent to which they do. About this there is little disagreement among criminologists. Even Bayley agrees with this statement, or else he would not have written a book replete with suggestions that police can, in fact, prevent crime and chock full of policy proposals about how they might do so.[7]

Indeed, the latest quantitative studies of violence over the course of human history now show that it was the emergence of the state as an armed, third-party referee regulating the use of violence in societies—Hobbes' Leviathan exercising a monopoly in the legitimate use of coercive force—that reduced violent deaths by 80 percent from pre-state, tribal societies, and later, the modern state's consolidation of law enforcement eventually brought down the homicide rate a further 96.7 percent.[8]

The weight of contemporary social science research (and common sense) rests quite solidly with the findings of the rational-choice theorists and the routine-activities criminologists who have demonstrated that law enforcement's capacity to ratchet up the criminal's costs and perceived risks reduces his willingness to commit acts of violence.[9] As Stephen Pinker concludes in his sweeping study of violence in *The Better Angels of Our Nature*:

> Analysis by Levitt and other statisticians of crime suggest[s] that deterrence works. Those who prefer real-world experiments to sophisticated statistics may take note of the Montreal police strike of 1969. Within hours of the gendarmes abandoning their posts, that famously safe city was hit with six bank robberies, twelve arsons, a hundred lootings, and two homicides before the Mounties were called in to restore order.[10]

Not only does the deterrent power of the criminal justice system work to reduce violence, it works like nothing else does. This is what makes it indispensable. Admittedly, it is also a dangerous power—which explains why people are so eager to find some other way to reduce the violence against the poor in the developing world. But wishful thinking should not lead us to pretend that we can substitute something else for the state's power to physically restrain and punish acts of illegal violence.

To be clear, a law enforcement response to violence will never be sufficient on its own. Law enforcement is necessary, but insufficient to adequately address violence. But it is *necessary*. To be effective, law enforcement must work in tandem with other interventions that address other complex social causes of violence—cultural norms, gender bias, economic desperation and inequality, lack of education, marginalization of vulnerable groups, etc. But these interventions will never be successful in the absence of a reasonably functional public justice system that restrains, brings to justice, and deters violent predators. As researchers with the World Bank concluded:

> While it is common to argue for either prevention or control responses to crime and violence, the two types of interventions are in fact

complementary. A more efficient and professional criminal justice system—and especially police forces—are essential to lower levels of impunity.[11]

As we discussed earlier, hunger has many exacerbating factors—but it has one primary and indispensable solution: food. One must address dysentery and food distribution problems and the cultural preference for feeding boys over girls—but at the end of the day, you are going to have to have food. Likewise with violence, one must address the social factors that increase violence and the vulnerability of poor people, but at the end of the day, you are going to need the properly exercised coercive power of the state to physically restrain violence and provide a credible deterrent to those prepared to use violence to advance their interests.

It is certainly true that cultural norms and attitudes that legitimate violence must be addressed—the notion that it's okay to beat your wife, the idea that raping your niece is a "family matter," the belief that Dalits (Untouchables) are worthy only of menial service to those of a higher caste, or the view that women are themselves property to be inherited. As long as these notions prevail in the community, law enforcement will be fighting an uphill battle to change behavior by punitive law enforcement deterrents alone.

On the other hand, one doesn't have to wait for cultural norms in the community to completely change before one may enforce the cultural aspirations expressed in law. In the United States, Americans did not wait for cultural attitudes toward segregation in the South (the prevailing, racist cultural norm) to change by gradual enlightenment before federal authorities began to enforce a competing cultural aspiration expressed in the Constitutional right to equal protection of the laws. As Martin Luther King, Jr. said with characteristic simplicity and clarity:

> It may be true that the law cannot change the heart but it can restrain the heartless. It may be true that the law cannot make a man love me but it can keep him from lynching me and I think that is pretty important.[12]

In fact, enforcement of the law can powerfully accelerate the transformation of cultural attitudes by bringing to bear public sanction—as Americans have seen in segregation, domestic violence, drunk driving and smoking. This synergistic relationship between law enforcement and the transformation of harmful cultural norms was noted by the World Bank in its World Development Report on Equity and Development when it observed: "The law can also accelerate shifts in norms, and justice systems can serve as a progressive force for change in the social domain by challenging inequitable practices."[13]

SIMPLY INDISPENSABLE

Some experts suggest that formal, state-based criminal justice systems are less important because indigenous communities have their own customary forums and procedures for resolving disputes and regulating behavior according to their own community norms and customs. In fact, it is observed that poor people in the developing world, especially in rural areas, rarely refer their disputes or even incidents of violence to the police (usually less than 10 percent of the time[14]), and that frequently the formal rules expressed in state criminal codes are inconsistent with prevailing local norms about right and wrong, about who bears responsibility for actions, and how they should be resolved. For example, local "peace committees" set up among pastoral tribal people in the arid north of Kenya have been suggested as an innovative mechanism for resolving disputes, regulating cattle rustling, and setting grazing permissions without using the police and courts—which are far away, expensive, and sometimes enforce legal norms in conflict with local customary norms.[15]

It can indeed be very efficient and effective for indigenous, non-state mechanisms and informal local procedures to perform the functions that a formal public justice system may perform in other settings. But when it comes to dealing with violence against the poorest and the weakest, it can be quite dangerous to underestimate the need for professional law enforcement functions to confront the realities of coercive force and to make sure that local cultural attitudes and power imbalances don't run over the rights of the women, girls, minorities, and others who may be marginalized in the local culture.

For instance, on its own, the local "peace committee" in Northern Kenya decided the murder of a male in the community would be dealt with not by criminal punishment but by payment of 100 cows from the perpetrator's family, with a 50-cow fine assessed for the murder of a woman. Such arrangements of monetary restitution for violence, while common in many traditional societies, have been rejected in developed societies through-out the world for a host of reasons—not the least of which is the way they disadvantage the poor by allowing those with greater financial resources to commit as much violence as they can afford, and the way they tend to reinforce the gross devaluation of certain members of the community (like the women whose lives in cow-dollars are only worth half that of the men). Indeed, in the case of the "peace committees" in Northern Kenya, it was eventually determined that murders would instead need to be referred to the police and the criminal justice system.[16]

Eventually, when it comes to violence against the poor, communities need access to the unique services of a criminal justice system to *enforce* the laws that prohibit acts of predatory violence. Law enforcement is indispensable—and as costly and risky as it may be, it is unrealistic and dangerous to imagine that the poor in the developing world can somehow get along without it.

Experts with a sophisticated understanding of the complex uncertainties and risks associated with building law enforcement systems in the develop-ing world affirm that "a well-functioning law enforcement apparatus is nec-essary to provide individuals with a stable and orderly living environment and to protect them from violence and exploitation"[17]—indeed, effective and legitimate law enforcement "makes development and poverty reduc-tion possible."[18] Likewise, poor people themselves are familiar with the risks and failures of law enforcement—and yet they say they want the police and authorities on their side protecting them from violence. As the authors of the *Voices of the Poor* study concluded: "Poor people need and want the police, but good police."[19]

But as we shall see—just because the poor want good law enforcement doesn't mean they get it.

THE EMPEROR HAS NO CLOTHES—AT ALL

So what does this lawlessness actually mean for the poor?

For poor people in Bolivia, for example, it means that child sexual assault is not actually prohibited by law. Not really. In a country of 10 million people, where tens of thousands of sexual assaults against children occur every year,[1] from 2000 to 2007 the Bolivian criminal justice system was able to convict fewer than three perpetrators of child sexual assault per year. If you sexually assault a child in Bolivia, you are more likely to die slipping in the shower or bathtub than you are of going to jail for your crime.

Likewise, for poor people in India, despite laws on the books condemning forced labor, those laws do not actually prohibit slavery because they are not enforced. With millions of poor people in India held illegally in forced labor, we can identify fewer than *five* perpetrators who have done any substantial prison time for this crime in the last 15 years. If you pick on the right people (low-caste people in poverty) and do it the right way (by disguising the slavery with a bogus debt) you can force people to work for you for no wages. You will be committing a serious crime under Indian law, but you are more likely to be struck by lightning than you are of going to prison for your crime.

Throughout the developing world, you can tell that poor people already know they don't have a functioning criminal justice system—because they don't even try to use it. Studies by the UNODC found that only a tiny fraction of crime in Africa is ever reported to police.[2] In Latin America, only a tiny fraction of sexual assaults are reported to the police because of "the expectation that law enforcement would be ineffective."[3] And if you look at the actual behavior of criminals in these countries, you'll see that they also know that law enforcement is no threat—many of them don't even go to the most rudimentary efforts to conceal their crimes.

The poor in the developing world and those who abuse them know the same thing: When it comes to their countries' justice systems, the emperor's "new" clothes aren't just hand-me-downs from the thrift shop—the scandalous truth is that the emperor is buck naked!

INTO THE PIPELINE

When I go into the kitchen, turn on the tap, and get a glass of fresh water, I generally don't have the foggiest idea about the massive subterranean system of aquifers, pumping stations, filtration systems, transmission mains, reservoirs, and thousands of miles of pipe that are at work to bring me my glass of water. And precisely because it works so well, I *never* think about it.

Similarly, there is another out-of-sight, out-of-mind system that physically protects us and our property from violence—the system that delivers the promised protections of law.

Like the water delivery system, the criminal justice system works as a series of interconnected "pipes." If you are a victim of a violent crime, this pipeline begins, generally, with the police—who first intervene on your behalf, physically rescue you from the violence, apprehend the perpetrator, conduct an investigation, and turn the factual evidence of the incident over to the prosecutor. The prosecutor then combines the factual evidence about what happened with what the law does and does not allow, and makes an argument before a court asserting that the accused violated the law. It is then the court's responsibility to decide guilt or innocence and to authorize an appropriate penalty, which the prison system then carries out.

In the developing world context, the process of investigation, prosecution and judgment often takes many years, is expensive (e.g., involves fees for travel and documents, missed days of work, etc.), and psychologically taxing and intimidating. And so, it is essential to add another indispensable actor in the system—the social services that support the victim through the various segments of the pipeline until justice is done. Without social workers and social services to make sure that these victims (who live on the edge of survival) are still alive, are still reachable, are in stable condition, and willing to pursue the case, the prosecution will fail.

This then is the criminal justice "pipeline."* Getting this system to work is extremely difficult, because a clog, leak or obstruction in any one segment renders the entire pipeline ineffective. Moreover, each segment is autonomous and has its own separate accountability structure—so, for example, the court in Cambodia generally has no power to discipline the police for failing to arrest the brothel owners, the police in the Philippines cannot discipline the judge for failing to show up for a hearing, and the judge in Peru cannot discipline the prosecutor for being too overwhelmed with cases to properly develop the evidence. What they all *can* do is blame each other for the overall failure of the pipeline and thus avoid difficult changes or reform.

But these maddening dynamics of both autonomy and interdependence apply to just about any public justice system in the world. When you step back from it, it is a miracle that a public justice system ever works at all. And yet they certainly do, and, in affluent societies, they are generally getting better and better, and the citizenry are getting safer and safer.[4] This, however, is *not* the case for public justice systems in the developing world. Indeed, perhaps no disparity is greater (and more compounding in its impact) than the yawning gap between the justice systems of the haves and the have-nots.

Of course, the developing world is full of struggling systems—food systems, health systems, education systems, sanitation systems, water systems, etc.—but it is fair to say that the most fundamental *and the most broken* system is the public justice system. It is the most fundamental because it provides the platform of stability and safety upon which every other system depends. Sadly, the public justice systems in the developing world not only fail to protect the poor from violence, but they actually perpetrate violence,

---

* This is, of course, a simplification of the complete public justice system which may also include many additional administrative or regulatory agencies that have a role in enforcing rules and addressing conflict—as well as a whole host of customary authorities, councils, and codes of traditional norms and sanctions that play a role in addressing violence.

protect perpetrators, and make poor people less safe. Other systems may be struggling in the developing world—but generally the education system doesn't make people more ignorant than they'd be without it, the road system doesn't make people less mobile and take them farther from the market, and the water system doesn't make the water dirtier and more remote than it would otherwise be.

But this can all sound unhelpfully vague, and so to make it more concrete we need to dive into the netherworld of criminal justice in the developing world—one segment of the dark pipeline at a time.

THE FIRST SEGMENT: THE POLICE

The first—and most important—segment of the public justice system "pipeline" is the police. They are the most important segment for two reasons: Because they are generally the first segment, nothing can get *into* the pipeline without passing through them. Secondly, they are the *only* segment with muscle (violent coercive power), which can be either used to stop violence or abused to hurt people.

Tragically, this first and most important segment of the most important system tends to also be its most dysfunctional element. The police, as experienced by poor people in the developing world, have almost no specialized crime-fighting training and can make more money hurting people than helping people; they generally lack the most rudimentary equipment; and, year to year, their presence in the community makes poor people *more* insecure.

This is not, of course, an accurate description of *all* the policing and *all* the police personnel in the developing world, but it is an accurate description of the quality of policing and police personnel that *poor* people in the developing world generally receive. There are, of course, individual officers and units of police in the developing world that are well-trained, well-equipped, motivated, highly intelligent, and competent. But to the extent they exist, they are not deployed to protect the common poor from crime and violence; rather, these rare and elite elements are deployed almost exclusively in three functions: 1) state security; 2) protecting elite economic and commercial assets; and 3) participating in *international* law enforcement programs that confront terrorism, narcotics-trafficking, arms smuggling, etc.

All three of these are important and legitimate functions for policing in the developing world and arguably may trickle down to benefit the billions of poor people who live in these countries. But the question is, what is left over to protect the common poor person from everyday predatory violence—the threat that matters most to her? The answer is: nothing that is very helpful, and something that is quite dangerous.

Ignorance and Incompetence

Perhaps the most glaring gap between what you and I expect from police and the reality on the ground for poor people in the developing world is simply *knowledge*. Restraining violent criminals and gathering enough evidence to prove their guilt are very hard things to do, which is why we expect the police to have some specialized knowledge or training—especially about how to carry out a criminal investigation. Modern, professional policing in the world's affluent societies is obsessed with training, and a police officer in your town will readily give you a rundown on the elaborate training received at the academy and the constant rounds of in-service trainings, skills-development courses and certifications he or she has acquired. By contrast, most of the police personnel in the developing world probably don't know anything more than you do about conducting a criminal investigation, because they have received almost no specialized training in the discipline. In fact, if you have been watching police shows on TV you probably know a good bit more about how to carry out a criminal investigation than the average police officer in the developing world. To be clear, there may be specialized groups of police personnel within a developing country or city who have received some significant investigative training—but the average police officer deployed to enforce the law in the villages, slums, barrios, and teeming streets of the mega-cities where billions of the world's poorest live has received almost none.

For instance, India has over a million police officers looking after well over a billion people—but 85 percent of those police officers are constables and have received virtually no training in criminal investigation.[5] Their induction training involves several months of colonial-era quasi-military training with only the briefest, elementary classroom lecturing on law and police regulations.[6] Even higher-ranking inspectors and sub-inspectors receive little investigative training and generally do not know the basic legal framework of the criminal law.[7] The vast majority will receive virtually no additional substantial investigative training. As one police inspector from Bangalore, the Silicon Valley of India, said: "We have to adjust to a modernizing world. But we are not given new skills."[8] In fact, India experts say things have gotten worse. Shortly after independence from the British Empire, experts described the grim state of India's police forces: "[Since independence] there has been no improvement in the methods of investigation or in the application of science to this work. No facilities exist in any of the rural police stations and even in most of the urban police stations for scientific investigation." That was 1953; amazingly, 60 years later, respected commentator Praveen Swami found that "the capacities of police to investigate crimes have incrementally *diminished*."[9]

When my colleagues in Cambodia first started working with the police ten years ago, basic recruits essentially received a uniform and on-the-job training with virtually no formal training in basic policing or criminal investigation. Police were expected to arrest sex trafficking suspects but had received little training in gathering intelligence, managing informants, conducting surveillance, or planning and executing a raid. Police in Peru were expected to gather evidence in child rape cases but had never received a single day of specialized training on how to investigate a rape case or interview a child witness. Police in Uganda were supposed to restrain perpetrators of land theft, but they had received virtually no training on safe tactics for arresting and controlling a suspect.

So what kind of training *do* police in the developing world get?

The answer is—they get trained in dysfunction. In the absence of helpful, professional, modern methods of policing, the training void is filled with a collection of attitudes, values, methods, standard operating procedures and practices that have been passed on from abusive colonial regimes of the past, outdated paramilitary models, reactive self-preservation instincts, and random nonsense. This "real world training" is so dominant that it overpowers the minimal formal training they receive. As one Indian police officer commented: "[W]hen I joined my first police station after the training, my superior officers all laughed and told me that I must now forget everything that I had been taught."[10]

Insecure about their own capacities, blamed for just about everything, disrespected by the public, and threatened by violent criminal elements, the police cover up their lack of training and knowledge by keeping outsiders at a distance with intimidation, rudeness, and a severe lack of transparency. The lack of specialized knowledge and training of the police has left them so weak and insecure that they can't afford to have people know what is going on.

The obvious outcome of this lack of training and specialized knowledge is a perfectly predictable but nevertheless shocking level of incompetence. The combination of pressured expectations and ignorance is deadly.

If they can't find a suspect, they may just round up a group of people nearby and torture them until someone confesses, or imprison suspects' *relatives* in their stead (and still may throw a suspect's family into jail for good measure even when they *do* locate the wanted man). Police in the Ivory Coast threw a 16-year-old child bride into jail, because her *husband* had been accused of murder. She rotted in jail—without any charges against her—for over a year before anyone noticed.

If scared and shy victims of sexual assault are difficult to interview, police slap them and yell at them as if they were interrogating the suspect of the crime. IJM staff in Southeast Asia have had to intervene to stop police when they slap, threaten to slap, and withhold food or bathroom breaks from child sex trafficking victims in order to get them to "tell the truth." In East Africa we have had to intervene when police officers got frustrated and abusive with the parents of child sexual assault victims in the midst of difficult interviews. The police lose patience and take their anger out on the parents, who then threaten to beat the children if they don't "tell what happened."

If police are conducting anti-trafficking or anti-slavery raids, they simply make a perfunctory appearance at the scene of the crime without any serious effort. Many times we have watched anti-human trafficking raids in South Asia and Southeast Asia in which the local police waited at the front door while the suspects ran away with their victims out the rear exit (and *not* because they were paid off—they just didn't know what to do). When owners of rock quarries, brick kilns and brick factories have sent mobs to interfere with anti-slavery operations, the police have simply fled and left the slaves to the mercy of the violent mobs. If they do manage to round up the suspects, police in the developing world routinely co-mingle victims and perpetrators together in the same room throughout the hours and days of processing at the police station, permitting perpetrators to intimidate, threaten, and dissuade the victims from cooperating with the investigation.

Many times police rely on the families of victims or victims themselves to find and apprehend the thugs accused of violent abuse and assault. We have seen police tell parents and relatives of children who have been sexually assaulted and frail old widows who have had their homes stolen that they must bring the perpetrators on their own to the police station to be interviewed. As African citizens in the *Voices of the Poor* report explained: "Normally, they send us back to catch the murderers and thieves and bring them to the police station."[11]

The lack of training produces a predictable catalogue of horrors and absurdities—lost files and evidence, dangerous suspects slipping out of the holding cell, misapplication of basic law, failure to pick up key evidence at the crime scene, mistakes covered up with falsified reports, and dangerous and excessive use of force. The experience for individual officers who are utterly ill-equipped for their jobs is miserable and unfair—and the misery and injustice is only multiplied a thousand-fold for the common citizenry that is left abused and utterly unprotected from violence. Slum dwellers in Bangladesh summed up police performance this way: "The police always catch the innocent people instead of the guilty ones."[12]

Corruption and Perversity

When outsiders breezily declare that police in the developing world are "totally corrupt," they are frequently overstating the universality of corruption and simultaneously underappreciating the true impact of law enforcement corruption. On the one hand, not all of the police personnel in the developing world are corrupt. I have met countless police officers of great courage and integrity in the developing world who daily take great risks to protect vulnerable citizens and to fight the prevailing culture of corruption and abuse. On the other hand, corruption and abuse *is* the prevailing culture among the police in the developing world, and the implications are far worse than what people commonly understand.

Corruption is a crime. It is a theft. It is a theft either by 1) extortion ("give me money or I will hurt you, detain you, fine you, or inconvenience you"), or by 2) selling the non-performance of a service that one has been paid to perform and which the public is entitled to receive. When corruption becomes endemic to a police force, it has become a criminal force. It is working *against* enforcement of the law.

Think of it this way: "Doctors" are not doctors anymore when they start making money off of making people sick. "Teachers" are not teachers any more if they accept payment from third parties to obstruct a child's education. "Water engineers" become something entirely different when they start taking money to contaminate the water. Likewise, poor people simply do not have "law enforcement" in their community when corruption becomes endemic to the police in their community.

Respected poverty expert Charles Kenny writes that, in developing nations, extortion and bribery are "the expected norm" for interactions with the police.[13]

Let's see: Extortion and bribery are *the expected norms* for interactions. If this is true of police in the developing world, and I think it is, then the poor really don't have law enforcement. They are without the fundamental protections against violence that you and I depend upon every day. And they are in big trouble.

Corruption of the police force in the developing world means that the poor are priced out of the very protections against violence upon which everything else depends. This was the unspeakably painful realization that pushed tears into the exhausted eyes of those mothers I spoke to in Peru when they realized that the police would do nothing to help their raped daughters, because they did not have money to pay. Likewise, researchers in India found that the poor could not afford to pay the bribes that the police demanded for simply filing a criminal complaint or for the costs of investigation.[14]

Corruption places the poor in a bidding war against perpetrators who are making counter offers to the police to *not* enforce the law. As sexual assault survivors from the slums of Nairobi explained to Amnesty International researchers: They did not report their employers' repeated sexual assaults (which left one of them pregnant and HIV positive) to the police "because our employers would have been able to bribe them."[15] In practical effect, corruption allows violent predators to purchase hunting licenses from the authorities to hunt down the poor.

It's a perfect storm: Ignorance and incompetence from a lack of training and knowledge combine with corruption (the discovery that you can make money from *not* doing your job) to produce a lethal chaos of perverse behaviors and outcomes.

With the expectation that law enforcement services are for paying customers only, there's little actual incentive to enforce the law: My colleagues
have repeatedly watched in amazement as police officers in the developing
world refuse to chase a suspect who runs away from them, refuse to fill out a
criminal complaint on behalf of a victim who has come to the station, refuse
to visit a crime scene, refuse to interview an eyewitness eager to provide
testimonial evidence, refuse to show up in court when ordered to testify, or
refuse to leave the police station to arrest a suspect.

Additionally, if you are under pressure to "reduce crime," but you
want to do as little actual crime-fighting as possible, you can make it look
like there is less crime by discouraging the reporting, registration, and
investigation of crime in the community.[16] Perversely, instead of exposing crime, the police cover up criminal activity as a way of reducing *the
appearance* of crime. Once corruption becomes endemic in the police
forces, the entire concept of "law enforcement" becomes inverted to
serve the money-making enterprise. Every law and regulation ceases to
be seen as an authorization to restrain a socially hurtful behavior and is
seen instead as an opportunity to extract money from the public. Police
even come to use the cloak of "law enforcement" to initiate and run their
own criminal enterprises such as sex trafficking, drug smuggling, illegal
mining, or logging operations. Police provide muscle and intimidation for
criminal enterprises, and gathering intelligence for gangs; and they act as
hitmen, assassinating and threatening those whom they are charged with
protecting.

In poor communities in the developing world where "law enforcement"
has been disconnected from the law by corruption and dysfunction, the
exercise of police power no longer works to elevate and protect those who
are weak and vulnerable. Rather, law enforcement works to reinforce the
subordination, abuse, and exploitation of those who are weak in the community. Instead of being motivated by an ethos of heroic protection of the
weak underdog, the police are co-opted by the powerful and put to work
oppressing and bullying the most vulnerable. This is perhaps most starkly
evident in the way women are generally treated by police in the developing
world. Painfully, researchers document the stunning regularity with which
law enforcement not only fails to adequately address but actively *condones*
violence against women.[17]

Because the police are the first segment in the public justice pipeline, they end up being the gatekeepers who determine who gets a crack at justice and who does not.[18] As a police sub-inspector in India explained after refusing to register a complaint from a woman claiming abuse: "In this area, the women come here all the time making all kinds of allegations. We listen to them and then tell them to go home. They are usually lies and exaggerations. We have experience. We know how to make the distinction."

In the slums of Nairobi, researchers found that "most of the women interviewed did not believe that female victims of violence could get any justice" from the police.[19] In Tanzania, when it came to women being thrown off their land and being dispossessed of their property, researchers likewise found that "women's cases are handled badly and the police often judge the cases themselves and decide not to take action."[20] Rape victim advocates in Indonesia describe the painful and demeaning gauntlet of questions young victims must typically endure from the police if they report an assault: "They ask whether she enjoyed it, what she was wearing at the time, and what she was doing outside at that time of night."[21] This gross insensitivity to the victims can viciously re-traumatize the survivors of these brutal assaults and serves as a powerful warning to future victims that they should not bother trying to seek any justice or relief in the public justice pipeline.

Over the years, countless traumatized women and girls from poor communities in Latin America and Africa have arrived in tears on the doorsteps of the offices of my IJM colleagues after they had taken great risks to report a sexual assault to the police but were then brutally turned away by officers who say it's just a "family matter" and not a crime. In India, NGOs and the police themselves reported that the police often tell female victims to work out a "compromise" with the families or relatives involved—even though there is reason to believe the victim has been repeatedly and severely abused.[22]

Another way that the police steer cases of violence out of the public justice pipeline is by inappropriately pressuring (and sometimes demanding) that the victim's family accept a financial settlement for the assault from the perpetrator's family in lieu of filing a criminal complaint. This allows wealthier people to simply purchase impunity for rapes and assaults against poor people, and it communicates to the victims that their dignity and physical integrity can be bartered away. Such settlements are particularly pernicious because the police frequently arrange to take a percentage of the financial settlement for themselves and pressure the victim's family to take the money rather than pursue justice. Victim advocates in the developing world see the parents of rape victims falsely arrested, imprisoned and beaten by the police for refusing to take a financial settlement for the rape of a family member—a settlement from which the police stood to make a good bit of money.

Scarcity

So, the entrance to the public justice pipeline is dangerous and toxic. But, in many cases, it's also so small and obstructed that nothing can get in it in the first place. That is to say, law enforcement is not only non-existent for most of the world's poor in *qualitative* terms because of incompetence, dysfunction, and corruption—it's also non-existent in *quantitative* terms.

Law enforcement is expensive—which makes it a scarce resource. My city of Washington, DC spends about $850 per person, per year on police— that's about $2.33 per day. By contrast, in Bangladesh, the government spends less than $1.50 per person per year for law enforcement. That's not even half of a penny per day and ends up providing one police officer for every 1,800 citizens, and in some districts only one police officer for every 8,000 citizens.[23] In the Philippines, the head of the National Police revealed that he only had one police officer for every 1,400 Filipinos and admitted that this was "far too low to meet the demands place[d] on the police."[24] India spends less than 13 cents per person, per day on policing for its citizens.[25] This translates into about one police officer for every 1,037 Indians (and 85 percent of those police officers have no significant training in criminal investigation or crime fighting skills).

A country like Kenya, however, has even fewer police per person than India—and overall, Africa has significantly lower police to public ratios than any other region of the world. What makes these numbers even worse is the fact that higher levels of violence actually require more police manhours to investigate the crimes. So while the worldwide average tends to be 188 police officers per homicide—the median for countries in Africa is only 22 police officers per recorded homicide.[26] We know that there is a minimum level of police presence below which "the criminal justice system cannot effectively deter future offenders," and it is now manifest that "many African countries reside below that threshold."[27] Latin American countries show better police-to-public ratios, but experts have found that many countries do not have sufficient personnel, equipment, or infrastructure to deal with the levels of violence that the police are facing in their countries.[28]

Moreover, *within* developing world countries, governments tend to deploy their scarce law enforcement resources to protect the things they value most—which generally are *not* common poor people. In Indonesia, for example, the tourist mecca of Bali gets about one police officer for every 300 people (a ratio on par with the United States), but the territory of Kalimantan (with a huge population of poor people) has one police officer for every 2,500 citizens.[29] Likewise, the Kibera slum in Nairobi, Kenya, with its one million residents, has virtually no regular police post or station—but the higher-income areas adjacent to Kibera with one tenth of its population have at least three police posts or stations.[30]

Of course, the number of police personnel is only the very beginning of the scarcity problem for policing in the developing world. A surgeon without a scalpel or a pharmacist without pharmaceuticals is just not very helpful. Likewise, police officers are simply not very useful if they don't have the basic equipment for their job.

A typical police station in the developing world gets about $100 to cover all non-salary expenses for a whole year, which is what a good Starbucks customer in the US spends every month.[31] This means that the police deployed to protect the poor in the developing world don't have the most basic tools to do their jobs, including transportation to go to the village where the widow is being thrown off her land, to go to the remote rock quarry where the slaves are being held, to transport the girls released from a brothel raid, to visit the witness who saw the rape, to go to the court to testify. They lack basic office supplies and technology, like forms for filing a criminal complaint, paper to make copies of evidentiary documents, or folders for maintaining files; phones for conducting interviews, contacting government offices, or contacting victims or witness; computers for keeping records, tracking performance data, or writing reports. When copy paper is hard to come by, it's not a surprise to learn that they also don't have basic evidence-gathering equipment such as rape kits, forensic evidence capacities, DNA testing, undercover cameras, undercover audio recording, or basic digital photography equipment.

On top of the inadequacy of police personnel and equipment, the *coup de grace* of scarcity is the devastating failure to pay police in the developing world a living wage above the petty corruption line. Most will get paid much less per month than what that good Starbucks customer pays per month in lattes. Repeatedly in the *Voices of the Poor* study, poor people described all of the conditions of incompetence and corruption that we have discussed here, but they also frequently expressed that they didn't actually blame the police officers for all of their failures because they are so poorly paid.[32]

Indeed, the police function in much of the developing world is so utterly severed from any accountability to the people in the communities they are supposed to serve, that not only has a half century of non-stop, common criminal violence kept billions of the world's poorest people in lawless poverty—but unlike so many issues in the developing world where conditions are improving for poor people, when it comes to basic law enforcement, things are getting progressively worse. The core systemic failure to provide even a minimally adequate police function for the poor in the developing world has given rise to a state of double impunity. There is impunity for the violent predators—*and* there is impunity for the government leaders who are responsible for this failure to provide the most fundamental protections to the poor. The stark reality is this: The poor don't have police protection. As a woman from a poor community in Brazil said, "Our public safety is ourselves. We work and hide indoors."

THE NEXT SEGMENT IN A BROKEN JUSTICE PIPELINE: PROSECUTORS

"In the Criminal Justice System the people are represented by two separate, yet equally important groups. The police who investigate crime and the District Attorneys who prosecute the offenders. These are their stories."

This is how *Law & Order*—the long-running U.S. television series that has spawned versions in the U.K., South Africa, Russia, France, and elsewhere—explains the criminal justice pipeline and the handoff from the police to the prosecutors in bringing violent criminals to justice. For more than twenty years, after the iconic *chung-CHUNG* sound effect, what followed were "their stories." The series made heroes out of the prosecutors because what they do—and don't do—matters.

What prosecutors do and don't do in the developing world matters as well. But it would be an interesting challenge, for instance, for the *Law & Order* screenwriters to hold our attention with the story that the *New York Times'* Michael Wines brought to light about Lackson Sikayenera and Ismael Wadi, two men in Malawi whose lives are wrapped up in a shared tragedy, and yet have never met and probably never will.[33]

Lackson's storyline would be a little tough to make interesting because for the last six years he's been spending 14 hours a day on a concrete floor, unable to move. He's jammed in a prison cell so overcrowded that he and the 160 other men he shares it with cannot move unless they all do so at once. Lackson has been holding this position for 14 hours a day, for six years. He is fed a single bowl of porridge once a day and some dirty water. Over the last six years, he has watched about 180 of his fellow prisoners leave the prison—dead—but the prison just keeps replacing its dead with new prisoners. In the meantime, Lackson hasn't seen his family in 2,100 days. He was the only breadwinner and has received word that his wife has had to move on and find another husband.

Like many of the other 10,000 prisoners in Malawi, Lackson has not been convicted of anything. He's been waiting these six years simply to appear before a court. But odds are that just isn't going to happen for Lackson—ever. The truth is, the Malawian justice system doesn't actually know that Lackson exists. The prison guards were told six years ago to keep Lackson locked up until the prosecutor summoned him to the court. And sometime after that, the justice "system" lost his file. And here is where our *Law & Order Malawi* episode gets a little stuck. The prosecutor can't summon Lackson to court because he doesn't know he exists—and Lackson, like almost everyone in Malawi, is too poor to afford an attorney to straighten this mess out, and none is appointed for him. So we are facing an hour-long episode in which a man is rotting his life away in a fetid prison because his paperwork got lost.

But maybe we cut away to Ismael Wadi—our other main character, and the man ultimately responsible for losing Lackson's file. As the Director of Public Prosecutions for Malawi, Ismael's office would have received Lackson's file from the police after they detained him, but like most prosecution offices in the developing world, Ismael's office is completely overwhelmed. His office is responsible for *all* criminal prosecutions across the *entire* country. While the New York District Attorney's office portrayed in

Law & Order has about 500 lawyers in real life, Ismael has to cover a territory seven times larger with twice the population with only ten prosecutors. There are vacancies for three times that many prosecutors, but the salaries are so low Ismael can't find lawyers willing to take the jobs—and there are only about 300 lawyers in the whole country.[34] Those ten prosecutors have a backlog of 1,500 serious felony cases, including about 900 murder cases—with about 600 new murders being added every year.

"When the offenses occur, they send the files to this office," Ismael told a reporter. "The files keep on coming, so the number keeps increasing. So what do you do? You accumulate the files, keep them nice and put them on the shelves."

At least one of those files was not kept so nice—and that was the one with Lackson's name on it. And with one prosecutor for every million and a half people in Malawi, it's safe to assume that there may be some other files that are not kept so nice either. And as bad as Malawi's pretrial choke point is, it's just as bad or worse in other parts of Africa. Two-thirds of Uganda's 18,000 inmates have also not been tried—and similarly, three-fourths of Mozambique's and four-fifths of Cameroon's detainees have been forced to endure harsh imprisonment without being convicted.[35]

The Second Half of the Tragedy

The brokenness of prosecution services in the developing world not only leaves innocent people who've had the misfortune of being wrongfully charged with a crime to languish in jail, but it also allows the violent abusers of the poor to run free. As in Dan's case in Kenya, most prosecutions in Malawi are actually carried out by police prosecutors without legal training; as a result, the most dangerous and sophisticated criminals can get off scot-free and remain undeterred. The chief of Malawi's High Court admits that cases against serious criminals "are extremely complicated cases for people who have not been trained sufficiently. We get convictions that aren't supposed to be convictions, and acquittals that aren't supposed to be acquittals."[36]

Throughout much of the developing world, the prosecution segment of the justice pipeline has been allowed to gradually collapse into a nearly impenetrable barrier to meaningful enforcement of the law.[37] The shortage of prosecutors is compounded in poorer countries by the disproportionately large volume of criminal violence (which produces more cases per prosecutor) *and* a massive pre-existing backlog. The end result is a colossal, painful farce.[38]

The raw numbers begin to tell some of the story. For instance, in the United States and Canada there are about 10.2 prosecutors for every 100,000 people. In the United States, this means that there are about 27,000 prosecutors for 312 million people, or one prosecutor for every 12,000 citizens. By comparison, in the developing world, the ratios look something like this:[39]

Ratio of Citizens per Prosecutor in Various Developing Nations

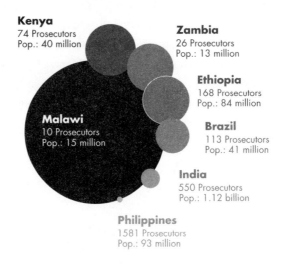

Kenya
74 Prosecutors
Pop.: 40 million

Zambia
26 Prosecutors
Pop.: 13 million

Ethiopia
168 Prosecutors
Pop.: 84 million

Malawi
10 Prosecutors
Pop.: 15 million

Brazil
113 Prosecutors
Pop.: 41 million

India
550 Prosecutors
Pop.: 1.12 billion

Philippines
1581 Prosecutors
Pop.: 93 million

Figure 5.1

These numbers reveal only a fraction of the disaster because of a compounding dynamic called "congestive collapse," which is perhaps best understood by recalling a classic scene from the 1950s television hit *I Love Lucy* in which Lucy Ricardo and her friend Ethel are assigned to wrap candies coming along a factory conveyor belt. As the chocolate candies come down the conveyer belt, Lucy and Ethel are supposed to wrap them quickly in paper and return them to the belt for the next stage of packing. At first, the two of them are able to handle the volume of candies coming at them; but then the belt speeds up, and the comedic absurdity begins. They try every possible way to cope with (and hide) their inability to keep up with the volume of candies, but once they are behind, they can only get more and more behind and they find themselves furiously stuffing the candies in their mouths, their blouses, their hats, the floor, and anywhere they can. Finally Lucy blurts out: "Ethel! I think we are fighting a losing game!" The live studio audience roars with laughter at the absurdity of their efforts to keep up. It's impossible—and only gets worse.

A criminal justice system is a relentless conveyor belt of criminal cases from the community. They just keep coming. If you do not have enough prosecutors to handle the volume, the prosecutors you do have will get increasingly behind *and* they will become *increasingly* unable to give any one case the attention it deserves.

For instance, in the numbers above, the Philippines might look like it is doing alright with one prosecutor for every 60,000 citizens—especially when compared to the ratios in many African countries. But with staffing levels that are one-fifth of those in the United States and a comparable or higher crime rate, the Filipino prosecutor has cases coming at him or her not twice as fast, but five times as fast. As a result, every year it gets worse on a compounding basis. Experts conclude that when they are overloaded with cases, these prosecutors "become a major obstacle, rather than aid, to redress" of abuses.[40] Indeed, studies now show that the average criminal case in the Philippines takes five to six years to reach judgment, with many cases taking as long as 10 years.[41]

And as we can see from the numbers, the Philippines prosecution service is in much better shape than most developing world countries. Even so, common Filipinos know that the system is so overwhelmed that the only way a victim of a crime can get his or her case properly prosecuted is if he or she hires a private prosecutor to do all the investigative work, the logistical legwork, the legal analysis and the argumentation for the public prosecutor. If, however, you are too poor to hire your own private prosecutor—which would certainly include the nearly 25 million Filipinos who live off about a $1.00 a day[42]—there simply is no prosecution service for you.

Experts at UNODC have looked at the massive criminal caseload facing the tiny number of prosecutors in Kenya and concluded that the odds of a Kenyan prosecutor being prepared to properly prosecute a case are simply "improbable."[43] Indian supreme court justices lament the "severe shortage of prosecutors"[44] and decry conditions in states like Maharashtra (with its mega-city of Mumbai) where the prosecutors fail to convict 91 percent of the criminal suspects they bring to trial.[45] Indeed, the conviction rate of prosecutors in India has been steadily falling for forty years, which the leader of India's elite Criminal Bureau of Investigation says clearly demonstrates what he calls "the non-efficacy of the public justice system."[46] In Latin America, the criminal justice system in Guatemala fails to convict 94 percent of the criminal suspects brought into the system—with the vast majority of cases being dropped before the case even appeared before the first instance judge[47]—and in Bolivia, prosecutors fail between 86 percent and 88 percent of the time.[48] As to Brazil, the U.S. State Department simply says that "criminal convictions for crimes are rare."[49]

Needless to say, however, the massive brokenness of rudimentary prosecution services gets almost no attention. It remains buried out of sight with the rest of the tedious plumbing of the criminal justice systems of the developing world. But for millions of common poor people, the result is terrifying: a perfectly upside-down world where falsely accused poor people rot in prison because their cases can't get processed, and violent predators run free to brutalize the poor because their cases can't get prosecuted.

The Final Segment: The Courts

A credible court system must be swift and true; that is, it must discern the guilt or innocence of an accused person with reasonable reliability—and do so in a reasonable amount of time. But, of course, ferreting out guilt or innocence is an extremely difficult enterprise, something societies have been trying to refine for thousands of years. And because it's so hard, the *quality* of the process must be quite high, or else the court *will* get it wrong—and if it gets that part wrong with anything remotely approaching regularity, the court is doing more harm than good. Secondly, the court must get this difficult job done with a reasonable amount of speed, because the coercive power of the state places lives in a terrible limbo until a case is resolved, because the deterrent value of criminal sanction is proportional to its frequency and certainty, and because the cases just keep coming.

Tragically for the poor in the developing world, the criminal courts are nearly paralyzed with dysfunction, reach the wrong results, and treat people badly. For our purposes, it doesn't matter if the courts occasionally can be made to work well for people of means—a meaningful *public* justice system must work for those who bring no money to the table. And to understand how the courts work for poor people, you have to crawl through the plumbing of the court system with them to see what they encounter and how they are treated.

While observing trials in developing countries around the world, I have often felt a bit like Alice in Lewis Carroll's *Alice in Wonderland* as she found herself watching the Knave of Hearts being put on trial for stealing tarts. Alice, who has read about courts in books, is "quite pleased to find that she knew the name of nearly everything there. 'That's the judge,' she said to herself, 'because of his great wig.'" She correctly identifies the "jury-box" and the "jurors"—and ends up feeling "rather proud of it: for she thought and rightly too, that very few little girls of her age knew the meaning of it all." Likewise I have entered these courts with my colleagues and thought: "I've read about this—and I'm a lawyer. I'll understand what's going on here."

And then the proceedings would begin, and like Alice, I would find myself perfectly lost in the swirl of confusion, non sequitur, and dysfunction. In Lewis Carroll's story, Alice watches as the Queen and King of Hearts preside over a spinning chaos of absurd exchanges, passionate gibberish, and strident malapropisms flying in rapid succession about the courtroom. Eventually, Alice takes the stand, the Queen threatens to behead her for insisting on logic, and Alice wakes up. It all reads as if Mr. Carroll were smoking something—or had some experience with the "logic" of the courts that the world's poorest are forced to rely on in matters of life and death. Scenes every bit as surreal as Alice's play out in the courtrooms of the developing world every day. In India, the man convicted of holding scores of children, women, and men in slavery for years is sentenced by the judge to detention "until the rising of the court"—that is, until the judge declares a short recess for any reason at all, including to take a bathroom break. In Uganda, where a penniless widow has to expend great effort and expense to travel to the court for a trial to get her land back from violent thieves, the magistrate fails to show up for trial *nine times* with no accountability. In Bolivia, hearings in a case against a teacher for raping children are rescheduled *80 times*— because the defense lawyer failed to show up, the accused feigned illness, the accused hid in the jail, and an endless array of inexplicable reasons. In a Kolkata courtroom, a mob of defense lawyers is allowed to physically attack and beat the lawyer representing a sex trafficking victim—engulfing the terrified survivor in the melee. After completing a trial, a court in the Philippines inexplicably takes more than three years to issue a judgment in a sex trafficking case—with no discipline. In African courts with mind-numbing case backlogs, court proceedings can only receive testimony and argumentation at the speed...that the judge...can personally write...by hand...because there is...no court...stenographer.

Truth be told, any court system anywhere in the world—even in the most affluent countries—can produce a series of outrageous anecdotes of gross incompetence and miscarriages of justice. But none of these stories will ever make headlines or generate any attention in the developing-world communities where they occur because they would seem much within a poor person's expectation for how they would be treated by those in power.

On a more systematic basis, judicial experts within these countries and the handful of international researchers who study these institutions readily identify the structural symptoms that make courts slow in their proceedings and perverse in their outcomes for poor people.

Gaping Holes Produce Perverse Outcomes

Leaving aside for a moment the massive problem of corruption in the criminal courts (that is, the problem of judges reaching the wrong result because they get paid to do so), these perverse outcomes arise from gaping holes in several core areas. A criminal trial requires a highly sophisticated and nuanced process that draws upon the disciplined knowledge and skills of professionals. While there are dangers in over-professionalizing any aspect of the public sphere, there are moments when the task of justice is so difficult and dangerous that the knowledge of professionals is simply indispensable. The problem for poor people in the developing world is that they cannot afford—and therefore, do not get—the benefit of this expertise when their interests are at stake in the criminal justice system, both when they are victims of crime and when they are accused of crime.

Therefore, the judge in the criminal court enters the trial process with access to only one side of the story—the side that can afford a lawyer—and will reach the wrong result. Not only do lawyers cost money that the poor do not have, but in the developing world, lawyers tend to be such a tiny guild of professionals that billions of poor people in the developing world will never meet a lawyer in their lifetimes.[50] In Chad, fewer than ten practicing lawyers serve six million people.[51] Nine African countries have a combined population of over 114 million people, and yet between them they only have 2,550 lawyers—the same number of lawyers that practice in the state of Vermont, which has a population of about 600,000 people.[52] The actual availability of lawyers to common citizens in Africa is even worse than these numbers indicate because most Africans still live in rural areas and overwhelmingly the lawyers are in distant cities. In fact, in Tanzania, with 42 million people, most of the country's 21 regions don't have *any* lawyers; in Uganda, lawyers can be found in *only nine* of the country's 56 districts.[53]

Americans will read these figures and perhaps joke about moving to rural Africa to get away from the lawyers—and we all get the joke. But if you personally knew Lackson and what it was like for him to rot for six years in that Malawian prison just because he had no lawyer to find his file, then the jokes sound as unfunny as an obese person jesting about going to Southern Sudan amidst a famine. Both obesity and starvation are real health crises—they just manifest, again, the two separate planetary systems of abundance and deprivation that divide human beings in our era.

But the problem is deeper than a lack of access to lawyers for victims and defendants in the courtroom. Lawyers can be so rare in the developing world that many *judges*—especially in Africa—have never been to law school and have no formal legal training. Again, lawyers aren't the only ones who can settle disputes and arbitrate conflicts in a community, but no one reading this book would tolerate living in a community where the coercive power of the criminal justice system was exercised without the specialized expertise of judges who have been formally trained and certified. When poor people (especially women) appear in court in the developing world, they frequently are forced to tolerate not only the absence of legal expertise but also brutal buffoonery from ignorant, bigoted, and bizarre judges.

We have watched poor people in the developing world appear before judges and magistrates who are utterly unfamiliar with the relevant passages of the criminal code; who declare from the bench that they "don't care" what the law says, or say that particular perpetrators are too powerful to have the law enforced against them, or explain that the rights in the law are written in books and therefore cannot be enforced for the illiterate; or who, in fits of punitive capriciousness, have threatened to throw out a child rape case when the victim does not appear in court *because she is in the hospital being treated for severe trauma*. Others who provide legal services in the developing world have similar stories to share.

In one African country in which we work, my local IJM colleagues conducted a baseline study with the national prosecution service in child sexual assault cases and found that in cases where the suspect denied the allegations—regardless of other evidence—the judges found the suspects not guilty 89% of the time. Furthermore, if the defendants simply claimed that the victim's family was lying about the abuse, *judges acquitted the defendants 100% of the time*, despite other evidence such as proof of penetration, finding of rape or thorough witness statements.

Again, every legal system in the world could produce its own litany of Judge Whacko stories, and the courts of the developing world are also filled with brilliant, hard-working, courageous judges. But the fact is, the lack of investment in judicial systems in the developing world means that the standards of judicial personnel processing the cases of millions of very poor people can be atrociously low. In many low- and middle-income countries, judges are largely the lawyers who could not find jobs in the private sector.

Even good judges, however, frequently lack the basic materials or facilities to do their job or to render good decisions. Judges have told my local IJM lawyer colleagues not to cite cases or legal authorities without providing a photocopy of the citation because they do not have access to such materials. Many developing countries lack the academic resources to produce legal textbooks—so it is not uncommon for judges in some former British colonies to rely upon textbooks commenting upon English law even though the substance of the rules may be very different in their countries today.[54]

And the courts in which these judges must render their decisions often lack the equipment and protocol to examine the evidence that is frequently the clearest, most compelling, and definitive—namely, video evidence. Judges can't or won't consider video of slave owners and traffickers bragging about their violent abuse because there is no equipment to view it in court, no familiarity with such evidence, or no procedure for authentication. Courts in the poorest countries lack even more basic equipment—like paper. In Malawi, courts tend to run out of paper halfway through the month and have to stop hearing cases until more paper arrives.[55] Victims will have to pay court personnel or police to serve warrants or summonses—or to have case records prepared because the court does have enough funds to pay for the paper or ink to document its own proceedings or orders.

The lack of resources for the *public* justice system means that the poor person must pay a variety of fees and costs (beyond any bribes that may be demanded) that are deemed necessary for the court to do its work. In Uganda for instance, my IJM colleagues have documented that an impoverished widow who seeks to secure her $500 piece of land against violent thieves must incur more than $200 in travel fees (with up to 16 trips to the capital city and more than 40 bus trips to her district court and office) and pay another $140 in fees and costs (not to mention any bribes that may be demanded of her.) On her own, a widow navigating this mess will just have to hope and pray that she and her children can have their shelter and vegetable garden for another day.

Another devastating deficiency in the court system's basic resources is the provision for basic security for the court, for victims, and for witnesses—from a lack of basic witness protection services to a lack of procedure requiring the allies of defendants to surrender their firearms in the courtrooms. The need for witness protection and court security in the criminal courts of the developing world is only mentioned here in passing; but in the courts of more affluent countries, one does not even contemplate the possibility of operating a functioning criminal justice system without such provisions.

Justice Moves at a Glacial Pace

The impoverished condition of the courts in the developing world and their high levels of dysfunction create massive delays and accumulate massive backlogs that for all practical purposes grind the system of justice to a halt for billions of poor people. Some of the delay and backlog comes from a shortage of judges and decades of underinvestment in the judicial system. In India, a third of judgeships are vacant, which means there are only about eleven judges for every million citizens. In the United States there are 10 times more judges per person; in Europe there are 12 to 20 times more.[56] This has created a backlog in India of more than 32 million cases, which leaves each judge with a stack of more than 2,000 cases to catch up on—while handling the daily intake. According to analysts, it would take the Indian courts 350 to 400 years to clear out the backlogged cases.[57]

The figures are even bleaker in Africa, which, when considered together as a region, has fewer judges than any other region in the world.[†] As analysts

---

[†] In Kenya, the staff establishment for the judiciary is 4,681 but there are only 1,456 people in posts. With regard to judicial officers, the total number of magistrates in post is 277 against an establishment of 554.

at UNODC found in their study of the impact of violence and crime on development in Africa: "Fewer judges mean that criminal cases are processed more slowly. This is important because the rate at which a case is processed is directly related to its prospects of success. Over time, victims lose their commitment and witnesses disappear, particularly in areas where they can be difficult to locate in the first place."[58]

A country like the Philippines only has 2.5 judges per 100,000 citizens, with almost a quarter of its judicial chambers left vacant and some provinces with no sitting judge at all. It has a national backlog of a million and a half cases, with criminal cases currently taking about six years to resolve.[59] Brazil produces a backlog of unresolved cases nearly four times as large in a single year—with surveys reflecting that the courts are the second-least-trusted government institution in the country—just after the police.[60] The Inter-American Commission for Human Rights found that Bolivian courts were only able to resolve 5 percent of the country's cases in a 21-month period of time, producing a massive backlog and delay.

Here is another devastating little detail of systemic dysfunction that people outside the developing world might never imagine: Trials are not conducted from start to finish in a few days, but one bit at a time over months and years. In countries like the Philippines, India, and other parts of the developing world, courts hear evidence and argumentation on one piece of the case on one day, and then stop the trial. The next portion of trial is then not heard until months later. When that portion is completed, the trial is stopped again and the next bit of the proceeding doesn't occur until months later. And on and on it goes. With common adjournments, postponements, and delays, there can easily be six, nine or 12 months *between each day* of the trial. So a four-day trial will easily take 12 to 24 months. The inefficiency of the approach is mind-numbing because it requires that the victim, the accused, the lawyers, witnesses, judge, etc. all reacquaint themselves with the case all over again; witnesses must be kept available for years; the victims and the accused must remain in painful limbo for years; and frequently the prosecutors and judges change and must learn the case from scratch.

In Mariamma's slavery and gang rape case, Sashmeeta had to help seven different prosecutors understand the law and evidence over the six years that it took to resolve the case, at which time the case was taken over by a brand new judge who acquitted the accused without personally hearing any evidence.

I sat with Sashmeeta and a senior Indian prosecutor one evening over dinner in Bangalore and listened as the prosecutor suggested that the reason for this piecemeal system of hearings was that the volume of cases was "too great" for a "day-to-day" approach.

"But how does it address the problem of too many cases to conduct the cases on a piecemeal basis?" a surprised Sashmeeta asked as politely as she could.

The earnest senior prosecutor just looked back at Sashmeeta with a furrowed brow and pained confusion on his face.

After politely rephrasing the question two or three more times without a response, Sashmeeta asked: "Let's say I am given 10 books to read by my teacher. Then he gives me 20 books to read. How would it help me deal with the increased number of books if my teacher told me I could only read one chapter of a book at a time before I must move on to read a chapter in the next book?"

This very senior prosecutor of more than 30 years' service looked over to his non-lawyer friend sitting next to him for help, but could find none. After a few awkward minutes, Sashmeeta diplomatically changed the subject. It was a jarring example of the way court systems in the developing world are subjected to severe habits of dysfunction that make *no sense at all*—but do not change.

On the other hand, if such a systemic folly were identified in one of the IT firms across town in Bangalore, it would be eliminated in half an hour.

The problem is not unique to India. As far back as the late 1980s, the Philippine Bar Association recommended that the court system abandon that nation's piecemeal approach and run continuous trials. The supreme court even issued an order for the courts to do so in 1990[61]—but it just hasn't happened. In testimony to the inertia that chokes these systems, my IJM colleagues have never seen a case run day-to-day in more than a decade of hundreds of trials in the Philippines.

Given the intensified importance of every hearing date that this piecemeal approach creates, it would probably surprise most outsiders to learn that, in practical terms, no one is really *required* to show up for trial in these courts—not the lawyers, not the witnesses, not the accused, not even the judge. If one of the parties does not show up, the proceeding is generally just postponed and rescheduled without any meaningful sanction.

For my colleagues in Bolivia, 85 percent of pre-trial hearings get cancelled—and 70 percent of trial hearings are cancelled and require rescheduling. One of IJM's successful slavery prosecutions in India required IJM lawyers make 45 trips to a court house over a 6-year period—and fully half of the hearings were cancelled after the 4-hour car ride to and from the courthouse. Child survivors of sex crimes and other vulnerable, traumatized victims have to testify two, three, or four times because of rescheduled hearings, changes of judges, lost transcripts, and new counsel. Doctors in East Africa are known to refuse service and examination of injuries and assaults just so they won't have to show up in court only to be told to come back another day. In both Africa and South Asia, my IJM colleagues have had criminal trials postponed because the defendant was able to hide in prison or simply refuse to board the prison transport to trial. In Bolivia, citizen jurors must serve with the professional judge to render a verdict in a criminal case (similar to a U.S. jury). But the court-run Notification Center doesn't alert citizens of their duty, so they never show up to serve—and if a citizen *does* get the notification but decides not to show, the court has no power to compel jury service. Criminal cases against dangerous predators and child rapists do not go forward simply because a jury cannot be assembled.

Outsiders would also be quite surprised to learn that in the courts of the developing world, people are not really required to tell the truth—that is to say, application of sanctions for perjury are almost unheard of. As a result, courts waste an enormous time chasing down the truth in an endless number of falsehoods that are shamelessly presented before the court without any fear of sanction.

For example, in one of IJM's typical child rape cases in the Philippines, our client, a 15 year-old girl, very bravely took the witness stand in court to describe how a man in her slum neighborhood had raped her when she was 13. However, the accused neighbor introduced reasonable doubt about the victim's direct testimony by having three friends take the stand and say that they all heard from the victim's aunt that it had been the victim's uncle who raped her. The uncle, of course, lived on a distant island province and was usually working as a cook on a cargo freight ship somewhere on the other side of the world. After months of effort and expense, IJM's legal team was able to secure proof that the accused uncle was actually on a ship in Baltimore at the time of the rape, but there was never any sanction levied on those three friends for telling the lie which, under normal circumstances, would have resulted in the rapist walking off scot free.

These tedious mechanics buried in the plumbing of the court systems must be understood because delay, in and of itself, can render a criminal justice system nearly useless. If the system doesn't operate with reasonable speed in catching offenders and in bringing them to justice, its usefulness drops off to somewhere close to zero, because an insufficient percentage of violent abusers are restrained, and the threat of punishment is too infrequent and uncertain to be a credible deterrent.[62]

Moreover, if the process of criminal adjudication takes too long, victims and witnesses in poverty cannot sustain their involvement in the process because of the costs and the extreme vulnerabilities of their day-to-day existence—and without victim participation it is difficult for the system to bring offenders to justice.

A system rendered ineffective by delays also does not attract community participation in reporting crime and supporting prosecution of offenders—which makes the system all the more ineffective.

In the words of two plain-spoken justices from the Indian Supreme Court: "The system has already become sick. What can be the expectation of the common man for speedy justice? Even in the Supreme Court, a special leave petition takes 8 years to reach final hearing. . . . 'We all give sermons. We go to the National Judicial Academy and give lectures to judicial officers asking them to speed up disposal of cases. But where is the infrastructure'?"

Responding to the question, the editorial writers from the *Indian Express* said: "The short answer is that it does not exist."

Indeed, Indians' outrage over the brokenness of their criminal justice system exploded in December 2012 with the gruesome news of a fatal gang rape of a young woman riding a bus in the nation's capital city of Delhi. Taking the case as a rallying point of protest, thousands took to the streets across India to condemn violence against women and the culture of impunity fostered by a corrupt political class and incompetent law enforcement authorities.[63] In words that sum up much of what we have been trying to discuss thus far, the high-profile Verma Commission established by the government in the wake of the tragedy concluded that a "[f]ailure of good governance is the obvious root cause for the current unsafe environment eroding the rule of law, and not the want of needed legislation." It's not that Indian experts don't know *how* to fix the criminal justice system, the report lamented; rather, because of the "the apathy of all the political dispensations," stacks of official reform recommendations simply "continue to gather dust for decades." As a result, when it comes to sexual violence, "it is clear to us that there is a fundamental incompetence in the ability of the police to deal with rape cases."[64]

FROM IMPUNITY TO PROTECTION

Almost everything useful the world has ever learned about fighting global poverty has come, one way or another, from walking intimately over a sustained period of time with the actual individual people who wake up every day to confront and push their way through the harsh and messy realities of being poor. Moreover, if you stay long enough and they let you get close enough, you will eventually catch glimpses of the vast subterranean world of appalling violence that lies hidden beneath the surface of their poverty

To address these forces of violence, experts are beginning to explicitly acknowledge that the global poor need the same thing that the experts themselves have forever believed indispensable in their own communities: reasonably functioning systems of law enforcement. The truth that has been slower to emerge for the outside world, however, is the degree to which such functioning criminal justice systems simply *do not exist* for most of the world's poor.

When the Pulitzer-Prize winning journalist Katherine Boo returned to the United States recently after spending three years sharing her life with families in an India slum, she was interviewed on National Public Radio about what she had learned. Much of what she had learned about the struggles, characters, and dramas of their world had been rendered in her magnificent book, *Behind the Beautiful Forevers*, but on NPR that day, Boo shared something she came to appreciate about her own country after returning home:

> But one of the things that I do appreciate in the United States now more than I did is that the relative functionality of the criminal justice system: the fact that even [though] the police stations in many low-income communities are not nice places to be [...], when somebody's a victim of a crime in a bad neighborhood, they will often call

911. And they won't feel that the police and the system will be out to victimize them again.

In India, the criminal justice system is so dysfunctional and so exploitative and so disinterested in even the murders of low-income people that for anyone to call for help is to risk their own livelihood. And that's an extremely pernicious situation. So [...] there are certain institutions that we have that I feel more appreciative of now.[65]

I don't think Boo is saying that American law enforcement is perfect, or the exact model for India or any other country—but simply that reasonably decent law enforcement does not exist for the poor families she came to know. And this fact is an urgent one—for it helps us appreciate not only the devastating downside of lawlessness, but also the enormous *upside* of decent justice systems that safeguard the pathway out of poverty for the poor. We've seen the way lawless violence can destroy economic opportunity for the poor and keep them trapped in poverty (see Chapter 3) and the way broken justice systems exacerbate the problem. But on the flip side, a massive, ambitious, and little-known study from the World Bank makes an intriguing argument that justice systems are themselves a key contributor to the development of nation's economic wealth. It turns out that addressing the dysfunctions of broken justice systems may be one of the most powerful ways to secure the poor's capacity for creating wealth.

In their study called *Where Is the Wealth of Nations*, the World Bank sets out to determine how different kinds of capital contribute to a nation's economic development. The sharp-penciled regression analysts at the Bank started with the familiar sources of a nation's capital: 1) natural resources (e.g., oil, gas, minerals, forests, croplands, etc.) and 2) built capital (e.g., machinery, equipment, infrastructure, urban land, etc.). But the economists found that these two sources of tangible capital accounted for only 20 to 40 percent of a nation's wealth. It turns out that the vast majority of the wealth comes from the *intangible* capital of institutions (e.g., education, governance, property rights, justice systems, etc.) that makes human labor and the natural and built capital increasingly productive.[66]

The Intangible Wealth of Nations

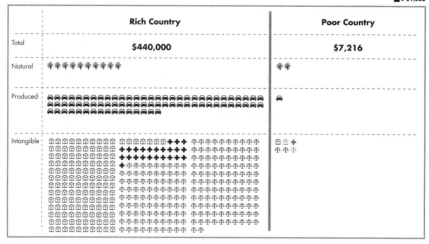

Figure 5.2

This makes intuitive sense in terms of education, right? A nation with rich natural resources and substantial equipment and infrastructure with people who can't read or without engineers or advanced expertise for technological innovation is simply not going to prosper at the same pace as the country with institutions that crank out a highly educated workforce. This explains the obvious emphasis on education for those who care about economic development, poverty alleviation, or empowerment of the girl-child. Education is critical.

Yes. In fact, educational institutions are the second largest factor in account for a country's intangible capital (36 percent), and a 1-percent increase in the value of nation's educational institutions will boost that nation's intangible capital by 0.53 percent. Such is the magic of education in creating wealth and lifting people out of poverty.

But what is the largest factor? Surprisingly, the World Bank drilled down and found that the most important institutions for generating economic development were the rule of law institutions (including the criminal justice system), accounting for a whopping 57 percent of a nation's intangible wealth! While an investment boosting educational institutions by 1 percent increased intangible capital by 0.53 percent, a 1 percent increase in rule of law institutions increases intangible capital by 0.83 percent.[67] The authors of the report summed up the conclusion of the study by saying that policy makers can be confident that investments in education and the justice systems "are the most important means of increasing the intangible-capital component of total wealth."

Admittedly, these regressions are highly complex, and the direct causal connection between rule of law and economic growth is famously elusive and difficult to parse. The criminal justice system is just one of the institutions of rule of law and the extent to which aggregate national economic growth alleviates the most stubborn poverty is not without controversy.

That being said, when combined with other accumulating data on the way lawless violence is undermining the economic advancement of the poor, with data on the dysfunctional collapse of the justice system protecting the poor, and the nearly universal acceptance of the foundational role justice systems play in any complex society—these recent empirical findings on the value of restoring fundamental justice systems to advance economic growth help to seal the argument. It's time to acknowledge and prioritize the difficult struggle to finally protect the poor from violence with justice systems that are at least worthy of the name.

As David Brooks of the *New York Times* has opined with characteristic common sense and clarity:

> You can cram all the nongovernmental organizations you want into a country, but if there is no rule of law and if the ruling class is predatory then your achievements won't add up to much...In short, there's only so much good you can do unless you are willing to confront corruption, venality, and disorder head-on.[68]

As Crisis Group board member Lord Paddy Ashdown, UN High Representative in Bosnia-Herzegovina, stated, "In hindsight, we should have put the establishment of the rule of law first, for everything else depends on it: a functioning economy, a free and fair political system, the development of civil society, public confidence in police and the courts."[69]

As we acknowledged earlier, however, even if we agree upon the indispensable priority of building effective and functional criminal justice systems in the developing world, such an enterprise is famously difficult, dangerous, and unlikely. Therefore, to engage these challenges with conviction, we need to see how the failure to build such systems in the developing world has undermined not only the dream to end severe poverty, but a second fundamental dream for human flourishing in the 21st century. It is to this second destroyed dream we now turn.

A DREAM DEVASTATED

The epic failure to provide billions of the world's poorest people with basic law enforcement systems so that they can be safe from the terror of lawless violence has had a devastating impact on the dream of ending severe poverty. Likewise, there is another great dream born in the last century that has made stunning historical progress over the last fifty years but for the poorest people on our globe remains a bitter, practical disappointment—and that is the modern struggle to secure for all people the most basic human rights. The human rights revolution of the twentieth century has been one of the most profound transformations over the millennia of human history, but like the unprecedented economic advances of this past century, this revolution has left billions of the poorest behind through a failure to secure justice systems that protect them from the chaos of common violence.

In the context of the American Civil Rights movement, it was Martin Luther King Jr. who explained the way a rights revolution could make epic progress in bringing freedom in some categories and for some people, and yet leave others behind in their chains. In his iconic "I Have a Dream Speech," King spoke of an American dream that had been fulfilled for many, but not for all:

> When the architects of our republic wrote the magnificent words of the Constitution and the Declaration of Independence, they were signing a

promissory note to which every American was to fall heir. This note was a promise that all men, yes, black men as well as white men, would be guaranteed the "unalienable Rights" of "Life, Liberty and the pursuit of Happiness." It is obvious today that America has defaulted on this promissory note, insofar as her citizens of color are concerned. Instead of honoring this sacred obligation, America has given the Negro people a bad check, a check which has come back marked "insufficient funds."[1]

From the steps of the Lincoln Memorial, King celebrated the historic victory won by the Emancipation Proclamation—that "momentous decree" which issued to millions of black Americans "a check that will give us upon demand the riches of freedom and the security of justice." But the scandal exposed in King's speech was the reality that America had defaulted on its promise to black citizens. Despite issuing eloquent declarations of rights in the Constitution and proclaiming emancipation from slavery, America had failed to make this dream meaningful for blacks because it had failed the practical task of *enforcing* these rights and providing "equal protection of the law." Declaring and legislating rights *without enforcement*, King said, is as useless to its intended beneficiaries as a check you cannot cash.

Today, if given the opportunity, the Yuris, Mariammas, and Lauras of the world might deliver their own "I Have a Dream" speech. The promissory note in their hands is not the U.S. Constitution and Declaration of Independence, but the Universal Declaration of Human Rights. For the holders of that note, the "bank of justice" is their public justice system, and it has long been bankrupt. The scandal at the heart of their speech would be that the failure to build effective public justice systems in the developing world has left them holding a bad check. It has made the great victories of the modern human rights movement largely irrelevant for addressing the most pressing human rights challenge of their daily lives—to be free from unchecked criminal violence.

Indeed, the architects of the modern human rights revolution seemed to understand that the fulfillment of their dream would proceed in three phases: from clearly articulating the *idea* of the right, to legislating the right into *law*, to the *enforcement* of the right through enforcement of the law.

Remarkably, against enormous odds, the modern human rights movement has achieved colossal victories in the first two stages of the movement—but tragically, it has fallen woefully short in the third. For the Yuris, Mariammas and Lauras of the world, the time has now come to channel our resources and energies toward the final indispensable phase of the struggle: building functional public justice systems that enforce the basic human rights now imbedded in national law.

IN THE TWENTIETH CENTURY, THE UNTHINKABLE BECAME MAINSTREAM

Shortly after World War II, the early pioneers of the modern human rights movement achieved a shocking and unlikely victory—passage of the Universal Declaration of Human Rights. To appreciate why such a thing would have been unthinkable even a few years before, we must go back to the mid-1940s—an era when it was inconceivable that a sovereign nation would have to answer to a higher authority for the way it treated those within its own borders. It is difficult for twenty-first-century readers to appreciate the degree to which, at that time, the very idea of human rights represented what one observer of the day called "a radical departure from traditional thinking and practice."[2] Even the most idealistic rights activist understood that getting states to acknowledge universal human rights claims would require a stunning reversal of centuries of geopolitical inertia: "We are in effect asking states to submit to international supervision of their relationship with their own citizens, something which has been traditionally regarded as an absolute prerogative of national sovereignty."[3]

The foundations of that sovereignty principle began to crack as the mass atrocities committed by the Nazis—many of which were consistent with their domestic law—came to light. So, under the sovereignty principle, by what authority could the Allied powers condemn them?

To make accountability to a higher law possible, the Allies crafted the Nuremberg principles of international criminal law, which would govern the trials of German and Japanese war criminals. The Nuremberg principles delivered the first blow to the sovereignty principle by affirming that there were some rights that no country could violate, even within their own borders, towards their own people, and consistent with their own laws.

At the Nuremburg trials, the grotesque atrocities of the Nazis were described as violations against the "inalienable rights" of members of the human family.[4] Grotesque photographs of the "Final Solution" displayed mounds of human bones, piles of eyeglasses and gold teeth fillings, and grooves in solid concrete made by the clawing fingers of those being dragged to the gas chambers.[5] Gruesome newsreels showed bulldozers unceremoniously shoveling heaps of naked and limp bodies of men, women, and children into mass graves.[6]

The defendants protested that they could not be held accountable for these atrocities. Hermann Goering, Hitler's deputy and the original head of the Gestapo, went so far as to complain that it was the Nazi defendants whose rights were being violated. At one point, rather than dispute the voluminous evidence presented by the prosecution of the Nazis' atrocities, Goering defended the atrocities themselves: "But that was our right! We were a sovereign state and that was strictly our business."[7]

Goering's reply may be morally jarring, but he was articulating the prevailing view of international lawyers of the day—that a nation's sovereignty was absolute. But for the rest of the world, the horrors unveiled at Nuremberg delivered a moral blow of such force that the sovereignty principle would remain irrevocably cracked. While Nuremberg left the issue of peacetime violations of human dignity untouched,[8] it paved the way for what would become a much deeper fissure in the sovereignty principle.

THE UNIVERSAL DECLARATION OF HUMAN RIGHTS

Up to this stage in the evolution of the modern human rights movement, the central cast of characters was largely comprised of diplomats who had been content to remain on the margins of serious philosophical discourse. They had never been required to define individual "human rights" and "fundamental freedoms" with rigor and precision, nor to wrestle with moral diversity on a global scale, nor to thoughtfully consider the implications of those rights and freedoms for the world as a whole.[9] This changed dramatically once the United Nations directed its Commission on Human Rights to draft an International Bill of Rights capable of securing universal acceptance. With that daunting mandate, it became clear that it would be impossible to avoid the array of challenging questions of moral and political philosophy that kept bubbling to the surface.

In response, governments appointed not the usual mouthpieces from their diplomatic corps, but an intellectual dream team—a remarkable collection of individuals of extraordinary erudition and political savvy who they believed would be discerning, articulate, and intellectually capable of navigating the difficult political and philosophical issues that would confront them.[10] Anticipating a lively and dramatic debate over highly charged moral and philosophical issues, observers packed the visitors' seats to capacity at the Commission's first meeting in January 1947 to witness what they knew would be an engaging and historic exchange.[11]

But for victims of violence across the world, the Commission's work was not a matter of intellectual entertainment. Even before its first formal meeting, the Commission was deluged with unsolicited petitions from victims of human rights abuses, many of them handwritten.[12] Literally thousands of victims from across the globe sent urgent appeals describing abuses that their government refused to address—or of which members of their government were themselves the perpetrators.[13] The petitions vividly expressed the pain and desperation of victims of violence around the globe and were a sobering reminder that the Commission's work was being watched with desperate anticipation by people who seemed to believe that their very lives and liberty could depend on its success.

But success did not come easily. Fierce realities of state power immediately threatened to drown out the cries of the weak and to crush the project before it ever drew breath and voice. The members of the Commission realized that if the rights in the Declaration of Human Rights were going to be meaningful to victims of abuses around the world, they would have to be enforced, but they clashed on whether the rights should take the form of a legally binding covenant or simply a declaration of principles, which set clear human rights standards without creating new legal obligations.

The fault lines that emerged pitted the stronger powers, which opposed formal legal obligations, against less powerful countries, which advocated for them. The Soviet representative, for example, warned that creating a legally binding covenant would begin "a voyage which would lead it in a direction where it might cross the border which divides international from internal law—the border which divides the interrelationships of governments from the field where the sovereign rights of nations must prevail."[14] In a sharp rejoinder, India's representative dispensed with flowery language, flatly declaring, "[U]nless it is binding on the members of the United Nations, it will have no meaning."[15] In the end, the Great Powers prevailed, insisting that the rights take the form of a non-binding declaration.

The Commission did not, however, relinquish its conviction that if the rights they proclaimed were to make a practical difference in the lives of human rights victims around the globe, they would have to be enforced. But its seasoned members had the political savvy to realize that a legally binding international bill of rights was simply infeasible at that time. Rather than recede into irrelevance by taking a hard line on a position that would inevitably fail, they realized that the modern human rights movement would have to proceed in stages. With prescient apprehension of the evolving political landscape, the Commission resolved during its second session in late 1947 that the project of creating an International Bill of Rights would be composed of three sequential parts: a clear declaration of rights, a legally binding convention, and, finally, specific measures for implementation.[16] This three-phase process became an unofficial blueprint for the modern human rights movement and, nearly 65 years later, remains a useful framework for understanding its past, present, and future.

For victims of violence, the Universal Declaration of Human Rights promised the dawn of a new day. A voice at last emerged to speak on behalf of those who had been silenced by the trump card of national sovereignty. Speaking for the billions of Yuris and Mariammas of the world, the Declaration affirmed with global authority that even those whom oppressors dismiss as "nobodies" have a right to life and personal security. For the likes of Jerardo and José—the men locked up and tortured by police until they "confessed" to the crimes of others in Yuri's case—the Declaration affirmed that no one shall be subjected to torture or arbitrary arrest, and that everyone charged with a crime has the right to be presumed innocent until proven guilty in a fair trial by an impartial court. Stepping forward on behalf of slaves like Mariamma, the Declaration proclaimed that "no one shall be held in slavery or servitude," and that everyone has the right to freedom of movement and free choice of employment. Behind those like Susan—the elderly Ugandan grandmother who suddenly became homeless when her land was seized by a violent neighbor—the Declaration stepped forward to affirm that women have a right to own property and that no one has the right to arbitrarily seize it from them. By acknowledging that these rights came simply as a birthright to every member of humanity, the world affirmed that no bully—whether a state, a private group, or a person—could strip them away.

The impact of the Universal Declaration of Human Rights extended far beyond its historic adoption in 1948. As Harvard law professor Mary Ann Glendon has observed, the Declaration inspired and influenced decades of political movements and spurred the fall of colonial empires, as well as amplified the long-silenced voices of the weak on the world stage; it remains "the primary inspiration for most rights instruments in the world today."[17]

With the Universal Declaration, the world spoke with one voice to assure the poor and vulnerable around the globe that every member of the human family had the right to be safe from predatory violence.

THE STRUGGLE: STAGE TWO

The adoption of the Universal Declaration without a single vote of opposition sparked a wave of euphoria among rights advocates that masked strong undercurrents of resistance. Powerful states willing to accept non-binding declarations of principle, for example, drew the line at transforming those principles into legally binding obligations that might expose their own failures and undermine their national sovereignty. Moreover, the Universal Declaration had been adopted during a narrow window of political viability between the end of World War II and the onset of the Cold War. Shortly thereafter, the window slammed shut, and the United Nations and the language of human rights were conscripted into serving the larger propaganda battle between East and West.

As a result, it took almost two decades before the rights of the Universal Declaration made their way into legally binding instruments. With the support of a large crop of newly independent countries and an ever-growing number of human rights non-governmental organizations (NGOs), the UN General Assembly adopted the historic International Covenant on Civil and Political Rights (ICCPR) and the International Covenant on Economic, Social, and Cultural Rights (ICESCR) and opened them for signature in 1966. Together with the Universal Declaration, these two covenants at last completed the International Bill of Rights.

The rights of the Universal Declaration were no longer abstract ideas that states could mechanically affirm without taking on any real legal responsibility. To the legions of poor people who felt chronically unsafe, the ICCPR required parties to implement legislation affirming their right to physical integrity, including the right to life and freedom from torture and slavery; the right to personal security and freedom from arbitrary detention; and the right to a fair and impartial trial. Not only were states parties required to implement legislation upholding these rights, but they were also required provide an effective legal remedy when those rights were violated.

The ICCPR and the ICESCR provided fresh energy to the second stage of the movement. In the wake of these two covenants came a spate of new human rights treaties on topics ranging from war crimes to apartheid to discrimination against women to torture to protection of migrant workers and the rights of children and other matters. Never before in history had so many human rights treaties been generated so quickly. However, as one delegate noted, the challenge was to acknowledge these achievements while at the same time avoiding "pompous statements" and "tempting promises" by seeing to it "that these new covenants are strictly observed everywhere."[18]

At the very least, that meant ensuring that rights were implemented into local law. A treaty becomes legally binding only after a predetermined number of states agree to accept its obligations.[19] With the international human rights covenants in place, the focus of the human rights movement began to shift from the corridors of the United Nations to the legislatures of the developing world, paving the way for a new set of actors to shape its future.

Grassroots Efforts Imbed Human Rights Standards into Local Law

Up to this point in the modern human rights movement, the power actors were largely government elites working under the auspices of the United Nations. But once the International Bill of Rights was in place, a new set of actors took center stage as individual grassroots movements sprung up across the developing world, pressing their legislatures to conform local laws to international human rights standards.

Although many developing countries inherited laws from their colonial predecessors that criminalized certain basic human rights violations, beginning in the 1960s and continuing through the present, countries in the developing world—many just emerging from colonial rule—gave rise to progressive political movements campaigning for legal reforms that would replace traditional or colonial standards with codifications of new international standards for political rights, civil rights, due process, labor rights, women's rights, children's rights, and others. Pursued mostly at a national level by country-specific political movements, the global human rights movement largely succeeded in conforming national laws to international standards.[20]

For instance, in conformity with international norms, South Asian countries passed laws outlawing bonded slavery.[21] African countries threw off centuries of traditional cultural practice and gave women rights to own and inherit land and to be free of ritual genital mutilation.[22] Southeast Asian countries elevated the status of women and girls, creating new laws to protect them from sexual exploitation and trafficking.[23] Latin American countries replaced authoritarian regimes and adopted international standards for arrest and detention procedures[24] and codified land reform rights.[25] Similarly, new laws and constitutions, including those of Costa Rica, El Salvador, Haiti, Indonesia, and Jordan incorporated specific language or principles of the Universal Declaration into their texts.[26]

Western human rights activists, lawyers, scholars, and statesmen played a supporting role behind the indigenous leaders of these political struggles and celebrated with local activists as they succeeded in incorporating international human rights standards into their domestic law.[27] As a result, hundreds of millions of the most vulnerable and abused became entitled to global standards of justice and equity under local law.

Enforcement: The Last Yard of Cable

It's a painful truth of life that some work only matters when the job is fully finished. It matters not at all to me, for example, that the cable company has managed to lay a million yards of cable across the country to bring the magic of fiber optics to my front yard if they do not provide that last yard of cable to connect to my television or computer. Likewise, all the genius and effort of making a life-saving antibiotic matters not at all to the dying man who cannot get it delivered into his veins.

The stunning and revolutionary triumphs won by human rights champions during the movement's first two stages are worth celebrating for sure, but the early architects of the human rights movement understood that these human rights standards would have no practical meaning to victims of abuse unless they were enforced. They would be delighted and astonished, therefore, by the robust international human rights system that exists today, the goal of which is to ensure that these standards are observed across the globe. Global NGOs and international bodies monitor and report on compliance with human rights standards. UN blue helmets around the globe carry out peacekeeping operations designed to stop mass atrocities.

International tribunals and courts try high-level state actors for their role in mass human rights atrocities like genocide or war crimes. By the end of 2015, the international community will have invested an estimated $6.3 billion in these international courts.[28] We owe a profound debt of gratitude to those who faithfully carried these efforts forward. Although the efficacy of this work will undoubtedly continue to improve, the project of building an international human rights system is well underway.

The astonishing proliferation of human rights standards and the international investment in the creation of a global human rights system are so impressive that they may obscure the gaping absence of enforcement for a massive group of human rights victims. There are billions for whom the promise of the human rights revolution remains a check they cannot cash.

International systems of enforcement do little to protect the huge group of average poor people victimized by common criminal violence in the developing world. The fact is, they were never expected or designed to do so. Accordingly, the next great movement of the modern human rights struggle must focus on collaborative efforts in the developing world to build effective public justice systems that make human rights meaningful for the common poor who suffer under chronic common violence.

There are understandable reasons why the broad human rights community has tended to focus more on international enforcement mechanisms than local public justice systems. Some of the leading human rights organizations of today grew up during the height of the Cold War when repressive regimes on the left and the right sought to quell opposition by oppressing those with dissenting voices. As a result, these organizations naturally began to focus on human rights abuses aimed at suppressing political rights, including illegal detention, torture, "disappearances," and extrajudicial executions.

These organizations saw their mission as serving as a check on repressive governments' power, so they naturally concerned themselves with human rights abuses by state actors. Because Cold War propaganda was such a controlling framework of foreign relations during that time, super powers and their client states were eager to use human rights rhetoric as a weapon against the other side, and to downplay or gloss over the human rights abuses of their allies. This dynamic sharpened the need for thorough and objective fact-gathering and reporting on human rights abuses and gave rise to the "monitoring and reporting" strategy that has become a signature tactic of leading human rights organizations. By carefully documenting the evidence of human rights abuses in ways that states could not credibly dismiss, burgeoning human rights organizations were able to rebut facile denials and the impression that there was an irresolvable stalemate resulting from a he-said-she-said game over the facts. The goal was to "name and shame" abusers in an effort to put public pressure on them to change their practices. Gradually, the human rights community brought this technique to abuses taking place during armed conflict.

The early focus on state political violence and human rights abuses during armed conflict helps us understand why improving local public justice systems in the developing world was not a major emphasis. For these categories of abuse, the most promising remedy is not likely to be a local public justice system. Stopping violence during armed conflict often requires intervention from other states or the international community at large. Similarly, state political violence is often not effectively remedied by local public justice systems because those carrying out the violence are typically agents of the state acting on its orders and for its benefit. When accountability for these forms of violence has been attempted, it has often been through an international tribunal or court or a truth and reconciliation process, rather than a local public justice system.

After the end of the Cold War, the human rights community began to focus on human rights abuses by non-state actors.[29] With the growing emphasis on women's rights as human rights in 1990s, human rights leaders brought their monitoring and reporting tactics over to address issues more likely to affect Yuri or Mariamma. But the modern human rights movement has not yet excelled at protecting poor people from common criminal violence. That task has been delegated chiefly to local state authorities (rather than blue helmets or international courts), and even the best norms and national laws cannot guarantee that a state will enforce them effectively. While the extensive array of human rights norms and the establishment of a robust international human rights system do vitally important things for human rights victims around the world, they don't do much to protect Yuri from the Ayalas, or Mariamma from her owner.

CATASTROPHIC NEGLECT OF THE JUSTICE DELIVERY SYSTEM

For victims of common criminal violence around the world, the tragic problem is that the protection of their rights under national law was placed in the hands of dysfunctional national law enforcement institutions. That is, vindication of basic human rights was left in the hands of local police, prosecutors, magistrates, social welfare administrators, councils, and courts that simply do not enforce the law. As a result, for the hundreds of millions of the world's poorest people who live outside the protection of the rule of law, the principal reason they suffer abuse is often not the absence of good laws, but the absence of a functioning public justice system to enforce those laws.[30]

International efforts succeeded in pressuring governments to change their laws but largely neglected the public justice systems required to enforce these laws. As a result, after six decades, many victims of criminal violence in the developing world have not enjoyed the benefits won during the first two stages of the human rights movement. Without a credible deterrent, poor people by the hundreds of millions are relentlessly subjected to assault, rape, imprisonment, extortion, enslavement, theft, dispossession, and removal.

Foreshadowing the second and third phases of their blueprint, the drafters of the Universal Declaration Human Rights included among the universal entitlements "the right to an effective remedy by the competent national tribunals for acts violating the fundamental rights granted him by the constitution or by law."[31]

Two generations of global human rights work have been predicated, consciously or unconsciously, upon assumptions about functioning public justice systems in the developing world, which, if incorrect, effectively gut the usefulness of those efforts for victims of common criminal violence. Absent an effective enforcement mechanism, the great work of the first two generations of the modern human rights movement will deliver to the world's poorest citizens only empty parchment promises.

The monumental achievements of the modern human rights era have re-ordered the world in many ways that men and women a century ago could not have dreamed. This march of freedom and human dignity has made great strides that must be honored and celebrated. But these achievements are in no way undermined by the frank acknowledgement that there is a core element of the struggle yet to be completed. Suppose, for example, that scientists worked feverishly for two generations to develop and fill warehouses with miracle vaccines that hundreds of millions of sick people in the developing world desperately needed but could not access. The absence of a delivery system would take nothing away from the medical advances the scientists had achieved, but it would suggest an urgent new priority for the international public health community. Likewise, it takes nothing away from the historic significance of the modern human rights movement to say that the brokenness of public justice systems in the developing world renders the promise of that movement largely undelivered to victims of common criminal violence across the globe, but it does suggest the urgent need for a fundamental shift in the agenda for human rights efforts in the twenty-first century. After more than 65 years of developing and refining vaccines that rarely reach their bloodstream, we must now focus resources on delivering the vaccines to those who are dying without them.

More than a half century after the miracle of the Universal Declaration of Human Rights, billions of the world's poorest people remain in a state of de facto lawlessness. For the Yuris, Mariammas, and Lauras of the world, the failure to build effective public justice systems in the developing world means that there is no system that can actually provide the protections that the human rights revolution promised to all but currently delivers only to some. Fierce battles were heroically fought to articulate and imbed fundamental human rights into national law, but such costly achievements are lost for all those who live without local justice systems that can actually deliver those protections.

In my own country's history, the most inspiring moments have come when the nation has confronted the reality of its unfinished business—and has struggled to extend its promise of freedom, dignity, and opportunity to even its most marginalized citizens. At a pivotal moment in that history, King forced the nation to confront the way its failure to actually enforce the promises of the U.S. Constitution and Bill of Rights denied black Americans access to the birthright of the American Revolution and "the riches of freedom and the security of justice." Likewise, in this era, we must with equal courage confront the way our failure to provide basic law enforcement for the poor has not only undermined their struggle to escape poverty but has left some of the most basic promises of the human rights revolution bitterly unfulfilled.

But to confront this failure, we must first be able to trace how we got here. How is it that justice systems in the developing world should be in such a state of dysfunctional collapse and total ineffectiveness for the poor? There are three surprising explanations that paradoxically offer a measure of hope—and expose the hard nut to be cracked.

COLONIAL LEGACIES AND A FAILURE THAT MAKES SENSE

The failure of a dysfunctional system is frequently just as rational as the success of a functioning system. This is why management experts will often say of some organizational mess: "Your system is perfectly designed to produce the results you are getting." Dysfunction is rarely random; it is driven by assumptions, motivations, fears, and calculations which are quite purposeful and rational for the people working inside the system. In fact, paradoxically, the greater the absurdity and utter failure of the dysfunctional system, the more one can expect to find a powerful and coherent internal logic and causality driving the system.

This was my own intuition as my colleagues and I began to absorb, year after year, the spectacular fiascos and seemingly insane behaviors of criminal justice systems in the developing world.

- Why aren't the police trained to investigate crime?
- Why does the legal system use a foreign language?
- Why are there such an absurdly low number of public prosecutors?
- Why aren't the police interested in trying to catching criminals?
- Why is there no transcript of the proceedings in court?

- Why are the police so gratuitously rude, abusive, and unhelpful to the public they are supposed to serve?
- Why are the police not given basic equipment or a living wage?

There must be reasons, I thought, why systems that are supposed to protect people are actually hurting them; but as an outsider, I just couldn't see what was really driving the dysfunction. Over time, however, several fog-clearing insights have emerged from surprising sources inside the developing world, and now much of the insanity makes perfect sense.

EXPORTING DYSFUNCTION

The first and most fundamental insight came from a gentle scholar from central India as he and his wife graciously served tea in the backyard garden of their quiet home in suburban Bhopal. With any dysfunctional system, it's indispensable to go back and find the story of origins, and when it came to justice systems in the developing world, here was the man who could help me.

Kirpal Dhillon is an 80-year-old historian and social scientist who has lived the story he tells. The span of his life makes the modern world seem young. When Dhillon was born in the Punjab in the 1930s, he and his fellow Indians were subjects of the British Crown; few people outside of India had heard of an obscure Indian lawyer named Mohandas Gandhi; and Pakistan, India, and Bangladesh were all part of a vast, unified British India. Eventually, the cataclysmic partition of India in 1947 set off massive communal violence between Muslims, Hindus, and Sikhs in which common people were massacred in numbers that equaled the Rwandan genocide, and 10 million people were forced to flee their homes in a scramble to get to the safe side of the imaginary lines drawn by a London barrister dividing Muslim Pakistan from Hindu India.

Both Dhillon and his wife Sneh were young people coming of age in different worlds in 1947, and both found themselves on the wrong side of those bloody partition lines for different reasons. Sneh's father was a prominent lawyer, Congress Party leader and Freedom Fighter against the British imperial occupation, but he woke up one morning in 1947 to find his city of Abbottabad now in a new country called Pakistan where he and his non-Muslim neighbors were not welcome. With murderous chaos descending on the city, 11-year-old Sneh was forced to flee with her brother and five sisters to a refugee camp across the border where thousands of her neighbors were desperately swarming onto trains seeking an escape to Delhi. But not all the trains made it to safety.

An elegant grandmother now in her seventies, Sneh recalled the distant nightmare as she served tea on her sunny garden porch from a China set that matched her blue and white sari: "There were whole trains being butchered. The train that left before we did was butchered and the train that left after us was butchered. We were the only train that escaped. There were lots of such instances on both sides."

Dhillon, by contrast, was a young high school graduate on the safe side of the line in 1947; but the medical school he hoped to attend was now on the wrong side of the line in the city of Lahore—the cultural and educational center of the Punjab now in Pakistan. "There was no question of going to Lahore at that time," Dhillon recalled. "In 1947 there were lots of killings taking place. So I went to the government college in Punjab."

A brilliant student, Dhillon was selected by exam to join the ultra-elite All India Services (the Indian Administrative Service and the India Police Service)—the centralized bureaucracy[1] by which the British colonial administration deployed hand-picked civil servants to administer unified imperial governance across the vast sub-continent of India. After Independence, the mechanism was retained by the new central government, and in 1952 Dhillon joined only 37 candidates selected that year from all across India to be trained for the Indian Police Service—the elite corps of police bureaucrats deployed throughout the states of India.

Happily, the epic rupture of Partition eventually ended in a love story for Dhillon and Sneh that was still playing out over tea 60 years later in their garden courtyard. Among a small number of new Indian political elites, Sneh's father was eventually recruited to replace one of the many British colonial administrators who had fled the country, and to occupy, literally, the palatial residence of the former imperial commissioner in Bhopal. Such a senior official was entitled to the posting of a police guard; as the young new police superintendent in the district, it was Dhillon's job to periodically check-up on the posted guard—and perhaps to check up on Sneh, the attractive young lady who had just returned to her father's house after earning her master's degree in English from the University of Allhabad.

"I was a very eligible bachelor," the tall, lanky Dhillon offered in explanation.

"He thought so," Sneh responded. "He has become so talkative now," she added with mocking wonder. "He gives lectures and writes books. He used to be so quiet," she teased.

"I'm still quiet," Dhillon insisted under his breath.

Indeed, over a half century, Dhillon quietly served in the most senior leadership posts in the Indian Police Service, including joint director of the Central Bureau of Investigation and director general of police for Punjab and his home state of Madhya Pradesh, as well as vice chancellor of Bhopal University. As the world's foremost historian of the Indian police, Dhillon eventually completed a massive two-part treatise tracing Indian policing from medieval times to the present. For me, this was the tome that began to make so much sense out of the absurd.

In response to the question "Why do criminal justice systems in the developing world fail so miserably to protect the poor from violence?" Dhillon's response was straightforward. *Those systems were never intended to protect the common people from violence—they were intended to protect the colonial rulers from the common people.* Moreover, we shouldn't be surprised today when those systems don't protect the common citizenry from violence, because those systems were never re-engineered to do so. In other words, the criminal justice systems in the developing world are perfectly designed to produce the results they are getting: namely, providing heavy protection for elites and no meaningful protection for the poor, because they have never been re-engineered to do anything different from their colonial design.

As Dhillon and a handful of other scholars give us the long view of history, a fascinating story unfolds of two parallel models of law enforcement that were born in the middle of the nineteenth century and still dominate much of the world today—but which produce wildly different results.

On the one hand, modern civilian policing is a surprisingly recent innovation that was substantially invented by the British in the mid-1800s in response to the social challenges of industrial-era urbanization and the increasing democratization of British society, which required a greater attentiveness to the community's need for public safety. In 1829, British Home Secretary Robert (Bobby) Peel introduced a model of policing to replace the traditional soldiers and private night-watchmen with unarmed, professional, uniformed civilian police (the "Bobbies") who would not only "keep the peace" but proactively suppress crime.² The British public was initially suspicious of and hostile to a uniformed police force, fearing it as a potential source of oppression and a threat to liberty. Over the ensuing decades, policing in Britain had to win the trust of an increasingly empowered citizenry who would not tolerate an abusive, extractive, or unhelpful police force for long.

Just as Britain and other Western powers were evolving systems of policing and criminal justice to be responsive to an increasingly enfranchised public at home, many of these same Western countries were preparing to export a very different form of policing around the world to the vast empires under their tenuous imperial control. Not surprisingly, the purpose and priority of this colonial model of policing would not be to protect the common citizenry from violence and crime—but to protect the colonial state and its narrow interests and beneficiaries *from the common citizenry.*

After a bloody and protracted effort to suppress the Indian Rebellion of 1857, the British government sought to ensure a more secure hold over its Indian subjects by dissolving the East India Company and seizing direct administration of colonial rule by the British crown. Two competing models emerged: the relatively new 1829 London model of professional, civilian policing that was steadily winning the trust of the local community; or the also relatively new Royal Irish Constabulary—which had been organized with great success as a centralized, paramilitary force to brutally suppress elements of Irish rebellion and opposition to the ruling British elite in Ireland.

Not surprisingly, given the unsettling events of 1857, the British Raj decisively reached for the Irish Constabulary model, imbedded it in India, and replicated it across Britain's non-white colonies around the world. As Dhillon observed, the Irish colonial police model implanted in India and across the Empire had a completely different purpose than the London metropolitan police model:

Such a[n Irish colonial] police with a distinct militaristic character and often led by army officers had no great motivation to watch the interests of or address the concerns of the local community, an obligation considered so vital in the mother country.... "With its diverse *services to the colonial power and the ruling elite* in a restless, often violent countryside, in its availability as an armed force under civilian control, and in its centralized structure, the Irish constabulary provided a model more *appropriate to colonial requirements* in India than the London police."[3]

So instead of replicating the policing model that the British leaders wanted for reducing crime in their own communities back home, they established the Irish colonial model of policing in India under the Indian Police Act of 1861.[4] As Dhillon makes plain, the Act of 1861 contemplated the Indian police system not "as an agency to protect the citizen from insecurity, crime and disorder," but "to protect and defend the ruler against all threats to their power and authority."[5]

> The Act, in fact, scrupulously avoids any reference to the people, except in respect to their liability to be questioned, or held under suspicion by the police. The new police was, in fact, meant to be a steadfast ally and dependable tool to firm the bonds of slavery.[6]

As Dhillon notes, the Act of 1861 had enormous historical impact because "the reorganized Indian police later provided models and precedents for many other colonial regimes in Asia, Africa and the Caribbean countries in the late nineteenth century."[7] As a former senior officer of that Indian police force, Dhillon adds wryly, "A distinction of sorts, one might say!"

So far, little of this historical tale is all that surprising. Colonialism was repressive and bad and resulted in the use of a form of policing that was likewise oppressive and utterly unconcerned about serving the common people. As might be expected, colonial powers built justice systems that were, in the parlance of Acemoglu and Robinson, patently "extractive" rather than "inclusive."

The part of the story that *is* surprising and explains so much of the criminal justice system dysfunction in India and many other parts of the developing world today is this: After the colonial powers went home, the colonial systems of policing and law enforcement were *never transformed to serve a new purpose.* Constitutions were changed and over the decades many laws were changed—but the actual machinery of law *enforcement* was generally never re-purposed for a post-independence mission of serving the (overwhelmingly poor) common public. Authoritarian regimes and political elites came to power in the post-colonial developing world and seemed to find the colonial law enforcement system just as useful for their purposes as the imperial powers did.

As Dhillon made clear to me, India was simply a vivid example of what did *not* change throughout the developing world with the end of colonial rule more than a half century ago:

> It is the very same Police Act, now 140 years old, which still governs the organization, structure, philosophy and functional modes of the Indian police, some 55 years after the British left, never mind the far-reaching changes in social, political, scientific, economic and cultural spheres over a century and a half. The major crime codes, laws of evidence and the entire judicial system are all frozen in time and hopelessly out of tune with contemporary theories of crime control, order management and dispensation of justice.... The police system all over South Asia, based as it is on the 1861 Act, provides for no weightage to community support or local accountability.[8]

It is simply fantastic to consider all the ways in which the world has changed since the *early* years of the reign of Queen Victoria when the 1861 Act established the Indian police (before the automobile, before the end of slavery in America, before the end of serfdom in Russia, before telephones, before the mass production of pencils); and then to imagine a fundamental government system that has not changed in the more than 150 years since that era. As another scholar of the Indian police has observed: "Independence brought revolutionary changes in the political structure of the government, [but] it brought none of any consequence to the structure of police administration.... What is particularly striking about contemporary police structure is its permanence. Its fundamental principles of organization have remained fixed for over a century."[9]

Suddenly, the litany of dysfunctions that define South Asian police forces make sense. *Of course* the vast majority of police officers are never trained to investigate common crimes against the public. That is not what colonial police do. They suppress riots and mobs. They guard expensive people and facilities. And they beat down disruptive challenges to the political regime. *Of course* the police aren't interested in trying to catching criminals. A colonial police force is not set up to do that, not trained to do that, and not rewarded for doing that—and they might get in trouble with their superiors if the criminals they catch are powerfully connected. *Of course* the police are gratuitously rude, abusive, and unhelpful to the public they are supposed to serve. Colonial police aren't actually supposed to serve the public: "Since voluntary community support was never forthcoming [for a colonial police force] except under coercion, ruthless, highhanded and brutal methods [are] commonly employed by the police to collect evidence and secure cooperation from an unwilling and often hostile public."[10] *Of course* the average police officer is not given basic equipment for professional criminal investigation, or even paid a living wage: "This is not surprising, given the characteristic mental and moral make-up of the lower [police] subordinates as a carry-over from colonial times. The lower subordinates form over 90% of the force and are the first, and normally the only, point of contact with law-enforcement organs, for the masses.... The dominant character of the organization, created under the Act, is of a socially-alienated, semi-military outfit, composed almost exclusively of a semi-literate, boorish, corrupt, ill-paid, ill-reputed and high-handed constabulary."[11]

Likewise, the farces that play out in South Asian courtrooms become perfectly logical. *Of course* the legal system is conducted in a foreign language. That's the language of the colonial power (and now of the political and economic elite). *Of course* there are an absurdly low number of public prosecutors. A colonial criminal justice system has no incentive for allocating expensive resources to provide the general public with excellent criminal justice services. *Of course* there is no transcript of the proceedings in court. A colonial administration will not be interested in having its magistrates subject to public scrutiny in protecting colonial interests or restricted in their discretion in administering state power through public exposure.

Indeed, a handful of scholars and researchers are beginning to fathom the stunning implications of the failure to transform the colonial and authoritarian criminal justice systems that the developing world inherited from its colonial past. As researchers with Human Rights Watch found in their extensive study of the Indian police: "A dangerous anachronism, the police have largely failed to evolve from the ruler-supportive, repressive forces they were designed to be under Britain's colonial rule. While sixty years later much of India is in the process of rapid modernization, the police continue to use their old methods."[12]

SAME HAT, DIFFERENT FACE

Across much of the developing world, the instruments of law enforcement failed to evolve because the authoritarian regimes and political elites that came to power in the developing world found that the colonial forms of policing very conveniently served their interests. Indigenous political and economic elites found that modern law enforcement models (with their emphasis on accountability to the community and general public) would be threatening.

Of course, the difficulty of re-engineering the administration of justice was exacerbated by the swiftness and lack of preparation with which the colonial powers departed the developing world. Imagine: One day in 1947 Sneh's father was a lawyer and Freedom Fighter on the run from the violence of Partition—the next day he was occupying the palatial residence of the British administrator who had fled the India he once ruled. Similarly, I remember perusing, one by one, the dusty portraits of the successive police commissioners of Kenya lining the walls of the staircase to the latest commissioner's office. Starting from the beginning of the colonial era, it was one white face after another—each looking serious and determined under his commander's hat. Then suddenly, under the same commander's hat with the same serious expression: a black face. Just that fast. Same hat, different face. In fact, the "history" of the Kenyan police force posted on the official website inadvertently describes the nature of the transformation quite perfectly:

> After Kenya gained her independence from Britain on December 12th, 1963, there was a need to make some drastic changes in the Administration of the Force. This led to the replacement of the expatriate officers in the senior ranks by Africans.[13]

End of description. That's it. That was the drastic change—"replacement of the expatriate officers in the senior ranks by Africans." This was indeed drastic, but without transformation of the police force from a colonial force serving a centralized power elite to a post-colonial force serving (and accountable to) the common citizenry, the replacement of the senior officers would prove to make little difference in protecting the common Kenyan from violence and crime.

In India, Dhillon described the Indian political classes as merely "step[ping] into the shoes of their British predecessors" as power transferred from the British to Indian elites, while the practical administration of the law "remained frozen in the mid-nineteenth century enactments, rules and regulations."[14]

And for this Indian scholar, decorated police professional, and patriot, the impact today is clear for India and the rest of the post-colonial developing world:

> Unsurprisingly then, the Indian police failed to evolve into a citizen-friendly force. Indian police are probably the most reviled government agency in India. Ordinary Indians consider brutality and corruption its most familiar features. The colonial image of a jackbooted agent of oppressive authority, rude and abusive, often acting unlawfully and sloppily, soliciting free eats and drinks, still clings to Indian policemen, despite substantial political and constitutional changes occurring since independence.[15]

Similar historical narratives across the developing world have provided powerful lenses through which to understand the systematic dysfunctions and brutal absurdities that might otherwise seem so inexplicable to outsiders. Indeed, a small number of historians are distinguishing with clarity the core purpose of the police and criminal justice systems that colonial powers left as a legacy in the countries of the developing world from that of the law enforcement systems that evolved in the colonial powers' home countries, which increasingly emphasized service to the community and accountability to the public.

With both the French and British empires, for example, the practical functions of the colonial "police" in Africa were to protect "the property, person and future prospects of the Europeans and those local groups who were dependent on them for power and livelihood," "enforce unpopular regulations, such as the collection of head taxes," "suppress the rise of nationalism," and "deal with political dissidents."[16]

Accordingly, as one scholar gently put it: "In the period immediately after independence from colonial rule, the Police in many countries in Africa are said not to always have played a completely neutral role." Indeed, after independence, the nature of their "indispensable" activities included: maintaining the power of dominant political parties (and wealthy landowning and industrial groups) by detaining opponents likely to be victorious, intimidating opponents into pulling out of elections and making it difficult for them to obtain parade or speaking permits, rigging election results, and responding with force when crowds protested social wrongs.[17]

Specific studies of the colonial experience in the developing world emphasize the gulf that developed over a century between what "policing" came to look like at home in Western countries and what it looked like in the colonies where those same Western countries had ruled by force.

In Nigeria, for example, colonial police were introduced to protect colonial interests—not ordinary Africans. But the "traditions of civility, efficiency, and submission to the rule of law that constituted the bedrock of the British police system"[18] weren't part of the export. Instead, the police force emphasized state security and riot suppression—two activities that provided little benefit (and some harm) to the average citizen.[19] Then, in the post-colonial era, these dysfunctions remained—now deployed by the locals who came to power at independence and continued the same patterns of terrorizing their opponents and brutalizing the citizenry in the successive waves of power struggles that followed.[20]

It turns out there is a reason why so many of the institutions in the developing world with names like "police," "prosecutors," and "courts" do almost none of the things you and I think those institutions should do or in the way we would expect them to be done. In most instances, these institutions in the developing world were set up by colonial or authoritarian regimes with purposes, mandates, missions, structures, procedures, and cultures that were completely different from those that evolved back home over the same historical time period.

The Language Barrier

As a result, many of the shocking dysfunctions we see in the criminal justice systems in the developing world are rooted in the colonial character under which these systems were designed and instituted—and perpetuated by the extraordinary failure (after so many decades) to throw off this colonial legacy.

Many of these lingering colonial dysfunctions are surprisingly obvious, devastating to poor people, and almost entirely ignored—all at the same time. One of the more obvious dysfunctions involves the most fundamental ingredient of the justice process—and that is words. Laws are written in words, evidence is gathered and presented in words, arguments are made in words, reasoning is exchanged in words, facts are described in words, and judgments are issued in words. But in much of the developing world, almost the entire legal process is conducted in a foreign language that most poor people do not speak or understand.

Through the Taft Commission of 1902, for instance, the American colonial rulers of the Philippines imposed English as the language of the legal system and the courts. Today, when large proportions of the poorest Filipinos do not speak English, even the Supreme Court of the Philippines has had to acknowledge the barrier this presents for the poor seeking justice through the system:

> The courts are perceived to be inaccessible especially by the marginalized sectors....Another constraint in communicating with the basic sectors is the issue of language. The *common tao* does not fully understand the law and court procedures because the latter are written in English and proceedings are in the same language. Most hearings are conducted in a language in which the litigants are not familiar. Hence, questions and answers had to be translated. Litigants have no recourse but to trust what their lawyers say in court even if the latter are unable to adequately explain what is happening.[21]

A series of regional consultations in the Philippines with grassroots organizations and communities in 2003 confirmed that "[t]he use of English instead of the local dialects in court proceedings [were] a major obstruction to the poor and marginalized groups' access to justice."[22]

Likewise, in Latin America, many countries have long used Spanish as the language of the courts and criminal justice process, even though much of the population—especially the indigenous poor—often uses a different native tongue (40 percent of Guatemalans) than the official language left by the Spanish imperial rulers. The need for translation in interviews, testimony, and court proceedings introduces significant delays and cuts off common poor people from being able to directly understand the process, to express their preferences, or to articulate their interests. It leaves them utterly dependent upon lawyers, translators, clerks, and other strangers to tell them what is happening, what their choices are, and the meaning of what is taking place in each step of the process.[23]

In Uganda, as in all former British colonies in Africa, English is the language of law enforcement and the legal system—but not of the common poor. A Ugandan legal scholar explained the impact on the poor's access to justice: "Language remains a barrier, since English is the language of the justice system, and is spoken well by only a minority of Ugandans. In addition to imposing a huge translation burden on all procedures, there is a suggestion that in some cases the judiciary themselves do not have sufficient proficiency in English to work effectively."[24] In Pakistan, where much of the country is either illiterate or barely literate, laws are written in highly technical and convoluted English.[25]

In Mozambique, Portuguese is the language of the courts despite the fact that about 60 percent of the population has no working knowledge of the language—75 percent in rural areas—and only 7 percent consider it their native tongue. As the Open Society Initiative for Southern Africa found, "Generally, courts do attempt to provide interpretation services as required, although the quality of the interpreters used is frequently poor. Particularly at the district level, interpreters are not professionals, and are usually simply drafted in on the day, as ad hoc staff."[26] As in other situations in Africa where ad hoc translation resources are used to try and help the poor navigate technical legal proceedings where their fundamental liberty, property, livelihood, and lives are on the line, the translator grabbed off the street is not only translating the words but is also trying to explain what they mean. But of course, they have no legal training and cannot properly interpret the legal terms in any helpful way to the client or to the court. Moreover, there are generally no translation services at all during the process of pre-trial arrest and detention, and the defendant will have no idea what the police are talking about when the officer charges him with crimes or describes a process in Portuguese.[27]

And in Malawi, the legal system is conducted in a language that only *one* percent of the population can understand: English. This means that many of the judges, magistrates, and court personnel do not even fully understand the language they are working in. The Open Society Initiative for Southern Africa notes of this nation: "According to a study conducted in 2002, the use of English in magistrates' courts hampers communication between magistrates and litigants—standards of interpretation were poor, particularly in relation to technical words—and limits the ability of magistrates to write clear judgments that analyse evidence adequately."[28]

In all of these contexts across the developing world, there is a sub-sector of the population that can understand the imperial language of the legal system very well—and that is the small class of economic, political, and social elites and the small number of expensive legal experts who serve them. Throughout the colonial era there was always a class of indigenous elites who were elevated to power by their association with the colonial culture and institutions—and after independence those exclusive advantages were largely locked in by retaining the colonial justice system. As one scholar observed of post-colonial Africa, "elites within the country became adept at negotiating the common law or civilian structures and, as a result, had a vested interest in seeing them continue."[29]

For the poorest and most vulnerable in the developing world, the foreign language of the post-colonial justice system is yet another crippling disadvantage in trying to leverage some protection against the forces of violence and abuse that are arrayed against them. From the very moment the first syllable is uttered in the arena of the criminal justice system, the common poor are rendered deaf and mute. As Michael Anderson has well described, "That the law is transacted in a foreign language, and often a language associated with the injustice of colonial rule, is doubly alienating for those who have no access to it."[30]

THE REVOLUTION THAT NEVER HAPPENED

In countries as diverse as Indonesia and Senegal, one can find painful and costly dysfunctions that flow from the colonial relics that have never been rooted out of the justice systems and which serve the interests of the powerful and leave the poorest without protection. In Indonesia, advocates from poor communities often find themselves unable to defend themselves against dispossession of their land (or to secure fair compensation for it) because of the government's manipulation of agrarian land laws rooted in the colonial regime's seizure of land by the state. British and Dutch colonial powers devised land policies by which ownership of indigenous lands fell by default to the state, which in turn leased it for exploitation by private logging, mining, and plantation interests. In the decades following independence, advocates in poor communities are finding that Indonesian authorities have continued to use the old colonial bias toward state land ownership embedded in the law to forcibly evict landowners without exhaustion of their legal remedies or to require them to accept sub-market compensation for their land.[31]

In Senegal, the notorious death of a 25-year-old man named Dominque Lopy while in police custody at the Central Police Station of Kolda in 2007 became a painful illustration of the colonial legacy of impunity for abusive authorities:

Dominique Lopy's family lodged a complaint and an investigation was opened but, three years later, the family of the deceased are still waiting for justice to be done. In May 2010, Dominique Lopy's mother told Amnesty International: "The family lodged a complaint, we have been heard by a judge one by one, but since that date, nothing else has happened. Everybody knows the circumstances of my son's death but nobody will throw any light on his disappearance. We think they buried the problem along with the body. The State does not want to talk about it."[32]

In Senegal, human rights advocates describe the way the former French administrators established a dual system of criminal justice that made it almost impossible for common poor people to hold colonial authorities (and local elites) accountable for violent abuses—while at the same time granting those same authorities and elites unfettered power in coercing compliance from the common poor. Independence was a power transfer from French to Senegalese elites and the continuation of French-bestowed legal structures that had been designed to control, rather than serve, the indigenous poor. Today, the Code of Military Justice "grants a de facto power of veto to the executive with regard to any judicial proceedings against members of the security forces . . . which leaves the judiciary helpless and deprives the victims and their families of any hope of redress."[33]

Across the developing world, one can find countless examples where the dysfunctional and predatory nature of the criminal justice systems is clearly rooted in a stunning historical failure to throw out the colonial system of law enforcement and to replace it with a system designed to serve the common people.

Colonialism does not, of course, explain everything about the brokenness of justice systems in the developing world. Indeed, there are some developing countries that were never fully colonized—e.g., Ethiopia and Thailand—and yet still struggle to provide the poor with functioning law enforcement, and it does not suggest that the pre-colonial justice systems in the developing world were any more effective in protecting the poor and weak from violence (generally they were not). But the colonial history does help us understand where many of the specific current dysfunctions came from—and should encourage national reformers to see that there is nothing unpatriotic about mounting an honest critique of their nation's failing justice system and pursuing a full-scale overhaul.

Sadly, however, one generally encounters a deafening silence of denial (or vigorous defensiveness) about the disastrous justice systems that carry on the curse of colonialism—even among people who should know better. As a result, a handful of marginalized prophets in the developing world find themselves crying in the wilderness. A wizened old scholar and patriot like Dhillon, for instance, looks out over the vast subcontinent of South Asia and sees a criminal justice system that "is on the verge of collapse."[34] And he chooses his words carefully when he describes the implications:

> It needs to be emphasized that the process of degeneration and decay afflicting the Indian criminal justice system will slowly engulf all areas of governance and soon negate all national endeavour and undermine the very roots of civil society.[35]

It does seem chilling to consider the implications of massive violence among the global poor coupled with the utter brokenness, dysfunction, and brutality of the systems that are supposed to be the solution.

The question is, why have things been allowed to get so bad and why don't they change? If these are colonial justice systems, why don't forces of national pride and progress throw off these imperial systems that choke the life out of the struggling poor? Especially in India and other emerging-market countries where there clearly are sectors of pace-setting economic dynamism, innovation, and growth, why has such a basic system as public justice been allowed to atrophy and decay into a national disgrace and a millstone around the neck of the poor?

In our search for answers, we next need to explore how developing countries (where so much seems to be going right) could permit the most basic system of society to go so wrong.

PRIVATE JUSTICE AND PUBLIC LAWLESSNESS

The first time I attended the World Economic Forum in Davos as an NGO leader, about five years ago, I was struck by the amazing clarity with which the organizers understood how to protect the participants from violence. Everywhere I looked, armed police lined the streets, manned layers of check-points, filled police vans waiting all day along the roads, watched from roof-top sniper points, and patrolled the skies by helicopter. From press reports I learned that there were approximately 10 security personnel assigned to the annual event *per attendee*. It was impossible to miss the police presence.

The extraordinary police ratio probably made sense given the extraordinary net worth and public profile of some of the attendees, but what did not make sense was the way this clarity about the fundamental importance of law enforcement seemed to disappear once participants stepped into discussions about violence against the poor in the developing world. In the few sessions where gender violence, sexual violence, or human trafficking was raised, there was a good bit of discussion from experts about education, human rights training, changing cultural norms, and reducing poverty; but there was *zero* mention of the poor needing law enforcement—the very service that saturated every square inch of this tiny Swiss ski village when the people of power and wealth came to town.

I vividly remember one particular Davos session where I found myself in a gathering of corporate executives who were leading colossal global corporations with massive investments in the developing world. All of them seemed to care deeply about responsible corporate citizenship in emerging market countries and appreciated the need to pursue economic growth in ways that were sustainable. Given what I had experienced of the utter brokenness and dysfunction of the criminal justice systems in these developing countries, I asked them a straightforward and practical question: "In the developing world, how do you provide protection from violence for your people and your property?"

Their unanimous answer was equally straightforward and practical. Casting glances at one another they answered nearly in unison: "We buy it."

Indeed, their answer is a manifestation of one of the most profound, devastating, and almost completely unnoticed social transformations that has taken place in the developing world over the last three decades: the nearly total displacement of public justice systems by private justice systems for elites in the developing world. Quietly and almost imperceptibly, those with wealth and power in the developing world have utterly abandoned the broken *public* justice system and have established a parallel system of *private* justice in which private security forces and alternative dispute resolution systems provide the services traditionally provided by public police and courts—namely security and the resolution of disputes.

This thorough privatization of justice services by elites throughout the developing world helps explain why public justice systems have been allowed to become so useless and dysfunctional—and why it has been so hard for outsiders to perceive what is happening. After all, if public justice systems are so dreadfully broken in the developing world, how is it that we see such booming rates of economic growth in many of these countries— places like India, Brazil, and most recently even much of sub-Saharan Africa? How could these societies be outpacing the economic growth rates of so many of the affluent countries if their public justice systems are so utterly dysfunctional?

Some of the rates of growth are higher by comparison because of the low baseline of economic development from which these countries begin. However, it still seems puzzling that countries without functional public justice systems should be able to see any significant economic growth at all—especially given the way we have seen that violence undermines economic growth. But with a parallel system of private justice, economic elites can protect their people and property from violence, resolve disputes, and thereby secure the conditions necessary for substantial economic enterprise and growth within their sphere, while billions of the poorest who cannot pay for their own security are left to fend for themselves.

While *aggregate* economic growth over the last two decades in some developing countries in Asia, Latin American, and sub-Saharan African has been quite impressive,[1] the growth has tended to occur disproportionately in the wealthier sectors within these countries—among those who can afford to pay for private security.[2] In fact, in this same era, more entrenched or increased income inequalities *within* countries in the developing world have become as noteworthy as the increases in aggregate economic growth.[3] Indeed, more of the world's poorest (those living in extreme poverty) now live in "middle income" countries than do in "low income" countries.[4] Economists worry about income inequality itself as an obstacle to broad and sustainable economic growth,[5] but the most straightforward problem is the way the divide between the safe rich and the undefended poor is simply leaving billions behind in harsh poverty. Growth among the safe affluent in Sub-saharan Africa, for example, is still leaving the unsafe *half* of the population living off $1.25/day or less. The recent years of fastest aggregate economic growth in India actually saw the rate of poverty reduction fall during the same period, "indicating that the poor have largely been left behind throughout India's growth."[6] While encouraging strides in poverty reduction have occurred in Latin America, the rate of poverty reduction is slowing and nearly 30 percent of the population remains in poverty, with the same 66 million in extreme poverty in 2012 as in 2011.[7] Worldwide, hundreds of millions who form the vast lower rungs of the economic ladder in these countries are left undefended by a useless *public* justice system and are being rapidly left behind in the same old desperate poverty in which they started.

Many of us are familiar with what happens to public school systems or public transportation systems when people of affluence and influence in the community abandon these systems. Predictably, when they stop using the public systems and pay for their own schools and personal transportation, the public schools get worse and worse and the public transportation gets run down and becomes less reliable. Few of us can contemplate, however, what would happen if the people of affluence and influence opted out of the public system of *law and order* and built an alternative system of private justice. Instead of relying on the police for security, wealthy individuals and private companies hire private security forces. Instead of submitting commercial disputes to clogged and corrupt courts, they establish alternative dispute-resolution systems. And instead of depending on lawyers to push legal matters through the system, those with the financial means use their wealth and social networks to secure privileged political influence that will resolve their disputes favorably. Business, commerce, and the wealthy in the developing world know that the public justice systems don't work—and so they don't use them.

As a result, without pressure from other powerful actors in society, elites have little or no incentive to build public criminal justice institutions that work.

In fact, some elites may affirmatively *prefer* the existing system. A properly functioning legal system would only limit their power—and require a substantial commitment of financial and human resources. And for some, a *functioning* public justice system might, in fact, be a problem.

PRIVATE SECURITY

Tragically, the brokenness of the developing world's public justice systems leaves the poor in a world in which they are vulnerable to violence at any moment—the Hobbesian "state of nature" in which existence for the weakest is "solitary, poor, nasty, brutish and short." Elites, on the other hand, are able to purchase the security of their person and property through a private system of security—and this story is not a new one. Indeed, in other eras, elites were reluctant to support and invest in the establishment of public security systems because they had their own private solutions. For instance, despite horrific levels of violence in eighteenth-century London, "the aristocracy was slow to implement police reform, as they were largely insulated from the violence and were otherwise able to afford private means of protection of themselves and their property."[8]

In our era, it is only very recently that a few experts have begun to sound the alarm about the fundamental re-ordering of the basis of security in the developing world away from public institutions and into private security arrangements.

In Asia, law enforcement experts warn that "the phenomenal rise in private security forces across the region, guarding the lives and assets claimed by those who employ them, may boost the gross national product (GNP) figures but it also hints at a disturbing trend toward the conversion of public safety—an essential public good—into a private commodity."[9] Likewise, in Africa experts observe that everyday security has been transferred from the state to thousands of private companies, and—despite the ubiquity of their uniformed guards—this profound shift has largely occurred without notice.[10]

Experts in Latin America have seen a similar transformation and note that it is a direct consequence of the near total loss of confidence in the public justice system. Accordingly, in these otherwise relatively stable developing countries with a semblance of democratic institutions, analysts observe such high levels of violence and chaos in the absence of functioning justice systems that they refer to them as "uncivil democracies"—where elites must purchase their own protections from violence, and, as a result, the basic "civil components of citizenship"—including being defended from slave-owners, rapists, land thieves, and traffickers—"are unevenly and irregularly distributed among citizens."[11]

Not only does delinking these *most basic* public services (public security and law and order) from public and political affairs in the developing world leave the poorest vulnerable to abuse—but, by turning basic safety into a commodity for purchase, it actually solidifies and widens the gap between rich and poor.[12]

Across the developing world, the booming markets in which private security companies out-man and out-gun the public police bear witness to the silent collapse of the public justice system.[13] The private security industry in India is valued at more than an estimated $2 billion and employs over 5.5 million people[14]—roughly four times the size of the Indian police force and five times the size of the central paramilitary forces.[15] Brazil has an even higher ratio of private security guards: Private forces are more than five times the size of the public police force, with nearly 2 million private security guards and more than 3,000 private security companies.[16] A city like São Paulo alone has about a half a million registered private security guards (four times the size of the state police force)—and more than another half million *unregistered* private security guards (many of whom are police officers serving as "rent-a-cops" and using public equipment for their security activities protecting private clients.)[17] The privatization of basic citizen security is even more pervasive in Guatemala, where there are nearly seven private security guards for every one public police officer.[18] In Honduras, the nation's private security forces are four times larger than the public police force. Likewise in Kenya, security guards outnumber the public police force by four to one.[19] More than 80 percent of businesses in Kenya feel they must pay for security measures[20]—and more than 90 percent in Malawi.[21] Indeed, the largest employer in all of Africa is a private security firm—Group4Security—with 115,000 security personnel across the continent providing protection to the people who can afford to pay for it.[22]

Of course, it is perfectly rational and appropriate for businesses and wealthy individuals in the developing world to spend money on security measures to protect their people and their property from violence and theft. Indeed, there has also been a boom in the private security industry in affluent countries—and under certain circumstances it makes sense for wealthier entities to privately foot the bill for their supplemental security measures rather than having common taxpayers bear the costs of maintaining the wealthiest in their desired state of security.

However, when the private security apparatus is being secured for the wealthy *in the absence of (and as a private substitute for)* a reasonably functioning public justice system that can provide basic law and order to the general public, then the society has descended into a spiral of lawlessness where public law enforcement systems decay to a point of functional failure and the poor are left without a defender.

In recent years, there have been outbreaks of dramatic violence in the developing world that even the private security arrangements of the elites have not been able to control; in these moments, the dreadful dysfunction of public law enforcement has been shockingly exposed for all to see. For decades, elites in Mexico did little to address the rampant corruption and pathetic incompetence of domestic law enforcement because they had secured their own private means of protection. However, when the forces of narco-violence began to overrun the country and the Mexican state reached for a law enforcement response to contain the violence—it became abundantly clear that there was nothing really there, and the fight against the drug cartels had to be militarized. In this experience, even the elites began to sense something of the lawless terror that the poor have always known in the absence of competent policing and criminal justice.[23]

Likewise, Katherine Boo, the journalist and author who immersed herself in the slums of India for 3 years, captured the way the 2008 terrorist attacks on the posh hotels in Mumbai exposed India's elites to the empty shell of public law enforcement upon which the poor are forced to depend:

> Officers in the train station didn't know how to use their weapons, and ran and hid as two terrorists killed more than fifty travelers. Other officers called to rescue inhabitants of a besieged maternity ward hospital stayed put at police headquarters, four blocks away.... The attacks of the Taj and the Oberoi [hotels], in which executives and socialites died, had served as a blunt correction. The wealthy now saw that their security could not be requisitioned privately. They were dependent upon the same public safety system that ill-served the poor.[24]

Alternative Dispute Resolution

Elites and those with means in the developing world not only rely on private systems of security rather than public police to protect their property and person, but they also increasingly rely on private systems of alternative dispute resolution (ADR) to resolve issues ordinarily adjudicated by public courts.[25] ADR has exploded in the developing world, and a small number of specialists who are familiar with the phenomenon are quite clear on why it is so attractive to elites: because the corroded, dysfunctional legal systems of their countries are so *unattractive*—with all their endemic bribery and corruption, gross inefficiencies, glacial pace, perverse outcomes from politicization, and insufficient frameworks to effectively adjudicate complex cases.[26]

Facing the crippling impact of broken judicial systems on business development, leaders of the development movement at agencies like the World Bank have supported the efforts of businesses and elites that choose to opt out of the public system and purchase "ADR services where the courts fail to perform their functions efficiently."[27] For those with means, the public justice system, given all its dysfunctions, "simply is not considered an alternative for the adequate resolution of commercial disputes."[28]

But, just as private security is out of reach for the poorest and the most vulnerable in the developing world, there are no meaningful "alternative dispute resolution" systems that reliably vindicate the rights of the poor against those who are stronger and more powerful. And so, with increasing frequency, in the absence of reliable policing for security and functioning legal forums for resolving disputes, poor citizens are taking matters into their own hands with acts of mob justice and a retreat to communal forms of justice that often do not provide due process or protection for the most marginalized members of the community (e.g. women, children, ethnic or religious minorities, or the very poorest). Without reasonably functioning public services for law and order, "private responses in the form of booming private security businesses and vigilantism by those who cannot afford to purchase security are increasing in many countries."[29]

A Downward Spiral

As individuals with high incomes pursue private substitutes to public goods and services, the influential elites undermine support for funding of public services—and, predictably, such systems get worse and worse.[30] Furthermore, as the wealthy lose interest in public services, so do the policy-makers responsible for providing high-quality public services.[31] Those who support increased investment in public services, primarily lower-income individuals, have the least political influence, and the result is a gradual deterioration of public services.[32] Other scholars have found that this dynamic is especially pronounced in developing countries where the poor make up the majority of the population but are politically marginalized.[33]

Some experts who are familiar with the benefits of privatizing some public services in affluent countries have flirted with the contrarian suggestion that maybe similar benefits might accrue from encouraging further growth of private systems of security and dispute resolution in the developing world. Researchers who have spent time studying these issues on the ground, however, warn development agencies against that approach. Taking the elites out of the public system and putting them in a private one simply hasn't improved the quality of justice for those stuck in the broken system.[34] Instead, it has spurred the descent of the public safety system down the spiral of decay and neglect, leaving the poorest sectors of the society utterly vulnerable to the devastating levels of violence. Indeed, establishing effective private substitutes for elites might communicate that the public system is not worthy of investment. As one expert warned: "Rather than stimulate reform, it threatens to take away the impetus for reform."[35]

THE BIGGEST OBSTACLE TO CHANGE:
THE BENEFICIARIES OF LAWLESSNESS

Because elites are able to purchase private protections without depending on the public justice system, they have become largely *indifferent* to its brokenness—having bypassed the morass, they have little incentive to invest in or support its reform.

But, having bypassed the morass, elites are not merely indifferent to the brokenness of the public justice system; the problem is even more profound—because, tragically, many elites actually benefit from *keeping* the public justice system broken. Elites do not need an *effective* public justice system to protect them from being victimized by others, but they may *need* a broken public justice system to protect them from being held accountable for victimizing others. Broken public justice systems auction impunity to the highest bidder, and when the victims are too poor to purchase protection from private substitutes, impunity comes cheap.

The Ayalas, whom we met in Chapter 1, for example, were not merely *indifferent* to the brokenness of the public justice system in Peru. They *preferred* it. In fact, they utterly *depended* on it. Instead of spending the balance of their lives in prison for Yuri's rape and murder, they were able to purchase the disappearance of damning physical evidence, the torture necessary to unwind the incriminating testimony of eyewitnesses, and even the framing of a hapless scapegoat, who would be forced to spend 30 years rotting in a harsh and dangerous Peruvian prison for their crimes. Their lawyer was well rewarded for orchestrating the cover-up. In such circumstances, the police and other actors in the public justice system make extra money for *not* doing their jobs. For these players, the broken public justice system wasn't a problem; rather, as they clearly understand, an honest and effective justice system would be a problem.

The names and details may change, but the same story is played out across the developing world day after day. Effective criminal justice systems take impunity off the market. Taking the get-out-of-jail-cheap card off the table radically changes the cost for oppressors like the Ayalas. Instead of a few extra dollars in bribes paid to a broken system, a functioning criminal justice system could cost them a lifetime behind bars. For many elites, an effective public justice system is much more costly than a broken one.

Indeed, the biggest obstacle to building effective public justice systems in the developing world will not come from the inertia of old colonial justice systems, the neglect of poverty alleviation agencies, or the private justice substitutes of elites. The fiercest opposition to change will come from social, political, and economic forces in the developing world that rightly perceive that their dominance and exploitation of the poor is threatened by a criminal justice system that actually enforces the law. As we shall see later on, overcoming these regressive power centers will require a coalition of forces in these communities to seize the initiative in a radical transformation of the political will to build functioning law enforcement systems that protect all citizens from violence.

The brokenness of public justice systems is not merely an irrational relic of the colonial era. Criminal justice systems in the developing world remain broken substantially because many elites with the power to change it don't need it, and other predatory elites actually need to keep it broken to secure their exploitive dominance over the poor. Consequently, if forces of goodwill do nothing or simply continue to do what they have been doing in this sphere, there is no reason to expect that public justice systems will change. Making public justice systems work for the poor will involve strategically confronting the incentives of elites who are opting out of the public system with private substitutes or securing their dominance through the impunity of a broken system. Either way, in the developing world, safety for the few elites is undermining the safety of the many poor.

YOU GET WHAT YOU PAY FOR

Billions of poor people in the developing world are struggling mightily to pull their families out of harsh poverty. But these efforts are being devastated by a free-for-all of lawless violence that overruns the poorest families in the absence of functioning law enforcement systems. Instead, the poor have dysfunctional criminal justice systems that *add* to the violence by protecting the perpetrators and rewarding the violence.

The question we are exploring now is: why? First, we've seen that most law enforcement systems in the developing world are colonial relics that were never set up to protect the poor from violence (but to protect the regime from the poor), and that, tragically, these systems have never been fundamentally re-engineered to serve the common people.

Secondly, elites with wealth and power in the developing world have abandoned these dysfunctional *public* justice systems and have set up systems of *private* security that protect them from violence. They have financed the growth of massive private security forces that replace the need to rely on public policing, and they have abandoned the clogged and corrupt court systems to dysfunction and decay because they have found private means for resolving disputes in their favor.

Now we turn to a third explanation for why basic law enforcement systems in the developing world have been allowed to atrophy and decay into such utter uselessness (and even danger) for poor people. In stark, simple terms, *the massive global movement to address poverty in the developing world over the last half century has not made a meaningful effort to address the problem.*

But what do we mean by "meaningful effort?"

When I ask my teenager, for instance, if he has studied for his final algebra exam, he can, with technical accuracy, say, "Yes, I have," even if he has spent only a few sleepy minutes thumbing through his textbook on the morning of the exam. But what I am actually asking is whether he has made a "meaningful" effort to study for the exam, given 1) the magnitude of the challenge (the exam will cover a whole semester of complex material), 2) the depth of the implications for everything else (it will be impossible to get a good grade in the course overall without doing well on the final exam), and 3) the relative level of effort and investment that has been made in other things (given all the time and effort he has given to studying with his girlfriend for his exam in his favorite history class).

In the same way, when we look over forty plus years of effort and more than $3 trillion[1] spent on development assistance in poor countries, and we ask whether any "meaningful" effort has been made to address broken law enforcement systems, we are looking for a level of effort and investment that is commensurate with: 1) the *magnitude of the challenge* (given that the brokenness and dysfunction is severe and nearly universal for the billions of poor people in the developing world), 2) the *depth of its implications* for everything else (given the way violence can destroy all other forms of human progress), and 3) the focus and investment in addressing *other needs* (given the very meaningful effort of the international community to help poor countries meet other needs in health, nutrition, housing, education, etc.).

As we shall see, the international community can say with technical accuracy that it has made *some* effort to address the problem, just as my son can say that he made *some* effort to prepare for his exam. However, when one examines the level of effort and investment the international community has made in prioritizing and helping build criminal justice systems that protect the poor from violence in the developing world against the backdrop of its investment in other needs, we are forced to confront the shocking truth that we haven't actually made a serious effort.

It may yet prove to be true that the international community actually *cannot* help fix broken criminal justice systems in the developing world, just as it may turn out that my son cannot succeed in math. But we cannot draw this conclusion based on the amount of effort extended thus far (on the contrary, given the meager effort to date, failure was practically *guaranteed*). And as we shall see later, there are actually very substantial reasons for believing that failing justice systems can be transformed to protect the poor from violence.

For the last half century, however, building functioning criminal justice systems in the developing world has received scandalously little attention, investment, or assistance from the movements and institutions dedicated to addressing poverty. It's a scandal because we know that such systems are utterly indispensable for the poor, for those of us in affluent countries have all treated law enforcement as *the* indispensable and first-priority public system in our own communities. It's a scandal because we know that the law enforcement systems are the most broken (and most dangerous) public systems in the developing world. But despite knowing all this, fixing broken criminal justice systems has not been the problem we have focused on, prioritized, or spent money on.

To be clear, this is *not* to say that we have spent too much money and effort on other challenges confronting the poor (like health, education, food, clean water, micro-loans, or housing needs). Surely, we have not. If one spreads that $3 trillion across the desperate poverty of the world's poorest billions over the last half a century, the per-person investment in aid has been modest by any measure.[2]

But—modest or not—we must confront the reality that these investments were made in the absence of any meaningful effort to provide a reasonable degree of security for poor people through basic law enforcement, and in the resulting chaos, much of the other assistance we extended could not possibly succeed in the way we hoped.

Clearing Away the Fog

But what about all the investment over decades in programs seeking to promote things like "rule of law," "good governance," "anti-corruption efforts," "access to justice," "gender equality," and "rights-based development?" Haven't the U.S. government and other institutions spent billions of dollars on international law enforcement efforts around the world? Hasn't the international community made significant efforts building justice systems and rule of law in the developing world that will protect the rights of the vulnerable poor?

Well, to answer this question we must clear away a lot of fog and untangle a great deal of confusion. The international community may have extended significant efforts in the general direction of governmental systems of various kinds in the developing world, while at the same time doing virtually nothing meaningful to build criminal justice systems that work reasonably well to protect the poor from violence.

To see matters clearly, let's begin with the biggest source of confusion: the hugely popular and compelling concept of "rule of law." To massively oversimplify, "rule of law" expresses the idea that, in a just society, what ultimately ought to rule or reign is not a person, or money, or might, or some other arbitrary factor, but law—and law that is fairly derived, fairly enforced, and protects fundamental fairness. Most people will readily associate the concept of rule of law with the basic power to restrain oppressive and unjust violence—the idea that violence is "against the law," that no one is "above the law," and that, therefore, no one (even if they are rich and powerful) can use violence against another person (even if they are weak or poor) to injure them, steal from them, enslave them, threaten, or oppress them. And if they do, "the law" will be enforced to stop such abuse. Accordingly, it is readily appreciated that the entire enjoyment of life, liberty and the pursuit of happiness fundamentally depends on effective rule of law to restrain the power of the strong to commit violence against the weak.

Therefore, when people hear about programs that support the "rule of law" they might readily assume that such programs address the most basic and core concept of using law enforcement to protect the poor and weak from violence. Likewise, if one hears that there is a public health program addressing an outbreak of an infectious disease for which there is a vaccine and a treatment, one might readily assume that the core of that program is getting that vaccine or treatment into the bloodstream of as many vulnerable people as possible. But in both situations, it's quite possible for such assumptions to be completely wrong—because among specialists, the concepts of "rule of law" and "public health" are significantly more expansive and may involve programs very far from the core concept that most of us have in mind. Public health plans to combat this hypothetical infectious disease, for example, might involve a great many things besides the direct administration of the vaccine or treatment—from public awareness campaigns to efforts to clean up or eradicate a source or carrier of the disease, to the promotion of better nutrition or healthier living to reduce vulnerability. But we'd consider the plans to be a tragic farce if we learned that the one thing *not* included was provision of the vaccine. Likewise, you would be outraged if 80 percent of the vaccine were being provided in two or three isolated countries where only a tiny percentage of the infected population lived (and where it was disproportionately expensive and difficult to provide it successfully), or if the cure were otherwise being restricted to those few poor countries where the disease threatens to spill over to rich countries.

This absurd scenario is unfortunately a fairly precise description of the international community's "rule of law" response to the epidemic of lawless violence against the poor in the developing world. To understand why, we have to appreciate how broad the concept of "rule of law" is in current development industry parlance. While many will readily identify that protecting the weak against the violence of the strong is perhaps the most basic and core concept at the heart of rule of law, in practice that idea is just a small part of the larger, richer concept of the rule of law. Indeed, in the broadly accepted explication of the rule of law offered by the American Bar Association's World Justice Project, there are nine discrete factors or dimensions that make up the rule of law:

1. Limited government powers
2. Absence of corruption
3. Order and security
4. Fundamental rights
5. Open government
6. Effective regulatory enforcement
7. Access to civil justice
8. Effective criminal justice
9. Informal justice

An effective criminal justice system that protects citizens from violence is only one of those nine factors, which are further disaggregated into 52 sub-factors.[3] As a result, nearly every kind of program—from election monitoring, to development of a free press, to fighting software piracy, to eliminating bribes for drivers' licenses, to writing clear intellectual property regulations, to televising coverage of parliamentary proceedings—can be rightly included in programs seeking to strengthen rule of law in the developing world. Indeed, a nearly infinite array of programs can be properly pursued under the banner of the rule of law that have little or nothing to do with the very specific challenge of protecting the poor from violence through effective enforcement of criminal law.

Again, to be clear, all nine of the listed factors play a critical role in the rule of law, and the international community is right to invest (with increasing vigor and commitment) in all of these areas. Moreover, given the complex way in which a criminal justice system is only part of a very intricate web of civil and cultural institutions that ultimately combine to provide the political will and operational capacity to protect the poor from violence, all nine of these factors can end up playing some role in providing a secure and peaceful community in which the poor can better their lives.

Nevertheless, we must hold on to two critical points. First, if international rule of law programs do not specifically and adequately invest in "effective criminal justice" systems, then the poor are not going to be protected from violence and—as we saw clearly in Chapter 3—they cannot thrive. This is why effective criminal justice systems are *indispensable*. Second, to determine the level of international investment in criminal justice programs in the developing world, we have to disaggregate these programs from the vast array of good and worthy "rule of law" investments that have nothing to with providing a system of criminal justice that effectively protects the poor from violence.

And when we clear away the layers of fog around "rule of law" investments, what do we find? Over the history of modern efforts at economic development and poverty alleviation in the developing world, rule of law investments have constituted a relatively small percentage of the overall effort, and within the fraction of aid investments that constitute rule of law expenditures, investments in effective criminal justice have been so small as to be immaterial—largely because significant development institutions like the World Bank and USAID (U.S. Agency for International Development— the U.S. government's primary foreign aid agency) have been *prohibited by their own policies* from making investments in law enforcement systems in the developing world. When international donors and agencies *have* made investments in rule of law or law enforcement systems, such efforts and investments have been swallowed up by three separate agendas that have very little to do with ensuring that the common poor person is protected from violence: rebuilding a small handful of post-conflict countries (like Iraq and Afghanistan); addressing transnational crimes of terrorism, and narcotics and arms trafficking; and building attractive and stable conditions for business, commercial activity, and capital investment.

As a result, when all the institutional and semantic fog is cleared away, the final analysis reveals a shockingly low investment: Only about 1 percent of aid from institutions like USAID or the World Bank can even be plausibly described as targeting improvements in justice systems in the developing world so that they better protect the poor from violence.

CRIMINAL JUSTICE SYSTEM INVESTMENTS PROHIBITED BY POLICY

In many respects, it should not be surprising that there has been such vast underinvestment in criminal justice systems in the developing world, because they are the one system in which international aid agencies have been *prohibited* from investing *as a matter of policy*. It's hard to imagine aid agencies banning investments in food systems, education systems, health systems, or water systems in the developing world, but this is precisely what happened with criminal justice systems in poor countries. And while there have been some very understandable reasons for this reluctance to spend foreign aid dollars in this area, the end result has been a tragic and unique neglect of criminal justice systems.

Over the past fifty years, the great aid agencies of the international community found that trying to improve food systems, health systems, educational systems and other systems of human well-being in the developing world was difficult and complex. However, when it came to improving law enforcement systems, they found that such efforts were also uniquely dangerous. Other systems fail poor people in the developing world—but they are not likely to turn on poor people and hurt them. In that sense, they are benign systems. Law enforcement systems, on the other hand, are not. They are systems of coercive power that can be used for good or for ill. A criminal justice system that is empowered, highly trained, well-resourced, and efficient can be used to repress the common people with violence as well as protect them from violence. Moreover, such systems are the coercive arm of the state (controlled by a ruling regime); while governments may be very happy to have outsiders come and tinker with their hospitals, schools, and farming techniques, they are much more reluctant to have outsiders mess around with their systems of justice, policing, and legal accountability.

Confronted with these challenges fairly early on in the history of international aid programs, leading foreign aid agencies decided to deal with the complexities and risks by simply banning investment in improving the criminal justice sector in the developing world.

The U.S. Government

The United States, by far the largest provider of international foreign aid, actually began its journey of engagement in the developing world with significant investment in improving criminal justice systems. Following World War II, the U.S. government invested heavily in training and equipping foreign police forces through the Office of Public Safety (OPS) within the Agency for International Development,[4] which often served as an intelligence-gathering agency for the CIA. By 1968, "the United States was spending $60 million a year to train police in 34 countries in areas such as criminal investigation, patrolling, interrogation and counterinsurgency techniques, riot control, weapon use, and bomb disposal."[5] Despite the efforts of some State Department and OPS advisors who argued for a training model built around civilian policing that would be accountable to the public and subject to law, in practice, OPS programming embraced a paramilitary model, with significant focus on counter-insurgency and intelligence measures. Not surprisingly, in countries with abusive governments, such a model took a disastrous toll. In the 1970s it emerged that, among other outrageous incidents of torture and abuse, OPS-purchased field telephones were being used to administer electric shocks during interrogations, and that the partially-OPS-funded Operation Phoenix in Vietnam had resulted in the torture and murder of thousands of suspected Vietcong after their imprisonment in the notorious "tiger cages" of Con Son prison.[6] As a result of these and other scandalous human rights abuses, OPS was dissolved and, in 1974, Congress amended the Foreign Assistance Act of 1961 with Section 660, which prohibited the United States from using foreign assistance funds to provide training, advice, or financial support for foreign police, prisons, or law enforcement organizations, except for international narcotics control.

Beginning in 1985, Congress authorized certain exemptions to the ban to allow funding for police assistance activities on a case-by-case basis, and new exemptions to the ban were legislated for U.S. involvement with overseas police in anti-narcotics operations and certain efforts to halt illegal immigration.[7] In 1996, Congress added an exception for reconstituting civilian police authority and capacity in post-conflict states. Finally, in 2005, more than thirty years after broadly banning law enforcement aid in the developing world, Section 564(a) authorized police assistance to "enhance the effectiveness and accountability of civilian police authority through training and technical assistance in human rights, the rule of law, strategic planning, and through assistance to foster civilian police roles that support democratic governance, including assistance for programs to prevent conflict, respond to disasters, address gender-based violence, and foster improved police relations with the communities they serve."[8]

Notwithstanding this new authority to aid police throughout the developing world, Congressional budgets, GAO reports, and other government documents make clear that the overwhelming majority of the governance and democracy, rule-of-law, and police assistance programs have been directed towards counter-terrorism, counter-narcotics, and a handful of post-conflict countries where the United States has had a massive strategic investment. As one American police training expert told us, U.S. aid to police forces in other countries overwhelmingly focuses on stopping cross-border crimes, like terrorism and drug trafficking, that threaten to bring their devastation to U.S. soil. The security needs of the people in the countries receiving the aid—much less the particular needs of poor communities vulnerable to criminal violence or exploitation—are generally not part of the equation.

The World Bank

Perhaps even more important to international aid policy than the longstanding U.S. ban on criminal justice investments has been the World Bank's ban on such investments—which for all practical purposes continues to this day. As the premier financial institution for international economic development, the World Bank not only stewards very significant resources, but also maintains a dominant influence on strategies and approaches to international assistance targeting the developing world.

Over the course of its history, the Bank has only belatedly and modestly made investments in the justice sector generally, and has steadfastly refused investment in the primary system entrusted with protecting the citizenry from violence in the developing world: law enforcement. The Bank's involvement in criminal justice sector reform has been fundamentally handicapped by its own charter, which requires all projects to have a direct economic impact and to refrain from interfering in the political activities of the state. These aspects of the charter have traditionally been interpreted as barring investments in criminal justice systems. As a result, while many of the Bank's rule-of-law projects have the intended purpose of helping the poorest and the most vulnerable groups, very few, if any, have partnered with law enforcement organizations to target criminal violence against the poor. The overwhelming majority of these projects have worked to build institutions to improve the commercial and business environment through anti-corruption efforts.[9]

In recent years, reformers within the Bank, led by the Justice Reform Practice Group, have worked to broaden the space in which assistance can be provided to the justice sector, including the police. Justice Reform Practice Group members Heike Gramckow, Christina Beibesheimer, and others at the Bank have built on the Bank's work on governance, and the Bank's "2011 World Development Report: Conflict, Security and Development" linked criminal violence to under-development,[10] providing a solid foundation for the Bank to address the issue of criminal violence forthrightly.

In February 2012, Anne-Marie Leroy, senior vice president and group general counsel of the World Bank issued a Legal Note on Bank Involvement in the Criminal Justice Sector.[11] Instead of a rigid and narrow requirement that investment decisions be guided solely by economic criteria, they may now be made in projects that have a reasonable "economic rationale." The Bank itself has concluded there is a "broad consensus that an equitable, well-functioning justice system is an important factor in fostering development and reducing poverty."[12] In fact, at the end of his term as World Bank president, Robert Zoellick concluded that "the *most* fundamental prerequisite for sustainable development is an effective rule of law."[13] Likewise, there is no doubt that the most fundamental prerequisite for effective rule of law is the most basic restraint, by effective law enforcement, of violence in the community. Again, as Christopher Stone advised the Bank, "In terms of social and economic development, high levels of crime and violence threaten to undermine the best-laid plans to reduce poverty, improve governance, and relieve human misery."[14]

If the World Bank's new interpretation of its mandate will allow it to move swiftly to engage directly with struggling justice systems—especially the police—it can make an inestimable contribution to the struggle for functional criminal justice in the developing world. The Bank's particular expertise in addressing infirmities in government institutions and systems, and its international stature would make it a highly valuable partner in addressing broken police and justice systems.

The risks and difficulties in working with law enforcement systems in the developing world are indeed substantial and real—but meaningfully engaging them will be far more difficult in the absence of bold leadership by the world's leading development institution. Other institutions and donors (perhaps following the World Bank's lead) are not meaningfully addressing the problem on a global basis either. Given the Bank's explicit goal of reducing poverty in the developing world, it makes no sense to disengage from a social system that the Bank now recognizes is indispensable to achieving that goal.

THREE AGENDAS THAT DO SEEM WORTH THE RISKS: POST-CONFLICT SITUATIONS, INTERNATIONAL CRIME, AND BUSINESS

Paradoxically, the history of policy bans on investments in improving justice systems and law enforcement have not kept aid agencies (especially from the United States) from making investments in these sectors when they involved the agendas that seemed to matter more deeply to policy makers: rebuilding a small handful of post-conflict countries (like Iraq and Afghanistan and a handful of other security vacuums); addressing international crimes that threaten to spill over into wealthier nations; and promoting business, commercial activity, and capital investment in the developing world.

Again, these may all be good things, but they are not targeted at the central problem facing most poor people in the developing world. What these programs do manifest is that when it comes to their own interests, wealthier nations have no doubt about the indispensability of effective law enforcement for being safe within their own borders and making economic growth viable.

Security Vacuums

Some of the most active donors funding relevant rule of law and justice sector reform in the past twenty years have been the UK's Department for International Development (DFID), the United States government, the

Inter-American Development Bank, the World Bank, and the UN Office on Drugs and Crime, which have together poured billions of dollars into programs supporting rule of law. However, almost all of these resources have been funneled into a handful of countries where post-conflict security vacuums became a strategic concern to the donor countries.

Relatively little funding has been allocated by these major donors to the development of criminal justice systems in otherwise stable, developing countries where the vast majority of the global poor live in lawless violence, and where it would be easier and cheaper to actually achieve significant and lasting transformations of criminal justice systems to protect the common poor.[15]

International Crime

There is a second circumstance in which wealthy countries are willing to suspend their concerns about the risks of law enforcement investment in the developing world, and that is when the criminal violence threatens to spill over and affect their own societies. To the extent wealthy countries have invested in rule of law and criminal justice systems in the developing world, it has overwhelmingly been for the purpose of combating criminal threats of terrorism and the narcotics trade.

For the United States, the largest funder of rule-of-law programs in the developing world, over the past decade, almost all rule-of-law funding has been poured into two or three countries that are perceived as harboring significant terrorism threats to the United States: namely, Iraq, Afghanistan, and Pakistan. For example, from 2004 to 2007, 53 percent (approximately $395 million) of the U.S. State Department's Bureau of Democracy, Human Rights and Labor (which leads the State Department's efforts of democracy and human rights promotion around the world) foreign assistance funds were directed to Iraq.[16] And, in 2011, Afghanistan and Pakistan received almost 50 percent of the funds allocated for "Governing Justly and Democratically"—an amount greater than the funding for the Western Hemisphere, Africa, East Asia, Europe, and Eurasia combined.[17]

The United States' efforts in combating drugs have often centered on foreign assistance to police and other law enforcement organizations, with Latin American and Caribbean countries receiving the greatest amounts of police training for this purpose. In just one recent investment, Congress approved the Merida Initiative, a partnership with the Mexican, Haitian, Dominican Republican, and other Central American governments to fund police training and rule of law. The funds were specifically earmarked to combat organized crime, weapon smuggling, and drug trafficking through professionalizing law enforcement—providing an annual average of more than $380 million to Mexico and more than $95 million to the other Central American countries from 2008 to 2010.[18]

Even these investments may not have the kind of impacts that benefit the common poor—despite the criminal violence connected to Central American drug smuggling gangs. Michael Shifter of the Council on Foreign Relations notes that U.S. assistance in the region has been more focused on "immediate results" like securing major arrests and blocking drug shipments, rather than building lasting "modern and professional" law enforcement functions in these countries.[19, *]

The U.S. Department of Homeland Security funds International Law Enforcement Academies (ILEA) in Bangkok, Budapest, Gaborone, and San Salvador, with $166.89 million invested between 2001 and 2011.[20] Overwhelmingly, the four offices offer training and assistance in transnational crimes such as narcotics, terrorism, money laundering, etc. (with an additional unit on human trafficking that does indeed address the local vulnerabilities of the poor).

Again, fighting international crime is a perfectly legitimate basis for funding rule of law and law enforcement efforts in the developing world, but to be clear, the purpose (and outcome) is not to protect the poor in the developing world from violence. The purpose and outcome of these investments are to protect people in the wealthy countries from violence and theft. As one expert analyzing this funding has commented: "Goals such as improving global security through police reform and antiterrorist laws are accomplished by reforming rule-of-law institutions—but they are targeted not at improving the rule of law *within* a particular state, but at achieving security for *other* states."[21]

Attracting Business and Commercial Investment

The third category that has generated substantial investment in rule-of-law and justice system reform has been efforts to provide an environment in

---

*One encouraging exception to this trend may be the small (e.g., 2010 investment of $20.4 million) Model Precinct program implemented by the U.S. State Department/ INL (Bureau of International Narcotics and Law Enforcement), which has been an effective deterrent of crime in some of the most violent communities of Guatemala, El Salvador, and Honduras.

the developing world that is secure, efficient, and attractive for business and commerce. This is a worthy goal, and one which, if successful, promises to raise the boats of the poor to new levels of prosperity with the rising tide of overall economic growth in emerging market countries. However, these investments are not targeted at and do not meaningfully address the issue of lawless violence—which, as we have seen, ends up undercutting the gains that the poor might otherwise be able to realize under an environment of economic growth.

For instance, most of the World Bank's activities in rule of law have focused on developing a fair and transparent business environment conducive to economic growth under its Governance and Anti-Corruption initiatives. A review of the World Bank's 2009 projects in justice reform revealed a few dominant themes, most relevant to the development of an attractive business environment, including reforming financial markets, resolving business disputes, reducing corruption, and reforming public administration regulations. Even projects designed to improve access to justice rarely focused on the needs of the poorest. World Bank expert Vivek Maru analyzed 16 major, completed judicial reform projects financed by the Bank in Latin America, the Middle East, Eastern Europe, and Asia—and found that only three of them considered the justice needs of poor people.[22] Again, an attractive business culture in the developing world is a worthy aim and may have benefits for the poor—but that result does not necessarily flow to them (since they are not the intended direct beneficiaries), and it certainly does not address the poor's critical need to be protected from lawless violence.

THE MATH

What happens if we look at the overall funding of the major foreign aid agencies and all of the purported funding for improvement of justice systems and rule of law in the developing world—but we strip out the worthy but off-topic funding for post-conflict security vacuums, international crime, and business investment? What is left for the massive global problem of addressing the absence of functioning criminal justice systems to protect the poor from lawless violence in the developing world? Well, it turns out, almost nothing.

By its own admission, although the World Bank has engaged in justice reform for two decades, "its justice reform portfolio remains relatively small."[23, *] One of the Bank's significant lending sectors is called "Law and Justice and Public Administration," but despite the name, almost none of that sum actually goes to projects the Bank categorizes under "Law and Justice." In the previous five years, Law and Justice averaged 2 percent of total lending, dipping as low as .03 percent in 2009.

Likewise, if we look again at funding from the United States for foreign assistance and try to drill down and see what funding has even come close to addressing the targeted problem of broken criminal justice systems in the developing world, we come up with virtually nothing. We first have to confront the awkward truth that it is nearly impossible for even the U.S. government to identify what all of its "rule of law" funding does—let alone account for how much of it actually addresses broken criminal justice systems in the developing world.

First, the various U.S. agencies working in the area of rule of law do not use a consistent definition of what constitutes "rule of law activities," and some organizations do not even use consistent definitions internally.[24] As a result, reporting on funding for police support and rule of law is often ad hoc and difficult to determine.[25] Second, U.S. government support for police assistance lacks coordination. A recent GAO report stated that in 2009, seven federal agencies and 24 components within those agencies funded or implemented police training programs, and it concluded that this diversity made it difficult to determine the precise amount the U.S. government has spent on police training.[26]

But by following the money as closely as we can, what we find is clear enough: The amount of investment in helping criminal justice systems protect the poor from violence is so small as to be immaterial. Given the opacity of data on spending, it's impossible to say with exactness, but a fair and conservative estimate is that somewhere between 1 and 2 percent of foreign assistance funds are directed towards programming that might have a direct impact on protecting the poor from common criminal violence. (See the Appendix for the math behind this conclusion.)

A welcome exception to the rule is police training funded by the State Department Office to Monitor and Combat Trafficking in Persons (TIP).

---

*From 2004 to 2008, "Rule of Law" lending averaged $460 million. It fell 97 percent in 2009 to $16 million, when $450 million of its loans categorized under Rule of Law were dropped. $190 million of that sum was specifically earmarked for Law and Justice projects. Since then, funding for rule of law projects has increased slightly, but is still less than half (down 64 percent between 2010 and 2012) of average rule of law spending from 2004 to 2008.

The Office has made numerous grants for anti-trafficking police training from its tiny grants budget (approximately $20 million per year). Anti-trafficking units in countries, including Cambodia and the Philippines, that received training from this account have made remarkable progress in professionalizing their operations, rescuing victims, apprehending perpetrators, and significantly deterring the crime of sex trafficking.

Excluding anti-trafficking funding, the United States and the World Bank appear to devote between one and two percentage points of their funding to justice system efforts that target the specific needs of the poor in the developing world. When it comes to helping the most important segment of the criminal justice system pipeline protecting the common poor, the police have received *zero* assistance from the World Bank and virtually none from the United States, apart from funding the TIP Office's tiny spigot of assistance for anti-trafficking.

A Sober Assessment—and a Fundamental Hope

Over the last several decades, even when the international aid agencies have stepped up to try to address the brokenness of criminal justice in the developing world, these efforts have frequently lacked even a pretense of seriousness—court reporter machines for Zambia that soon break and are left unrepaired, a one-man UN monitor of the courts in Cambodia who faithfully "monitors" just how bad they are, police or prosecutor training from Western counterparts that results in four and a half nice days at the Sheraton for everybody, but no useful changes of behavior back out in the streets.

International aid agencies can say that they have tried to address the brokenness of criminal justice systems in the developing world, but looking back at the overall effort over the past fifty years while billions of the poorest have lived under a constant vulnerability to violence, the effort cannot be found to be serious. And help isn't coming from somewhere else. While the largest and most influential NGOs addressing the needs of the poor (e.g., CARE, Save the Children, Oxfam, World Vision, etc.) have saved millions of lives through improvements in nutrition, clean water, health care, education, sanitation, cultural transformation, political empowerment, and other achievements over the last half century, they have not (nor do they claim to have) made significant efforts to transform the working criminal justice system to protect the poor from violence.

While there certainly has been a growing appreciation among these NGOs for the problem of lawless violence among the poor (especially against women and children), their actual programmatic activities aimed at the problem of violence are generally focused on what are sometimes called the "underlying causes of violence"—like desperate poverty, lack of education, lack of awareness of rights, cultural attitudes, political disempowerment, gender inequity, etc. These programs therefore focus on awareness, education and advocacy campaigns, counseling services for victims, economic assistance to groups especially vulnerable to violence, changing social attitude and discriminatory laws, and sponsorship of legal aid. While these programs may help to reduce the vulnerability of victims, they simply will not make poor people meaningfully or sustainably safe in the absence of a functioning criminal justice system that actually enforces laws against violence. And most critically, none of these programs are targeted at getting the criminal justice system to actually work better—certainly not in any ways that have been shown to meaningfully reduce violence against the poor.

This is not to say that programs that effectively transform criminal justice systems do not exist; in fact, towards the end of this volume we shall look at a number of very promising projects from both international aid agencies and NGOs that provide tremendous encouragement that corrupt and failing law enforcement systems can actually be transformed to protect the poor from violence in the developing world.

But for now, our aim is to make a sober assessment of the fact that there has been no meaningful, large-scale attention or resources focused on protecting the common poor in the developing world from violence with basic law enforcement. Paradoxically, this stark appraisal provides a fundamental point of hope, for it belies the paralyzing cynicism that arises from the notion that we are throwing everything we have at the problem and have not even made a dent. Serious efforts to build criminal justice systems that work for the poor have not been tried and found impossible—they have been found hard, and left untried. Accordingly, the time has surely come for the international aid community to revise its investment priorities to address the lawlessness that is undermining so many other efforts to assist the poor.

IT'S BEEN DONE BEFORE

Let's begin with a short quiz. Below are five descriptions of profoundly dysfunctional criminal justice systems from a variety of cities that we have not yet discussed. The brokenness and injustice in each city is shocking—but the descriptions are not considered factually controversial and each represents the consensus view of experts who have studied conditions in each city. See if you can guess which city is being described:

1. Corruption in this city police force is endemic—from the chief of police who has made millions providing private services to elite criminals, to the precinct captains who borrow hundreds of thousands of dollars (from criminals) to purchase their appointments in bribe-rich districts, and then rake in immense payoffs from illicit enterprises. A famous local journalist has written that the police of this city "have practiced corruption so long that they now believe it is good; they know it is…for it pays." The police do not view themselves as working for the general public but for the political faction that appoints them, and experts have exposed their integral role in voter fraud and intimidation. Studies have found police brutality rampant and unchecked—in fact, the chief of police has openly stated: "There is

more law at the end of a policeman's nightstick than in all the decisions of the courts." As a result, an investigative commission concluded that "every interest, every occupation, almost every citizen is dominated by an all-controlling and overshadowing dread of the police department." The city's Magistrates' Courts are no better—"known to be corrupt, inefficient, and ineffective." One expert has concluded that "as producers of travesties upon law and justice, the [Magistrates'] courts of [this city] are unequalled." The vast majority of those who are dragged before the courts are poor, and 95 percent are "arrested summarily and without process." Experts observe that while the rich are "typically able to buy their way through the criminal justice system when arrested, the poor usually suffer injustice by it."

2. In this town, experts have documented rampant forced prostitution and the commercial sexual exploitation of children. They also find that brothel keepers and sex traffickers regularly pay bribes to judges to obtain bogus arrest warrants against sex trafficking victims who have run away, and to police to chase down the escapees and to return them to the brothel keeper or sex trafficker. In this town of economic boom and bust, there is also much communal violence directed against one particular ethnic minority group. One night the mayor and police chief deputized a mob and supervised a pogrom in the minority neighborhood that resulted in the public massacre of 19 citizens—17 by hanging and two by butchery with knives (including a doctor, one woman, and a 14-year-old boy). In full view of the police chief and mayor, the mob then pillaged through the minority neighborhood and stripped the community of anything of value. Eight men out of the mob of hundreds were eventually arrested, but their convictions were overturned by the nation's highest court. Not a single person was brought to justice for these atrocities. In this city's country, there is a public mob lynching approximately once every third day.

3. In this country, owners of large extractive industries can raise a private police force to deal with labor unrest simply by petitioning the local law enforcement official for permission to deputize a gang of hired men to be given police powers under the direction of the company. In this region, where mining has driven the local economy to new heights, company police can act with little concern for workers' rights because

they know that the miners are little more than indentured servants whose livelihoods depend on the company.... "[The private police] can conduct daily business knowing that they are virtually untouchable." Abuses have included the murder of 19 unarmed, striking miners whom forensic investigators determined were all shot in the back when they were running from an attack by the local police personnel and the deputized private police force. The law enforcement chief and his deputies were arrested for the killings, but all were acquitted.

4. In this megacity, the poor have become common targets of police action as law enforcement brings to bear unnecessary force against marginal groups amidst popular agitation over economic conditions and political unrest. The police service, which was once regarded as the "people's police," has been transformed into a security apparatus for the protection of the regime. The police have become an object of widespread fear, and revisions of the law have made nearly any offense against the regime punishable by death. The Special Higher Police has been expanded and charged with controlling "dangerous thought," and it is now especially notorious for its use of torture, abusive detentions, unauthorized entry of residences, and illegal censorship practices.

5. The uniformed police in this vast city are primarily recruited from illiterate men just released from four years of conscripted service in the army. Experts regard them as poorly trained and ill-equipped, with low morale and serving under very bleak conditions. Not surprisingly, the public regards them with contempt and distrust. The common person experiences the police as insolent, incompetent, aggressive drunkards and abusive to women. A prominent local economist and journalist has described the local police as "villainous, boastful, cowardly, aggressive...detested and abhorred by everybody."

* * *

If you have found it difficult to match these descriptions with any current cities in the developing world, you should not feel badly. They are in fact descriptions of the police, prosecutors, and courts in the developing cities of the United States, France, and Japan over the past 150 years—each manifesting a level of corruption, dysfunction, incompetence, brutality, and lawlessness that rivals anything seen in the developing world today.

Description #1 is of New York City in the 1890s. This was an era when the police were notoriously and openly corrupt, abusive, incompetent, and utterly owned by kleptocratic political machines and criminal rackets—all of which was impervious to the efforts of crusaders like Theodore Roosevelt who sought to reform the system. Likewise the "police courts" (as they were called) were a circus of corruption, incompetence, inefficiency, and absurdity that victimized the poor and granted license to the rich and powerful (for a fee).[1]

Description #2 portrays the horrifying story of law enforcement complicity in sex trafficking and violent pogroms against the Chinese population of Los Angeles in the 1870s. Federal law might have prohibited such atrocities, but enforcement of such protections for vulnerable minorities was in the hands of corrupt and racist local officials who simply refused to enforce the law and committed abuses with impunity.[2] Indeed this was an era of lawlessness in which, on average, someone in America was lynched about once every third day.

In fact, in the very bad old days of the Wild West in the United States—specifically in the Pacific Northwest—a series of violent pogroms and forced expulsions were carried out against more than 200 different Chinese communities across the region in the second half of the nineteenth century.[3] In 1885 in Seattle and Tacoma, a city mayor appointed himself police chief and deputized a hundred men to carry out an orgy of ethnic cleansing, murder, looting, forced expulsion, and torching of the Chinese community.[4]

Description #3 takes us to the state of Pennsylvania during an era in which tens of thousands of laborers died in the dangerous mines of the northeast counties of the state and where the Coal & Iron Police Act of 1865 authorized local sheriffs to deputize the private security forces of major mining and industrial companies with police powers. For the next 65 years, the Act authorized local vigilantes to use force against uncooperative workers and their families during a period of intense exploitation and abuse of industrial laborers. This culminated in the "Lattimer massacre," which began with protests over conditions of child labor and ended in the deaths of 19 miners and the wounding of up to 50.

Description #4 takes us to Tokyo in the early decades of the twentieth century, when Japanese policing was an infamously fierce institution of imperial oppression. Amazingly, however, by the 1980s Japan had the lowest crime rate in the industrialized world and its police force was widely considered (rightly or wrongly) a model for crime prevention and building public trust. But the abusive police force described in our quiz had itself come a long way in a hundred years from "policing" during the Edo Period when the *samurai* were the strong arm of the law, when torture was legal, and when most crimes were punishable by gruesome executions. As Japan opened up to the world during the "enlightened rule" of the Meiji period that followed, its leaders embarked on a massive study of modern police models from Europe and adapted a centralized and professional police force. While it proved to be a marked improvement over the unchecked violence of the *shogunate*, the police service was still considered oppressive and abusive of marginalized groups and the poor. As Japan fell under the forces of an imperial military dictatorship in the 1920s, the police in Japan were transformed yet again into the force of mass fear among the common people depicted in Description #4.[5]

Description #5 is a picture of policing in Victor Hugo's Paris during the tumultuous years of the nineteenth century when the city was full of fierce poverty, social upheaval, and political instability. "Policing" in this era was generally focused on regime survival, protection of state authority, and suppressing the threat of the *dangerous classes* against the *respectable classes*. The common Paris constable in this period was viewed (quite accurately) as an illiterate drunk of infuriating incompetence. Police in nineteenth-century Paris provided a thin and shabby line of defense against "disorder" for the governing authorities and the affluent classes, but they provided little protection against everyday crime for the masses of common Parisians, and almost no protection for the poor underclasses, whom the police were largely content to have fight among themselves.[6] However, as more meaningful universal male suffrage emerged among the French electorate in the second half of the nineteenth century, Parisians came to demand more from the police service.[7] Accordingly, by 1893, the famous Paris police chief Louis Lepine had begun the process of dramatically transforming the French police into a modern and professional police force that had, by 1914, gained an extraordinary level of respect and trust from the common people. At precisely the same time, France was exporting an extremely repressive form of policing into the countries of its expanding colonial empire overseas—a form of policing utterly unresponsive to the disenfranchised masses over which it ruled.

DYSFUNCTION IS NORMAL

Obviously the point of all this is to take what we have seen of public justice dysfunction and brokenness in the developing world today, and to place it within the larger reality of history. The truth is, very few of today's residents in New York, Seattle, LA, northwest Pennsylvania, Japan, or Paris—who currently enjoy some of the highest levels of public safety and the lowest levels of crime in human history—would have any idea how utterly corrupt, incompetent, abusive, lawless, and criminal the public justice systems in their cities once were.

This is not to say, of course, that the criminal justice systems in these countries are without their own flaws and dysfunctions today. Indeed, the authors of this volume have spent careers at the U.S. Department of Justice serving on teams that do nothing but fight the corruption, abuse, lawlessness, and criminality that persists within the American public justice system. But two things are undeniably true. First, as journalist and author Katherine Boo observed upon returning to the United States after sharing life with the poor in Mumbai, common residents (even the poorest) in the most prosperous countries currently enjoy the services of criminal justice systems that provide an extraordinary level of protection from crime and violence—especially when compared to what common citizens in the developing world received from their criminal justice systems. Secondly, it is simply true that residents of these same cities 100 years ago would have found the broken public justices systems of today's developing world much more similar to their own than the modern, professional justice systems that now prevail in their cities. That is to say, Theodore Roosevelt, the New York City police commissioner of 1895, would find the police and courts of, say, Mumbai, India in 2012 much more familiar to him than the professional, well-equipped, reasonably accountable (albeit imperfect) law enforcement institutions of New York City today.[8]

It turns out that dysfunction in criminal justice systems is *normal*. Reasonably functioning law enforcement systems do not descend from the heavens fully formed with effectiveness, fairness, honesty, and functionality; rather, they are built and fought for out of environments of corruption, absurdity, dysfunction, brutality, and incompetence. Uniformly, this seems to be the story of history: Wherever you now have a reasonably functioning criminal justice system that provides common citizens with a basic level of protection from violence, at some time in history, in that exact same place, you once had a criminal justice system that was thoroughly corrupt, abusive, incompetent, in exclusive service to a political or economic elite, and a failure at protecting the poorest and most vulnerable from violence.

This suggests that very few of the difficulties and dysfunctions currently facing criminal justice systems in the developing world are fundamentally different than those that have been faced and substantially overcome in other contexts in history.

For example, while policing in the United States today is a highly sophisticated science and profession, police work in American cities in the nineteenth century was a form of unskilled, casual labor for which one received virtually *no* formal training. Being a policeman was not a career, a profession, or a public service, but a temporary job providing street muscle for the political faction that had prevailed in the most recent municipal election.[9] Policing was a job for rank amateurs and required no specialized training or knowledge. Political loyalty was literally the only real qualification.[10]

Not surprisingly, as in the developing world of today, police officers in the American West, who received no training, were famously incompetent when it came to crime fighting and criminal investigation. The American police reformer of the early twentieth century Raymond B. Fosdick argued that the police were "perhaps the most profound failure in all our unhappy municipal history."[11] What they actually did "bore little relationship to the official mandate of the police" and was guided simply by the informal customs, practices, and procedures of a force organized for purposes of political muscle and graft.[12] Accordingly, historians find it "doubtful" that the police of this era had any meaningful effect at all on reducing or preventing crime.[13]

This high level of incompetence helps explain two phenomena of the era: the public's low regard for the police and the high level of police violence. As ignorant, incompetent brutes, the police earned no respect from the public. In fact, the iconic, comedic image of incompetence and buffoonery from the era is none other than the Keystone Cops.[14] This image of bumbling idiots armed with coercive powers was a bad combination: "Policemen on the beat were subject to a remarkable degree of disrespect and outright abuse. To gain even a nominal amount of respect for their authority, policemen frequently resorted to violence—to gain, by means of the nightstick, the respect that was not freely granted. Thus began a cycle of disrespect and brutality on both sides"[15]

Likewise, the level of corruption among police in the developing world in our era is impressive, but even so, they would have a hard time keeping up with America's "finest" in the big cities of the nineteenth century. As the historian Samuel Walker concluded:

> From the beginning the police became the central figures in an intricate system of racketeering and municipal corruption. In short, the American police represented the antithesis of professionalism.... Corruption was endemic to the entire criminal justice system.[16]

In the 1890s, for example, it was the famous Lexow Commission that exposed the massive system of corruption within the New York City police force, which generated millions of dollars in revenue for the police chief and huge payouts for everyone down the chain of command—pay-offs from illicit businesses, extortion, racketeering, and expensive special services to the city's wealthiest citizens and visitors. Eventually a similar commission or investigative body would expose the same pattern in just about every major city in America:

> [T]he police were part of a larger criminal justice system that was essentially a form of systematic racketeering. The attractions of positions of authority lay primarily in the opportunities they offered for business ventures.[17]

Without a doubt, one of the most lucrative money-making ventures for the American police was their partnership in protecting the massive commercial sex industry that thrived at unprecedented levels in the U.S. cities of the late nineteenth century.[18] In fact, the common term for the commercial sex district in New York City (and some other cities like San Francisco) became "the Tenderloin" when a famously corrupt and brutal police inspector commented that his promotion from a waterfront crime precinct to the midtown red-light district along Broadway would vastly increase his income from bribes. "I've been living on rump steak since I been on the force," Captain Alexander S. ("Clubber") Williams said. "Now I am going to have a bit of Tenderloin."[19]

In addition to this open corruption, if we observed American "police" work in the nineteenth and early twentieth centuries, we would be completely taken aback by the primary function of the police—namely, the provision of coercive and logistical manpower for the political party machine. As one expert notes, "the police had only minimal commitment to the enforcement of the law. As political operatives, they were more interested in furthering the interests of their political sponsors."[20] One of the primary jobs of the police force was to carry out the labor-intensive tasks of voter fraud, ballot box stuffing, and voter intimidation.

We would also be shocked by the pervasive levels of police violence and brutality. As a political operative and bruiser for the political machine, the police officer in the street did not have institutional legitimacy with the public; he would seek to establish his own, personal legitimacy—through force. It requires little imagination to guess the origins of the notorious Captain "Clubber" Williams' nickname. In his autobiography, American journalist Lincoln Steffens recalled, "Many a morning when I had nothing else to do, I stood and saw the police bring in and kick out their bandaged, bloody prisoners."[21]

Police of this era were also the enforcers of violence against marginalized groups and the laboring classes, the protectors of ethnic gangs, and the facilitators of racist brutality against minorities. As we have seen, the American criminal justice system of the nineteenth and early twentieth centuries was deeply complicit in shockingly brutal forms of racial violence, from thousands of public lynchings and burnings at the stake, to hundreds of pogroms against minority communities like the Chinese in the American West.

Looking back on the history of policing in America, one historian depicted conditions that might aptly describe circumstances in poor communities of the developing world today: "Since police brutality was so pervasive, large segments of the public accepted it; they had no standard of fair and impartial public service against which to measure it."[22] Like their counterparts in the developing world today, the criminal justice systems in the United States and other affluent countries 150 years ago were not only brutal, but also shockingly ill-equipped, overwhelmed, and under-staffed for the size of the populations they were expected to protect. In fact, in most instances the creation of official police forces to replace the old volunteer systems did not actually result in an increased number of men on the patrol. Indeed, the police forces of most nineteenth-century American cities were so small that, while municipalities may have attempted to embrace the new and revolutionary idea of a crime-*preventing* police patrol, in practice, these minuscule efforts were meaningless in the face of a tidal wave of crime.[23]

In New York City, there was an officer on patrol for about every 1,300 residents—fewer police per citizen than in India today and about what the Philippines provides.[24] In the 1880s, a police officer in Chicago was responsible for patrolling four and a half miles of city streets by himself— on foot.[25] Historians tell us that the idea that the urban policeman was intimately acquainted with the citizens on his beat is a "romantic notion" utterly unsupported by the facts: "The ratio of police to population suggests that there could have been only minimum contact at best."[26] In Minneapolis, the police were so understaffed that three quarters of the city streets had no police patrol at all.

With so few officers stretched so thinly across exploding city populations, police of this era (like many police in the developing world today) worked extremely long hours. Most police departments established a two-platoon system in which police personnel worked 12-hour shifts and then remained at the station "on reserve." Without modern means of electronic communication, officers could only be available "on call" if they were physically at the station—which meant they worked a 110-hour week or more. In the 1890s New York policemen slept together in foul-smelling, overcrowded barracks in the precinct house. And when on patrol before the era of electronic communication, officers were almost entirely unsupervised as they covered the vast long miles of their beat by themselves.[27]

Obviously, the police had almost none of the basic technological tools of criminal investigation and crime fighting. Even at the end of the nineteenth century there was nothing akin to a police "science;" officers had no access to the equipment now viewed as most basic to crime prevention and criminal investigation; and the police stationhouse was itself frequently a run-down, overcrowded building devoid of equipment, facilities, or amenities to strengthen or assist police personnel. At the opening of the twentieth century, the New York City chief of police described conditions at the typical station house as "a positive disgrace ... unsanitary, poorly ventilated, and without modern improvements ... heated by stoves in winter which give out a poisonous coal-gas. They are damp, gloomy, forbidding."[28]

Of course, the result of all the corruption, politicization, incompetence, and dysfunction of policing a hundred years ago was the same double impunity that broken law enforcement produces in the developing world today.

Criminals (especially those victimizing the poor and marginalized) were unrestrained by the criminal justice system, and law enforcement itself was (for a long time) not held accountable for its corruption, abuse, and failure to enforce the law. In the chronicles of nineteenth- and early-twentieth-century America, historians find that the crisis of "lawlessness" in the cities was not just about levels of crime, but more about "the failure of the police to enforce existing law."[29] Even when the police did attempt to enforce the law, their efforts were frustrated by the lower courts.[30] For the coercive enforcement of social norms and behaviors, the power of private vigilante action (organized and provisioned by private elites or spontaneously generated by community mobs) played a much more significant role in nineteenth-century America than the criminal justice system.[31] When things got out of control, "order" was "restored" by communal mob action or private vigilante forces organized by elites that took the law into their own hands.

THE POWERFUL TRUTH: IT'S POSSIBLE

With all this in mind, the long view of history seems to offer a powerful lesson: namely, that reasonably functioning justice systems are *possible* even in circumstances in which they do not currently exist or seem unlikely to emerge. Historically, criminal justice systems that protected the poor and the weak did not exist *anywhere* and, to contemporaries, always seemed highly unlikely. Now they *do* exist, in lots of places, for billions of people. But in each case, a pitched battle was fought to rescue the public justice system from abuse for private gain, from misuse for political power, from the dysfunction of neglect, and from slavish bondage to outdated, unprofessional, and ineffectual practices.

The vantage point of history allows us to see that the dysfunctions in the criminal justice systems of the developing world today are *normal*. That is to say, they are to be expected—not only because utterly dysfunctional criminal justice systems were imposed on most of these countries by occupying colonial powers, but also because it seems that *every* society must very intentionally and vigorously rescue its criminal justice system from dysfunction and abuse.

This lesson from history provides a critical starting point for addressing the debilitating despair that has seized many in this era when it comes to building functioning criminal justice systems in the developing world.

Building such systems is admittedly costly, difficult, dangerous, and unlikely. History does not make the struggle seem easier, cheaper, or safer—but it does make it seem *possible.*

In the eyes of many people, reforming criminal justice systems in the developing world seems like a dangerous waste of time. Critics will suggest that governmental institutions in today's developing world are simply too dysfunctional and corrupt, or that political cultures are too captive to narrow and oppressive interests (that benefit from a broken system) for a healthy criminal justice system to ever emerge. They will imply that a country is too poor, under-developed or under-resourced, or too beset with oppressive cultural values to ever prioritize and support a modern, professional, and effective criminal justice system. Each of these grim appraisals can feel devastatingly true when you are standing amidst the violence, squalor, and rank injustice of the poorest communities in the developing world today, but I think that is largely because we are unable to be transported back with equal vividness to the realities of the "developed world" a century or more ago, where bloodthirsty mobs summarily executed suspects in acts of grotesque vigilante justice and abused, oppressed, and looted their ethnic minority neighbors, with no accountability from—and often with the endorsement of—the criminal justice "system;" where police were little more than untrained, un-resourced street thugs in the pocket of the ruling political faction; and where absurd and brutal farces played out every day in the courtrooms of corrupt and ludicrously incompetent judges.

Those who led reform in these historical settings would readily appreciate the challenges reformers face in the developing world today—but I think they would have very little sympathy for arguments that change is impossible or unworthy of extreme and sacrificial efforts.

Sadly, the fascinating, strange, and inspiring stories of these reformers of the past are almost entirely lost on us today. Very few of the billions of people in our world who enjoy a reasonable degree of security, freedom, dignity, and protection from a healthy law enforcement system would have any idea where those systems came from or any mental picture of the ugly chaos and lawless violence out of which they emerged.

For Americans, the earliest forms of formal policing seem to have emerged in the mid-nineteenth century, when cities got fed up with the way every dispute seemed to produce a rioting mob in the streets. In every country, the story of how policing emerged and why is organically connected to the distinctive story of the society at large—and for many historians, the distinctive story of U.S. policing emerges from the fact that American society was "more violent" than other western countries.[32] To be more precise, by the middle of the nineteenth century, it was becoming clear that Americans habitually rioted about almost everything: from political rivalries to street gangs' territorial skirmishes; from racial tensions to labor disputes; from reform movements to denominational theological disagreements—there was almost no source of conflict in American society that did not bubble over into street violence. In the 1830s, thoughtful Americans like Andrew Jackson and Abraham Lincoln began wondering aloud if the young republic could survive "the spirit of mob law," and the "disregard for law which pervades the country."[33]

By the end of the 1850s, most American citizens—especially business leaders and property owners—were tired of paying the property damage bills and had had enough. The business leaders of St. Louis were the first to take the initiative and raised up a volunteer vigilante force in 1854 to try to prevent election-day rioting. The next year, they made the force permanent and created the first modern-style, standing police force in a major American city—and then Baltimore, Philadelphia, New York, Boston, Cincinnati, and other cities followed suit across the country, with 57 of America's largest cities developing police departments between 1850 and 1880.[34]

But the creation of these new forces came with great challenges, first, because policing was an utterly new institution. What most American and European cities had prior to the "new policing" of the mid-1800s was basically unchanged from the medieval era—a system of volunteer, rotating constables or a sheriff who would, upon a complaint, apprehend an offender for a fee, combined with a neighborhood night watchman who, if not drunk or asleep, might react to a call for help. At the same time, America was going through a process of exploding industrialization and urbanization that was giving rise to large cities crowded with masses of vulnerable poor people, new immigrants, and migrants—as well as large-scale, complicated, and volatile social problems. Boston, New York, and Philadelphia grew from cities of less than 100,000 in the early 1800s to more than a million by 1890—and the percentage of Americans living in cities would explode from 5 percent to 45 percent by 1910.[35] The night-watchman and the militia were not going to get the job done.[36]

But most American cities, despite the growing crime and violence, did not eagerly embrace the new concept of a consolidated, full-time, uniformed, armed, and permanent police force in their midst. Americans (like their British counterparts) were famously suspicious of coercive state power. Indeed, once formed, the police force in most American cities became captured by the dominant political regime of the day, the jingoistic haters, and the corrupt moneyed interests of the city, quickly developing the dysfunctions vividly described in our opening quiz. They were untrained, abusive, brutal, and ineffectual—manifesting virtually all the symptoms of dysfunction that we associate with broken criminal justice systems in the developing world today.

In other countries, the story was somewhat different, but the end result of dysfunction was the same. In France, for instance, the foundations of policing were actually laid by the monarchy when Louis XIV created the office of Lieutenant-General of Police in 1667 with a broad portfolio of duties for addressing just about anything that was a source of disorder in Paris—lighting for dark streets, aid to beggars, food supplies, public health, *and* responding to crime in a growing city.[37] On the one hand, the establishment of a centralized government office for addressing urban crime (nearly two hundred years before the Americans or British) produced pioneering innovations in policing (e.g., deterrent patrols, the police station, surveillance methods and tools).[38] But it also became associated with the heavy-handed rule of the *ancien régime* and was substantially dismantled by the forces of liberty that blew through Paris with the French Revolution of 1789.[39] Famously, Napoleon the Emperor would reassert the mandate and machinery of centralized "high policing" in Paris and throughout France, which would lead to a form of policing in the late nineteenth century that was very useful for regime survival and protecting the "respectable classes" but not much use (and frequently the source of much harm) for the teeming masses of urban poor.[40]

As we saw earlier, a completely different story emerged in Japan, where a window of radical modernization opened up in the 1870s with a fresh opportunity to fashion a form of policing to replace the harsh medieval rule of the *samurai*. A new police system was designed in 1874, on the advice of a small group of officials who had spent several months in Europe observing modern practices there.[41] The reforming Meiji-era leaders looked to the highly centralized French model, inspired by its wide-ranging administrative functions and strong surveillance role—both appealing to a paternalistic government with an overriding concern with order. By 1890, the force had evolved toward a Prussian model featuring a large number of police boxes (*koban*) distributed throughout society under central supervision.[42] Staff numbers had skyrocketed, and training schools, standardized codes, and professional associations had developed.[43] By the end of the Russo-Japanese war (1904–1905), a centralized and professional police force operated in Japan.[44] Like the police force of mid-nineteenth-century France, however, much of this modernized police power in Japan was exerted in the maintenance of order and regime stability to the advantage of the elite classes and at the expense of marginalized groups in Japanese society. In fact, by the 1930s, the Japanese police force would be utterly captured by the centralizing, imperial military dictatorship and would become a force of brutal, totalitarian repression.

But the Japanese, French, and American stories of criminal justice over the past hundred years were not left forever mired in debilitating corruption, political repression, and chronic violence against the poor and marginalized. Rather, each eventually developed criminal justice systems that provided their common citizens with a reasonable degree of protection from violence and abuse—and a reasonable degree of security in their person and property sufficient to allow even the poor a substantial opportunity to improve their lot. Again, there is nothing perfect about the criminal justice systems in these countries, and each has its own dysfunctions and abuses. But that is not the point. The point is, criminal justice systems can change from very bad to pretty darn good—in fact, so good that poor people living in the violent chaos of the developing world today would be quite grateful to receive such service.

So how did this transformation come about?

Perhaps the only thing we know for sure is that there is no uniform answer to this question. The story of transformation in each context is itself a massively complex combination of historical factors, unique social conditions, institutional dynamics, intervening events, cultural responses, intentional efforts, and unintended consequences. A silver bullet solution from history is unlikely to emerge as the answer for transforming criminal justice systems in the immensely diverse and complicated contexts of the developing world today.

But all of the stories say it's *possible*. It is possible for a law enforcement system to start out backwards, broken, and dangerous for poor people, and yet be transformed by intentional effort into one that provides common citizens with the basic protections and dignity they need. By analogy, I may be struggling to work my way up a mountain path to the summit and losing faith that I am on the right path, that there actually is a path to the summit, or that such a path is accessible for humans—but all those doubts are forced into re-orientation when I meet other hikers coming back down the trail *from the summit*. They confirm that it is possible to reach the summit, that there are pathways, and that those pathways do work for some. It still doesn't necessarily mean it's possible for me, and it is no guarantee of ease—but I am motivated to look harder for a path and to stick to the pursuit.

Likewise, when we consider the brokenness of criminal justice systems in otherwise stable developing countries like Kenya, Guatemala, India, the Philippines, Cambodia, Indonesia, Zambia, Peru, or Ethiopia—and place them in the light of history—the challenges and barriers to transformation seem less extraordinary or overwhelming. In fact, they seem to fit right into the predictable set of challenges that face a society forging its own path to make increasing opportunity, prosperity, and freedom accessible for larger and larger proportions of its people.

COMMON THEMES

Indeed, perhaps it is time to recover the story of how these pathways were carved out in other contexts in history to see what useful lessons, insights, or cautions might be gathered from the past. Over the last decade, out of our study of the historical record and interface with the daily, hands-on struggle for functioning criminal justice systems in the developing world several encouraging—and cautionary—themes have emerged.

Each movement of criminal justice reform required local ownership and leadership of a very intentional effort to transform the justice system

Here is a hard truth from history. Criminal justice systems do not naturally evolve by their own dynamics toward fairness, accountability, effectiveness, and broad public service, because there are always powerful people, interests, and institutions that don't want that to happen—and they are willing to work very hard to make sure it doesn't. This makes the struggle for functioning criminal justice systems different from other struggles to empower the poor in the developing world—requiring an extraordinary level of intentionality and costly commitment. Generally, there are not a lot of powerful people in the developing world waking up every day to try and make sure that the health system does not work for poor people—or working hard to make sure the food system, or the sanitation system, or the education system fails for the poorest. In fact, there are generally professional and cultural dynamics at play in these other public systems that drive them forward to be better and more effective. Such systems are hard enough to make work on their own—but how much harder would it be if there were people who were highly motivated to work every day to make poor people sicker, or to undermine their education, or to contaminate their water? Thankfully, this is generally not the case.

By contrast, in every society there are people, interests, and institutions that are intentionally trying to make the justice system fail and to make poor people and marginalized groups weaker and more vulnerable to violence. They are seeking to advance their personal, economic, political, and exploitive interests through violence and fear—and they are threatened by a functioning criminal justice system that would restrain their coercive power. And so they will vigorously oppose reform. In nineteenth-century America, political bosses, police, plantation owners, sex traffickers, industrialists, tenement owners, racists, misogynists, criminal gangs, and racketeers who were seeking to advance their interests with violence vigorously opposed Progressive Era reforms that sought to build justice systems that were politically independent, professional, free of corruption, and accountable to the common people.

Wresting the criminal justice systems from the corrupt and moneyed interest, therefore, required an extremely vigorous fight that was very intentional, strategic, and costly—and took many years, sometimes decades. Such a difficult fight over a long period of time had to be locally owned—that is to say, New York, Seattle, and Cincinnati changed because there was a critical mass of local citizens and leaders who were willing to lead and sustain the struggle in their city—against the forces *in their city* who opposed a functioning public justice system. Forces outside the community also played a role (as we will discuss in a few pages)—but such a difficult and protracted fight was successfully carried out only with the commitment of local leaders and community members who had as much invested in the outcome as the opposing forces did.

Likewise, struggles to build functioning justice systems in the developing world are likely to succeed only where there are local leaders and community forces willing to carry the fight on a very committed, costly, sustained, and sacrificial basis. This prioritizes the identification, support, encouragement, and strengthening of local leaders and community forces that manifest a vested interest and passionate commitment to what is, at its core, a *fight* against vigorous opposing forces of corruption, lawlessness, and violence. Because the struggle for re-engineering the plumbing of public justice systems is almost entirely off the world's radar screen (even among those passionate about global poverty), the struggles and needs of such local leaders and community forces tend to be unknown, unsupported, under-resourced, and undefended. This will need to change.

Each public justice system had its own particular problems, symptoms of dysfunction, and obstacles to reform that required highly contextualized solutions

Even a cursory review of the struggle to build functioning criminal justice systems out of context of abuse and chaos in cities around the world exposes the unique set of challenges and strengths in each context. New York and Chicago dealt with systematic venality and corruption among the police in a way that the legacy of *samurai* ethics in Tokyo did not.[45] On the other hand, the Tokyo law enforcement system had to deal with a tradition of policing "dangerous thought" and a military dictatorship that was unimaginable in New York or Chicago. Paris policing struggled with the legacy of Napoleonic centralization of authority in a way that Seattle or Texas did not—but neither did French policing (at the time) share the struggle that American law enforcement did with racism and despised minority communities. Criminal justice systems in most American cities had to overcome the way the police tended to become tools of local party politics in a way that police in London did not.

Criminal justice systems were corrupted, distorted, or rendered ineffectual for different reasons—and they did not all fight the same kinds of enemies or make use of the same remedies. There are certainly interesting commonalities that were occasionally shared—and there is much evidence that reform was accelerated (in some cases greatly accelerated) by the sharing of information, lessons learned, and best practices across the various cities (even internationally). Nevertheless, each city and country required a unique diagnosis of its problem and a tailor-made set of solutions—which also uniquely changed with each city's circumstances over time.

Likewise, the struggle to build functioning public justice systems in the developing world will require not only localized ownership and leadership, but also a localized diagnosis of the problem and exploration of solutions. There will be accelerations of the struggle that come from shared insights, awareness, momentum, innovations, technologies, and resources, but history (and current experience) does not suggest that we should be looking for massive, one-size-fits-all, magically replicable and scalable remedies that sweep out corruption, dysfunction, and abuse from developing world justice systems in one fell swoop. Meaningful transformation is not likely to come from the miracle vaccine, the new high-yield seed, the mass production of water-pumps or treated bed nets, or effective awareness campaigns. It is going to come from support of a local movement that is rigorously tracking the precise reason why its particular justice system is failing the poor, and developing targeted efforts to address both what is broken and the unique set of forces that prevent it from getting fixed.

Committed community leaders and reform-minded elites played a critical role

It is striking to observe the very significant role that exceptional leaders played in the struggles for criminal justice reform around the world in the nineteenth and early twentieth centuries. Even discounting for the way we tend to tell stories from history in a way that exaggerates the pivotal influence of individual (and interesting) leaders, one is struck by the difference that brave, innovative, passionate, clear-thinking leaders made in the transformation of corrupt, broken, and abusive justice systems.

These movements of reform were frequently given critical initial momentum from extraordinary journalists, preachers, reformers, academics, investigators, lawyers, politicians, and rabble-rousers who suddenly flipped on the lights to expose what had been hiding in the shadows. In almost every case, they took the truth that everybody knew (about corruption, incompetence, and abuse), and they made it a truth that no one could ignore.

Over time, a pattern emerged around the turn of the century in which a vocal journalist, preacher, or civic leader (from groups with names like Citizens' Municipal League, the Allied Reform League, or the Law and Order Society) would get the ball rolling through dramatic exposure of a scandalous event (like Reverend Charles Parkhurst exposing the blatant corruption of Tammany Hall and the New York City Police by personal investigation, or the journalist Lincoln Steffens uncovering police complicity in Philadelphia's voter fraud). Or a shocking riot, mob action, or public theft would seize the public's attention.[46] Then a special commission or investigation would be authorized and a detailed study of the underlying corruption, graft, violence, and abuse would lay bare the egregious nature of the specific abuses and their perpetrators with such clarity that it would create immense popular pressure for reform.

This cycle of scandal, exposé, and calls for reform from religious leaders and upper- and middle-class business people came to replicate itself across cities of the United States as police reform rolled along with the broader reform movement of the Progressive Era.[47]

Interestingly, in the U.S. context, the initial waves of police reform were substantially the passion of elites and middle class leaders rather than the focus of the working class and poor citizens. As American cities became dominated by partisan political machines that substantially drew their support from the impoverished masses of new immigrants, the urban working class, and uprooted underclass, in most cities, the police force would become a corrupt and abusive tool of these partisan political forces. Accordingly, calls for reform of the police (and wresting it from the political control of the working-class party bosses) came from the opposing political forces (usually Republicans), business elites (who found the politicized police unreliable), and middle-class and elite progressive or moral reformers.[48]

Over time, calls for police reform also came from the brand-new class of police "professionals"—a set of police chiefs (mostly) who began to emerge with an agenda for professionalizing the service of policing, bringing to bear the era's new ideas of managerial excellence, police "science," bureaucratic efficiency, civil service reform, and autonomy from politics.[49] Leaders included Major Richard Sylvester (founder of the International Association of Chiefs of Police), August Vollmer (police chief from

Berkeley, California, who helped establish the academic discipline of criminal justice), and Louis Lepin in Paris (who modernized the French police and pioneered forensic science, criminology, finger-printing, and the study of criminal psychology).

Business leaders also played a very significant role in the reform story and ended up bankrolling most of the significant investigative commissions that exposed abuses (the Lexow Commission that led to Theodore Roosevelt's tenure as commissioner of police in New York, the Cleveland Study headed up by the eminent jurists Felix Frankfurter and Roscoe Pound, the Page Commission that revolutionized the New York courts, etc.), the political movements to support reform, and the study and pursuit of modern, professional, and rationalized police services. Volunteer organizations of the era (or what we would call not-for-profits today) also assisted in the development and funding of specialized police units (for women and juveniles, for example) which later became permanent fixtures of almost all police departments in the modern era.

It's difficult to draw clear lessons about the role of leaders and elites in these stories from the past when contemplating the struggle for criminal justice reform in the developing world today, but we would note some commonalities throughout stories of successful historical reform that can guide us today.

Journalists, media leaders and outlets, advocacy organizations, community leaders, and thought leaders in the developing world have an indispensable role in exposing (with great specificity, accuracy, and vividness) the raw story of public justice corruption and dysfunction in their nation and community. Especially important are the voices of indigenous leaders already *within* the criminal justice systems, who have an opportunity to rise up and be catalysts and drivers of change. They bring to bear professional credibility, official standing, and positional authority to articulate what is broken from the inside, to seek reforms, to experiment with new programs, to support (and protect) voices of change, and to work for the transformation of the organizational culture and practices from within the existing systems. Private enterprise and the business community in these contexts have an historic and conspicuous opportunity to make a choice: Do they continue to undermine the public justice systems by investing in purely privatized solutions to the problems of violence, instability, and crime? Or do they play the critical role they have played in other eras by making the integrity and effectiveness of the *public* justice system a foundational priority in emerging market countries?

External contributions can also have powerful influence on the direction and pace of change. This truth manifests itself throughout the reformation history, from the powerful influence that the British reforms of 1829 had on New York and other U.S. cities, to the impact of French and Prussian policing models on Japan in the late nineteenth century, and the catalytic power of the U.S. occupation authorities in the re-engineering of the Japanese police service after World War II.

This suggests that there are robust opportunities for many external and international actors to find an appropriate place for supporting and encouraging local struggles for criminal justice transformation in the developing world.

Effective criminal justice systems improved the working conditions of the people working in the system

Effective efforts to transform criminal justice systems in the past focused not only on the way those systems mistreated, neglected, humiliated, and failed the common public—but also on the way those systems similarly mistreated the people *working in* those systems. Reformers addressed themselves to the needs of the police officers, lawyers, judges, social workers, and supporting personnel who were responsible for delivering public justice services.

As we have seen, the people working in the public justice systems in the developing world are generally very poorly paid, overworked, ill-trained, poorly managed, under-resourced, forced to serve the whims and arbitrary demands of dysfunctional leaders, and trained in cultures of abuse, gratuitous rudeness, violence, and theft. History suggests that little meaningful improvement in the *external* performance of a criminal justice system will come without addressing these issues of *internal* performance toward its own personnel.

Successful reformers in the past frequently began by 1) reducing the unmanageable working hours and array of unfocused duties, 2) providing a living wage, improved benefits, and assistance to widows and children of police, and 3) providing everyone in the justice "pipeline" with professional education and training that matched the demands of their work in a way that allowed them to serve the public effectively and gain respect from the community. Groundbreaking work recently done by MIT's Abdul Latif Jameel Poverty Action Lab with the Rajasthan police in India provides provocative evidence of the way improvements in the training and treatment of police officers may translate into improvements in the way the public feels served by the police.[50]

The priority goal of effective transformation efforts was a criminal justice system that prevented violence and crime and built trust with the public

Meaningful reforms of dysfunctional criminal justice systems were given energy, focus, and force by aiming at two goals that mattered to the customer public: 1) improved *prevention* of crime, and 2) improved relations of *trust* with the public. The earliest days of reform rose out of a yearning from the community that the authorities would not just come to their aid in a moment of peril (like the night watchman) or have their abuser brought to justice (like the sheriff or constable would do for a fee), but that a new law enforcement system would actually proactively *prevent* crime, rather than simply react to it.[51]

Over time, reformers found that effective crime prevention was being undercut by corruption, dysfunction, abuse, poor training, and a lack of resources, so they were forced to deal with these symptoms of brokenness as well. Moreover, the goal of prevention opened up discussion of all the complex causes of crime and all the complex interventions (beyond mere investigation, apprehension and punishment) that might reduce crime as well. These reformers began to examine interventions and strategies that prevent vulnerable individuals from being drawn into a life of crime—to "go upstream" to the source of crime—as the "father of modern policing," August Vollmer, emphasized as far back as 1918. Out of this line of thinking, innovations such as parole, probation, juvenile courts, women's police, and children's bureaus were born.

While many of these "rehabilitative" themes would be eventually overshadowed by a focus on "crime-fighting" techniques in American law enforcement—the notion of going upstream to the source of crime in the community would re-emerge in the themes of "community policing" and "problem solving" of the 1980s and would be counted among the most advanced approaches to effective policing.

Likewise, it would seem that criminal justice reform efforts in the developing world would do well to focus on all the possible strategies, programs, and approaches (whatever they may be) that seem most effective in 1) actually preventing violent crime in poor communities, and 2) increasing the trust and confidence of those who must depend on the system—two outcomes that are likely to be mutually reinforcing.

Building an effective, professional, well-resourced law enforcement capacity was risky

The earliest proponents of police modernization encountered strong opposition from those who well appreciated the dangers of powerful and effective law enforcement systems. Indeed, history would bear out the seriousness of these dangers. As we have seen, almost immediately upon their establishment, police forces in the United States became captive to local political parties and racketeering networks. Local American police became the abusive muscle of corruption, graft, election fraud, extortion, racist terrorism, illicit criminal enterprises, and the violent suppression of the labor movement. World class innovations and advances in law enforcement professionalization of the Federal Bureau of Investigation were misused for inappropriate political purposes and to intimidate dissent. Likewise, Napoleon's centralized police in Paris helped restore civil order following the chaos of the French Revolution but then became the instrument for violently repressing political dissent, social unrest, and the underclass throughout much of the rest of the nineteenth century. The modernized police of the Meiji era in Japan became the instruments of brutal political and social repression under the imperial military dictatorship that emerged in the 1920s.[52]

Moreover, the elitist roots of much criminal justice reform in America also brought with it a "jingoistic militarism, the soaring and self-righteous idealism, an implicit but deeply rooted contempt for the mass of humanity"[53] that ended up impeding its effectiveness in achieving and retaining its own goals, and eventually produced a police culture in the United States that by the 1960s was dangerously isolated from external feedback loops and not able to deftly adapt to significant social change.[54]

With eyes wide open to all of these dangers, however, what the best leaders seemed to appreciate was that while *bad* law enforcement systems were dangerous, the absence of such indispensable systems (or the provision of such protection on a privatized basis) was even more perilous. And so they made it their responsibility to build *good* systems, to fight continuously to ensure that the systems served their intended public function, and to vigilantly defend those systems against the *natural* dysfunctions that always stood ready to consume them.

Transformation of a public criminal justice system can happen faster than expected—but usually in punctuated bursts, and frequently with two steps forward and one step back

Through the longer lens of history, it is quite remarkable how quickly some of these transformations of criminal justice systems occurred. It's hard to imagine now, but in the beginning of the 1800s, contemporary observers in London credibly described the city as "practically at the mercy of bands of thieves and marauders, which the existing guardians of the peace were utterly unequal to cope with." London was a place "[o]n the whole.... passing through an epoch of criminality darker than any other in her annals."[55] In response to these conditions, Robert Peel instituted his new police in 1829, and while it still took many years before the new police gained the trust and confidence of the people, and riots continued to plague England for the next several decades, contemporaries noted the surprisingly swift success of the London Metropolitan Police. One author said, "The immediate result of the institution of an effective police force, whose main object was prevention, was precisely that which was to be expected: convictions for crimes of violence decreased, because evil-disposed persons knew that they could no longer commit them with impunity."[56] In 1903, one author investigating the current state of the police concluded that Londoners received "a protection of life and property which [made] London one of the safest cities in the world."[57]

Cincinnati, Ohio would be another experiment in criminal justice reform that would exceed anyone's fair expectations. A voter fraud scandal in 1885 gave rise to the nonpartisan Committee of One Hundred to clean up the city, but the corrupt police refused to arrest the corrupt officials who the Committee identified. Outraged, the highly motivated Committee appealed to the state legislature to place the Cincinnati police under a Board of Commissioners appointed by the governor (not the local political bosses). Duly appointed, the Board proceeded to dismiss 80 percent of the police force and install a new police chief who pursued aggressive reforms, including public inspection of the police force, requirements for physical fitness, military drill discipline, a three-platoon system, American's first police school of instruction (with significant sustained training and instruction), and a probationary period for new recruits to test out their mental and physical fitness for duty. As a result of these reforms, the Cincinnati police force was, in a very short time, vaulted decades ahead of its counterparts in other American cities.

Such quick and relatively effective reform, however, was relatively rare. The more common pattern of reform looked like this: great frustration in the face of resilient forces of corruption, politics and racketeering, followed by hard-fought breakthroughs achieved through a coalition of forces (business leaders, civic leaders, political leaders, and police professionals) that usually sponsored an investigative body, an oversight body, and police leaders with a passion for professionalization. This typically transpired over a decade or two of frustration, a handful of years of accelerated reform, followed by setbacks and deterioration, followed by renewed struggle, setbacks, and then advancement once again. All the while, the bar of expectation and performance was advancing forward to a point where the community, while not fully satisfied, lost virtually all memory of the chaos, corruption, abuse, and dysfunction that once plagued their neighborhoods.

The revolution of expectations that occurred over the decades was reflected in the famous Cleveland Survey, which reviewed the status of that city's police force in 1922. The report concluded by saying: "A general picture of the police service in Cleveland gives the impression of a group of men, singularly free from scandal and vicious corruption, but working in a rut, without intelligence or constructive policy, on an unimaginative, perfunctory routine."[58] As Walker emphasizes, "It was no longer sufficient that the police were not doing something blatantly wrong; they were now expected to take an imaginative and innovative approach to crime control."[59]

What a tremendous revolution it would be if it could be said of the police in a large city in the developing world that they are "singularly free from scandal and vicious corruption" but simply in an unimaginative "rut" about creative crime control. In 1930 August Vollmer could say: "In no other branch of government have such remarkable changes been made as those made in the field of police organization and administration during the last quarter of a century...One can hardly believe that such great advances could be made is so short a time."[60] Again, what a tremendous gift it would be to the people in the developing world's poorest communities if the next quarter century were likewise characterized by "such great advances" in the systems that are supposed to protect them from the terror of violence.

DEMONSTRATION PROJECTS
OF HOPE

We have come to see with some urgency that criminal justice systems are indispensable for the poor, and we know from history that it's possible to build them. But we also know that building them is difficult, costly, dangerous, and unlikely. What we need, therefore, are bold projects of hope: projects of transformation that bring real change, that teach us, and that inspire hope—because the vulnerable poor need all three.

The problem of broken criminal justice systems in the developing world is too massive and deep to address everywhere at once. Moreover, we don't even know exactly what to do. So wisdom suggests that we pick some places in the world where we can pursue targeted, experimental projects that relentlessly push through in transforming a targeted dysfunctional justice system into one that actually protects the poor from violence. From these projects we learn what we didn't previously know about the problem, and what seems to help and what does not. And from these projects, we inspire hope, and address this era's deepest barrier to change—the fundamental despair that law enforcement in the developing world can never change to actually protect the poor from violence.

There are already a number of these projects going forward in the world, and each looks different, ranging from governments and NGOs at work in Brazil, the Democratic Republic of the Congo, Sierra Leone and Cambodia, to an International Justice Mission project with community groups and government agencies in the Philippines. Each of these projects in the developing world is producing authentic and surprising change in the criminal justice system's capacity to protect the poor from violence. Each is producing edifying lessons worthy of global attention. And each is working in its own way to dispel the myth that criminal justice systems cannot be made to work for the poor.

INTERNATIONAL JUSTICE MISSION AND PROJECTS OF STRUCTURAL TRANSFORMATION

By way of background, IJM began with me and a few friends in 1997 as a very modest effort to replicate the early Amnesty International model of providing direct advocacy on behalf of individual victims of human rights abuse, and to do so through local, indigenous teams in the developing world. While Amnesty began its work focusing on prisoners of conscience from all around the world, we began by focusing on victims of everyday violent abuse in poor communities in the developing world—common poor people who were being held in slavery, sexually assaulted, thrown off their land, abused by the police, or illegally detained. To make the services meaningful and sustainable, we sought to build teams of local lawyers, investigators, social workers, and community activists who would, on a full-time basis, take on individual cases of injustice and work with local authorities to: 1) rescue victims from the hand of abuse, 2) bring the criminals to justice, and 3) restore survivors to safety and strength through the provision of meaningful aftercare services.

Like Amnesty International's founder, Peter Benenson, my friends and I personally came to the human rights struggle out of a Christian conscience. Because our own Christian communities were largely disengaged from the human rights struggles of the era, we had a particular passion for helping them move into active service on behalf of human rights victims. While we find strength for difficult work in our shared faith and we continue our special outreach to the Christian community in challenging them to support the cause of human rights, our local IJM teams in the developing world have been providing direct services for more than 15 years to thousands of human rights abuse victims of any, all, and no faith and in partnership with community groups, government agencies, NGOs, and civil society groups that may not share anything of our faith but share a common commitment to protecting the poor from violence.

IJM now has nearly twenty field offices in Africa, Latin America, South Asia, and Southeast Asia supported by a headquarters in Washington, DC and partner offices in Canada, the UK, the Netherlands, Germany, and Australia. After spending more than a decade walking thousands of individual cases through the brokenness of criminal justice systems in the developing world, IJM's local teams are now working to leverage their experience to construct a clear picture of the precise points where that system fails to protect the poorest in their communities from violence. They then seek to use this unique knowledge to catalyze local coalitions to fix what is broken in the criminal justice system so it can protect vulnerable populations from being abused in the first place. We call this process of change Structural Transformation.

For example, in the Philippines, our local team of Filipino lawyers, investigators, and social workers have been working for years with local authorities to rescue impoverished children from sex trafficking, to bring individual perpetrators to justice, and to walk with these child survivors through the long journey to recovery and restoration. Building on years of experience in the trenches, we wanted to see if we could actually stop the violence before it began. We wanted to see if our local Filipino team with international assistance could catalyze a coalition of forces in the community to actually transform the corrupt and ineffective local law enforcement system so that the police, prosecutors, courts, and social services would work effectively to protect poor children from sex trafficking in the first place. We wanted to see if the dysfunctional local law enforcement system could be transformed to actually enforce the law—and, crucially, if they did so, to find out: *would this deter would-be traffickers and actually reduce the number of poor children victimized in the sex trade?* Finally, we wanted to see if this reduction in victimization could be objectively and quantitatively measured—by outside auditors.

This would be—to the best of our knowledge—the first attempt in the history of the world to objectively measure whether a project improving law enforcement in a developing world city could produce a demonstrable reduction in the number of children victimized in the commercial sex trade throughout the targeted city. If successful, such a project would provide powerful evidence of two things: 1) that it is possible to meaningfully change a dysfunctional justice system in the developing world, and 2) that a transformed justice system can contribute to a meaningful reduction in the violent abuse afflicting poor people.

As we've said, we knew that transforming a dysfunctional criminal justice system would be difficult, costly, dangerous, and unlikely; but as with so many other ground-breaking innovations in service to the global poor in this era, it was the Bill and Melinda Gates Foundation that was willing to help underwrite the experiment. In 2006, IJM was given resources from the Gates Foundation to build a Filipino team and start the project from scratch in a brand new city—in Cebu City, the nation's second largest metropolitan area. They were given a four-year timeframe to do two things: 1) to transform the performance of local law enforcement in fighting the sex trafficking of minors, and 2) to demonstrate to outside auditors a measurable 20-percent reduction in the availability of children in the commercial sex trade.

When the four years were up—we were stunned. The team had exceeded all expectations. They increased local law enforcement's rescue of sex trafficking victims by about 1,000 percent (bringing release to more than 250 confirmed trafficking victims) and they secured criminal charges against more than 100 suspected sex traffickers, with prosecutions ongoing at a highly successful rate. Most importantly to the project's unique purpose, at the end of the four-year time frame, the outside auditors documented a stunning 79 percent reduction in the availability of children in the commercial sex trade—an impact nearly four times larger than the stretch goal they had been given. As Leila de Lima, secretary of the Philippine Department of Justice, observed, "The cooperation of the government and International Justice Mission exemplify a new model of law enforcement, where government and civil society work as puissant allies not only to punish the perpetrators of trafficking but also to empower their victims."

Their story is worth looking at more closely for several reasons: first, as an example of how NGOs can directly partner with government authorities to not just respond to violent abuse on a case by case basis, but to actually transform what's broken in the criminal justice system so the violence stops before it starts; second, as an early but tangible demonstration project that can serve as a helpful starting point to explore improved projects in the future; and third, as an example of the hope such projects offer for driving innovation, dispelling unhelpful myths, and constantly improving a methodology.

"Something Big Was Building"

The first person hired for the new project was Sam Inocencio, a local Filipino lawyer from IJM's office in Manila, who agreed to go to Cebu and lead the project's legal team. In 2007, Sam uprooted himself and his new bride to move to a brand-new city, to start the project from scratch, and to help assemble a whole new team to take on an ugly problem of violence, corruption, and despair. Of those early days, Sam recalls, "There were obstacles—but there was a great sense of possibility, a sense that something big was building, and a hope that something could be different for the Philippines."

It was that hope that gave Sam and the team the audacity to attack such a massive issue by starting with a bite-sized piece of the problem: one metro area (Cebu City has about 2 million people, 40 percent of whom are in poverty[1]) and one category of violent abuse (the commercial sexual exploitation of children). This was the targeted project that came to be called Project Lantern—after the lanterns that were once used on the Underground Railroad to show the way to freedom.

To show change, one needs a baseline against which to measure progress, but drawing such a baseline level of crime and proving that the law enforcement actions worked to reduce it is extremely difficult and complex. The best that social scientists can do is derive the clearest indicators and evidence of prevalence and attribution possible, open these findings up to scrutiny, and continually improve them. Precisely because such matters are so complex and require high levels of expertise, the Gates Foundation grant provided funding to retain an external consulting firm of social scientists (Crime & Justice Analysts) to conduct a baseline study of the level of commercial sexual exploitation of children in Cebu, and then to retain a second set of experts to conduct an evaluation of the baseline and any reported change against that baseline. Finally, a third level of consultations with experts and stakeholders were convened at the completion of the evaluation of the project to seek additional analysis, evaluation, and lessons learned.*

* At this point in our story, two reading audiences are likely to emerge and radically diverge; those of you for whom the appearance of the words "prevalence" and "attribution" have finally begun to make the book interesting and those of you for whom the appearance of precisely those same words suggest that it is time to set the book aside. In the hope of satisfying both, we have made the detailed baseline study and follow-up surveys by Crime & Justice Analysts, as well as the 122-page expert evaluation of the baseline study and larger project, available online at www.ijm.org/projectlantern. The point we wish to make here is that our Structural Transformation projects rigorously seek to *demonstrate change* (first through expert baselines and then monitoring and evaluation) because we cannot be satisfied that we have *achieved change* unless we have done our best to *demonstrate* that change to ourselves and to others.

With the outside auditors having drawn the baseline, Sam and his team knew that they could only hope to lower that line by catalyzing a coalition of forces in Cebu to take on this mission of transformation together. Consequently, Project Lantern began with a survey of the multiple stakeholders that would play a variety of roles in improving law enforcement performance and reducing the vulnerability of Cebu's children to sex trafficking:

- *Victims and people vulnerable* to violent crime are at the center of all of IJM's Structural Transformation projects. The ultimate question is: How well does the system serve them in rescuing them from violent abuse, treating them appropriately, bringing their perpetrators to justice, and ensuring protection through the creation and deepening of a deterrent effect?
- *Public justice system actors* are likely to be the prime partners and tangible input recipients of Structural Transformation projects, so they can bolster the functional capacity, increase the skills, and influence the attitudes and behaviors of their staff.
- *Local[†] political actors and duty-bearers* control or influence the criminal justice system through policies and resource decisions that affect the functionality, focus, capacity, operational work, public perception, and ultimate impact of the criminal justice system.
- *Local socio-cultural actors* (e.g., civil society organizations, media, business leaders, religious leaders, thought leaders, and celebrities) have an impact on the priorities and actions of political actors and duty-bearers and can motivate the wider public to demand improvements to the criminal justice system.
- *International actors* (e.g., foreign donor governments, multilateral agencies, regional bodies, etc.) influence the priorities and actions of political actors and duty-bearers and can form direct partnerships to work with the criminal justice system.

Working Cases

With a constant eye toward catalyzing and leveraging larger partnership for the struggle, Sam and the Cebu team entered into the core methodology of a Structural Transformation project—what we refer to as "Collaborative

[†] Local actors can be at national, regional, or grassroots levels.

Casework" with local authorities and stakeholders. This is perhaps the most distinctive aspect of International Justice Mission's approach. We have found that working a critical mass of *individual cases* of violent abuse with the criminal justice authorities (from beginning to end, over several years, with *specific* victims and perpetrators) is the most effective way to accurately diagnose what is broken in the criminal justice "pipeline" and precisely understand how the victims and perpetrators actually experience this system. It's how we get to know the people working in the criminal justice system (their motivations, strengths, weaknesses, perspectives, attitudes, anxieties, ambitions, relationships, etc.) and earn relationships of trust with them that lead to transparency, authentic engagement, and meaningful training experiences. It also allows us to concretely identify partners in various spheres who are already working on the same or related problems. And, crucially, we've found that prevailing in even a modest number of individual cases helps prove that justice for the poor is possible, which ignites hope in the stakeholder environment that broader change might be possible.

Running cases through the system via Collaborative Casework is like filling a bicycle tube with air and running each section of the tube underwater when you think you have a puncture. Soon enough, what once was a vague hissing noise suddenly appears as an unmistakable torrent of bubbles shooting out through a very specific hole. Likewise, repeatedly accompanying impoverished victims of crime through the criminal justice system from beginning to end allows us to see where the system is leaking, obstructed, hurtful, and broken.

To help launch the process of Casework Collaboration in Cebu, Sam had several key colleagues on the team. Mae Sampani—the head of the Cebu Aftercare Team—was born in the Philippines but worked for many years as a social worker in Northern California. She originally got to know IJM and the brokenness of justice systems in the developing world when she volunteered to help train social workers serving sexual assault victims in Huánuco, Peru—where she was supporting José and Richard as they responded to Yuri's case and the epidemic of child sexual violence in that community. Mae later learned of IJM's need for an aftercare director, applied, and found herself returning to the very region in the Philippines where her own family was from.

Immediately Mae began working with Sam and the growing team to meet aftercare providers and other stakeholders in the area and to build a vision for what restoration services could look like for impoverished girls trafficked in

Cebu. If the project succeeded in bringing rescue to even a fraction of the children who were being sexually exploited in Cebu, there were going to be massive needs for quality, long-term aftercare to make those rescues meaningful.

Likewise, if the project was successful, then there was going to be a flood of prosecutions that would need to be fought through the local criminal courts. To help handle the caseload, Mae helped Sam recruit a winsome local litigator named Mark del Mundo—a young attorney, born and raised in Cebu, who was thriving at his firm but was hungry for more. And in taking on the child sex trafficking industry in Metro Cebu, Mark definitely got "more." With his IJM colleagues in Cebu, Mark would come to manage scores of prosecutions against violent and well-financed criminals, build an intense partnership with the local prosecutors, see first-hand (from the perspective of hundreds of clients victimized by sex trafficking) what was working in the justice system and what was not, and eventually, after death threats and tense encounters, require a 24/7 security detail. As Mark discovered in vivid fashion, sooner or later, the true nature of a Structural Transformation project becomes clear: It is a fundamental, life-or-death struggle for rule of law.

To kick-start the Collaborative Casework process, the IJM team in Cebu gathered detailed information on the commercial sex industry to identify where and how children were being exploited. Painfully, they found hundreds—and began to provide the local authorities with detailed information about where they were being kept, who was controlling them, and how. Sam, Mae, Mark, and the rest of the Cebu team then began to walk alongside the local authorities as they worked through each stage of each case—from rescue to prosecution and all the way to survivor restoration.

Over time, this Collaborative Casework with the authorities and other stakeholders performed its tedious magic. A diagnosis of priority breakdowns, dysfunctions, and failures in the system began to emerge in a way that made abundantly clear why sex traffickers in Cebu didn't fear going to jail—and why the child victims were afraid of everybody (their traffickers, the police, the social services, and anyone in "the system"). Through Collaborative Casework, here are some of the breakdowns they found in Cebu.

Commingling Suspects and Victims

At the police station after a rescue operation, the local police were placing the child victims and the accused traffickers and abusers *in the same tiny room* waiting for hours while the initial critical investigation was being conducted. The terrified trafficking victims would have no idea whether they were in trouble or getting help, could not get any rest, and would be intimidated, threatened, and harassed by the suspects. The unsurprising result of this practice was that victims would deny that they had been abused and would be too scared and confused to accept care.

Lack of Law Enforcement Resources, Training, or Mandate

The police lacked training—they didn't have a clear understanding of the anti-trafficking law, procedures, or criminal investigations techniques. The police had not been taught how to conduct an effective sting operation, and in case after case they showed they didn't know how to gather the evidence that really mattered for proving guilt. Because senior police leadership had never given them a clear mandate to conduct these risky anti-trafficking investigations, officers were afraid their superiors wouldn't back them up.

Prosecutors and Judges Don't Know the Law

In case after case, prosecutors would misunderstand or misstate the law in making decisions about the cases or in making arguments before the court. They would fail to apply key provisions of the law, like charging the suspect with child abuse (under which the suspect could be released on bail and would run away) rather than charging them with trafficking, under which bail is denied.

Aftercare Providers Unprepared, Untrained

The rescue operations prompted by Sam's team also forced a stress-test of Cebu's social work capacity to care for child trafficking survivors. Mae and her team quickly discovered gaping holes in the system of post-rescue care—and child survivors had almost no chance of thriving or acquiring the strength to go through the prosecution process.

Mae and her team found that social work providers in the Cebu region had almost no knowledge of or training on how to handle trafficking survivors. "They were actually quite afraid of accepting such difficult cases into shelters," Mae remembers. "So, the simplest thing to do was just to send the girls back home"—regardless of how unstable "home" was—or even if "home" was straight back to their traffickers.

Trafficking Not a Crime—or "Not Here in Cebu"

Sam and his team found that many authorities in Cebu didn't see sex trafficking as a crime or denied that it was a problem in their city. "Many senior police officials and stakeholders in Cebu thought sex trafficking was just a social issue—and not a violent crime," Sam explains. "They thought they should devote their resources to 'more important' crimes like drugs and homicide." Other public officials in Cebu simply responded with denial, and made unhelpful public statements that there were "zero trafficking victims" in their jurisdictions—or that there was no need for training.

Corruption

Inevitably Sam's team found that outright corruption was also obstructing enforcement of the law against child sex traffickers in Cebu. "The very people who needed to be champions to end it had become the reason that the problem was so entrenched," Sam remembers. In one key rescue operation with an elite police agency, 15 confirmed trafficking victims were rescued, and the powerful owner of a brothel was arrested with his managers. But at the stationhouse, officers let the owner slip out while the lower-level managers were being processed. Confronting the agency with this embarrassing example of corruption only made the working relationship difficult for IJM.

* * *

The purpose of running all this diagnostic casework through the criminal justice pipeline is not to gather material to publicly shame the leaders of the system; rather, it is to gain an accurate diagnosis of what is broken and to form a relationship of trust *so that* an NGO like IJM can be an authentic partner in finding practical solutions. Obviously, there will be leaders in the system who *do not want* to fix the problems—but then the diagnostic material is used by other leaders within the system who *do* want to fix the system to fight for change. This can be a longer process than the approach of the dramatic, damning exposé, but the truth is, it's simply naïve to believe that meaningful transformation of a dysfunctional criminal justice system can ever occur without champions taking up the fight from the inside.

Pivoting toward Hope and Real Solutions

With a clear diagnosis of the critical breakdowns in the criminal justice pipeline, Sam and the Cebu team began to catalyze a coalition of forces at the local, national, and international level to fix the problems alongside the local authorities in Cebu. As Mae recalled, "Our obstacle was really the lack of hope. People were stuck in a cycle of negativity. A lot of the solutions we discovered aren't revolutionary. They are simple approaches to fixing obvious gaps in the system. We don't need a rocket scientist to implement the solutions—we need someone who will just dream that it's possible to get the job done. It doesn't take a billion dollars. It just takes a few resources, and *a lot* of hope."

Mae and her team worked hard to unify the social service providers in Cebu with that hope, offering significant investments in education and training on victim-centered approaches to treatment. "We encouraged aftercare partners with different programs that have worked elsewhere in the world," Mae recalled. "Most of our partners were really hungry for information and skills—they wanted to learn. That has made a difference in slowly turning the ship around. We helped debunk a lot of myths."

With its partners in the aftercare community, IJM launched an Economic Self-Sufficiency and Re-Integration project to increase realistic and sustainable work opportunities for trafficking survivors and to enhance holistic re-integration support. Mae and IJM's partners saw survivors thrive through these programs, and today the program has been fully taken up by another local, non-profit organization that provides career-preparation services for survivors.

Mae and her team also worked with the local Department of Social Welfare and Development (DSWD) to establish a separate post-rescue processing center so that the victims would never have to be taken to the police station and could be safely separated from the perpetrators throughout the entire process (see figure 11.1). From this safe place—now called HerSpace—the compelling testimonies of violent abuse flowed freely and started sending traffickers to prison. "HerSpace has become a good model," Sam says, "because Mae and DSWD stuck with it and invested in it and poured a lot into it." The Philippines government is now replicating the HerSpace facility elsewhere in the country. As HerSpace was launched, Mark, Sam, and the other attorneys had also noticed that victim witnesses were placed in a very insecure situation during inquest and trial proceedings. So, taking the success of HerSpace as an inspiration, they worked with the prosecutor's offices to designate and renovate a secure area for other vulnerable witnesses at the courthouse. Today, public prosecutors conduct inquest proceedings in the new waiting room, and the government has fully taken over responsibility for the facility's upkeep and is upgrading it.

Figure 11.1   *Figure 11.2*

After being rescued, girls and young women experience their first days of freedom in the safety of the Cebu government's HerSpace Shelter

One of the most pivotal sources of hope came as the team saw proof that law enforcement *could* effectively deter would-be traffickers, restrain perpetrators, and rescue victims. As Sam and his team learned, you don't have to address police corruption everywhere all at once. The sex trafficker's protection payments to the street-level police become useless when there is a specialized unit that is vetted, well-trained, and well-managed to perform targeted anti-trafficking enforcement actions. Accordingly, Sam and his team signed a Memorandum of Understanding with the regional Philippine National Police leadership to establish, train, and support a new Regional Anti-Human Trafficking Task Force (or "RAT Force," as they call themselves). IJM provided intensive training, equipment, office space, and operational support and consultation; but the indispensable key to building trust and effectiveness came from months and months of *working cases together*—not from three days of training and buffets at the Sheraton, after which the experts all fly back home. The end result was a strong wave of enforcement actions that resulted in the rescue of large numbers of victims and saw scores of traffickers arrested, charged, and detained for successful prosecution.

To speed up the disposition of trafficking cases, Mark and the larger IJM team—along with the U.S. government—successfully lobbied the Office of the Supreme Court Administrator to require all judges in the Philippines to prioritize human trafficking prosecutions. As a result, courts have processed trafficking cases more efficiently and this has led to a major increase in convictions—61 in the two years following the Supreme Court order compared with 42 in the previous *seven* years. At the same time, the Cebu team worked closely with a coalition of forces in the community to advocate for the passage of local Anti-Trafficking in Persons Ordinances in all three of the jurisdictions that make up Metro Cebu.

Figure 11.3
Suspects await their trials in a small courtroom in Cebu, Philippines

To raise public awareness, the IJM team actively pursued responsible media coverage of anti-trafficking operations, trained local journalists on how to educate the public about the problem and how to tell these stories in ways that preserved the dignity of the survivors. Heightened awareness fed public demand for counter-trafficking action, and stories of trafficking convictions maximized the deterrent impact of law enforcement activity.

Over time, as case after case broke through the myths and denials, government officials began to change from being brick walls to being partners. "It took us lots of coaching and talking to our partners," Sam says, "but they don't treat it as an abstract social problem anymore. They prioritize it as a heinous, violent crime."

This bottom-up methodology of sustained Collaborative Casework builds relationships of trust with the full environment of service providers and stakeholders, and it produces a steady flow of small but meaningful breakthroughs that encourage hope—and in the end reach a tipping point of change. Indeed, there is an inflection point of transformation that is almost imperceptible when it happens—but it is the moment when local champions emerge to take the fight to its finish.

Shifting the Center of Gravity

The notion that all public authorities in the developing world are hopelessly corrupt, apathetic, and brutish is simply not true. Wherever we have seen success, it has been because of local authorities who acted with courage and competence. They are there, but they are frequently toiling away without the political support, training, and resources to experience success and to lead on their own. Once these leaders are empowered, violent crimes against the poor are no longer shunted aside as a low priority compared to "real" crimes like narcotics trafficking and terrorism—rather, they become categories of crime-fighting that get attention, special training, international resources, and professional regard. Eventually officers, prosecutors, and judges experience success, and people all along the criminal justice pipeline start to see what their job was supposed to look like (having never really seen it before), and many begin to take great initiative to learn and do their job well.

Over time, we have noticed a dynamic we call the 15-70-15 Rule. The rule has no real scientific precision, but it expresses the observation that, within criminal justice systems in the developing world, it seems that about 15 percent of the personnel wake up every day intent on using their coercive power and authority for purely predatory purposes. Another 15 percent wake up every day with an earnest intent to do good and to serve the public. The vast majority—the remaining 70 percent—are simply waiting to see which of these two factions is going to prevail in dominating the organizational culture and its system of rewards. As long as the brutal and corrupt 15 percent is prevailing, the rest of the 70 percent are going to go along and join in the dysfunction and abuse—because it will benefit them to do so and it would be risky to oppose the dominant ethos. In such a context, it then looks and feels as if 85 percent of the entire law enforcement force is aggressively and irredeemably committed to the ways of venality and violence.

In fact, the situation is actually much more dynamic than it may at first appear. Indeed, if it appears to the middle 70 percent that the virtuous 15 percent are going to prevail and control the culture and systems of rewards and punishments (job retention, promotion, benefits, assignments, discipline, termination, etc.), then they will, with surprising alacrity, begin to clean up their acts to stay out of trouble. And a system that once looked like it was 85 percent full of crooks and brutes can rather quickly look like it is made up of a critical mass of tolerably decent public servants. A virtuous circle can emerge in which the political will to support a reasonably functional criminal justice system develops and is strengthened 1) by cadres of progressive national leaders, 2) by a middle class that is sick of endemic corruption, and 3) by the competitive advantages that await developing economies with functional rule of law.

Reasonable Risks?

Many readers will be concerned that the enhanced capacities of the criminal justice system will actually be used to hurt citizens—or even to oppress or disadvantage the very poor communities they are supposed to be protecting.[2] Indeed, these risks are very real and need to be addressed, but a few preliminary observations might be helpful. First, we should remember that donor nations and multilateral institutions are already taking on huge risks to provide police aid in the developing world to protect *themselves* from terrorist violence and the narcotics trade, clean up the mess after wars in Iraq and Afghanistan, and enhance business and commercial security. Are we unwilling to manage the risks of police aid when the targeted beneficiaries of the police aid are simply common poor people? If reasonably functioning criminal justice systems are *indispensable* for poor people (as we believe they are), then the attendant risks provide a compelling reason to be thoughtful, rigorous, attentive, and prepared for managing and mitigating those risks, rather than a reason for abandoning the enterprise altogether. Unfortunately, the world's largest international development institution, the World Bank, has chosen not to rigorously engage programs to transform criminal justice systems in the developing world—*not* because it doesn't think such systems are indispensable for the poor, but because it has found the risks too high.[3] Again, these risks are real and suggest great caution—but the stakes are simply too great for billions of the world's poorest, and experts have articulated ways to proceed that are both thoughtful and responsible.[4]

Collaborative Casework provides an incremental and contextual way to assess and manage the risks of programs that strengthen police capacity. It allows donors to incrementally test the trustworthiness and integrity of the institutions and leaders it is supporting, and it builds a constituency of accountability among local, national, and international stakeholders.

In a Structural Transformation project, addressing the abuse of vulnerable people is always *the main objective* of the project—rather than the harm that is hopefully avoided when serving some other primary objective like counter-narcotics, terrorism, or commercial stability. This allows the project to build in activities and investments that mitigate the risk of law enforcement abuse of the poor or other "collateral" harm in an intentional way, and that don't feel like trade-offs from the primary objective. For instance, Sam and his team in Cebu built in specific activities and metrics that reduced the risks of police abuses against people collaterally affected by law enforcement actions in the commercial sex industry. These projects include activities that train and actively monitor the police on proper conduct toward vulnerable populations in the commercial sex trade, post-raid de-briefing and feedback sessions with advocacy groups working in the affected area, and even economic and employment assistance programs for people in the affected area of enforcement.

An International Role

The success in Cebu came from local ownership and leadership. But there was a second powerful force at play: international assistance. Because these external forces intended for good can actually cause harm, however, the wise approach emphasizes appropriate roles for external players, proceeding with incremental tests and innovations, and long-term investment in developing local leadership and sustainable local coalitions.

In Cebu, and in other Structural Transformation projects, external forces played a critical role in building on the momentum created by the local NGO team and partners through financial support; training, capacity building, and program assistance for local NGO staff, social service providers and law enforcement; bilateral and multilateral support for increasing local political will; and monitoring and evaluation services. As IJM's Filipino team and their local partners worked within Cebu, the U.S. government leveraged its annual Trafficking in Persons Report to encourage the further development of anti-trafficking initiatives nationwide, and the new U.S. ambassador to the Philippines, Harry K. Thomas, placed special emphasis on the issue. Other external forces, including the Australian and Canadian governments, the European Union, and the United Nations also worked to support the growing political will within the Philippines to seriously confront trafficking.

Indeed, in the coming era, development assistance from donor nations and institutions should be significantly linked to the willingness of authorities in the developing world to commit to the kind of transformation process that is possible (with donor country investments in capacity building) to make law enforcement work for the poor. One of the fundamental principles of donor aid, economic assistance, favorable trading status, and diplomatic partnership with developing countries should be a willingness on the part of partner countries to make concrete commitments to build criminal justice systems that bring effective law enforcement to the poor. In the absence of such commitments, much of our twenty-first-century efforts in the developing world are likely to run swirling down the same drain of lawless chaos they did in the last century.[5]

ADDITIONAL PROJECTS OF HOPE

My colleagues are certainly not alone in this work. Important projects of hope are bringing concrete change to criminal justice systems throughout the developing world, producing important lessons about protecting the poor from violence, and helping dispel the paralyzing myth that effective criminal justice is impossible for the poor.

MOBILE COURTS IN THE DRC

Around 7:00 P.M. on New Year's Day of 2011 more than a hundred Congolese army soldiers violently tore through the small village of Fizi, located in the eastern part of the Democratic Republic of the Congo (DRC). These soldiers were on a specific mission ordered by their commanding officer, Lieutenant Colonel Kibibi Mutuara: namely, to terrorize, rape, loot, and pillage the defenseless Fizi community in retaliation for the death of one of their fellow soldiers. Mass rape was carried out against girls and women, ranging in age from 16 to 60.[6] At least 50 women were reported as raped in the incident.[7]

In recent years, such atrocities had taken place with utter impunity in this region of the DRC. Victims had no place they could trust to turn for justice. To address the problem, a coalition of partners have come together to provide an innovative system of mobile courts which the local presiding judge says "has had an impact. Sexual violence is serious. This crime is committed less frequently because of the impact of this tribunal."[8] The mobile courts project was designed by the Open Society Justice Initiative (OSJI), funded by the Open Society Initiative for Southern Africa (OSISA), and implemented in late 2009 by The American Bar Association Rule of Law Initiative (ABA ROLI). It has produced encouraging results in one of the world's most difficult contexts.

Mobile courts are formal courts that travel to rural communities that lack formal or unbiased justice systems in order to provide a fair and rapid verdict. Operating within the Congolese justice system and utilizing national prosecutors, judges, magistrates, and other professionals, these courts are specifically designed by OSJI and OSISA to try gender crimes and organized attacks on groups, a capacity lacking in the existing justice system. In the DRC a mobile court will typically stay in a rural community for one to two months and hear as many cases as possible.

In the case of the Fizi raid, for example, a mobile court set up in this remote region allowed 49 rape victims to bravely testify about the raid. The testimony from the young girls and elderly women who survived the horrific violence was enough to secure convictions of Kibibi, three of his officers, and five additional soldiers—just a few weeks after the violence.[9]

These convictions were truly remarkable for the DRC. Margot Wallström, the UN Secretary-General's Special Representative on Sexual Violence in

Conflict, stated that "the sentences send a strong signal to all perpetrators in the DRC and beyond that conflict-related sexual violence is not acceptable and will not be tolerated."[10] Madame Tabena-Isima Mikongo, who works for a local NGO that attends to victims of sexual assault, said the set of convictions "was the best thing that happened until now" because, even a hundred miles away, "soldiers are now afraid [to commit sexual violence]. After Kibibi was sentenced, people saw that the government could react even against a colonel."

In the first 22 months of implementation from October 2009 to August 2011, mobile courts heard 248 cases and achieved 140 convictions for rape and 49 convictions for other offenses.[11] Experts also praise the way the program was designed to incorporate local participation through a consultation process with local stakeholders and implementation of the program through genuine "local ownership, both in terms of the structures within which they exist, and the personnel upon which they depend."[12] This investment in local ownership increases social demand for justice sector services, and is enhanced through training, legal clinics, and community education to build awareness of the courts and encourage norms that condemn sexual violence.[13] Mobile courts in the DRC exemplify a new kind of approach which combines formal mechanisms with local participation and a holistic approach to cultural and normative changes necessary for communities to develop social demand for justice.[14]

PROTECTING THE POOR FROM SLAVERY IN BRAZIL

In a world where millions of poor people are held in slavery, a coalition of forces in Brazil has united to mount an aggressive and highly effective assault upon long-standing systems of forced labor. Their story demonstrates the way national leadership can bring swift change when a problem is boldly acknowledged and forcefully addressed with law enforcement that puts an end to a culture of impunity.

Brazil's response to the overwhelming problem of forced labor has been multifaceted and holistic. Its National Commission to Eradicate Slave Labour (CONATRAE) is responsible for implementing and monitoring Brazil's National Plans to prevent and eradicate forced labor slavery, while the Ministry of Labour operates Special Mobile Inspection Groups (GEFMs), which conduct surprise inspections on estates suspected of using forced labor, as well as publishes a "dirty list," which names and shames perpetrators.

Under the country's 2005 National Pact for the Eradication of Slave Labour, approximately 200 enterprises representing 20% of Brazil's GDP voluntarily agree to be monitored for trafficking. The nation "developed perhaps the most effective media campaign in the world" to raise public awareness about and create social demand for the eradication of the problem.[15]

It was the José Pereira case that finally brought the problem of forced labor to the forefront in Brazil. In 1989, 17-year-old José and a friend attempted to escape from the estate where they and 60 other workers were held captive as slave laborers. They were met with rifle fire, which killed José's friend and wounded José. After barely escaping with his life, José filed an official complaint against the landowners who had held him captive. While the Brazilian government freed the rest of the laborers at the estate, no one was ever held criminally responsible for the crimes.

Indeed, the case illustrated many of the ways the Brazilian government was failing to protect its poorest citizens from slavery. There are an estimated 1.8 million victims of forced labor in Latin America and the Caribbean alone.[16] Thousands of these slaves are Brazilian and are exploited in the northern Amazonian states of Pará, Mato Grosso, and Tocantins, working in cattle, logging, deforestation, charcoal production, soy, and sugar-cane production.[17] The poor are often enticed by recruiters known as "gatos" who convince desperate workers to travel to areas with the promise of good pay and housing.[18] Once they arrive, the new slaves are informed that they now owe the landowner for transportation and food—finding themselves trapped in an ever-growing debt the landowners ensure will never be repaid, and denied their freedom by armed thugs.[19] The voluntary recruits have become slaves "through the final authority of violence."[20]

Largely because of advocacy from the Pastoral Land Commission, a Catholic agency dedicated to defending the land rights of the poor and the eradication of slavery, the Centre for Justice and International Law, and Human Rights Watch, in 2003 the Brazilian government finally accepted responsibility for the José Pereira case by signing an amicable settlement agreement in addition to a series of commitments concerning the protection of human rights in Brazil. This series of commitments later solidified into the responsibilities outlined for CONATRAE, which has since been at the forefront in the fight against forced labor in Brazil.[21] In 2002 President Inacio Lula da Silva promised to abolish slavery in his state[22] and in 2003 the president launched the first National Pact for the Eradication of Slave Labor, which has since served as a template for other states fighting against modern slavery.[23]

The primary vehicle for countering slavery in Brazil has been the Special Mobile Inspection Groups (GEFMs) of the Ministry of Labour and Employment (MTE), which conduct surprise investigations on landowners and employers suspected of using slave labor.[24] These units use anonymous tips to pinpoint cases of slavery, investigate the allegations, release victims, impose fines, and arrest perpetrators. The mobile units rescued 38,031 laborers between 1995 and 2010[25] and their work has been replicated across Brazil. The mobile units have elevated the issue of forced labor and produced an "increase in confidence in public power and, as a consequence, . . . a change in attitude for the workers and employers throughout the country."[26] The social impact of the mobile units has been enhanced by MTE-promoted awareness campaigns executed in partnership with civil society groups and other governmental divisions,[27] as well as the provision of legal assistance, medical care, and schooling for former slaves by groups like the Pastoral Land Commission.

Although the GEFMs have been quite successful in identifying and freeing thousands of forced laborers, the Brazilian government has not been particularly ardent in prosecuting perpetrators. Media reports indicate that only seven slave labor convictions were achieved in 2011, although one was of a former congressman.[28] It is very likely that the low number of convictions is due to the fact that labor prosecutors (who can only apply civil penalties) and public ministry prosecutors (who have the ability to initiate federal criminal cases) lacked coordination.

Brazil's approach in seeking to eradicate forced labor has been strengthened by the MTE's "dirty list" which publicly names and shames employers that use slaves to increase profits. Employers remain on the list for two years and are able to have their names removed only if the offense has not been repeated, fines have been paid in full, and certain other criteria are met. Perhaps one of the deepest successes of Brazil's efforts has been the way it has "slowly but steadily weakened the culture of impunity that protects employers from state action" in the area of forced labor and "helped to restore the workers' faith in the state apparatus" to protect them.[29] Not surprisingly, much of this success can be attributed to "the immense capacity for coordination displayed by the various social actors involved"[30] and the way the Brazilian government, civil society groups, private enterprises, financial institutions, and universities have been able to work together.[31]

ADDRESSING POLICE CORRUPTION IN GEORGIA

Perhaps the most discouraging obstacle to the transformation of criminal justice systems in the developing world is corruption. As we have seen, many criminal justice systems in the developing world are indeed "criminal" because they relentlessly and routinely commit crimes of corruption against poor people—extorting money from poor people under threat of false arrest or false charges, or accepting money from wealthy people in order to *not* enforce the law when they commit crimes against poor people. Moreover, corruption of the law enforcement system is different than corruption of other public systems because it is the system specifically tasked with fighting the crime of corruption in every other system. So if your corruption-fighting system is corrupt, you are stuck in a closed loop of criminality that may appear impossible to break out of. Indeed, such corruption is perhaps the chief reason that people have given up on trying to reform broken public justice systems in the developing world.

In the midst of that despair, a story has emerged of stunning and provocative transformation and hope. With everyone talking about the devastation of corruption in conversations about global poverty and development, it is surprising that everybody *isn't* talking about the nation of Georgia and its spectacularly successful fight against police corruption.

Thankfully, the World Bank has recently released a characteristically careful report on Georgia's experience fighting corruption, which should be a profound encouragement around the world. As explained in the foreword to the report, the Georgia experience demonstrates that developing nations *can* break out of the death loop of corruption.[32]

Often, administrative corruption is seen as endemic, a product of traditional local culture, and—as such—inevitable. In turn, political leaders often use citizens' perceived tolerance of corruption as an excuse for inaction. Global experience is replete with stories of reform failures and dashed expectations, but relatively few successful anticorruption efforts. Georgia's experience shows that the vicious cycle of ostensibly endemic corruption can be broken and—if sustained with appropriate institutional reforms— turned into a virtuous cycle.[33]

Prior to 2003, the former Soviet republic and now independent nation of Georgia was one of the most corrupt nations in the world. According to Transparency International, it ranked 124th among nations in the world for corruption (worse than Kenya, India, Bolivia, and the Congo), and was particularly egreguious[34] when it came to police corruption and abuse—surveys indicated that police demanded bribes in more transactions (7 out of 10) than just about any other police force in the world. The U.S. State Department repeatedly documented violent abuses of citizens by the Georgian police in its annual Human Rights Report. According to a World Bank Report, "corruption permeated nearly every aspect of life in Georgia,"[35] but the most visible and most hated aspect of the corruption was seen in the police, who "wielded wooden batons to flag down hapless motorists and extort bribes, usually for fabricated infractions."[36]

By 2010, however, Transparency International ranked Georgia as *first* in the world in reducing corruption—and second in the world in terms of the government's effectiveness in fighting corruption.[37] Astonishingly, by 2010, Georgia's police were viewed as less corrupt than the most respected police forces in Europe—manifesting less corruption than the police in Germany, France, and the UK.[38]

Some may be tempted to imagine that Georgia's police corruption problem couldn't possibly have been as bad as the corruption we see in countries like India, Kenya, or Peru, but that would be a mistake. As the World Bank study made plain, police corruption in Georgia was as bad as any place in the world:

> Corruption was at the core of Georgia's policing system. Police could not survive on the tiny salary they received—when they were paid at all (sometimes they went months without a paycheck). To make ends meet, many worked for organized crime or sold drugs or, as was common among traffic cops, accused citizens of breaking laws (whether they had or not) and then pocketed the fines.[39]
>
> People paid as much as $2,000 to $20,000 in bribes for jobs as policemen, earning the money back through an internal pyramid scheme funded by illegal pursuits. Each week, for example, patrolmen paid a fixed amount from the bribes they extracted from citizens for various "offenses" to their immediate supervisors, who in turn were expected to share a cut

with their bosses, and so on. [...] The corrupt system created a vicious cycle in which money rarely reached state coffers, salaries were not paid regularly, and police turned to crime to make money. There was nothing secret about this.[40]

Distrust ran so deep that crimes went unreported. People were afraid to mention even minor infractions, such as unruly teenagers breaking windows, for fear that culprits would be tortured in detention. Their fears were not unfounded. A 2002 UN Human Rights Committee report expressed concern about "widespread and continuing subjection of prisoners to torture and cruel, inhuman or degrading treatment or punishment by law enforcement officials and prison officers."

Police were also considered hopeless at solving crimes. If someone's house was robbed, citizens typically turned to people linked to criminals to offer a reward to get their belongings back. Worse, many police were themselves criminals, involved in kidnapping, drug dealing, and racketeering.[41]

How then did Georgia transform its police and criminal justice system from one of the worst in the world into a force with higher integrity ratings than most police in Western Europe?

Build Social Demand

The indispensable foundation of transformation seems to have come from the power of grassroots social demand. The common people of Georgia had reached a tipping point of frustration with corruption in every corner of their national life, and they translated that frustration into an expression of united, social demand for change. In the national election of 2003, Georgians voted in overwhelming numbers (more than 90 percent) for a new president, Mikheil Saakkashvili, and his United National Movement as they campaigned under a single, explicit call: "Georgia without Corruption." As Nika Gilauri, who initially served as minister of energy in the new regime and later became prime minister, made clear, successful reform would have been impossible without an overwhelming mandate from the Georgian people for fundamental change.[42]

Look for Decisive, Courageous Reformers Inside the System

Once in power, the new administration took bold, decisive, and controversial action to address corruption, but the leaders implementing the reform had actually served previously within the governmental system. Under the previous regime, President Saakashvili had served as justice minister; the first new prime minister, Zurab Zhvania, had been chairman of the Parliament; and, the new minister of energy, Nika Gilauri (who would later become prime minister himself), had been a financial controller in the state electricity system. The whole system under the old regime *looked corrupt*, but not everybody in that system *was corrupt*. Many reform-minded leaders were *in the system*—but they had been marginalized and disempowered.

Attack Corruption in the Criminal Justice System First

It is instructive that, among all the corrupt public systems that needed transformation, the Georgia reformers went after corruption in the criminal justice system first. They seemed to understand that if they were going to go after the crime of corruption in other public systems, they would need a crime-fighting capacity in the criminal justice system that was free of corruption. They understood that public confidence in the risks required to fight corruption would only come if the public trusted that law enforcement had been cleaned up. "From this desperate beginning, the new government started its work, adopting a simple strategy. It sought to establish the credibility of the state from the outset by focusing on tax collection *and the prosecution of criminals and corrupt officials*."[43] [emphasis added.]

Clean House and End Impunity for Police Corruption

Georgian leaders knew that a critical mass of the traffic police were corrupt, and so they fired them—all of them! The system was so corrupt, they believed, from top to bottom, that any attempt to introduce new recruits would fail, as new officers would soon succumb to the corrosive atmosphere of corruption. So in perhaps the boldest move of the young government, in a single day, it fired and took off the streets 16,000 officers. To soften the blow, the government provided two months' pay and amnesty from past crimes. Some officers went without fuss, and others joined the opposition. Chaos did not ensue—many observers believe that the roads were actually safer without the traffic people waving motorists over all the time—and a new patrol police force was created.

Zero tolerance did not stop with the firing of the traffic police and the hiring of new blood. Undercover officers were assigned to ensure the police followed the rules. Police officers caught taking bribes were fired. Such practices sent a strong message to new recruits that the ministry was serious about its code of conduct and the ethical practices of its police. Fines were no longer collected on the spot but paid at commercial banks, eliminating opportunities for the police to pocket the money.

Treat the New Police with Respect

The reformers also committed to treating the new Georgian police force with respect. Salaries were increased ten-fold. Police were provided with top-line uniforms and equipment to do their jobs, their training academy was revamped, and 60 police stations were built or renovated to provide open and inviting facilities for both the police and the public.[44] Financial savings were realized by shrinking the corruption-bloated police force. Staffing of all law enforcement agencies was reduced from about 63,000 in 2003 to 27,000 in 2011. Before the reforms, Georgia absurdly had one police officer for every 21 citizens; "today, that ratio has fallen to one police officer for every 89 citizens"[45] (which is still plenty; the United States, for example, has one police officer for every 450 citizens).

Win Public Trust through Effective Crime Fighting and Public Relations

At the end of the day, the government won the public's trust for the new police force by doing what was necessary to empower a force that effectively protected them from crime. Overall, crime was cut in half, and armed robberies were reduced by 80 percent. Moreover, 95 percent of residents in Georgia's capitol city of Tbilisi reported "feeling safe at all times."[46] Police leaders also engaged an intentional media relations campaign to build a community-friendly image for the police that accompanied the substance of improved crime fighting.

The end result of the Georgian reforms—in seven short years—is breathtaking to a world paralyzed by despair over police corruption. As the World Bank report found:

> Crime rates have dropped, corruption in the patrol police has declined, a service culture has been developed, trust has been restored, and an

accountability framework for the patrol police has been strengthened. Perhaps most important, one of the most visible signs of corruption in Georgia has been removed.[47]

As an article in *The Economist* observed, the smashing success of Georgia's fight against corruption is a "mental revolution" that explodes the notion that corruption is a "cultural phenomenon."[48] As former Prime Minister Gilauri said, "Corruption is a not a culture; it's a choice."[49]

INTERNATIONAL BRIDGES TO JUSTICE

To address the global epidemic of violence suffered by poor people *at the hand of their own criminal justice systems* (through abusive detention and torture), an innovative NGO called International Bridges to Justice (IBJ) strives to guarantee the right to competent legal representation, the right to be protected from torture and other cruel and unusual punishment, and the right to a fair trial. IBJ President and CEO Karen Tse was inspired to found the organization after an encounter in 1994 with a 12-year-old Cambodian boy accused of stealing a bicycle who had been tortured during a prolonged pre-trial detention. Tse recognized that while several organizations were successfully advocating for the human rights of political and other high-profile prisoners, there was a gap in human rights protection for the ordinary individuals who are charged with crimes every day.

IBJ works in partnership with countries seeking to improve their criminal justice systems, identifying leaders capable of sparking reform in their countries, collaborating with like-minded government ministries to seek consensus for change, providing key support through local and international partnerships, and joining them all together under the umbrella of its online defender portal.

Defender Trainings

IBJ believes that skilled defense attorneys, equipped with adequate training and support, are the key to unlocking the full potential of criminal justice reforms. Consequently, a critical IBJ objective is to increase defender capacity by providing training to new and experienced criminal defense attorneys, both increasing the number of lawyers taking criminal cases and improving each lawyer's ability to provide competent representation. IBJ also trains other actors within the justice system, such as police, prison officials, and judges, in best practices for safeguarding the rights of the accused.

Justice Sector Roundtables

IBJ believes that implementing a more humane vision of criminal justice is best accomplished with cooperation throughout the entire legal community, and so it works to convene roundtable meetings where defense lawyers, judges, prosecutors, police, and prison officials can engage with one another and identify common ground.

Rights Awareness Campaigns

IBJ also works in the developing world to equip ordinary individuals with awareness of their legal rights so they are more likely to assert those rights when arrested. By publicizing the role that lawyers play in protecting the accused from illegal detention and torture, IBJ encourages individual defendants to demand representation and seeks to increase community understanding of the importance of defense attorneys, developing public support for their work. IBJ employs a variety of media platforms to raise awareness, from posters to radio broadcasts.

Defender Resource Centers and the Provision of Legal Services

IBJ currently has in-depth programs in six of the world's most challenging countries, including three that have been scarred by genocide: Cambodia, China, India, Burundi, Rwanda, and Zimbabwe. Defender Resource Centers (DRCs) are IBJ's principal vehicle for achieving transformative change in these countries. Serving as the centers of IBJ's in-country activities, the DRCs enable IBJ to complement its legal defense trainings with mentoring and one-on-one case consultations, opportunities for networking and skill-sharing, and the provision of technical support for defense lawyers. The DRCs also operate as community legal centers—the first place to go for those seeking help for themselves or accused family members. Through the DRCs, IBJ-trained lawyers take hundreds of cases annually, increasing access to justice for the indigent accused and strengthening the country's pro bono culture. Thus, they provide a model for the implementation of a properly functioning legal aid system.

Cambodia provides the best example of the progress IBJ has made. As the only NGO in the country that focuses exclusively on criminal legal aid work, IBJ now represents the indigent accused in 18 out of 24 provinces, and says that torture has been reduced in the provinces where IBJ has had the longest presence. Moreover, there has been a steady increase in the percentage of cases where IBJ lawyers achieve an acquittal or reduced sentence.

In the years ahead, IBJ is seeking to scale up and adapt its techniques until investigative torture becomes a distant memory and the provision of basic due process rights becomes the new global norm.[50]

JUSTICE IN SIERRA LEONE

Sierra Leone offers a window into groundbreaking criminal justice projects from two very different organizations: Timap for Justice (Timap)—a small, young Sierra Leonian organization headed by the inspiring Vivek Maru; and the UK's Department for International Development (DFID)—one of the world's leading international development agencies.

Unlike almost all other bilateral international aid programs focused on law enforcement in the developing world, DFID's approach looks at the entire justice sector and is explicitly designed to consider the specific needs that poor and marginalized communities are likely to encounter. DFID's multiple justice reform initiatives in Sierra Leone, known as Security Sector Reforms (SSR), and Safety, Security and Access to Justice (SSAJ), are two separate but overlapping programs that provide an excellent case study of DFID's approach to sector-wide structural transformation. Although the two strategies overlap in their efforts to reform police institutions, SSR initiatives focus primarily on police, intelligence, and military institutions while SSAJ efforts focus on the justice sector as a whole by strengthening courts, penal systems, civil justice, and dispute resolution mechanisms.[51]

In 1999, DFID began its first highly structured justice system transformation initiative, known as the Commonwealth Community Safety and Security Project. This project focused on Sierra Leone police reform by providing the training and equipment necessary for the maintenance of peace, increasing trust between the police and grassroots communities, and conducting leadership training.

Perhaps the two most distinctive aspects of the police reforms were the emergence of Local Police Partnership Boards and Family Support Units. Both of these initiatives focused on building a positive relationship of trust between the police and the community, and they promoted active citizen engagement in the provision of their own security. The Family Support Units target cases of domestic violence and have been successful enough to attract the support and cooperation of various NGOs working in the area of sexual abuse.[52] The most promising characteristic of the Local Police Partnership Boards and the Family Support Units is the potential of these components to create social demand for justice systems that work for the poor—because, as DFID has emphasized: "conventional supply-side institution building interventions are unlikely to have much beneficial impact without a social demand for reform."[53]

As Sierra Leone emerged from bloody conflict in January of 2002, DFID began to lead the way in explicitly integrating security and comprehensive justice sector concerns into its approach to development.[54] Today poor people in Sierra Leone benefit from improved security from a reformed national police, a more effective judicial system, and security forces that provide reasonable stability. The aggregate result of these accomplishments has been significant, so much so that the "perceptions of the people of Sierra Leone…indicate that there has been a significant positive change in levels of security on the ground."[55]

For a very different approach to the common problem of protecting the poor from violent abuse we turn to Vivek Maru, the energetic and passionate CEO of Namati, an international organization dedicated to legal empowerment of the poor.[56] Maru is one of the co-founders of Timap for Justice, a non-profit, independent Sierra Leonean paralegal and advocacy organization which partners with Namati, the government of Sierra Leone, the World Bank, DFID, and other civil society organizations.

From Maru's perspective, legal empowerment offers a way to both achieve long-term institutional reform and at the same time provide immediate relief to victims of a broken justice system.[57] His approach seeks to have victims of injustice perceived as agents capable of initiating and building social demand for properly functioning justice systems. Maru says that "lasting institutional change depends on a more empowered polity," and empowered victims are an integral part of producing such a polity.[58]

He emphasizes that, while human rights education is a critical part of that empowerment, a short supply of qualified lawyers and the expenses associated with a heavy reliance on lawyers are key limiting factors in build-ing functioning judicial systems in the developing world. To meet this need, Maru has pioneered a program that places highly-trained paralegals at the center of its strategy for providing justice for the poor. "The paralegal," Maru explains, "offers a promising methodology of legal empowerment that fits between legal education and legal representation, one that maintains a focus on achieving concrete solutions to people's justice problems but which employs, in addition to litigation, the more flexible, creative tools of social movements."[59]

The innovative tools—including mediation—used by paralegals in the Timap model are ultimately focused on creating and sustaining a social demand for justice. The World Bank has praised Timap's "avoid[ance of] reliance on the laborious and expensive process of litigation through the fre-quent use of mediation for the resolution of individual level cases."[60] But Timap also recognizes the indispensability of the formal criminal justice system: When it finds unchecked violence, including sexual assault and traf-ficking, it refers such clients to lawyers.[61]

The Timap approach also offers a useful template for taking small-scale structural transformation initiatives to scale. "I don't want second- or third-class solutions for the poor," Maru says, "but injustice is at scale, so justice should be at scale." Maru explains that the Timap model began on a small scale in order to focus on the development and refinement of its meth-ods,[62] but now that these methods have been sufficiently refined, 40 percent of Sierra Leone now has community paralegals.[63] Scalability is aided by a central role for the more accessible and cost effective paralegal; a willing-ness to utilize unconventional tools such as mediation, traditional law, and even religious belief, when it is appropriate in non-violent conflicts; a recon-ceptualization of victims as agents capable of producing change; and spe-cific methods for targeting community-level issues aimed to produce social demand for institutional reform. The forethought put into the model has allowed it to become, in the words of one client, "the voice of the voiceless."

Ending Impunity in Huánuco, Peru

One of the most hopeful models of criminal justice transformation has emerged out of the horrific story of Yuri's rape and murder in the Andean region of Huánuco, Peru. Yuri's story is an iconic narrative of the brutal dysfunction of the public justice system in the developing world, but thanks to the work of Paz y Esperanza and other leaders in the Huánuco region, Yuri's story is also emerging as an encouraging example of the way local movements in the developing world can unite diverse stakeholders, draw upon international resources, and reform the criminal justice system in a way that begins to bring credible protection to the poor.

Indeed, many of the elements of IJM's Structural Transformation model were inspired and refined by what we learned over many years of working with Paz y Esperanza in Huánuco. The twin strategies of catalyzing a coalition of forces in the community and using Collaborative Casework to diagnose systemic dysfunctions and to pursue solutions have been powerfully pioneered by Paz y Esperanza.

As we saw from Yuri's story, when Paz y Esperanza started working in Huánuco, there was an epidemic of sexual violence against women and girls,and successful prosecutions of perpetrators were virtually unheard of. Over the last decade, however, José and Richard and their Paz y Esperanza team have worked with hundreds of individual women and girls who have been victimized by sexual violence, and have walked with the authorities and local social services in the Huánuco region through hundreds of these sexual assault cases, seeking justice against the perpetrators of these horrific crimes. They have led campaigns of awareness and public action which have vastly increased the social demand in the community to address the problem—and have translated that social demand into the political will to fix what is broken in the criminal justice system. They have also worked with a coalition of forces to help provide training to the authorities and to increase knowledge and resources for addressing sexual violence.

As a result, in this remote Andean district, Paz y Esperanza has successfully secured *more than 152 convictions* of sexual predators since 2003—and has ensured high-quality aftercare services for hundreds of victims and their families. As with IJM's Structural Transformation projects, Paz y Esperanza has achieved these results by first catalyzing a coalition of forces in the Huánuco region to lead a movement of awareness and public action, which transformed the political will to address these crimes. Paz y Esperanza partnered with other advocacy groups, schools, medical providers, churches, local government and international humanitarian agencies to transform the level of awareness of the problem and to build the social demand in the community to address it. This coalition of efforts led by Paz y Esperanza:

- Conducted education and awareness programs and events on sexual violence in hundreds of schools.
- Formed and resourced Women's Rights Networks in 13 districts of the Huánuco region.
- Conducted workshops and exhibitions on sexual violence at the universities, educational institutions, social service organizations, and local government.
- Provided training on sexual violence to hundreds of teachers, school principals, health workers, and members of the justice system.
- Established local Vigilance Committees with mayors, civil society leaders, and government authorities.
- Brought the epidemic of sexual violence into the open and into the public discourse through a sustained media campaign that publicized cases of abuse and trained the media on how to cover the issue in an effective and responsible manner.
- Transformed days of tragedy—like the yearly anniversary of Yuri's death—into iconic days of public awareness, remembrance and protest s (December 18: Day of Impunity—No Child Sexual Abuse; November 19: International Day Against Child Sexual Abuse; April 11: Peruvian Children's Day).

As a woman from a poor community in the region told Paz y Esperanza leaders after one of their workshops," It's the first time I hear about my rights. Now I know it was my right to defend my sister who suffered sexual abuse."

As Paz y Esperanza led its coalition partners in this campaign to build local political will to address sexual violence, they also led a parallel effort to build the capacity of each section of the public justice pipeline that must address sexual violence offenses. For police, prosecutors and judges, Paz y Esperanza provided hands-on training and Collaborative Casework. to secure confident competence in handling sexual assault cases. As a result of the training and improved case preparation, Paz y Esperanza leaders report that they have seen a transformation in the performance measures of the justice system.

Perhaps most spectacularly, Paz y Esperanza and its coalition partners successfully led an unprecedented campaign to remove four judges from the Huánuco courts who have failed to enforce the laws against sexual violence with integrity—including the president and another member of the court who presided over the gross miscarriage of justice in Yuri's case. As Paz y Esperanza leaders announced in 2012, "Their removal came as a direct result of pressure by Paz y Esperanza and other NGOs, along with an outraged public,who advocated over the course of several months to remove them from office."

Finally, Paz y Esperanza and its partners also led a critical effort to improve the social services that must support a child in poverty as she goes through the difficult process of seeking justice in the criminal justice system and in finding restoration from abuse. Paz y Esperanza provides direct services of support for more than 250 women and girls who are victims of abuse, trains and supports local social service providers, and has partnered with local and international agencies to establish a full-service residential facility for children who are victims of sexual violence.

These locally owned and led efforts by Paz y Esperanza and their partners are transforming the landscape of despair in Huánuco, where impoverished Peruvian children like Yuri once endured sexual violence in a brutal, lawless chaos. Concrete hope is now emerging for a justice system that can provide the kind of basic protections against violence that so many of us take for granted for our own children.[64]

Legal Empowerment of the Poor

Timap's work in Sierra Leone illustrates an encouraging trend in development circles to pursue legal empowerment of the poor. As we at IJM have done in a targeted way with the criminal justice system, the emerging model of legal empowerment of the poor examines the way broader legal issues directly impact the poor, and it seeks to engage the poor in helping themselves where possible and acting on their behalf where necessary. Gradually, major development agencies have grown to appreciate the diverse ways in which legal empowerment can help the poor gain greater control over their lives. Development expert Stephen Golub, who has been studying this evolution, explains that legal empowerment can include such diverse activities as a farmers' association helping its members gain greater control of their land, a local women's organization using advocacy to enhance the physical security and independence of wives in their area, parents learning how to register the births of their children to ensure their access to education, government public health programs enabling impoverished beneficiaries to understand and act on their rights to basic medical services, or grassroots groups making traditional justice systems—the only law many rural poor can access, afford, and understand—less gender-biased.

With increasing research manifesting the concrete way in which legal empowerment benefits the poor, the UN Secretary General, the World Bank, the UN Development Programme, USAID, DFID, the Open Society Foundations, the International Development Law Organization, and a host of other international actors have endorsed the concept. This is a massively encouraging step forward. But to decisively address the common violence threatening billions of our poorest neighbors, the broad efforts of the "legal empowerment" movement must include targeted attention to broken criminal justice systems, as several of the projects highlighted in this chapter have.[65]

Indeed, the critical question of our era is before us. At this historic inflection point in the struggle against severe poverty, are we prepared to do something different? Are we prepared to honestly acknowledge that the abandonment of criminal justice systems in the developing world has been a disaster? And are we prepared to leverage what we now know to finally begin securing for the poor that safe passage out of the violence that history tells us is both indispensable and possible?

CONCLUSION

So now what? What do we do with what we now know?

We have taken a long hard look at the hidden plague of violence and lawlessness that quietly terrorizes the global poor.

Somehow the world missed the fact that most of the global poor lack the most basic ingredient of forward progress: personal security. We now can see what was so hard to see before—that most of the global poor live outside the protection of rudimentary law enforcement and are utterly vulnerable to the locusts of violence that can come on any given day and sweep all other good efforts to improve their lives away.

We see something of the violence now—and perhaps more importantly, we are beginning to understand something of its catastrophic implications. As we draw close to the locusts of violence, we begin to fathom something of their cost in unspeakable human suffering. And as we draw back and look at the bigger picture, we can see the devastating impact that violence has on the poor's struggle to move forward, and the way it undermines so much of what we otherwise try to do to assist them. For the slave locked in the brick factory, the widow and orphans thrown off their land, for the girl raped at school and infected with HIV, for the breadwinning husband rotting in jail—it turns out that if you're not safe, nothing else matters.

We have also come to see more clearly the basic system of law enforcement that many of us have been relying upon all along for our own safety—and we have worked through the rather shocking realization that poor people in the developing world simply do not have such systems. Indeed, perversely, their systems of "public safety" are, for them, systems of public harm.

We've seen more deeply where many of these dysfunctional systems came from in the first place (the insidious legacy of colonial justice systems that have never been overthrown). We have seen what has made these systems worse (the use of private substitutes that allow people of wealth and power to abandon the public systems) and why they have not gotten better (because the "plumbing" of public justice delivery systems has been neglected by traditional human rights and poverty alleviation efforts—and most importantly, because the local political and economic elites who figured out how to thrive in lawlessness would be threatened by rule of law).

We have also stumbled upon a surprising hope. First, from history, we have encountered the unexpected story that just about every criminal justice system that can now be relied upon to work reasonably well was once utterly corrupt, abusive, and dysfunctional. History clearly teaches that local movements of criminal justice reform in developing societies can achieve radical transformation. And few things are more profoundly encouraging to the despairing hiker than meeting summiteers on the return trip who can testify that the climb is *possible*. Second, there is paradoxical hope in the fact that the world has not really even begun to apply its best thinking and commensurate resources to support such movements—except for in a few places where attempts have been made minimally, badly, or in a hurry-up panic to clean up a post-conflict chaos.

So where do we go from here? What do we need to do now?

Transform the Conversation about Global Poverty

First, we need to fundamentally change the conversation. Whenever we speak of global poverty, we must speak of the violence imbedded in that poverty. And we must speak the awkward truth—the emperor-has-no-clothes truth—that there is no meaningful system of law enforcement in the developing world to protect the poor from that violence. In every forum, conference, classroom, policy discussion, think tank, blog, or dinner table conversation where global poverty is center stage, the problem of violence deserves equal time with hunger, dirty water, disease, illiteracy, unemployment, gender discrimination, housing, or sanitation because for the poor, violence is every bit as devastating and is frequently the hidden force undermining solutions to these other needs.

The locusts of violence are devastating the poor in the developing world, and they aren't getting any help stopping the descending plague. An effective defense against the plague exists—we know this because you and I get it. It's called law enforcement. But the poor in the developing world do not have access to these basic services, and they are suffering and dying as a result.

With the AIDS pandemic, the world got to a place where it became an embarrassing oversight to carry on a conversation about economic development and poverty alleviation in the developing world without mentioning that there was a raging AIDS epidemic that was destroying millions of poor people every year. You just were not in touch with reality if you weren't in touch with the global ravages of AIDS. Likewise, our conversations about global poverty are not in touch with reality if the plague of violence does not surface as an urgent, fundamental reality that brutally contorts everything else. Moreover, with the AIDS epidemic, the world eventually came to grips with the fact that antiretroviral drugs could keep babies safe from HIV and could keep HIV-infected people safe from AIDS. And even though these treatments were available, the world came to see that poor people in the developing world just didn't get access to these protections. The world came to see that the poor were needlessly wasting away by the millions as a result—and the world has substantially reversed course.

Likewise, we all know that law enforcement systems are indispensable for keeping us and those we love safe in our communities, but we seldom speak of the fact that poor people in the developing world don't get these protections and so suffer in terror by the millions. But now we know, and we must speak of it—and we must transform the conversation.

Bring New Expertise to the Conversation about Global Poverty

Next, we must not only integrate a discussion of violence into every broad conversation about global poverty; we also must begin to integrate the relevant expertise into the conversation—especially expertise from the disciplines of criminal justice.

Over the last half century, amidst endless conferences and consultations on poverty, everyday lawless violence against the poor has barely registered a mention compared to all the other issues that confront the poor. Fortunately, this has begun to change, and over the last few years I have begun to hear the subject of violence occasionally raised in forums on global poverty (especially violence against women and girls). What is stunning, however, is that there is almost never anybody in the room with any law enforcement expertise. It's like we are having a discussion about AIDS without doctors and public health professionals in the room. Violence, like AIDS, *is* a complex social phenomenon—and experts from a wide array of disciplines have a great deal to contribute. But something very odd is at play when criminal violence is the topic and the core discipline of law enforcement and criminal justice is not present. It's especially odd because it's not the way such conversations take place in affluent countries. In affluent communities, there are no forums on rape, domestic violence, armed robberies, assaults, or gang violence that don't include law enforcement expertise in the room; in fact, law enforcement experts are frequently the ones invited to lead the dialogue.

Likewise, the expertise of law enforcement and criminal justice needs to be integrated into the leading agencies that address economic development, poverty alleviation, and human rights in the developing world. As we have seen, the aspirations of all three of these fields are profoundly affected in the poorest communities by the violence that thrives in the absence of functioning criminal justice systems—and yet these agencies tend to have very little or no in-house expertise in the disciplines relevant to the technical administration of justice and law enforcement, which are the core social instruments for addressing criminal violence.

In fact, both the human rights field and the development field have had awkward relationships with criminal justice systems, for understandable reasons. Development agencies, on the one hand, have become experts in devising ingenious work-arounds and coping mechanisms to deal with failed criminal justice systems in the developing world. They have spent decades innovating ways to help poor people survive *in the absence* of a working "pipeline" of justice, and it may be a disorienting shift to move towards efforts to *fix* the pipeline. Development agencies have vast expertise in economic systems, food systems, health systems, education systems, housing systems, sanitation systems—and almost every other system *apart* from society's fundamental system of public safety. This will need to change.

Human rights agencies likewise have had an awkward relationship with systems of criminal justice and traditionally have not invested in deep expertise and experience in the technical work of delivering justice through police and court systems on behalf of common citizens. The international human rights community tends to be dominated by researchers, scholars, legal theorists, media advocates, diplomats, and policy experts who are experts at developing and assessing compliance with international legal standards—but not in the practical work of building and supporting local law enforcement mechanisms by which common poor people can have their rights vindicated. All of this has been made even more difficult by the fact that law enforcement and justice systems are traditionally among the chief *perpetrators* of human rights abuses; so it will be an awkward pivot to turn with conviction to the realization that the local *enforcement* of international human rights standards has actually been placed in the hands of local law enforcement—and there will ultimately be no substitute for helping them to do their job.

Projects of Hope

But what happens after that? Let's say that the world is awakened to the vast plague of violence like never before and the conversation is transformed. Lawless violence has taken its proper place in the mainstream priorities to be addressed in the developing world, and broad investment is made in bringing new and relevant criminal justice expertise to the table. Let's say the world was even ready to step up and devote serious resources to address the problem. Would we even know what to do with these resources?

Well, here's what we know—bad news first. The problem is massive: There are billions of poor people living under abusive and dysfunctional criminal justice systems all around the world in thousands of different settings. Secondly, we really don't know what to do about it. We know from history that indigenous movements can radically reform these systems and that external players can have a positive role—but that doesn't mean we actually know the path to transformation for the massive and diverse societies in need today or the right role for outsiders. As we've said, we know these criminal justice systems are indispensable for the poor, and we know it's possible to build them—but we also know that building them is difficult, costly, dangerous, and unlikely.

In the face of these realities, what seems most needful and doable are experimental projects of transformation that bring real change, that teach us, and that inspire hope—because the vulnerable poor need all three. In realistic appreciation of the inherent difficulty of these projects, however, we recommend prioritizing these experiments in contexts where there is a higher likelihood of success rather than those most likely to fail (i.e., not in failed states or in countries in conflict or emerging from natural disaster). While these latter contexts also desperately need functioning criminal justice systems, it would be a pity to pour limited resources exclusively into these *immensely* more challenging contexts, while missing out on the opportunity to see inspiring and instructive success in the large number of relatively stable countries that nevertheless have massive populations in poverty and criminal justice systems that utterly fail to protect them from violence. Within these imminently doable contexts, we need to invest in the kinds of bold and rigorous experiments we have just reviewed in the previous chapter.

In particular, we would encourage projects that use a version of the Collaborative Casework approach. There is a tremendous need for methodologies that patiently allow a diagnosis of what is broken in the criminal justice system to emerge from the authentic human experience of the most vulnerable end-users of that system (i.e., poor people who are victims of violent crime) and then build solutions that meet the specific needs of those users in collaborative, problem-solving relationships with the people who are inside the system and tasked to make it work.

We need to discover what methodologies might be replicated and adapted to new contexts, and to discover and support those local champions of reform who can lead their communities to finally fulfill the desire of the poor for a justice system that is truly their own, that fights for them, defends them, and keeps them safe. Moreover, in some of the areas where innovations in reforming the public justice system have already shown promise, there is a desperate need to scale-up political will and resource investment in a way that is commensurate with the need and the opportunity. It's time to take that decisive turn down the long road we've been avoiding—by investing aggressively in what already seems to be working, by continuing to innovate through short and long term experiments in criminal justice, and making that commitment of compassion to secure what we have always treasured for ourselves: the freedom from violence and fear through which the global poor might finally find their opportunity to flourish and thrive.

THE MATH: U.S. GOVERNMENT SPENDING ON RULE OF LAW INITIATIVES

Given the opacity of reporting and the variety of terminology used, it is challenging to determine the precise amount of U.S. government spending on rule of law efforts that impact the common poor. However, a careful study of the data is revealing.

For the 2010 budget, the State Department, USAID, and Public Law 480 resources requested $32.3 billion (a 4 percent increase from 2009). Of these requests, $12.7 billion—or 39.4 percent of U.S. foreign aid—can fairly be considered "Broad" Rule of Law aid. (This $12.7 billion is comprised of the program areas in the "Peace and Security" objective and the "Governing Justly and Democratically" objective, along with "Private Sector Competitiveness"—a subset of the "Economic Growth" funding objective.) To help us understand where this "broad" spending goes, we can break it down into five general categories:

		% of total U.S. foreign aid
International Security	$7,172m	
Weapons of Mass Destruction	314	1%
Stabilization Operations and Security Sector Reform (*Afghanistan*)	6,345	19.60%
Conflict Mitigation and Reconciliation	513	1.60%
International Crime	**2,000**	
Counter-Terrorism	403	1.20%
Counter-Narcotics	1,538	4.80
Other Transnational Crime*	60	0.20%
Recruiting Business	**698**	
Private Sector Competitiveness	698	2.20%
Democracy	**2,060**	
Good governance	1,074	3.30%
Political Competition and Consensus-Building	377	1.20%
Civil Society	609	1.90%
Narrow Rule of Law	**786**	
Rule of Law and Human Rights	754	2.30%
Trafficking in Persons element of transnational crime	31	0.10%
Total	**12,716**	**39.40%**

*Financial crime and money laundering, but excluding human trafficking

Figure Appendix.1 General Categories of "Broad" Rule of Law Spending

On this accounting, $786 million of the 2010 budget went towards "Narrow" Rule of Law spending. That represents only 2.4 percent of total foreign assistance, or 6 percent of the "Broad" Rule of Law budget—but it's important to realize that, even within this very small and specific subset of funding, not all of the funds are targeted to promote access to criminal

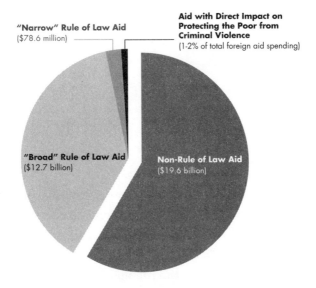

**Total U.S. Foreign Aid Spending
$32.3 billion**

Figure Appendix.2 Breakdown of U.S. Foreign Aid
Spending

justice for the poor. The figure includes programs aimed at high-level trans-national trafficking that are unlikely to directly affect the poorest, and even programs aimed at fomenting transnational cooperation around issues like protecting the ozone layer and safeguarding air traffic. Given the opacity of data on spending, it's impossible to say with exactness, but a fair and conservative estimate is that somewhere between 1 and 2 percent of foreign assistance funds are directed towards programming that might have a direct impact on protecting the poor from common criminal violence.

ACKNOWLEDGEMENTS

I owe a tremendous debt of gratitude to those who have generously assisted and encouraged me in this project over the past decade. First and foremost, I am grateful to the hundreds of men, women, and children in the developing world who have shared with me their deeply personal stories of grief, terror, loss, struggle, resilience, and triumph in the face of violence—stories that opened my eyes to the terror of poverty, to the promise of change, and to lives worth fighting for. They were willing to share these intimate stories because of mutual friends who earned their trust amidst the pain and immense dignity of their struggles: my colleagues serving in the field with International Justice Mission (IJM) and the hundreds of friends who serve with other NGOs, government agencies, and faith communities in the poorest corners of our world.

I am thankful for the encouragement, collaboration, and friendship of my brilliant, careful, and gracious co-author, Victor Boutros, without whom this project simply would not have been possible.

I am deeply grateful for the very kind invitation by Saul Levmore, then-Dean of the University of Chicago Law School, to teach a course on human rights in the developing world during the Spring of 2010, which afforded both the opportunity and impetus to lay the intellectual foundation for our argument here. Fortunately, this invitation was suggested to Dean Levmore by two highly persuasive scholars, Samantha Power and Cass Sunstein (my former law professor)—both of whom provided indispensable guidance and encouragement in shaping the earliest vision of this volume that eventually emerged from those lectures. I was very thankful for the great privilege of debuting the argument at the Ulysses and

Marguerite Schwartz Memorial Lectureship at the University of Chicago Law School, and at Yale Law School at the invitation of James Silk, Clinical Professor of Law and Executive Director of the Orville H. Schell, Jr. Center for International Human Rights, and with the encouragement of former University of Chicago classmate Tracey L. Meares, now the Walton Hale Hamilton Professor of Law at Yale University Law School. Thanks, again, to the encouragement of Samantha Power and the invitation of James F. Hoge, Jr., then-editor of *Foreign Affairs*, Victor Boutros and I were able to provide a summary of this book's argument in an article in that journal under the title "And Justice for All" in May/June 2010. Much of the research for the course at the University of Chicago and the article in *Foreign Affairs* was made possible through a generous grant from the Microsoft Corporation and the encouraging friendship and intellectual companionship of Brad Smith, General Counsel and Executive VP for Legal and Corporate Affairs at Microsoft. I was also deeply encouraged by the personal time generously shared by Laurence Tribe, esteemed Carl M. Loeb University Professor at Harvard University and relentless advocate for the poor, in reviewing and discussing the argument that was taking shape in this formative stage. Ally McKinney and Jonathan Crowe provided foundational research assistance in the very earliest stages of the project as well.

The process of researching and writing the book was a true team effort shared with my colleagues and friends at IJM—meaning, this book simply would not exist without them. I am especially grateful to Ruthie McGinn for organizing and accompanying me and the team on every aspect of the project—from advancing trips to the field for research, investigation, and interviews, to developing systems for electronically collecting and accessing tens of thousands of pages of research, to organizing massive volumes of course materials, lecture notes and visuals—and everything in between. Lori Poer was the indispensable team leader and delightful editor in the arduous but critical internal editing process at IJM. I am joyfully indebted to Holly Burkhalter for leveraging her sterling reputation and networks in the human rights and development fields to develop the rigor, clarity, and sophistication of our argument. Holly helped master several critical fields of argument and research, and she facilitated interactions with a broad range of relevant experts to place the argument on solid ground. Among the external experts who graciously, critically, and constructively reviewed our arguments along the way were: Kate Almquist Knopf, Eric Beinhart, Allyson Collins, Eric Friedman, Anne Gallagher, Steve Golub, Tom Malinowski, Bob Perito, Anthony Randazzo, Stephen Rickard, Len Rubenstein, Susan Vitka, and Jennifer Windsor. Mark Lagon and the Council on Foreign Relations provided an early forum to test the ideas with human rights experts.

I am grateful for research associates Tim Gehring and Ryan Lang, who brought great intellectual rigor, thoughtful precision and deep dedication to this project over many months. IJM mobilized a grand army of researchers and fact-checkers who also rendered indispensable assistance, including Natalie Bruce, Lindsay Henson, Jessica Kim, Rebecca Lollar, Katherine McCulley, Melody Miles, Kim Pendleton Bolles, and Nicole Provo.

The entire global family of IJM painstakingly shared their experiences serving victims of violence in their journeys through abuse and broken justice systems, delivering the human face and heart to our story. My colleagues in nearly 20 field offices around the world who took the time to help me get my facts straight, host me in their offices and share the stories of their work are too numerous to name individually—but their generous and patient assistance was indispensable to this project and a singular encouragement to me. Fellow IJMers Kay Anuluoha, Karen Barnes, Bill Clark, Pamela Gifford, Lacey Hanson, Bethany Hoang, Vera Leung, Amy Lucia, Jim Martin, Michelle Quiles, Amy Roth, Melissa Russell, Sheeba Philip, and Chong-Ae Shah provided special leadership and insight in advancing the book concept, direction, and publishing process. All of us at IJM are indebted to Stephanie Reinitz for shepherding the larger book process and the delightful relationship with Oxford University Press, and we are very thankful to have Dan Raines and Meredith Smith of Creative Trust representing us with OUP with such excellence, professionalism, and friendship. It has been a dream come true to publish *The Locust Effect* with Oxford University Press—the gold standard in intellectual and publishing excellence—and to have had the benefit of our editor, David McBride, Editor-in-Chief, Social Sciences, in bringing our project up to meet that lofty standard.

I am personally indebted for the grace and generosity of many friends who provided space for my mobile "book bunker" and the coordination of Dawn Gary—especially friends at Potomac Baptist Church, Osprey Point, Jim and Susan Swartz, Carr Workspaces—and to Virginia Theological Seminary for providing work space for Victor Boutros. Many respected friends provided insight and much-needed support and encouragement throughout the process including Nicole Bibbins-Sedaca, Dale Hanson Bourke, Andy Crouch, Donald Harrison, Mark Labberton, Andrew Legg, D. Michael Lindsay, Anne Michael, Donald Miller, Bob Mosier, Art Reimers, Jim Swartz, David Weekley, and many others. The excellent faculty and students at Pepperdine University Law School also provided valuable feedback and dialogue over the issues and arguments. Andrea Cheuk, Andrew Bertolli, and John Newell with Latham & Watkins were extremely generous in contributing their world-class professional skills in providing critical legal counsel.

Needless to say, while all of these friends, colleagues, and experts named above have made *The Locust Effect* possible and infinitely better than it would otherwise be, the remaining infirmities and inadequacies of the book are solely the responsibility of Victor Boutros and myself.

—Gary A. Haugen, 2013

NOTES

CHAPTER 1

1. Rukmini Callimachi. "Congo Rape Rate Equal To 48 Women Attacked Every Hour: Study." *Huffington Post*, May 11, 2011. Web. Available online at http://www.huffingtonpost.com/2011/05/11/congo-rape-48-women-every-hour_n_860581.html.
2. "50 casos de violacíon sexual en solo 5 días." Diarie Ahora. June 19, 2002.
3. Supreme Court of Huánuco, August 14, 2009, Testimony of Doctors Velaochaga Grimaldi Ricardo Manuel and Leocio Moreno Valverde: "These were submitted to the Laboratory La Unión, since the sample came out positive for sperm."
4. Supreme Court of Huánuco, Verdict No. 20-2009: "Instructive Declaration of ALFREDO AGAPITO CONDORI BUENO, who says that he asked the Director of the Hospital what the reason was for taking out the samples if they had already carried out the legal autopsy. He was given a very vague response, indicating that the samples had been lost, so he investigated the cause for the loss and was told that the doctor had ordered the samples to be thrown out because they had already rejected the samples on medical orders."
5. "WHO Multi-country Study on Women's Health and Domestic Violence against Women." Geneva: World Health Organization (2005). Available online at http://www.who.int/gender/violence/who_multicountry_study/fact_sheets/Peru2.pdf.
6. World Health Organization. "Facts: Sexual Violence." Geneva: World Health Organization (2002). Available online at http://www.who.int/violence_injury_prevention/violence/world_report/factsheets/en/sexualviolencefacts.pdf.
7. United Nations Rule of Law. Commission on Legal Empowerment of the Poor. *Making the Law Work for Everyone: Report of the Commission on Legal Empowerment of the Poor, vol. 1.* New York: United Nations Development Programme (2008). 2. Web. Available online at http://www.undp.org/content/dam/aplaws/publication/en/publications/democratic-governance/dg-publications-for-website/making-the-law-work-for-everyone---vol-i/Making_the_Law_Work_for_Everyone.pdf.
8. World Bank. "Poverty Overview." Web. Available online at http://www.worldbank.org/en/topic/poverty/overview.

9. Rediff Business. *Surat, Fastest Growing City in India.* 2008. Web. Available online at http://in.rediff.com/money/2008/jan/29gdp.htm.

10. *Times of India.* "Bangalore's 13 Richies on Forbes List." 2011. Web. Available online at http://articles.timesofindia.indiatimes.com/2011-10-30/bangalore/303 38903_1_forbes-india-rich-list-mn-wipro-chairman.

11. *Times of India.* "10,000 Dollar Millionaires Here." 2007. Web. Available online at http://articles.timesofindia.indiatimes.com/2007-03-31/bangalore/27887212_ 1_millionaires-wealth-mutual-funds.

12. Indian Health News. "Malnutrition among Indian Children Worse Than in Sub-Saharan Africa." *Med India,* December 22, 2007. Web. Available online at http://www.medindia.net/news/Malnutrition-Among-Indian-Children-Worse-Than-in-Sub-Saharan-Africa-30955-1.htm.

13. Action Aid. *Study of the Homeless.* Report, 2003.

14. Kevin Bales. *Disposable People: New Slavery in the Global Economy.* Berkeley and Los Angeles: University of California Press. Rev. ed, (2012). 9.

15. United Nations. *State of the World's Cities 2010/2011—Cities for All: Bridging the Urban Divide.* Nairobi: UN-Habitat, (2010). 32.

16. Amnesty International. *Insecurity and Indignity: Women's Experiences in Slums in Nairobi, Kenya.* London. Amnesty International. (2010). 7. Web. Available online at http://www.amnesty.org/en/library/info/AFR32/002/2010. Korogocho stands on both private and public land (in almost equal measure) with an estimated 120,000 people living in about seven villages.

17. United Nations Human Settlements Programme. *The Challenge of Slums- Global Report on Human Settlements 2003.* Nairobi: UN Habitat, 2003. 59. Web. http://www.unhabitat.org/pmss/listItemDetails.aspx?publicationID=1156

18. Ibid., 78.

19. Oxfam GB Urban Programme. *Urban_Poverty_and_Vulnerability in Kenya.* Oxfam GB Urban Programme, 2009. Web. Available online at http://www.irinnews.org/pdf/Urban_Poverty_and_Vulnerability_in_Kenya.pdf.

20. Center on Housing Rights and Eviction. Women and Housing Rights Programme. *Women, Slums and Urbanisation Examining the Causes.* Geneva: The Centre on Housing Rights and Evictions (2008). 14. Web. Available online at http://www.alnap.org/POOL/FILES/ COHRE- WOMEN SLUMSANDURBANISATIONEXA MININGTHECAUSES AND CONSEQUENCES.PDF.

21. Center for Rights Education and Awareness. *Status of Women & Girls in Kenya Urgent Need to Uphold Human Rights.* 12. Available online at http://www.creawke-nya.org/pdf/The_status_of_women_and_girls_in_Kenya.pdf.

   See also Amnesty International. *Insecurity and Indignity: Women's Experiences in the Slums of Nairobi, Kenya.* London: Amnesty International (2010). 12. Web. Available online at http://www.amnesty.org/en/library/asset/AFR32/002 /2010/en/12a9d334-0b62-40e1-ae4a-e5333752d68c/afr320022010en.pdf.

22. Ibid., 17.

23. Few outside of these slums would think of studying such things but fortunately Amnesty International has. Ibid., 5.

24. UN Habitat. *State of the World's Cities 2010/2011.*

25. UN Women. *Violence Against Women Prevalence Data: Surveys by Country.* (2012). Web. Available online at http://www.endvawnow.org/uploads/browser/files/vaw_prevalencematrix_dec2012.pdf.

26. Dorothy Kweyu. "P3 Forms in the Spotlight as Women Are Denied Justice." *The Nation.* April 30, 2010. Web. Available online at http://www.nation.co.ke/News/P3-forms-in-the-spotlight-as-women-are-denied-justice/-/1056/909850/-/2igob2/-/index.html.

CHAPTER 2

1. The World Bank. "World Bank Sees Progress Against Extreme Poverty, But Flags Vulnerabilities." February 29, 2012. Web. Available online at http://go.worldbank.org/2MU9XBWGX0.

   See also Shaohua Chen and Martin Ravallion. "An Update to the World Bank's Estimates of Consumption Poverty in the Developing World." Development Research Group, World Bank (2012). Available online at http://siteresources.worldbank.org/INTPOVCALNET/Resources/Global_Poverty_Update_2012_02-29-12.pdf.

2. "Multidimensional Poverty Index." *Human Development Reports.* United National Development Programme (2011). Web. Available online at http://hdr.undp.org/en/statistics/mpi/.

3. USAID. *Two Decades of Progress: USAID's Child Survival and Maternal Health Program.* Washington, DC: USAID (2009). Web. Available online at http://pdf.usaid.gov/pdf_docs/PDACN044.pdf.

   James P Grant. *The State of The World's Children 1981–82.* Leicester: United Nations Children's Fund (UNICEF) (1981). Web. Available online at http://www.unicef.org/sowc/archive/ENGLISH/The%20State%20of%20the%20World's%20Children%201981-82.pdf.

   See also http://www.unicefusa.org/campaigns/believe-in-zero/.

4. UNICEF and the World Health Organization. *Progress on Drinking Water and Sanitation: 2012 Update.* WHO/UNICEF Joint Monitoring Programme for Water Supply and Sanitation. (2012). Web. Available online at http://www.unicef.org/media/files/JMPreport2012.pdf.

   United Nations. *The Millennium Development Goals Report 2011.* New York: United Nations (2011). Web. Available online at http://mdgs.un.org/unsd/mdg/Resources/Static/Products/Progress2011/11-31339%20(E)%20MDG%20Report%202011_Book%20LR.pdf.

5. Food and Agriculture Organization of the United Nations, World Food Programme, International Fund for Agricultural Development. "The State of Food Insecurity in the World." Rome: Food and Agriculture Organization of the United Nations (2012). Web. Available online at http://www.fao.org/docrep/016/i3027e/i3027e.pdf.

   See also "Hunger Stats." World Food Programme. (2012). Web. Available online at http://www.wfp.org/hunger/stats.

6. UNESCO. "The Hidden Crisis: Armed Conflict and Education." *Education for All Global Monitoring Report 2011*. Paris: UNESCO (2011). Web. Available online at http://unesdoc.unesco.org/images/0019/001911/191186e.pdf.

   See also Roy Carr-Hill. "Finding and Then Counting Out-of-School Children." *Compare: A Journal of Comparative and International Education*. 42.2 (2012): 187–212. Web. Available online at http://www.tandfonline.com/doi/abs/10.1080/030 57925.2012.652806#preview (suggests 115 million).

7. United Nations. "Press Briefing by Special Rapporteur on Right to Adequate Housing." November 05, 2005. Web. Available online at http://www.un.org/News/briefings/docs/2005/kotharibrf050511.doc.htm.

8. United Nations. *The Millennium Development Goals Report 2011*. Web. Available online at http://mdgs.un.org/unsd/mdg/Resources/Static/Products/Progress2011/11-31339%20(E)%20MDG%20Report%202011_Book%20LR.pdf.

9. In 1820, about 75 percent of humanity lived on less than a dollar per day; as of 2013, about 20 percent live under that amount. In 2008, there were 6.7 billion people and 805 million of them lived of $1.00/day.

   Ian Vásquez. "Ending Mass Poverty." *Cato Institute*. September 2001. Web. Available online at http://www.cato.org/research/articles/vas-0109.html.

   Population Reference Bureau. "2008 World Population Data Sheet." 2008. Web. Available online at http://www.prb.org/Publications/Datasheets/2008/2008wpds.aspx.

   Chen and Ravallion. "An Update to the World Bank's Estimates."

10. Ibid.

11. The absolute number of people in the developing world living off less than $2 per day actually increased from 1981 (2.6 billion) to 2000 (2.9 billion) before falling back to 2.5 billion in 2008.

12. Michael R Anderson. "Access to Justice and Legal Process: Making Legal Institutions Responsive to Poor People in LDCs." *World Development Report Meeting*. 1999. Web. Available online at http://siteresources.worldbank.org/INTPOVERTY/Resources/WDR/DfID-Project-Papers/anderson.pdf (Note: 2003 update is available at http://www.ids.ac.uk/files/dmfile/Wp178.pdf).

13. The World Bank. "Poor People Endure Many Struggles; New Bank Study Cites Powerlessness And Domestic Violence." Voices of the Poor II. September 21, 2000. Web. Available online at http://web.worldbank.org/WBSITE/EXTERNAL/NEWS/0,,contentMDK:20013280~menuPK:34463~pagePK:34370~piPK:344 24~theSitePK:4607,00.html,

14. Deepa Narayan, Raj Patel, Kai Schafft, Anne Rademacher and Sarah Koch-Schulte. *Voices of the Poor: Can Anyone Hear Us?* New York: Oxford University Press (2000). 194. Web. Available online at http://siteresources.worldbank.org/INTPOVERTY/Resources/335642-1124115102975/1555199-1124115187705/vol1.pdf.

   Deepa Narayan, Robert Chambers, Meera K. Shah, and Patti Petesch. *Voices of the Poor: Crying Out for Change*. New York: Oxford University Press (2000). 126. Web. Available online at http://siteresources.worldbank.org/INTPOVERTY/Resources/335642-1124115102975/1555199-1124115201387/cry.pdf.

15. Ibid., 120.

16. Deepa Narayan and Patti Petesch. *Voices of the Poor: From Many Lands.* New York: Oxford University Press (2002). 69. Web. Available online at http://siteresources. worldbank.org/INTPOVERTY/Resources/335642-1124115102975/1555199-1124115210798/full.pdf.

17. Ibid., 368.

18. Narayan, et al. *Voices of the Poor: Can Anyone Hear Us?*, 181.

19. Narayan and Petesch, *Voices of the Poor: From Many Lands*, 99.

20. Ibid., 403.

21. "World Report on Violence and Health: Summary." Geneva: World Health Organization (2002). Web. Available online at http://www.who.int/ violence_injury_prevention/violence/world_report/en/summary_en.pdf.

22. United Nations Human Settlements Programme. "The Challenge of Slums: Global Report on Human Settlements 2003." London: Earthscan Publications Ltd. (2003). xxvii. Web. Available online at http://www.unhabitat.org/pmss/listItem-Details.aspx?publicationID=1156.

23. P. Amis and C. Rakodi. "Urban Poverty: Concepts, Characteristics and Policies." *Habitat International* 19.4 (199): 403–405.

24. Nicholas Kristof and Sheryl WuDunn. *Half the Sky: Turning Oppression into Opportunity for Women Worldwide.* New York: Vintage Books, Random House, Inc. (2009). xiv.

25. Narayan, et al. *Voices of the Poor: Crying Out for Change.* 122.

26. "Fact Sheet: Violence against Women Worldwide." New York: United Nations Development Fund for Women (2009). Web. Available online at http://www.uni-fem.org/campaigns/sayno/docs/SayNOunite_FactSheet_VAWworldwide.pdf.

27. "World Report on Violence and Health: Summary." 57–60.

   UN Millennium Project. *Taking Action: Achieving Gender Equality and Empowering Women.* London: Earthscan Publications Ltd. (2005). Web. Available online at http://www.unmillenniumproject.org/documents/Gender-complete.pdf.

28. Claudia García-Moreno, Henrica A. F. M. Jansen, Mary Ellsberg, Lori Heise, and Charlotte Watts. *WHO Multi-Country Study on Women's Health and Domestic Violence against Women.* Geneva: World Health Organization (2005). Web. Available online at http://www.who.int/gender/violence/who_multicountry_study/en/.

   Benjamin Petrini. "Domestic Violence Dataset: 1982–2007." 2010. Web. Available online at http://siteresources.worldbank.org/EXTCPR/Resources/ 407739-1267651559887/Domestic_Violence_Dataset_combined.pdf.

29. "Fact Sheet: Violence against Women Worldwide."

30. Kristof and WuDunn, xv.

31. United Nations General Assembly. *In-depth Study on All Forms of Violence against Women: Report of the Secretary-General.* 61st session. 2006. Web. Available online at http://www.un.org/womenwatch/daw/vaw/SGstudyvaw.htm.

32. UN Women. *Indicators on Violence Against Women.* Web. Available online at http:// www.un.org/womenwatch/daw/vaw/v-issues-focus.htm.

33. Shireen J. Jejeebhoy and Sarah Bott. *Non-consensual Sexual Experiences of Young People: A Review of the Evidence from Developing Countries.* New Delhi: Population Council (2003). Web. Available online at http://www.popcouncil.org/pdfs/wp/ seasia/seawp16.pdf.

Tracy McVeigh. "World Turning Blind Eye to 10 Million Child Brides Each Year, Charity Warns." *The Guardian.* June 25, 2011. Web. Available online at http://www.guardian.co.uk/society/2011/jun/26/10-million-child-brides-each-year-charity-warns.

34. Amnesty International. "Impunity – violence unchecked and unpunished," *It's in our Hands: Stop Violence Against Women.* Amnesty International. London: Amnesty International Publications. (2004) Available online at: http://amnesty.org/en/library/asset/ACT77/001/2004/en/d711a5d1-f7a7-11dd-8fd7-f57af21896e1/act770012004en.pdf

35. CDC. *Together for Girls: We Can End Sexual Violence.* Atlanta: Center for Disease Control and Prevention (2010). Web. Available online at http://www.cdc.gov/violenceprevention/pdf/TogetherforGirlsBklt-a.pdf.

36. "World Report on Violence and Health: Summary." 18.

37. Jill Keesbury and Ian Askew. *Comprehensive Responses to Gender Based Violence in Low-resource Settings: Lessons Learned from Implementation.* Population Council (2010). Web. Available online at http://www.popcouncil.org/pdfs/2010RH_CompRespGBV.pdf.

International Women's Health Coalition. "Triple Jeopardy: Female Adolescence, Sexual Violence, and HIV/AIDS." New York: International Women's Health Coaltion (2008). Web. Available online at http://www.iwhc.org/index.php?option=com_content&task=view&id=2693&Itemid=824.

38. U.S. Department of State. *2009 Human Rights Reports: Ethiopia.* Washington, DC: U.S. Department of State (2010). Web. Available online at http://www.state.gov/g/drl/rls/hrrpt/2009/af/135953.htm.

39. Anne M. Moore, Kofi Awusabo-Asare, Nyovani Madise, Johannes John-Langba, and Akwasi Kumi-Kyereme. "Coerced First Sex among Adolescent Girls in Sub-Saharan Africa: Prevalence and Context." *African Journal of Reproductive Health* 11.3 (2007). Web. Available online at http://www.guttmacher.org/pubs/journals/reprints/AJRH.11.3.62.pdf.

40. du Venage, Gavin. "Rape of children surges in South Africa/Minors account for about 40% of attack victims." San Francisco Chronicle. February 12, 2002. Web. Available online at http://www.sfgate.com/news/article/Rape-of-children-surges-in-South-Africa-Minors-2875310.php

41. Juan M. Contreras, Sarah Bott, Alessandra Guedes, and Elizabeth Dartnall. *Sexual Violence in Latin America and the Caribbean.* Sexual Violence Research Initiative (2010). Web. Available online at http://www.svri.org/SexualViolenceLACaribbean.pdf.

42. World Health Organization. "World Report on Violence and Health." Chapter 6. (2002). 156. Web. Available http://www.who.int/violence_injury_prevention/violence/world_report/chapters/en/

43. Medicines Sans Frontieres. "Sexual Violence. Web. Available online at http://www.doctorswithoutborders.org/news/issue_print.cfm?id=3466

44. Ibid.

45. Jejeebhoy and Bott. 8.

46. World Health Organization. "World Report on Violence and Health." Chapter 6. (2002). 156. Web. Available http://www.who.int/violence_injury_prevention/violence/world_report/chapters/en/

47. Shireen J. Jejeebhoy and Sarah Bott. *Non-consensual Sexual Experiences of Young People: A Review of the Evidence from Developing Countries.* New Delhi: Population Council (2003). Web. Available online at http://www.popcouncil.org/pdfs/wp/seasia/seawp16.pdf.

48. Ibid.15

49. "World Report on Violence and Health: Summary."

50. Donald E Brown. *Human Universals.* New York: McGraw-Hill (1991).

51. The ILO reports that there are 12.3 million in forced labor, of whom around 43 percent are forced to work in the sex trade.

International Labour Organization. "Fighting Human Trafficking: The Forced Labour Dimensions." January 28, 2008. Web. Available online at http://www.ilo.org/global/topics/forced-labour/publications/WCMS_090236/lang--en/index.htm.

Ethan B. Kapstein. "The New Global Slave Trade." *Foreign Affairs* 85.6 (2006): 106. Web. Available online at http://www.cgdev.org/doc/KapsteinfaslaveryFA.pdf.

Approximately 43 percent of [forced laborers] in the global market are used for sex.

52. Brian M Willis. "Child Prostitution: global health burden, research needs, and interventions." The Lancet. April 20, 2002. Available online at http://www.thelancet.com/journals/lancet/article/PIIS0140-6736(02)08355-1/fulltext

53. UNICEF. "State of the World's Children 2005." Web. Available at http://www.unicef.org/sowc05/english/sowc05.pdf

54. U.S. Department of State. "Country Reports on Human Rights Practices." March 31, 2003. Web. Available online at http://www.unicef.org/sowc05/english/sowc05.pdf

55. Patrick Belser. "Forced Labour and Human Trafficking: Estimating the Profits." Geneva: International Labour Office (2005). 14. Web. Available online at http://www.ilo.org/wcmsp5/groups/public/—ed_norm/—declaration/documents/publication/wcms_081971.pdf. (To say nothing of the additional $15.4 billion generated by forced commercial sexual exploitation in the industrialized nations).

56. HRW exposed the horror of forced prostitution in Thailand in 1994 and rightly identified it as a "Modern Form of Slavery."

Human Rights Watch. *A Modern Form of Slavery: Trafficking of Burmese Women and Girls into Brothels in Thailand.* New York: Human Rights Watch (1994). Web. Available online at http://www.hrw.org/legacy/reports/1993/thailand/.

57. United Nations Global Initiative to Fight Human Trafficking. "The Vienna Forum to Fight Human Trafficking." Background Paper. February 13–15, 2008. 2. 016 Workshop: Profiling the Traffickers. Vienna: UNODC (2008). Web. Available online at http://www.unodc.org/documents/human-trafficking/2008/BP016ProfilingtheTraffickers.pdf.

57. Available at TheLocustEffect.com.

59. Almost all the studies and reports under review found that a high percentage of trafficked people belong to lower income groups. The greater the degree of impoverishment, the higher is the risk of falling prey to trafficking.

Mukherjee and Das 1996. K.K. Mukherjee and Deepa Das, Prostitution in Six Metropolitan Cities of India, New Delhi, Central Social Welfare Board, 1996.

DWCD 1998. Department of Women and Child Development, Ministry of Human Resource Development, Government of India, Report on the committee on prostitution, child prostitutes and children of prostitutes & Plan of Action to combat trafickers and commercial sexual exploitation of women, New Delhi, India, 1998.

UNDCP, ILO, UNDP 2002, Survey of Opium Cultivation in Lohit District, Arunachal Pradesh, New Delhi, 2002.

Sankar Sen and P. M. Nair. "A Report on Trafficking in Women and Children in India 2002–2003." NHRC, UNIFEN, ISS Project, vol. I. New Delhi: UNIFEM (2004). Web. Available online at http://www.ashanet.org/focusgroups/sanctuary/articles/ReportonTrafficking.pdf.

60. Ibid.

60. Nakul Bera has since been convicted of rape and other trafficking-related offenses in Maya's case. Judgment from Court of Additional District & Sessions Judge, Fast Track, 2nd Court, Haldia, Purba Medinipur. March 15, 2013.

62. Belser.

63. Kevin Bales. "How We Can End Slavery." *National Geographic Magazine*. 2003.Web. Available online at http://ngm.nationalgeographic.com/ngm/0309/feature1/online_extra.html.

64. John D. Sutter. "Slavery's Last Stronghold." *CNN Freedom Project*. 2012. Web. Available online at http://www.cnn.com/interactive/2012/03/world/mauritania.slaverys.last.stronghold/index.html.

65. Ethan B. Kapstein. "The New Global Slave Trade." *Foreign Affairs* 85, no. 6 2006. 103-115.

66. David Eltis. "The Volume and Structure of the Transatlantic Slave Trade: A Reassessment." *William and Mary Quarterly* 58,no. 1 (2001): 17–46.

67. Bales, 15–17. ILO. "A Global Alliance against Forced Labour." International Labour Conference. 93rd Session. Report I(B). 18. Geneva: International Labour Office (2005). Web. Available online at http://www.ilo.org/public/english/standards/relm/ilc/ilc93/pdf/rep-i-b.pdf.

68. Kevin Bales. *Ending Slavery: How We Free Today's Slaves*. University of California Press, 2008.

69. "Bonded Labour Touches the Figure of 1m in Pakistan." *Daily Times*. February 26, 2005. Web. Available online at http://www.dailytimes.com.pk/default.asp?page=story_26-2-2005_pg7_15.

70. John D. Sutter. "Slavery's Last Stronghold." *CNN Freedom Project*. 2012. Web. Available online at http://www.cnn.com/interactive/2012/03/world/mauritania.slaverys.last.stronghold/index.html.

71. Samuel Grumiau. "UNICEF Aids Restavek Victims of Abuse and Exploitation in Haiti." *At a Glance: Haiti*. January 31, 2012. Web. Available online at http://www.unicef.org/infobycountry/haiti_61518.html.

72. Robyn Dixon. "Africa's Bitter Cycle of Child Slavery." *Los Angeles Times*. July 12, 2012. Web. Available online at http://articles.latimes.com/2009/jul/12/world/fg-ghana-slavery12; See also "George Achibra." *Not My Life*. http://notmylife.org/participants/george-achibra.

International Labour Organization. "Combatting Forced Labour and Discrimination in Africa". Web. Available online at http://www.ilo.org/sapfl/Projects/WCMS_082041/lang--en/index.htm.

73. "Brazilian Pact to Eradicate Slave Labour." Pacto Nacional. Web. Available online at http://www.reporterbrasil.com.br/pacto/conteudo/view/9.

74. Br. Xavier Plassat. "Brazil Slave Labor: Hero Honored for Battling Human Trafficking." *Interview by Catholic Relief Services.* June 15, 2010. Web. Available online at http://crs-blog.org/brazil-slave-labor-hero-honored-for-battling-human-trafficking/.

75. Johannes Koettl. "Human Trafficking, Modern Day Slavery, and Economic Exploitation." *SP Discussion Paper.* No. 0911. May 2009. 10, 13. Web. Available online at http://siteresources.worldbank.org/SOCIALPROTECTION/Resources/SP-Discussion-papers/Labor-Market-DP/0911.pdf.

"Bonded labor, in particular in South Asia, is the most important form of forced labor."

Beate Andrees and Patrick Belser. *Forced Labor: Coercion and Exploitation in the Private Economy.* Boulder: Lynne Rienner Publishers (2009). 51. "Bonded labor in Pakistan and India almost certainly accounts for the largest number of forced labor in the world today."

Kevin Bales. *Disposable People: New Slavery in the Global Economy.* (Berkeley and Los Angeles: University of California Press. Rev. ed. (2012).

"The biggest part of that 27 million, perhaps 15 to 20 million, is represented by *bonded labor* in India, Pakistan, Bangladesh, and Nepal."

76. Aneel Karnani. "Microfinance Needs Regulation." *Philanthropy News Digest.* October 31, 2011. Web. Available online at http://foundationcenter.org/pnd/ssir/ssir_item.jhtml?id=359800001. Even microfinance efforts in the developing world are coming under fire because of concerns about coercive loan recovery methods.

77. UN-HABITAT. *Secure Land Rights for All.* HS/978/08E. 2008. Web. Available online at http://www.responsibleagroinvestment.org/rai/sites/responsibleagro-investment.org/files/Secure%20land%20rights%20for%20all-UN%20HABITAT.pdf.

Nicole Anand. "To Fight Poverty, Give Secure and Long-term Land Rights to the Poor." *OneWorld South Asia.* November 13, 2010. Web. Available online at http://southasia.oneworld.net/weekend/to-fight-poverty-give-secure-and-long-term-land-rights-to-the-poor.

78. David Bledsoe and Michael Brown. *Land and Conflict: A Toolkit for Intervention.*USAID (2005). Web. Available online at http://transition.usaid.gov/our_work/cross-cutting_programs/conflict/publications/docs/CMM_Land_and_Conflict_Toolkit_April_2005.pdf.

Land Governance for Equitable and Sustainable Development. "Kenya: Food Security and Land Governance Factsheet." 2010. Web. Available online at http://www.landgovernance.org/system/files/Kenya%20Factsheet%20landac%20april%202011.pdf.

Caroline Moser and Dennis Rodgers. "Change, Violence and Insecurity in Non-Conflict Situations." *Overseas Development Institute Working Paper 245.* March 2005. Web. Available online at http://www.odi.org.uk/resources/docs/1824.pdf.

79. UN-HABITAT.

80. Hamid Rashid. "Land Rights and the Millennium Development Goals: How the Legal Empowerment Approach Can Make a Difference." *IDLO Legal Empowerment Working Papers No. 15.* Rome: International Development Law Organization

(2010). Web. Available online at http://www.idlo.int/publications/LEWP/ LEWP_Rashid.pdf.

81. "Africa's Homeless Widows." *The New York Times.* Opinion. June 16, 2004. Web. Available online at http://www.nytimes.com/2004/06/16/opinion/africa-s-homeless-widows.html.

82. Sylvia B. Ondimba. "The World Must Support Its Widows." *The Guardian.* June 23, 2011. Web. Available online at http://www.guardian.co.uk/commentisfree/2011/jun/23/international-widows-day-support.

83. UN Division for the Advancement of Women. "Widowhood: Invisible Women, Secluded or Excluded." *Women 2000.* December 2001. Web. Available online at http://www.un.org/womenwatch/daw/public/wom_Dec%2001%20single%20pg.pdf.

84. Kachika, Tanyade. "Land Grabbing in Africa: A Review of the Impacts and the Possible Policy Responses" Oxfam (2010). http://www.oxfamblogs.org/east-africa/wp-content/uploads/2010/11/Land-Grabbing-in-Africa.-Final.pdf //

85. Kaori Izumi, et al. "Protecting Women's Land and Property Rights in the Context of AIDS." Module 4/Thematic Note 5. (2008). Web. Available online at http://siteresources.worldbank.org/INTGENAGRLIVSOUBOOK/Resources/AfricaIAP.pdf.

86. UN Division for the Advancement of Women.

87. S. Vanessa von Struensee. "Widows, AIDS, Health, and Human Rights in Africa." (2004). Web. Available online at http://www.genderandaids.org/index.php?option=com_content&view=article&id=90:widows-aids-health-and-human-rights-in-africa&catid=34:africa&Itemid=114

88. Rashid.

89. Ibid.

89. Oxfam. "Oxfam warns that modern day land rush is forcing thousands into greater poverty." Oxfam (2011). Web. Available online at http://www.oxfam.org.uk/media-centre/press-releases/2011/09/modern-day-land-rush.

91. Narayan, Chambers, Shah, and Petesch (emphasis added).

92. Narayan and Petesch, 471.

93. Ibid.

94. Narayan, Chambers, Shah, and Petesch.

95. Narayan and Petesch.

96. Ibid.

97. Open Society Justice Initiative. "Criminal Force: Torture, Abuse, and Extrajudicial Killings by the Nigeria Police Force." Open Society Institute and NOPRIN. New York: Open Society Initiative (2010). Web. Available online at http://www.soros.org/initiatives/justice/articles_publications/publications/nigeria-police-abuse-report-20100519.

98. Narayan, Chambers, Shah, and Petesch.

99. Ibid., 163. Amnesty International. "Rape: The Silent Weapon." Amnesty International (2006). 3. Web. Available online at http://www.amnesty.org/en/library/info/AFR44/020/2006

100.   Open Society Justice Initiative. "Pretrial Detention and Torture: Why Pretrial Detainees Face the Greatest Risk." New York: Open Society Initiative

(2011). 23. Web. Available online at http://www.unhcr.org/refworld/category,COI,OSI,,,4e324fa22,0.html.

101. Ibid., 20.

102. Ibid.

102. "Unclog the Courts: Law Ministry Proposes Measures to Clear Backlog of Cases." *The Times of India*, October 27, 2009.

104. "Pretrial Detention and Torture: Why Pretrial Detainees Face the Greatest Risk."

105. Alfred de Zayas. "Human Rights and Indefinite Detention." s/files/other/irrc_857_zayas.pdf.

106. Open Society Justice Initiative. "The Socioeconomic Impact of Pretrial Detention." New York: Open Society Initiative (2010). 13. Web. Available online at http://www.undp.org/content/dam/undp/library/Democratic%20Governance/a2j-%20Socioeconomic%20impact%20of%20PTD%20OSI%20UNDP.pdf.

107. Ibid.

108. Michael Wines. "The Forgotten of Africa, Wasting Away in Jails Without Trial." *The New York Times*, November 6, 2005. Web. Available online at http://www.nytimes.com/2005/11/06/international/africa/06prisons.html?pagewanted=print.

109. Police Staff College. "Locked up and Forgotten." October 2010. Web. Available online at http://www.penalreform.org/files/GTZ_locked_UP_forgotten.pdf.

110. Open Society Justice Initiative, 2010. 8.

110. United Nations. "Interim report of the Special Rapporteur on torture and other cruel, inhuman or degrading treatment or punishment." United Nations. (2009) Web. Available online at http://antitorture.org/wp-content/uploads/2012/07/V-Thematic-Report-Conditions-of-Detention-Children-in-Detention.pdf

112. Ibid., 34.

113. Alfred de Zayas. "Human Rights and Indefinite Detention."857_zayas.pdf

114. Open Society Justice Initiative, 2011. 17.

115. Ibid., 30.

116. Ibid., 11.

117. Nowak, Manfred. "Fact-Finding on Torture and Ill-Treatment and Conditions of Detention." *Journal of Human Rights Practice* 1, no. 1 (March 2009): 113. Web. Available online at http://jhrp.oxfordjournals.org/content/1/1/101.full.pdf+html.

CHAPTER 3

1. Lyndon N Irwin and Douglas Pascoe. "Grasshopper Plagues and Destitute Farmers." Missouri State University Agricultural History Series: Grasshopper Plagues. Web. Available online at http://www.lyndonirwin.com/hopdesti.htm.

2. "When The Skies Turned To Black: The Locust Plague of 1875: A Study of the Intersection of Genealogy and History." Hearthstone Legacy Publications.

2004–2012. Web. Available online at http://www.hearthstonelegacy.com/when-the-skies-turned-to-black-the_locust-plague-of-1875.htm.

3. Daniel Hubbard. "Locusts on the Plains." *Personal Past Meditations: A Genealogical Blog.* 2009. Web. Available online at http://www.thepersonalpast.com/2009/08/14/locusts/.

   See also Yoon, Carol Kaesuk. "Looking Back at the Days of the Locust." *The New York Times.* 23 April 2002. Web. Available online at http://www.nytimes.com/2002/04/23/science/looking-back-at-the-days-of-the-locust.html.

4. Lyndon N Irwin and Douglas Pascoe. "Grasshopper Plagues and Destitute Farmers." Missouri State University Agricultural History Series: Grasshopper Plagues. Web. Available online at http://www.lyndonirwin.com/hopdesti.htm

5. *The History of Henry and St. Clair Counties, Missouri.* St. Joseph, MO: National Historical Company, 1883. 959. Web. Available online at http://www.archive.org/stream/historyofhenryst00nati#page/958/mode/2up.

6. Christopher Stone. "Crime, Justice Systems and Development Assistance." *World Bank Legal Review: Law, Equity, and Development,* vol. 2. Washington: World Bank and Martinus Nijhoff, 2006. 215, 216. Web. Available online at https://openknowledge.worldbank.org/bitstream/handle/10986/6899/568260PUB0REPL1INAL0PROOF0FULL0TEXT.pdf?sequence=1.

7. (Narayan 1999) and (Sage et al. 2006) in Open Society Justice Initiative and Department for International Development 2008:7.

   Roger Bowles, Joseph Akpokodje, Emmanuel Tigere. *Evidenced-based Approaches to Crime Prevention in Developing Countries.* Centre for Criminal Justice Economics and Psychology, University of York, (2002).

8. Pablo Fajnzylber, Daniel Lederman, and Norman Loayza. *Determinants of Crime Rates in Latin America and the World: An Empirical Assessment.* Washington, DC: World Bank (1998). 1. Web. Available online at http://www-wds.worldbank.org/servlet/WDSContentServer/WDSP/IB/2000/02/23/000094946_9903040 6230127/Rendered/PDF/multi_page.pdf.

9. The World Bank. *The World Bank Legal Review: Law, Equity, and Development.* vol. 2. Ed. A. Palacio. Washington: The World Bank (2006). 18. Print.

10. United Nations Office on Drugs and Crime. *Crime and Development in Central America: Caught in the Crossfire.* Vienna: UNODC (2007). 11. Web. Available online at http://www.unodc.org/documents/data-and-analysis/Central-america-study-en.pdf.

    Antonio Maria Costa. *Localizing the Millennium Development Goals.* United Nations, 2008. 2.

11. Department for International Development. *Eliminating World Poverty,* 2006. London: DFID (2006) 37.

12. United Nations Office on Drugs and Crime. *Crime and Development in Africa.* Vienna: UNODC (2005). 101. Web. Available online at http://www.unodc.org/pdf/African_report.pdf.

13. Deepa Narayan, Robert Chambers, Meera K. Shah, and Patti Petesch. "Anxiety, Fear, and Insecurities." *Voices of the Poor: Crying Out for Change.* New York: Oxford University Press (2000). 152. Web. Available online at http://siteresources.

worldbank.org/INTPOVERTY/Resources/335642-1124115102975/1555199-1124115201387/cry.pdf.

14. Michael R. Anderson. *Access to Justice and Legal Process: Making Legal Institutions Responsive to Poor People in LDCs.* Sussex: Institute of Development Studies (2003). 2. Web. Available online at http://www.ids.ac.uk/files/dmfile/Wp178.pdf; Easterly, 87 ("Another problem society must solve is the protection of property and person.")

See also Amartya Sen. "What Is the Role of Legal and Judicial Reform in the Development Process." *The World Bank Legal Review: Law, Equity, and Development,* vol. 2. Ed. A. Palacio. Washington: The World Bank (2006). 215–216. ("Let me pause here a bit to recollect how capitalism came into such a successful system. Capitalism did not emerge until the evolution of law and order and the legal and practical acceptance of property rights had made an ownership-based economy feasible and operational. The efficiency of exchange could not work until contracts could be freely made and effectively enforced, through legal as well as behavioural reforms.")

15. Daron Acemoglu and James Robinson. *Why Nations Fail, The Origins of Power, Prosperity & Poverty.* New York: Random House (2012).

16. George Soros and Fazle Hasan Abed. "Rule of Law Can Rid the World of Poverty." *Financial Times,* September 26, 2012. Available online at http://www.ft.com/intl/cms/s/0/f78f8e0a-07cc-11e2-8354-00144feabdc0.html#axzz2NcxJB1Wi.

17. World Bank. *World Development Report.* 2011. 64–65. Web. Available online at http://siteresources.worldbank.org/INTWDRS/Resources/WDR2011_Chapter1.pdf.

("While all the costs cannot be quantified, conservative estimates of the economic costs of lost production range from 2 to 3% of GDP both for civil war and for very high levels of violent crime.")

18. Ginger Thompson. "In Guatemala Village, a Scramble for Bodies." *The New York Times,* October 11, 2005. Web. Available online at http://www.nytimes.com/2005/10/10/world/americas/10iht-flood.html.

19. *World Development Report,* 65.

20. Juan Luis Londoño and Rodrigo Guerrero. "Violencia en América Latina: epidemiología y costos." In *Asalto al Desarrolla: Violencia en América Latina.* Ed. Juan Luis Londoño, Alejandro Gaviria, and Rodrigo Guerrero. Washington D.C.: Inter-American Development Bank (cited in http://idbdocs.iadb.org/wsdocs/getdocument.aspx?docnum=36835069 p. 6).

21. IDB Institutions for Development—Institutional Capacity of the State Division. *The Cost of Crime and Violence in Latin America and the Caribbean.* 5. Web. Available online at http://idbdocs.iadb.org/wsdocs/getdocument.aspx?docnum=36835069.

See also United Nations Organization on Drugs and Crime and the Latin America and the Caribbean region of the World Bank. *Crime, Violence, and Development: Trends, Costs, and Policy Options in the Caribbean.* 2007. 59. Web. Available online at https://openknowledge.worldbank.org/bitstream/handle/10986/7687/378200LAC0Crim1white0cover01PUBLIC1.pdf?sequence=1.

22. Pfizer (2001) estimates that the aggregate cost of crime and violence is tantamount to 5 percent of industrialized countries' GDP or 14 percent of low-income countries' GDP.

Inter-American Development Bank. Institutions for Development—Institutional Capacity of the State Division. 5.

23. Mayra Buvinic and Andrew Morrison. *Technical Note 4: Violence as an Obstacle to Development*. Inter-American Development Bank (1999), 4. Web. Available online at http://idbdocs.iadb.org/wsdocs/getdocument.aspx?docnum=362887.

24. Ibid.

25. World Health Organization. "Violence by Intimate Partners." *World Report on Violence and Health* (2002), 102–103. Web. Available online at http://whqlibdoc. who.int/publications/2002/9241545615_chap4_eng.pdf.

26. Buvinic, 5.

27. United Nations Office on Drugs and Crime. *Crime and Development in Africa*. Vienna: UNODC (2005). 67.

28. United Nations Office on Drugs and Crime. *Crime and Development in Central America*: Caught in the Crossfire. Vienna: UNODC (2007). 73.

29. *Crime and Development in Africa*.

30. Human Rights Watch. "South Africa: Sexual Violence Rampant in Schools." March 27, 2001. Available online at http://www.hrw.org/news/2001/03/26/south-africa-sexual-violence-rampant-schools.

31. *Crime and Development in Africa*, 72.

32. World Health Organization. *Thirds Milestone of a Global Campaign of Violence Prevention Report* (2007), 7. Web. Available online at http://whqlibdoc.who.int/publications/2007/9789241595476_eng.pdf.

33. *Crime and Development in Africa*, 67; *Crime and Development in Central America: Caught in the Crossfire*, 73. Web.

34. World Bank. *Crime and Violence in Central America: A Development Challenge*. World Bank (2011). 5, 11, 17. Web. Available online at http://siteresources. worldbank.org/INTLAC/Resources/FINAL_VOLUME_I_ENGLISH_ CrimeAndViolence.pdf.

35. *Crime and Development in Africa*, 68.

36. Ibid., xiii, 71.

37. Michael R. Anderson. *Access to Justice and Legal Process: Making Legal Institutions Responsive to Poor People in LDCs*. Sussex: Institute of Development Studies (2003). 20. Web. Available online at http://www.ntd.co.uk/idsbookshop/details. asp?id=729.

38. World Health Organization. "Violence by Intimate Partners." (2007). 101–102. Available online at http://www.who.int/violence_injury_prevention/violence/activities/intimate/en/index.html.

39. Buvinic, 4.

40. Judith Herman. *Trauma and Recovery: The Aftermath of Violence-from Domestic Abuse to Political Terror*. New York: Basic Books (1992). 86.

41. Ibid. 90.

42. Ibid. 94.

43. Centre on Housing Rights and Evictions Women and Housing Rights Programme. *Women, Slums and Urbanisation:Examining the Causes and Consequences*. 2008. 13. Web. Available online at http://sheltercentre.org/sites/default/files/COHRE_ WomenSlumsAndUrbanisationExaminingTheCausesAndConsequences.pdf.

44. UN-Habitat.*State of the World's Cities 2010/2011—Cities for All: Bridging the Urban Divide*. London: Earthscan Publications Ltd. (2010).117. Available online at http://www.worldcat.org/title/state-of-the-worlds-cities-20102011-bridging-the-urban-divide/oclc/506252802

45. Human Rights Watch. *Policy Paralysis: A Call for Action on HIV/AIDS-Related Human Rights Abuses Against Women and Girls in Africa* (December 2003), 10. Web. Available online at http://cfsc.trunky.net/_uploads/Publications/5.A_Call_for_Action_on_HIVAIDS-Related_Human_Rights_Abuses_Against_Women_and_Girls_in_Africa.pdf.

46. International Labour Conference. *A Global Alliance Against Forced Labour*. 93rd Session, 2005. Geneva: International Labour Office (2006). 30. Web. Available online at http://www.ilo.org/public/english/standards/relm/ilc/ilc93/pdf/rep-i-b.pdf.

47. Johannes Koettl. *Human Trafficking, Modern Day Slavery, and Economic Exploitation*. The World Bank 2009). Web. Available online at http://siteresources.worldbank.org/SOCIALPROTECTION/Resources/SP-Discussion-papers/Labor-Market-DP/0911.pdf.

48. Open Society Foundations. The Global Campaign for Pretrial Justice. *Collateral Consequences: How Pretrial Detention Stunts Socioeconomic Development*. Open Society Justice Initiative (2013). Web. Available online at http://www.open-societyfoundations.org/publications/collateral-consequences-how-pretrial-detention-stunts-socioeconomic-development

49. Christopher Stone. *Crime, Justice, and Growth in South Africa: Toward a Plausible Contribution from Criminal Justice to Economic Growth*. Center for International Development at Harvard University. 2006. 10. Web. Available online at http://www.hks.harvard.edu/var/ezp_site/storage/fckeditor/file/pdfs/centers-programs/centers/cid/publications/faculty/wp/131.pdf.
See also Lloyd, Susan. "The Effects of Domestic Violence on Women's Employment." *Law and Policy* 19, no. 2 (1997): 156.

50. Christopher Stone. "Crime, Justice Systems and Development Assistance." *World Bank Legal Review: Law, Equity, and Development*, vol. 2. Washington: World Bank and Martinus Nijhoff, 2006. 216. Web. Available online at https://openknowledge.worldbank.org/bitstream/handle/10986/6899/568260PUB0REPL1INAL0PROOF0FULL0TEXT.pdf?sequence=1.

CHAPTER 4

1. Patricia Kameri Mbote and Migai Akech. *Kenya: Justice Sector and the Rule of Law*. Johannesburg: The Open Society Initiative for Eastern Africa (2011). 12, 149. Web. Available online at http://www.ielrc.org/content/a1104.pdf.

2. Ibid., 123.

3. Ibid., 124.

4. World Health Organization. "Summary and Key Points." *World Malaria Report 2011*. World Health Organization (2011). Web. Available online at http://www.who.int/malaria/world_malaria_report_2011/wmr2011_summary_keypoints.pdf.

5. "Malaria Overview." Bill and Melinda Gates Foundation. 1999–2012. Web. Available online at http://www.gatesfoundation.org/topics/pages/malaria.aspx.

6. David H. Bayley. *Police for the Future*. Oxford University Press: New York (1994); Carl B. Klockers. "The Rhetoric of Community Policing." In J.R. Greene and S.D. Mastrofski (eds), *Community Policing: Rhetoric or Reality*. New York: Praeger (1988) 239-258.

    See also *Thinking about Police: Contemporary Readings*. Ed. C. B. Klockers and S. D. Mastrofski. New York: McGraw-Hill, Inc. (1991). 537. Print.

7. Richard A. Leo. "Police Scholarship for the Future: Resisting the Pull of the Policy Audience." Law and Society , vol. 30 (1996): 871. Web. Available online at http://papers.ssrn.com/sol3/ papers.cfm?abstract_ id=1144325. In fact, Bayley has written another book specifically on how to build police forces in the developing world. See David H. Bayley. *Changing the Guard: Developing Democratic Police Abroad*. New York: Oxford University Press (2005). (For reviews of this work see http://www.politicalreviewnet.com/polrev/reviews/PUAR/R_0033_3352_277_1007578.asp and http://www.jstor.org/discover/10.2307/4623353?uid=3739936&uid=2129&uid=2&uid=70&uid=4&uid=3739256&sid=56280155533.)

    See also two related articles by Bayley: David H. Bayley and Christine Nixon. "The Changing Environment for Policing, 1985–2008." *New Perspectives in Policing*. Harvard Kennedy School, September 2010. Web. Available online at https://www.ncjrs.gov/pdffiles1/nij/ncj230576.pdf; and David H. Bayley. "Democratizing the Police Abroad: What to Do and How to Do It." *Issues in International Crime*. U.S. Department of Justice. Web. Available online at https://www.ncjrs.gov/pdffiles1/nij/188742.pdf.

8. Steven Pinker. *The Better Angels of Our Nature: Why Violence Has Declined*. New York: The Viking Press (2011). 681. Print.

9. In the past decade, empirical economists have made substantial progress in identifying the effects of punishment on crime by finding new ways to break the simultaneity of crime rates and punishments. The new empirical evidence generally supports the deterrence model but shows that incapacitation influences crime rates, too. Evidence of the crime-reducing effect of the scale of policing and incarceration is consistent across different methodological approaches.

    Steven D. Levitt and Thomas J. Miles. "Empirical Study of Criminal Punishment." *Handbook of Law and Economics* Ed. A. M. Polinsky and S. Shavell. Amsterdam: Elsevier, 2007. 455–495.

    For example, criminologists of the rational-choice perspective, such as Derek Cornish and Ronald Clarke, have written convincingly of the process of choice that a criminal makes when he or she is contemplating the commission of a crime. The risk of apprehension, according to Cornish and Clarke, is but one criterion that must be weighed by the would-be criminal before he or she decides to commit the crime (Adler, Mueller, and Laufer 1995). Increasing the risk of apprehension, for example, through focused police patrols or hot spot surveillance, will influence the rational choices available to the offender and, assuming the correct choice is then made, prevent crime. Bayley's assertion that police do not prevent crime is also refuted by the routine-activities perspective theory of crime asserted by noted criminologists Lawrence Cohen and Marcus Felson. Similar to the rational-choice theory, the routine-activities perspective focuses on the characteristics of the crime, rather than those of the offender. Cohen and Felson point out that crime rates rise along with the number of suitable targets and the absence of people to protect those targets (Adler, Mueller, and Laufer 1995).

See Derek Cornish and Ronald V. Clarke eds. *The Reasoning Criminal: Rational Choice Perspectives on Offending.* New York: Springer-Verlag (1986).

See also John J. Coleman. Book Review: Police for the Future by David H. Bayley. The National Executive Institute Associates Leadership Bulletin, March 2001. Web. Available online at http://www.neiassociates.org/bookreview.htm.

10. Pinker, 122.
11. World Bank. *Crime, Violence and Economic Development in Brazil: Elements for Effective Public Policy.* Washington: World Bank (2006). ii.
12. King, Martin Luther, Jr. "Social Justice." Conscience of America Series. Western Michigan University, Read Fieldhouse. Kalamazoo, MI. December 18, 1963. Lecture. Web. Available online at http://www.wmich.edu/sites/default/files/attachments/MLK.pdf.
13. World Bank. *World Development Report 2006: Equity and Development.* World Bank (2006). 13. Web. Available online at http://siteresources.worldbank.org/INTWDR2006/Resources/WDR_on_Equity_FinalOutline_July_public.pdf.
14. Center for Rights Education and Awareness. *Status of Women and Girls in Kenya: Urgent Need to Uphold Human Rights.* Center for Rights Education and Awareness (2007). 12. Web. Available online at http://www.creawkenya.org/creaw-publications/the-status-of-women-and-girls-in-kenya.html.
15. Caroline Sage, Nicholas Menzies, and Michael Woolcock. "Taking the Rules of the Game Seriously: Mainstreaming Justice in Development: The World Bank's Justice for the Poor Program." *IDLO Articles.* Rome: International Development Law Organization (2010). 6.
16. Ibid., 8
17. United Nations Rule of Law. Commission on Legal Empowerment of the Poor. *Making the Law Work for Everyone: Report of the Commission on Legal Empowerment of the Poor, vol. 1.* United Nations Development Programme (2008). 47.
18. Christopher Stone. "Crime, Justice Systems and Development Assistance." *World Bank Legal Review: Law, Equity, and Development,* vol. 2. Washington: World Bank (2006). 217. Web. Available online at https://openknowledge.worldbank.org/bitstream/handle/10986/6899/568260PUB0REPL1INAL0PROOF0FULL0TEXT.pdf?sequence=1.
19. Deepa Narayan, Robert Chambers, Meera K. Shah, and Patti Petesch. "A Call to Action: The Challenge to Change." *Voices of the Poor: Crying Out for Change.* New York: Oxford University Press (2000). 280. Web. Available online at http://siteresources.worldbank.org/INTPOVERTY/Resources/335642-1124115102975/1555199-1124115201387/cry.pdf.

CHAPTER 5

1. Child Rights International Network. *Denouncing Sexual Violence Against Adolescent Girls in Bolivia.* Child Rights International Network (2012). Web. Available online

at http://www.crin.org/docs/Thematic_Hearing_Submission_DRAFT_03-08-12_3pm.pdf.

2. United Nations Office on Drugs and Crime. *Crime and Development in Africa.* United Nations (2005). Web. Available online at http://www.unodc.org/pdf/African_report.pdf.

3. United Nations Office on Drugs and Crime. *Crime and Development in Central America: Caught in the Crossfire.* United Nations (2007). 30.

4. Steven Pinker. *The Better Angels of Our Nature: Why Violence Has Declined.* New York: Viking Press (2011).

5. Human Rights Watch. *Broken System: Dysfunction, Abuse, and Impunity in the Indian Police.* New York: Human Rights Watch (2009). 7, 26–28. Web. Available online at http://www.hrw.org/sites/default/files/reports/india0809web.pdf.

6. Administrative Staff College of India. *Training Module for Sub-Inspector.* Web. Available online at http://bprd.nic.in/writereaddata/linkimages/4596119307-Training%20Module%20for%20Sub-Inspector.pdf.

7. *Broken System: Dysfunction, Abuse, and Impunity in the Indian Police,* 32.

8. *Broken System: Dysfunction, Abuse, and Impunity in the Indian Police,* 33.

9. Praveen Swami. "Why Rape Victims Aren't Getting Justice." *The Hindi,* March 11, 2012. Web. Available online at http://www.thehindu.com/news/national/article2982508.ece.

10. Naureen Shah and Meenakshi Ganguly. *India: Broken System: Dysfunction, Abuse, and Impunity in the Indian Police.* New York: Human Rights Watch (2009). 68.

11. Deepa Narayan and Patti Petesch. *Voices of the Poor: From Many Lands.* New York: Oxford University Press (2002). 71.

12. Ibid., 128.

13. Charles Kenny. *Getting Better: Why Global Development Is Succeeding—And How We Can Improve the World Even More.* New York: Basic Books (2011). 170.

14. Human Rights Watch. *Broken System: Dysfunction, Abuse, and Impunity in the Indian Police.* New York: Human Rights Watch (2009). 9. Web. Available online at http://www.hrw.org/sites/default/files/reports/india0809web.pdf.

15. Amnesty International. *Kenya: Insecurity and Indignity: Women's Experiences in the Slums of Nairobi, Kenya.* London: Amnesty International (2010). 15.

16. "Police officers can thus manipulate the crime rate in their jurisdictions by simply refusing to register victims' complaints." Abhijit Banerjee, Raghabendra Chattopadhyay, Esther Duflo, Daniel Keniston, and Nina Singh. *Can Institutions Be Reformed from Within? Evidence from a Randomized Experiment with the Rajasthan Police.* Poverty Action Lab, Massachusetts Institute of Technology (2012). 7. Web. Available online at http://www.povertyactionlab.org/publication/can-institutions-be-reformed-within-evidence-randomized-experiment-rajasthan-police

17. Ian Clegg, Robert Hunt, and Jim Whetton. *Policy Guidance on Support to Policing in Developing Countries.* Swansea: Centre for Development Studies, University of Wales (2000). 23–24. Web. Available online at http://www.gsdrc.org/docs/open/SEC4.pdf.

18. Ibid., 56.

19. *Kenya: Insecurity and Indignity: Women's Experiences in the Slums of Nairobi, Kenya,* 12.

20. Tamar Ezer. "Inheritance Law in Tanzania: The Impoverishment of Widows and Daughters." *The Georgetown Journal of Gender and the Law* 7 (2006): 599–662. Web. Available online at http://winafrica.org/wp-content/uploads/2011/08/Inheritance-Law-in-Tanzania1.pdf.

21. IRIN. "Women Struggle to Survive Sexual Violence in Indonesia." *Jakarta Globe,* April 10, 2012. Web. Available online at http://www.thejakartaglobe.com/lawandorder/women-struggle-to-survive-sexual-violence-in-indonesia/510427.

22. Human Rights Watch. *Broken System: Dysfunction, Abuse, and Impunity in the Indian Police.* New York: Human Rights Watch (2009). 9. Web. Available online at http://www.hrw.org/sites/default/files/reports/india0809web.pdf.

23. Asm Shahjahan. "Police Reform: A Bangladesh Concept." "Improving the Police's Role and Performance in Protecting Human and Economic Security." *Report from the ADB Symposium on Challenges in Implementing Access to Justice Reforms.* Asian Development Bank (2005) 39–40. Web. Available online at http://www2.adb.org/documents/reports/law-policy-reform/chap4.pdf.

24. Gen. Edgardo Aglipay. "Police Effectiveness and Accountability: Ideas to Launch Police Reform." *Improving the Police's Role and Performance in Protecting Human and Economic Security,* Report from the ADB Symposium on Challenges in Implementing Access to Justice Reforms. Asian Development Bank (2005). 48. Web. Available online at http://www2.adb.org/documents/reports/law-policy-reform/chap4.pdf.

25. The State Governments and UT Administrations incurred an expenditure of R` 31,748.3 crore on the police—which is $56,794,812,164, divided by 1.2 billion Indians, equals $47 per person. India: National Crime Records Bureau. "Police Strength, Expenditure, and Infrastructure." *National Crime Records Bureau Report 2010.* Web. Available online at http://ncrb.nic.in/CII2010/cii-2010/Chapter%2017.pdf.

   Compare to Washington, DC's $851 per person (18 times more), or New York State's $393 per person (8 times more), or California's $381 per person. (United States; Dept. of Justice. *State and Local Government Expenditures Per Capita by Criminal Justice Function and State: 2007,* Table 345. U.S. Department of Justice, September 2010. Web. Available online at http://www.census.gov/compendia/statab/2012/tables/12s0345.pdf.

26. United Nations Office on Drugs and Crime. *Crime and Development in Africa.* Vienna: UNODC (2005). 101. Web. Available online at http://www.unodc.org/pdf/African_report.pdf.

27. Ibid., 10.

28. United Nations Office on Drugs and Crime. *Crime and Development in Central America: Caught in the Crossfire.* Vienna: UNODC (2007). 30.

29. Adrianus E. Meliala. "Police Reform: The Indonesian Context." *Improving the Police's Role and Performance in Protecting Human and Economic Security,* Report from the ADB Symposium on Challenges in Implementing Access to Justice Reforms. Asian Development Bank (2005). 37. Web. Available online at http://www2.adb.org/documents/reports/law-policy-reform/chap4.pdf.

   Nicolas Florquin. "Global Private Security/Police Officer Personnel Levels by Country/Per Capita 2011." *2011 Small Arms Survey. Public Intelligence.* Web. Available online at http://publicintelligence.net/global-private-securitypolice-officer-personnel-levels-by-countryper-capita-2011/

30. *Kenya: Insecurity and Indignity: Women's Experiences in the Slums of Nairobi, Kenya,* 38.

31. Asian Development Bank. *Law and Policy Reform,* Report from the ADB Symposium on Challenges in Implementing Access to Justice Reforms. Asian Development Bank (2005). 10. Web. Available online at http://www.asianlii.org/asia/other/ADBLPRes/2005/2.pdf.

   "Calculating Lifetime Value: A Case Study." *KISSmetrics.* Web. Available online at http://blog.kissmetrics.com/wp-content/uploads/2011/08/calculating-ltv.pdf.

32. Deepa Narayan, Raj Patel, Kai Schafft, Anne Rademacher, and Sarah Koch-Schulte. *Voices of the Poor: Can Anyone Hear Us?* New York: Oxford University Press (2000). 280. Web. Available online at http://siteresources.worldbank.org/INTPOVERTY/Resources/335642-1124115102975/1555199-1124115187705/vol1.pdf.

33. Michael Wines. "The Forgotten of Africa, Wasting Away in Jails Without Trial." *The New York Times,* November 6, 2005. Web. Available online at http://www.nytimes.com/2005/11/06/international/africa/06prisons.html?pagewanted=all.

34. Hillery Anderson. "Justice Delayed in Malawi's Criminal Justice System Paralegals vs. Lawyers." *International Journal of Criminal Justice Sciences* 1 (January 2008). Web. Available online at http://www.sascv.org/ijcjs/anderson.pdf.

35. Wines, "The Forgotten of Africa, Wasting Away in Jails Without Trial."

36. Ibid.

37. In terms of government budgetary investment, studies suggest that the prosecution service may be the most neglected segment of the pipeline in the developing world. Jan Van Dijk. "Law Enforcement, Crime Prevention, and Victim Assistance." *The World of Crime: Breaking the Silence on Problems of Security, Justice and Development Across the World.* London: Sage Publications (2007). 207–244.

38. United Nations Office on Drugs and Crime. *International Statistics on Crime and Justice.* Ed. S. Harrendorf, M. Heiskanen, and S. Malby. Helsinki: European Institute for Crime Prevention and Control, Affiliated with the United Nations (2010). Web. Available online at http://www.heuni.fi/Satellite?blobtable=MungoBlobs&blobcol=urldata&SSURIapptype=BlobServer&SSURIcontainer=Default&SSURIsession=false&blobkey=id&blobheadervalue1=inline;%20filename=Hakapaino_final_07042010.pdf&SSURIsscontext=Satellite%20Server&blobwhere=1266335656647&blobheadername1=Content-Disposition&ssbinary=true&blobheader=application/pdf.

39. Ibid.

40. Danilo Reyes. "Prosecution in the Philippines." *Focus: Prosecutions in Asia,* special issue, *Article 2* 7 (March 2008). Web. Available online at http://www.article2.org/mainfile.php/0701/307/.

41. Rommel Alim Abitria. "How Speedy are Philippine Criminal Cases Disposed of?" Humanitarian Legal Assistance Foundation. Web. Available online at http://primary.hlafphil.org/index.php?option=com_phocadownload&view=category&id=1:research&download=1:speedy-trial-survey&Itemid=76.

42. Dr. Romulo A. Virola. "2009 Official Poverty Statistics." NSCB Operations Room, Makati City. National Statistical Coordination Board (February 8, 2011).

Presentation. Web. Available online at http://www.nscb.gov.ph/poverty/2009/Presentation_RAVirola.pdf.

43. "Launch of Joint UNODC and DPP Report: Toward Professionalized Prosecution Services in Kenya." United Nations Office of Drug and Crime, Eastern Africa. Web. Available online at http://www.unodc.org/easternafrica/en/criminal-justice.html.

44. "SC Raps States for Shortage of Prosecutors." *The Times of India*, September 22, 2011. Web. Available online at http://articles.timesofindia.indiatimes.com/2011-09-22/india/30188553_1_public-prosecutors-spectrum-scam-2g.

See also Rebecca Samervel. "Prosecution & Cops Need to Work as Team." *The Times of India*, February 29, 2012. Web. Available online at http://articles.timesofindia.indiatimes.com/2012-02-29/mumbai/31110257_1_neeraj-grover-murder-case-adnan-patrawala.

45. "Behind Maharashtra's Plummeting Conviction Rate." *Rediff News*. 02 Feb. 2012. Web. Available online at http://www.rediff.com/news/report/behind-maharash-tras-plummeting-conviction-rate/20120202.htm

46. Madan Lal Sharma. "The Role and Function of Prosecution in Criminal Justice." *Resource Material Series No. 53. 107th International Training Course Participants' Papers*. United Nations Asia and Far East Institute. Web. Available online at http://www.unafei.or.jp/english/pdf/RS_No53/No53_21PA_Sharma.pdf.

"Little Justice for Rape Victims." *The Hindu*. Table. Web. Available online at http://www.thehindu.com/multimedia/archive/00948/Little_justice_for__948144a.pdf.

47. "Guatemala." *The International Commission against Impunity in Guatemala*. Web. Available online at http://cicig.org/index.php?page=guatemala.

48. "Bolivia." United Nations Office on Drugs and Crime. 2005–2006. Web. Available online at http://www.unodc.org/documents/data-and-analysis/Bolivia.pdf.

49. "Brazil: Country Specific Information." *Travel.State.Gov*. Web. Available online at http://travel.state.gov/travel/cis_pa_tw/cis/cis_1072.html.

50. "Most African nations cannot afford to provide a defense for indigent defendants or assistance to others in need of legal information." United Nations Office on Drugs and Crime. *Crime and Development in Africa*. Geneva: UNODC (2005). 97.

"The only dealings the poor may have with the official justice system may be as defendants in criminal cases, in which they will normally have to cope without legal representation." United Nations Development Programme. *Making the Law Work for Everyone: Volume 1—Report of the Commission on Legal Empowerment of the Poor*. New York: UNDP (2008). 14.

51. Michael R. Anderson. *Access to Justice and Legal Process: Making Legal Institutions Responsive to Poor People in LDCs*. Sussex: Institute of Development Studies (2003). 19. Web. Available online at http://www.ids.ac.uk/files/dmfile/Wp178.pdf.

52. The combined populations of Burkino Faso, Burundi, Cote Ivoire, Liberia, Malawi, Mali, Niger, Rwanda, Zambia equal approximately 114 million people, with 2,550 lawyers. Vermont, with its population of 622,000 people, has 2,166 lawyers. California, Texas, New York, Florida, Illinois have a combined population of 112 million people with 136,880 lawyers.

"Lawyers Per Capita By State." *The Law School Tuition Bubble*. Web. Available online at http://lawschooltuitionbubble.wordpress.com/original-research-updated/lawyers-per-capita-by-state/.

United Nations Office on Drugs and Crime. *Access to Legal Aid in Criminal Justice Systems in Africa: Survey Report*. New York: United Nations (2011). Web. Available online at http://www.unodc.org/pdf/criminal_justice/Survey_Report_on_Access_to_Legal_Aid_in_Africa.pdf.

53. Ibid., 14.

54. Michael Anderson. *Access to Justice and Legal Process: Making Legal Institutions Responsive to Poor People in LDCs*. Institute of Development Studies, Sussex. (February 2003). 19.

55. *Crime and Development in Africa*, 13.

56. United Nations Office on Drugs and Crime. *International Statistics on Crime and Justice*. Ed. S. Harrendorf, M. Heiskanen, and S. Malby. Helsinki: European Institute for Crime Prevention and Control, Affiliated with the United Nations (2010). Web. Available online at http://www.heuni.fi/Satellite?blobtable=MungoBlobs&blobcol=urldata&SSURIapptype=BlobServer&SSURIcontainer=Default&SSURIsession=false&blobkey=id&blobheadervalue1=inline;%20filename=Hakapaino_final_07042010.pdf&SSURIsscontext=Satellite%20Server&blobwhere=1266335656647&blobheadername1=Content-Disposition&ssbinary=true&blobheader=application/pdf.

57. Press Trust of India. "Court Will Take 320 Years to Clear Backlog Cases: Justice Rao." *The Times of India*, March 6, 2010. Web. Available online at http://articles.timesofindia.indiatimes.com/2010-03-06/india/28143242_1_high-court-judges-literacy-rate-backlog.

Bar & Bench News Network. "Pending Litigations 2010: 32,225,535 Pending Cases; 30% Vacancies in High Courts: Government Increases Judicial Infrastructure Budget by Four Times." *Bar & Bench* (June 3, 2011). Web. Available online at http://barandbench.com/brief/2/1518/pending-litigations-2010-32225535-pending-cases-30-vacancies-in-high-courts-government-increases-judicial-infrastructure-budget-by-four-times-.

58. United Nations Office on Drugs and Crime. "Why Fighting Crime Can Assist Development in Africa: Rule of Law and Protection of the Most Vulnerable" United Nations Office on Drugs and Crime. Web. Available online at http://www.unodc.org/pdf/research/Africa_Summary_eng.pdf

59. Antonio T. Carpio. "Judicial Reform in the Philippines." Central Luzon Regional Convention of the Integrated Bar of the Philippines. (June 29, 2012). Speech. Web. Available online at http://www.scribd.com/doc/98639760/Justice-Antonio-T-Carpio-Judicial-reform-in-the-Philippines.

See also "Philippine Justice Slowed by Judge Shortage." *Middle East North Africa Financial Network*. Singapore: *The Straits Times*, Mar 28, 2011. Web. Available online at http://www.menafn.com/menafn/qn_news_story.aspx?storyid={c094a43b-1f36-40b0-8965-b75893560a63}.

60. International Bar Association Human Rights Institute. *One in Five: The Crisis in Brazil's Prisons and Criminal Justice System*. London: International Bar Association (2010).

61. R. Hunter. "Reconsidering 'Globalisation': Judicial Reform in the Philippines." *Law, Text, Culture* 6, no. 1 (January 1, 2002): 6. Web. Available online at http:// ro.uow.edu.au/ltc/vol6/iss1/5/.

62. "In such a climate of impunity, the deterrent effect of the law is minimal." United Nations Office on Drugs and Crime, *Crime and Development in Central America: Caught in the Crossfire*. United Nations (2007). 13. Web. Available online at http://www.unodc.org/documents/data-and-analysis/Central-america-study-en. pdf.

"If the chances of a murder resulting in a conviction are less than one in 20 the deterrent effect of the criminal justice system is likely to be very weak, and serial offenders may have long careers before being apprehended." United Nations Office on Drugs and Crime. Figure 9: Homicide Conviction Rates: Europe *Crime and Development in Africa*. United Nations (2005). 69. Web. Available online at http:// www.unodc.org/pdf/African_report.pdf.

63. Heather Timmons. "Rape Trial Challenges a Jam in India's Justice System." *The New York Times*, January 23, 2013. Available online at http://www.nytimes. com/2013/01/24/world/asia/gang-rape-trial-tests-indias-justice-system. html?pagewanted=1.

64. Justice J. S. Verma (ret'd), Justice Leila Seth (ret'd), and Gopal Subramanium. *Report of the Committee on Amendments to Criminal Law.* (January 23, 2013). Available online at http://www.scribd.com/doc/121798698/ Justice-Verma-Committee-report.

65. WAMU-FM. Kojo Nnamdi Show. "Interview of Katherine Boo regarding her book *Behind the Beautiful Forevers: Life, Death, and Hope in a Mumbai Undercity.*" (February 29, 2012). (audio excerpted at 26:51–28:52).

66. Ronald Bailey. "The Secrets of Intangible Wealth." Reason.com, (October 5, 2007). Web. Available online at http://reason.com/archives/2007/10/05/ the-secrets-of-intangible-weal.

67. The World Bank. *Where is the Wealth of the Nations?* Washington, DC: The World Bank (2006). Web. Available online at http://siteresources.worldbank.org/INT EEI/214578-1110886258964/20748034/All.pdf.

68. David Brooks. "Sam Spade at Starbucks." *The New York Times*, April 12, 2012.Web. Available online at http://www.nytimes.com/2012/04/13/opinion/brooks-sam-spade-at-starbucks.html?_r=1.

69. Mark L. Schneider. *Placing Security and Rule of Law on the Development Agenda.* Washington, DC: World Bank (2009). 14. Print.

CHAPTER 6

1. Martin Luther King, Jr. "I Have a Dream." Lincoln Memorial, Washington, DC, (August 28, 1963). Available online at http://www.americanrhetoric.com/ speeches/mlkihaveadream.htm.

2. UN Archives/Geneva, SOA 317/4/01(C), speech by John Humphrey, January 1, 1952, cited in Paul Gordon Lauren. *The Evolution of International Human Rights: Visions Seen.* 3d ed. XX: Philadelphia: University of Pennsylvania (2011). 232.

3. Ibid.

4. Robert Jackson, Opening Statement, in International Military Tribunal, *Trial of the Major War Criminals* 2 (November 21, 1945): 98–99, 130, cited in Lauren. *The Evolution of International Human Rights*, 198.

5. Lauren, *The Evolution of International Human Rights*, 198.

6. Ibid.

7. Herman Goering, as cited in G. M. Gibert. *Nuremberg Diary.* New York: New American Library, (1961), 39, cited in Paul Gordon Lauren, *The Evolution of International Human Rights: Visions Seen,* 198.

8. Mary Ann Glendon. *A World Made New: Eleanor Roosevelt and the Universal Declaration of Human Rights.* New York: Random House, 2001.

9. Lauren, *The Evolution of International Human Rights,* 207.

10. Ibid.

11. Ibid.

12. Glendon, *A World Made New,* 36.

13. Ibid.

14. Vladimir Koretsky, as cited in Humphrey, *Human Rights and the United Nations,* 40. *See also* U.S., NARA, RG 59, Box 2256, 501.BD Human Rights/6-2147, Telegram 7594 from W. Austin to Department of State, Restricted, (June 21, 1947) in Lauren, *The Evolution of International Human Rights,* 217.

15. Hansa Mehta, as cited in "Economic and Social Council," *United Nations Weekly Bulletin,* March 25, 1947, in Lauren, *The Evolution of International Human Rights,* 217.

16. Ibid.

17. Glendon, *A World Made New,* xvi.

18. E. N. Nasinovsky, December 16, 1966, in UN/GA, *Official Records, Plenary Meetings,* 1966, at 13, cited in Lauren, *The Evolution of International Human Rights,* 242.

19. Lauren, *The Evolution of International Human Rights,* 242.

20. Martha Finnemore and Kathryn Sikkink. "International Norm Dynamics and Political Change." *International Organization* 52 (1998): 887–917. Available online at http://graduateinstitute.ch/webdav/site/political_science/shared/political_science/Multilateral%20Governance%20Autumn%202010/finnemore%20and%20sikkink%201998.pdf.

21. Human Rights Watch. "The Small Hands of Slavery: Bonded Child Labor In India" *Human Rights Watch Children's Rights Project.* New York: Human Rights Watch (1996). Web. Available online at http://www.hrw.org/reports/1996/India3.htm

22. Women in Law and Development. *Protocol to the African Charter on Human and People's Rights on the Rights of Women in Africa (Simplified).* Lomé, Togo: Women in Law and Development. (2005). Web. Available online at http://www.peace-women.org/portal_resources_resource.php?id=939.

23. Abigail Schwartz. "Sex Trafficking in Cambodia." *Columbia Journal of Asian Law* 17, no. 2 (2004): 373–431. Web. Available online at http://www.columbia.edu/cu/asiaweb/v17n2_371_Schwartz.html.

24. Jonathan L. Hafetz. "Latin America: Views on Contemporary Issues in the Region Pretrial Detention, Human Rights, and Judicial Reform in Latin America." *Fordham International Law Journal* 26, no. 6 (2002): 1754–1777.

25. Karl DeRouen Jr. and Uk Heo. "Modernization and the Military in Latin America." *British Journal of Political Science* 31 (2001): 475–496. Available online at http://www.jstor.org/discover/10.2307/3593286?uid=3739584&uid=2129&uid=2134&uid=2&uid=70&uid=4&uid=3739256&sid=21101371053863.

26. Lauren, 228.

27. Andrea M. Bertone. "Transnational Activism to Combat Trafficking in Persons." *Brown Journal of World Affairs* 10 (2004): 9–22.

28. Stuart Ford. "How Leadership in International Criminal Law is Shifting from the United States to Europe and Asia: An Analysis of Spending on and Contributions to International Criminal Courts." *Saint Louis University Law Journal* 55 (2011): 953–999. Web. Available online at http://papers.ssrn.com/sol3/papers.cfm?abstract_id=1674063.

29. Hans Peter Schmitz. "Transnational Human Rights Networks: Significance and Challenges." *The International Studies Encyclopedia.* Vol. XI, ed. Robert A. Denmark. New York: Wiley-Blackwell, 2010. 7189–7208.

30. Commission on Legal Empowerment of the Poor. *Making the Law Work for Everyone.* Report vol. 1. United Nations Development Programme, June 2008. 31–32. Web. Available online at http://www.unrol.org/doc.aspx?n=Making_the_Law_Work_for_Everyone.pdf.

31. United Nations General Assembly. *Universal Declaration of Human Rights.* Paris: United Nations (1948). Article 8. Web. Available online at http://www.un.org/en/documents/udhr/index.shtml.

CHAPTER 7

1. Called the "Indian Civil Service" under British rule.

2. The French introduced its first uniformed professional police in the same year.

3. Kirpal Dhillon. *Police and Politics in India: Colonial Concepts, Democratic Compulsions, Indian Police, 1947–2002.* New Delhi: Manohar (2005). 35. Print. Emphasis added.

4. Ibid., 329.

5. Ibid., 23, 41.

6. Ibid., 41.

7. Ibid., 36.

8. Ibid., 33.

9. David Bayley. "The Police and Political Development in India." Patterns of Policing: A Comparative International Analysis. New Brunswick: Rutgers University Press. (1985). Print. 51.

10. Ibid., 42.

11. Ibid., 45.

12. "History of the Kenya Police." Kenya Police. Web. Available online at http://archive.is/eoer

13. Human Rights Watch. *Broken System: Dysfunction, Abuse, and Impunity in Indian Police.* New York: Human Rights Watch (2009).

14. Dhillon, *Police and Politics in India,* 28.

15. Ibid.

16. Patrick Edobar Igbinovia. "Pattern of Policing in Africa: The French and British Connections." *Police Journal* 54, no. 2 (1981): 150–151.
17. Ibid., 150–152.
18. Emmanuel C. Onyeozili. "Obstacles to Effective Policing in Nigeria." *African Journal of Criminology and Justice Studies* 1, no. 1 (2005): 32.
19. Ibid., 37.
20. Ibid., 36.
21. Edna E. A. Co et al. *Philippine Democracy Assessment: Rule of Law and Access to Justice.* Stockholm: International Institute for Democracy and Electoral Assistance (2010). 98–99. Web. Available online at http://www.idea.int/publications/philippine_democracy_assessment/loader.cfm?csmodule=security/getfile&pageid=42088.
22. Ibid.
23. S. E. Hendrix. "Innovation in Criminal Procedure in Latin America: Guatemala's Conversion to the Adversarial System." *Southwestern Journal of Law and Trade in the Americas* 5 (Fall 1998): 381. Print.
24. Simon Robins. "Restorative Approaches to Criminal Justice in Africa: The Case of Uganda." *The Theory and Practice of Criminal Justice in Africa.* Pretoria, South Africa: Institute for Security Studies (2009). 61.
25. Iffat Idris. *Legal Empowerment in Pakistan.* Islamabad: United Nations Development Programme Pakistan (2008)
26. Open Society Initiative for Southern Africa. *Mozambique: Justice Sector and the Rule of Law.* Johannesburg: Open Society Initiative for Southern Africa (2006).111. Web. Available online at http://www.afrimap.org/english/images/report/Mozambique%20Justice%20report%20(Eng).pdf.
27. AfriMAP et al. *Ghana: Justice Sector and the Rule of Law.* Dakar: Open Society Initiative for West Africa (2007).104. Web. Available online at http://www.afrimap.org/english/images/report/AfriMAP_Ghana%20JusticeDD.pdf.
28. F. E. Kanyongolo. *Malawi: Justice Sector and the Rule of Law.* Johannesburg: Open Society Initiative for Southern Africa (2006). 114–115. Web. Available online at http://www.afrimap.org/english/images/report/Malawi%20Report%20justice.pdf.
29. S. F. Joireman. "Inherited Legal Systems and Effective Rule of Law: Africa and the Colonial Legacy." *The Journal of Modern African Studies* 39, no. 4 (2001): 571–596.
30. "Access to Justice and Legal Process: Making Legal Institutions Responsive to Poor People in LDCs," 21.
31. Daniel Fitzpatrick. "Beyond Dualism: Land Acquisition and Law in Indonesia." *Indonesia: Law and Society,* 2d ed. Ed. Tim Lindsey. Sydney: The Federation Press (2008). 1.

    See also D. Henley. "In the Name of Adat: Regional Perspectives on Reform, Tradition, and Democracy in Indonesia." *Modern Asian Studies* 42, no. 4 (2008): 815–852. Print.

    Kurnia Toha. *The Struggle over Land Rights: A Study of Indigenous Property Rights in Indonesia.* Seattle: University of Washington (2007).
32. Amnesty International. *Senegal: Land of Impunity.* London: Amnesty International Publications (2010). 14. Web. Available online at http://www.amnesty.org/fr/

library/asset/AFR49/001/2010/fr/6dcdd964-211b-4269-9cab-32b9d6f28a99/afr490012010en.pdf.

33. Ibid., 6.
34. Dhillon, *Police and Politics in India*, 42.
35. Ibid., 29.

CHAPTER 8

1. Albeit with the biggest growth engines, the so-called BRIC countries (Brazil, Russia, India, China) are slumping back to much more modest, historic levels of growth. Ruchir Sharma. "Broken BRICs: Why the Rest Stopped Rising." *Foreign Affairs* (November–December 2012).
2. *International Law and the Third World: Reshaping Justice*. Ed. Richard Falk, Balakrishnan Rajagopal, and Jacqueline Stevens. New York: Routledge-Cavendish (2008), 1–2.
3. "In sum, while world poverty—especially extreme poverty—has been significantly reduced in the past three decades, income disparities among global citizens seem to have remained unchanged, despite a reduction in international (between countries) inequality. More importantly, this widening gap between international and global inequality appears to have come from increased income disparities within countries—notably in large emerging Asian economies such as China, India, and Indonesia, as well as many OECD countries—and not differences among them." Pedro Olinto and Jaime Saavedra. *Inequality in Focus: An Overview of Global Income Inequality Trends*. Washington: The World Bank April 2012). Available online at http://siteresources.worldbank.org/EXTPOVERTY/Resources/Inequality_in_Focus_April2012.pdf.
4. Andy Summer. *Where Will the World's Poor live? An Update on Global Poverty and the New Bottom Billion*. Working Paper 305. Center for Global Development, (September 13, 2012). Available online at http://www.cgdev.org/content/publications/detail/1426481/.
5. World Bank. "Equity and Development." *World Development Report2006*. *New York*: Oxford University Press (2006).
6. Jayati Ghosh. "Poverty reduction in China and India: Policy Implications of Recent Trends." New York: United Nations (January 2010). 17. Available at http://www.un.org/esa/desa/papers/2010/wp92_2010.pdf
7. Reuters. "Latin American Poverty Rate Ebbs to Lowest in 3 decades—UN." November 27, 2012. Available online at http://www.reuters.com/article/2012/11/27/latinamerica-poverty-eclac-idUSL1E8MR34B20121127.
8. W. Clinton Terry and Karelisa V. Hartigan. "Police Authority and Reform in Augustan Rome and Nineteenth-Century England." *Law and Human Behavior* 6, no. 3–4 (1982). 307.
9. Law and Policy Reform at the Asian Development Bank. "Report from the ADB Symposium on Challenges in Implementing Access to Justice Reforms." Asian Development Bank (2005). 10. Available online at http://www.asianlii.org/asia/other/ADBLPRes/2005/2.pdf.

10. Rita Abrahamsen and Michael C. Williams. "Privatising Africa's Everyday Security." *Open Security*, (July 1, 2010). Web. Available online at http://www.opendemocracy.net/opensecurity/rita-abrahamsen-michael-c-williams/privatising-africas-everyday-security.

11. Rachel Neild. "From National Security to Citizen Security: Civil Society and the Evolution of Public Order Debates." *International Center for Human Rights and Democratic Development* (1999). 16. Web. Available online at http://www.umass.edu/legal/Benavides/Fall2005/397U/Readings%20Legal%20397U/9%20Richard%20Neild.pdf.

12. James Holston, quoted in ibid., 11.

13. Neild, "From National Security to Citizen Security," 16.

14. Manu Kaushik. "A Force to Reckon With." *Business Today*, October 31, 2010. Web. Available online at http://businesstoday.intoday.in/story/a-force-to-reckon-with/1/9591.html.

15. Ibid.

16. Luciana Coelho. "Brazil Has Almost 5 Private Security Guards for Each Police Officer." *Folha De S. Paulo*, September 14, 2012. Web. Available online at http://www1.folha.uol.com.br/internacional/en/dailylife/1153834-brazil-has-almost-5-private-security-guards-for-each-police-officer.shtml.

17. William C. Prillaman. "Crime, Democracy, and Development in Latin America." *Policy Papers on the Americas*, vol. XIV, study 6. Washington, DC: Center for Strategic and International Studies (2003), 13. Web. Available online at http://csis.org/files/media/csis/pubs/ppcrime_democracy_inlatinamerica%5B1%5D.pdf.

18. Coelho, "Brazil Has Almost 5 Private Security Guards for Each Police Officer."

19. World Bank. *Kenya—Economic Development, Police Oversight, and Accountability: Linkages and Reform Issues*. Washington, DC: World Bank (2009), ii. Web. Available online at https://openknowledge.worldbank.org/bitstream/handle/10986/3174/445150ESW0P1061C0disclosed031161101.pdf?sequence=1.

20. World Bank. *Enhancing the Competitiveness of Kenya's Manufacturing Sector: The Role of the Investment Climate*. Washington, DC: World Bank (2004). 78. Web. ftp://www.soc.cornell.edu/cses_research/Yenkey/investment%20climate%20assessment%20kenya.pdf.

21. Peter Schouten. "Political Topographies of Private Security in Sub-Saharan Africa." *African Engagements: Africa Negotiating an Emerging Multipolar World*. Africa–Europe Group for Interdisciplinary Studies, vol. 5 (2011): 58. Web. Available online at http://www.academia.edu/1544401/Political_topographies_of_private_security_in_Sub-Saharan_Africa.

22. Abrahamsen and Williams, "Privatising Africa's Everyday Security."

23. Michael Weissenstein. "Mexico Drug War: Common Crime Rates Rise." *Huffington Post*, October 20, 2012. Web. Available online at http://www.huffingtonpost.com/2012/10/20/mexico-drug-war_n_1992497.html#slide=1630080;

Katharine A. Lorr. Review of *Gangland: The Rise of Mexican Drug Cartels from El Paso to Vancouver* by Jerry Langton. The Washington Independent Review of Books. Web. Available online at http://www.washingtonindependentreviewofbooks.com/bookreview/gangland-the-rise-of-mexican-drug-cartels-from-el-paso-to-vancouver/.

Jeanna Cullinan. "A Look at Police Reform." *Tinker Foundation Incorporated.* Web. Available online at http://www.tinker.org/content/look-police-reform.

24. Katherine Boo. *Behind the Beautiful Forevers.: Life, Death, and Hope in a Mumbai Undercity.* New York: Random House, 2012.

25. Anthony Wanis-St. John. "Implementing ADR in Transitioning States: Lessons Learned from Practice." *Harvard Negotiation Law Review* 5 (2000). 339, 342.

26. Ibid., 342–343.

27. Ibid., 346.

28. Ibid., 368.

29. Neild, "From National Security to Citizen Security," 2.

30. Kathryn Neckerman. *Social Inequality.* New York: Russell Sage Foundation, 2004; see also Katrina Kosec. "Relying on the Private Sector: The Political Economy of Public Investments in the Poor." Unpublished PhD dissertation. Stanford University (2011). 1. Web. Available online at http://works.bepress.com/cgi/viewcontent.cgi?article=1015&context=katrina_kosec.

31. Kosec, "Relying on the Private Sector, 5, 6.

See also Tugrul Gurgur. *"The Political Economy of Public Spending on Publicly-Provided Goods in Developing Countries."* Unpublished PhD dissertation. University of Maryland (2005). Web. Available online at http://drum.lib.umd.edu/bitstream/1903/2601/1/umi-umd-2495.pdf.

32. Miguel Sánchez and Roby Senderowitsch. "The Political Economy of the Middle Class in the Dominican Republic Individualization of Public Goods, Lack of Institutional Trust and Weak Collective Action." *World Bank Policy Research Working Paper.* Santo Domingo, Dominican Republic: World Bank (2012). 39, 40. Web. Available online at http://www-wds.worldbank.org/external/default/WDSContentServer/IW3P/IB/2012/04/24/000158349_20120424091546/Rendered/PDF/WPS6049.pdf.

See also The World Bank. *"Alternative Dispute Resolution Workshop."* January 6, 2000. Room MC4-800, 1818 H Street, N.W. Washington, D.C. Washington: Miller Reporting Co. (2000). Web. Available online at http://siteresources.worldbank.org/INTLAWJUSTINST/Resources/TranscriptOfWorkshop.pdf.

33. Carol Graham. *Private Markets for Public Goods: Raising the Stakes in Economic Reform.* Washington, DC: Brookings Institution Press (1998);

See also Gurgur, "The Political Economy of Public Spending on Publicly-Provided Goods in Developing Countries."

34. World Bank, "Alternative Dispute Resolution Workshop."

35. Ibid.

CHAPTER 9

1. "Foreign Aid for Development Assistance." *Global Issues,* (April 8, 2012). See chart entitled "Comparing Official Aid Given vs. Shortfall 1970-2011, (USD Trillions at 2010 Prices." Web. Available online at http://www.globalissues.org/article/35/foreign-aid-development-assistance#ForeignAidNumbersinChartsandGraphs.

2. While some critics (e.g., Moyo Easterly) have argued that this aid may have been ill-spent or counter-productive, given the massive human suffering flowing from

global poverty, we do not think it was too large of an investment for humanity to make in seeking to end it.

3. Protecting the poor from violence is also implicated in Factor No. 2 Order and Security (sub-factor 3.1, Crime is effectively controlled) and sub-factor 4.2 of "Fundamental Rights" where the Index indicates that rule of law effectively guarantees "the right to life and the security of person."

4. General Accounting Office. *Foreign Aid: Police Training and Assistance.* Report GAO-92-118. Washington, DC: General Accounting Office (1992). 1. Web. Available online at http://archive.gao.gov/t2pbat7/145909.pdf.

5. Ibid.

6. Ethan Avram Nadelmann. *Cops Across Borders: The Internationalization of U.S. Criminal Law Enforcement.* University Park: Penn State Press, 1993. 113–116.

7. Congress enacted exemptions to the Section 660 ban on police aid to allow funding for anti-narcotics and anti-terrorism training and assistance. That aid has been provided largely through the State Department International Narcotics and Law Enforcement. USAID limits its police assistance to a small program designed to exert civilian control over police in community policing programs.

8. U.S. Agency for International Development. *Assistance for Civilian Policing: USAID Policy Guidance.* Washington, DC: U.S. Agency for International Development (2005). 1. Web. Available online at http://pdf.usaid.gov/pdf_docs/PNADU808.pdf.

9. The World Bank. *Initiatives in Justice Reform.* Washington, DC: The World Bank (2009). 4. Web. Available online at http://siteresources.worldbank.org/INTLAWJUSTINST/Resources/JRInitiativestext2009.pdf.

10. The World Bank. *World Development Report: Conflict, Security and Development.* Washington, DC: The World Bank (2011). 5. Web. Available online at http://siteresources.worldbank.org/INTWDRS/Resources/WDR2011_Full_Text.pdf.

11. Anne-Marie Leroy. "Legal Note on Bank Involvement in the Criminal Justice Sector." Washington, DC: The World Bank (2012). Web. Available online at http://siteresources.worldbank.org/INTLAWJUSTINST/Resources/CriminalJusticeLegalNote.pdf.

12. The World Bank. *World Bank Directions in Justice Reform: Discussion Note.* Washington, DC: The World Bank (2012). 1. Available online at http://siteresources.worldbank.org/EXTLAWJUSTINST/Resources/wb_jr_discussionnote.pdf.

13. Robert Zoellick, quoted in *World Bank Directions in Justice Reform: Discussion Note*, 1.

14. C. Stone. "Crime, Justice Systems, and Development Assistance." *The World Bank Legal Review: Law, Equity, and Development*, vol. 2. Ed. A. Palacio. Washington, DC: The World Bank (2006). 215–216.

15. Nicole Ball et al. "Security and Justice Sector Reform Programming in Africa." *Evaluation Working Paper 23.* London and Glasgow: DFID (2007). ix. Available online at http://www.dfid.gov.uk/Documents/publications1/evaluation/sjr.pdf.
   See also Adam Isacson and Nicole Ball. "U.S. Military and Police Assistance to Poor-Performing States." *Short of the Goal.* Ed. Nancy Birdsall, Milan Vaishnav, and

Robert Ayres (2006): 414. Available at http://www.cgdev.org/doc/shortofthe-goal/chap13.pdf.

16. United States Department of State. "DRL Programs, Including Human Rights Democracy Fund (HRDF)." *U.S. Department of State Archive.* (2001–2009). Web. Available online at http://2001-2009.state.gov/g/drl/p/index.htm.

17. Freedom House. *Investing in Freedom: An Analysis of the Obama Administration FY 2011 Budget Request for Democracy and Human Rights.* Washington, DC: Freedom House (May 2011). 10. Web. Available online at http://www.freedomhouse. org/sites/default/files/inline_images/Investing%20in%20Freedom%20 Analyzing%20the%20FY%202012%20International%20Affairs%20Budget%20 Request.pdf U.S. State Department. *The Merida Initiative - Fact Sheet.* Washington, D.C.: U.S. State Department (2009). Web. Available online at http://www.state. gov/j/inl/rls/fs/122397.htm.

18. U.S. State Department. *The Merida Initiative - Fact Sheet.* Washington, D.C.: U.S. State Department (2009). Web. Available online at http://www.state.gov/j/inl/ rls/fs/122397.htm.

19. Michael Shifter. *Countering Criminal Violence in Central America.* New York: Council on Foreign Relations (2012). 18. Web. Available online at http://www.cfr.org/ central-america/countering-criminal-violence-central-america/p27740.

20. Taken from State/INL Congressional Budget Justification Reports. FY 2001–2009 were taken on a two-year lag.

United States Department of State. *Congressional Budget Justification: Fiscal Year 2001.* Washington, DC: GPO (2000).

United States Department of State. *Congressional Budget Justification: Fiscal Year 2003.* Washington, DC: GPO (2002). 507, 515. Web. Available online at http:// www.state.gov/documents/organization/9478.pdf.

United States Department of State. *Congressional Budget Justification: Fiscal Year 2005.* Washington, DC: GPO (2004). 585, 593. Web. Available online at http:// www.state.gov/documents/organization/28982.pdf.

United States Department of State. *Congressional Budget Justification: Fiscal Year 2007.* Washington, DC: GPO (2006). 665, 673. Web. Available online at http:// www.state.gov/documents/organization/60658.pdf.

United States Department of State. *Congressional Budget Justification: Fiscal Year 2008.* Washington, DC: GPO (2007). 76. Web. Available online at http://www. state.gov/documents/organization/84462.pdf.

United States Department of State. *Congressional Budget Justification: Fiscal Year 2009.* Washington, DC: GPO (2008). Web. http://www.state.gov/documents/ organization/100326.pdf

United States Department of State. *FY 2010 Program and Budget Guide: Centrally-Managed Programs.* Washington, DC: GPO (2009). 41. Web. Available online at http://www.state.gov/documents/organization/131027.pdf.

United States Department of State. *FY 2012 Program and Budget Guide: Centrally-Managed Programs.* Washington, DC: GPO (2011). 201. Web. Available online at http://www.state.gov/documents/organization/185822.pdf.

FY2010 and 2011 were taken from State/INL Budget Justification Report 2012

United States Secretary of State. *Congressional Budget Justification Volume 1: Department of State Operations: Fiscal Year 2012.* Washington, DC: GPO (2011). 423–426. Web. Available online at http://www.state.gov/documents/organiza-tion/156215.pdf.

21. Rachel K. Belton. "Competing Definitions of the Rule of Law: Implications for Practitioners." *Carnegie Papers: Rule of Law Series,* No. 55 (2005): 23. Web. Available online at http://www.carnegieendowment.org/files/CP55.Belton. FINAL.pdf.

22. Vivek Maru. "Access to Justice and Legal Empowerment: A Review of World Bank Practice." *Hague Journal on the Rule of Law* 2 (2010): 259–281. Web. Available online at http://journals.cambridge.org/action/displayAbstract?fromPage=online &aid=7942021.

23. *World Bank Directions in Justice Reform: Discussion Note.* 1. Available online at http://siteresources.worldbank.org/EXTLAWJUSTINST/Resources/wb_jr_ discussionnote.pdf.

24. Belton, "Competing Definitions."

25. United States General Accounting Office. *Foreign Assistance: Rule of Law Funding Worldwide for Fiscal Years 1993-98.* Washington, DC: GPO (1999). 12. Web. Available online at http://www.gao.gov/archive/1999/ns99158.pdf.

26. John F. Tierney. *Multiple U.S. Agencies Provided Billions of Dollars to Train and Equip Foreign Police Forces.* GAO Report. Washington, DC: GPO (2011). 2. Web. Available online at http://www.gao.gov/new.items/d11402r.pdf.

CHAPTER 10

1. Richard Zacks. *Island of Vice: Theodore Roosevelt's Quest to Clean Up Sin-Loving New York.* Garden City, NY: Anchor Books (2012). 84. Print.

2. Jean Pfaelzer. *Driven Out: The Forgotten War against Chinese Americans.* University of California Press. (2008) Print. 75–84.

3. *Ibid.,* 25.

4. *Ibid.,* 243–251.

5. Elaine Tipton. *The Japanese Police State: The Tokkō In Interwar Japan.* London: Athlone Press (1990). 66–67.

   Christopher Aldous. *The Police in Occupation Japan: Control, Corruption, and Resistance to Reform.* London and New York: Routledge, Chapman & Hall (1997). 32–33.

6. J.P. Burdy. "Social Control and Forms of Working-Class Sociability in French Industrial Towns between the Mid-Nineteenth and the Mid-Twentieth Centuries." *Social Control in Europe 1800–2000,* vol. 2. Trans. Helen Arnold, ed. H. Roodenburg, P. Spierenburg, C. Emsley, and E. Johnson. Columbus: Ohio State University Press (2004). 25–69. Print.

   P. Lawrence. "Policing the Poor in England and France, 1850–1900." *Social Control in Europe 1800-2000,* vol. 2. Ed. H. Roodenburg, P. Spierenburg, C. Emsley, and E. Johnson. Columbus: Ohio State University Press (2004). 210–225.

7. Jean-Marc Berlière. "L'Institution policière en France sous la Troisième République, 1875–1914." Unpublished PhD dissertation. University of Bourgogne, Dijon (1991). 36.

8. Samuel Walker and Charles Katz. *The Police in America: An Introduction.* New York: McGraw- Hill (2007). 4.
9. Ibid., 9.
10. Ibid., 16.
11. Ibid., 9.
12. Ibid., 14.
13. Ibid., 24.
14. Ibid., 62.
15. Ibid.
16. Ibid., 9.
17. Ibid., 40.
18. Ibid., 100.
19. Zacks, *Island of Vice,* 88.
20. Walker and Katz, *The Police in America,* 9.
21. Ibid., 20.
22. Ibid., 16.
23. Ibid., 20.
24. Ibid. There were 769 police patrolling in New York in 1876 when the City had a population of about a million—which is one officer for every 1,300 citizens. India now has one police for every 1,037 and the Philippines one per 1,400.
25. Walker and Katz, *The Police in America,* 20.
26. Ibid., 21.
27. Ibid., 18 and Zacks, *Island of Vice,* 103.
28. Walker and Katz, *The Police in America,* 24.
29. Ibid.
30. Ibid., 25.
31. Ibid., 30.
32. Robert F. Vodde. *Andragogical Instruction for Effective Police Training.* Amhurst: Cambria Press (2009). 5–6 (quoting Stephens).
33. Walker and Katz, *The Police in America,* 10.
34. Vodde, *Andragogical Instruction,* 7 (quoting Bailey).
35. Ibid.
36. Vodde, *Andragogical Instruction,* 1–17.
37. John Roach and Jürgen Thomaneck. *Police and Public Order in Europe.* Croom Helm. (1985) Print. 107.
38. David H. Bayley. "The Police and Political Development in Europe." *The Formation of National States in Western Europe.* Princeton University Press. (1975) Print. 345.
39. Phillip J. Stead. *The Police of France.* Macmillan Publishing Company. (1983) Print. 34.
40. *Ibid.,* 68-69.
41. D. E. Westney, "The Emulation of Western Organizations in Meiji, Japan: The Case of the Paris Prefecture of Police and the Keishicho." *Journal of Japanese Studies, 8.* (1982), 311.
42. Christopher Aldous. *The Police in Occupation Japan: Control, Corruption, and Resistance to Reform.* London and New York: Routledge, Chapman & Hall. (1997). 24.
43. Ibid., 19–31.

44. Katzenstein, Peter J., and Yutaka Tsujinaka. ""Bullying, "Buying," and "Binding": US-Japanese Transnational Relations and Domestic Structures." *Cambridge Studies in International Relations*, 42. (1995). 36.

45. Craig L. Parker. *The Japanese Police System Today: A Comparative View*. Armonk, NY: M. E. Sharpe, 2001. 21–22.

46. Walker and Katz, *The Police in America*, 25–26.

47. Vodde, *Andragogical Instruction*, 8 (quoting Roberg from Roberg, Crank, & Kuykendall (2000). 45).

48. Walker and Katz, *The Police in America*, 31.

49. Ibid.

50. Abhijit Banerjee. "Police Performance and Public Perception in Rajasthan, India." Web. Available online at http://www.povertyactionlab.org/evaluation/police-performance-and-public-perception-rajasthan-india.

51. Walker and Katz, *The Police in America*, 7.

52. L. Craig Parker. *The Japanese Police System Today: A Comparative View*. Armonk: East Gate Publications (2001), 21.

53. Walker and Katz, *The Police in America*, 44.

54. Vodde, *Andragogical Instruction*, 11.

55. Ibid., 149.

    J. L. Lyman. "The Metropolitan Police Act of 1829: An Analysis of Certain Events Influencing the Passage and Character of the Metropolitan Police Act in England." *The Journal of Criminal Law, Criminology, and Police Science* 55, no. 1 (1964): 151.

56. Josiah Flynt. "Police Methods in London." *North American Review* 176, no. 556 (1903): 440.

57. Ibid., 447.

58. Leonard Porter Ayres. "The Cleveland survey of the administration of criminal justice." Cleveland: The Cleveland Trust Company. (1922) Web. Available online at http://archive.org/details/clevelandsurvey00clevgoog

59. Samuel Walker. *A Critical Theory of Police Reform*. Lexington Books. (1977) Print. 127.

60. Walker and Katz, *The Police in America*, 135.

Chapter 11

1. Rhea Ruth V. Rosell. "40% Cebu City households are poor—DSWD." *Cebu Daily News*, October 6, 2011. Available online at http://newsinfo.inquirer.net/71311/40-cebu-city-households-are-poor-dswd.

2. Christopher Stone. "Crime, Justice Systems and Development Assistance." *World Bank Legal Review: Law, Equity, and Development*, vol. 2. 217.

3. Ibid.

4. Ibid., 228.

5. For more information on IJM projects in other geographies, readers may wish to visit www.TheLocustEffect.com.

6. David Batty. "More than 30 Women Raped and Beaten in DR Congo Attack." *The Guardian*, January 6, 2011. Web. Available online at http://www.guardian.co.uk/world/2011/jan/07/congo-women-raped-beaten.

7. Associated Press. "Congo Army Colonel Guilty of Ordering Mass Rape on New Year's Day." *The Guardian*, February 21, 2011. Web. Online at http://www.guardian.co.uk/society/2011/feb/21/congo-rape-trial

8. Open Society Justice Initiative. *Justice in the DRC: Mobile Courts Combat Rape and Impunity in Eastern Congo.* June 2012. 2. Print.

9. UN News Centre. "DR Congo mass rape verdict sends strong signal to perpetrators—UN envoy." *UN News Service*, February 21, 2011. Web. Available online at http://www.un.org/apps/news/story.asp?NewsID=37580&Cr=sexual.

10. Ibid.

11. Open Society Justice Initiative. *Justice in the DRC: Mobile Courts Combat Rape and Impunity in Eastern Congo.* 5.

12. Tessa Khan and Jim Wormington. "Mobile Courts in the DRC- Lessons from Development for International Criminal Justice." Oxford Transitional Justice Research Working Paper Series, July 9, 2012. 23. Web. A vailable online at http://www.csls.ox. ac.uk/documents/OTJR-KhanandWormington-MOBILECOURTSINTHEDRC-LESSONS FROMDEVELOPMENTFORINTERNATIONALCRIMINALJU.pdf.

    See also Patrick Vinck and Phuong Pham. "Ownership and Participation in Transitional Justice Mechanisms: A Sustainable Human Development Perspective from Eastern DRC." *International Journal of Transitional Justice*, vol. 2 (2008): 401. Print.

13. Khan and Wormington. "Mobile Courts," 27.

14. Ibid., 2.

15. Patrícia Trindade Maranhão Costa. *Fighting Forced Labour:The Example of Brazil.* Geneva: International Labour Office (2009). v. Web. Available online at http://www.ilo.org/wcmsp5/groups/public/---ed_norm/---declaration/documents/publication/wcms_111297.pdf.

16. International Labour Office. *ILO 2012 Global Estimate of Forced Labour Executive Summary.* Geneva: International Labour Office (2012). Print. 2.

17. Costa, *Fighting Forced Labour*, 9.

18. Ibid., 8.

19. Ibid.

20. Kevin Bales. *Disposable People: New Slavery in the Global Economy.* Berkeley and Los Angeles: University of California Press (1999). 5. Print.

21. Ibid., 78.

22. Nick Caistor. "Brazil's 'Slave' Ranch Workers." *BBC News*, May 11, 2005. Web. Available online at http://news.bbc.co.uk/2/hi/americas/4536085.stm.

23. Presidência da República do Brasil. "Plano Nacional Para a Erradicação do Trabalho Escravo." Presidência da República do Brasil (2003). Web. Available online at http://www.oit.org.br/sites/all/forced_labour/brasil/iniciativas/plano_nacional.pdf.

24. Costa, "Fighting Forced Labour."

25. International Labour Organization. "The Good Practices of Labour Inspection in Brazil: The Eradication of Labour Analogous to Slavery." Geneva: International Labour Organization (2010). Available online at http://www.ilo.org/wcmsp5/groups/public/---ed_norm/---declaration/documents/publication/wcms_155946.pdf.

26. Ibid., 39.
27. Ibid., 36.
28. United States Department of State. "Trafficking in Persons Report 2012" Washington, DC: United States Department of State (2012). Available at http://www.state.gov/documents/organization/192594.pdf. "There were no comprehensive data on how many labor traffickers federal and labor courts prosecuted during the reporting period; however, media reports indicated that authorities convicted seven possible labor trafficking offenders, including one former congressman, under the trabalho escravo statute" (96).
29. Costa, "Fighting Forced Labour," 28.
30. Ibid., 77.
31. Ibid.
32. The World Bank. "Fighting Corruption in Public Services: Chronicling Georgia's Reforms." Washington, DC: The World Bank (2012).
33. Ibid., ix.
34. Transparency International. "Corruption Perceptions Index 2003." Available online at http://archive.transparency.org/policy_research/surveys_indices/cpi/2003.
35. World Bank, "Fighting Corruption," 1.
36. Ibid.
37. Ibid., 7.
38. Ibid., 21.
39. Ibid.
40. Ibid., 13
41. Ibid., 14.
42. Personal conversation with former Prime Minister Gilauri. World Economic Forum, January 2012.
43. World Bank, "Fighting Corruption," 6. Emphasis added.
44. Ibid., 18.
45. Ibid., p. 8
46. Ibid.
47. Ibid., 19.
48. "Seven Years after the Rose Revolution, Georgia has come a long way" The Economist. August 19, 2010. Web. Available online at http://www.economist.com/node/16847798
49. Personal conversation with former Prime Minister Gilauri. World Economic Forum, January 2012.
50. Learn about IBJ at http://www.ibj.org/Meet_IBJ.html.
51. Christopher Stone, Joel Miller, Monica Thornton, and Jennifer Trone. "Supporting Security, Justice, and Development: Lessons for a New Era." New York: Vera Institute for Justice (2005). 12. Web. Available online athttp://www.vera.org/sites/default/files/resources/downloads/Supporting_security.pdf.
52. Ibid., 58.
53. Department for International Development. *Safety, Security, and Accessible Justice: Putting Policy into Practice.* Department for International Development (July 2002). Web. Available online at http://www.gsdrc.org/docs/open/SSAJ23.pdf
54. Ibid., 12–14.

55. Peter Albrecht and Paul Jackson. "Executive Summary." *Security System Transformation in Sierra Leone, 1997–2007*. Global Facilitation Network for Security Sector Reform (2009). 6. Web. Available online at http://www.ssrnetwork.net/documents/Publications/SierraLeoneBook/Security%20System%20Transformation%20in%20Sierra%20Leone,%201997-2007.pdf.

56. "About Us." *Namati*(2012). Web. Available online at http://www.namati.org/about/.

57. Vivik Maru. "Between Law and Society: Paralegals and the Provision of Justice Services in Sierra Leone and Worldwide." *The Yale Journal of International Law* 31 no. 2 (2006): 427–476.

58. Ibid.

59. Maru, "Between Law and Society," 428.

60. Pamela Dale. "Delivering Justice to Sierra Leone's Poor: An Analysis of the Work of Timap for Justice." World Bank Justice for the Poor Research Report. (2009). 21.

61. Vivek Maru. Personal interview by Holly Burkhalter. May 15, 2012.

62. Maru, "Between Law and Society," 441.

63. Personal interview with Vivek Maru. 2012. Interview conducted by Holly Burkhalter.

64. To learn more about Paz y Esperanza, visit www.pazyesperanza.org.

65. Golub, 9.

BIBLIOGRAPHY NOTE

For a complete list of sources used in the research and writing of *The Locust Effect*, please visit TheLocustEffect.com.

THE AUTHORS

Gary A. Haugen is founder and president of International Justice Mission (IJM), a global nonprofit organization dedicated to protecting the poor from violence by rescuing victims, bringing the criminals to justice, restoring survivors to safety and strength, and helping local law enforcement build a safe future. Haugen received the Trafficking in Persons Hero (TiP Hero) award, presented by former U.S. Secretary of State Hillary Clinton in 2012, for the work of his organization in combating human trafficking around the world. Prior to founding IJM in 1997, Haugen was Senior Trial Attorney with the Police Misconduct Task Force of the Civil Rights Division of the U.S. Department of Justice. He was detailed from the Justice Department to serve as Officer in Charge of the United Nations' investigation in the aftermath of the Rwandan genocide. A graduate of Harvard University and the University of Chicago Law School, Haugen has been honored for his human rights leadership by the University of Chicago, Pepperdine University, and Prison Fellowship and Sojourners, among other institutions. Haugen and the work of IJM have been featured by *Foreign Affairs*, *The New Yorker*, *The New York Times*, *U.S. News and World Report*, *Forbes*, *The Times of India*, CNN, Dateline NBC, FOX News, MSNBC, and National Public Radio, among many other media outlets

Victor Boutros is a federal prosecutor who investigates and tries nationally significant cases involving police misconduct, hate crimes, and international human trafficking around the United States on behalf of the U.S. Department of Justice. He is also a member of the Justice Department's Human Trafficking Prosecution Unit, which consolidates the expertise of some of nation's top human trafficking prosecutors and enhances the federal government's ability to identify and prosecute large human trafficking networks. Boutros trains federal and local law enforcement professionals on investigating and prosecuting federal civil rights crimes and has taught trial advocacy to indigenous lawyers working on similar issues in the developing world. Prior to his work with the Justice Department, Boutros worked on prison reform in Ecuador, documented bonded slaves in India, and helped strengthen anti-trafficking efforts as a visiting lawyer with the National Prosecuting Authority of South Africa. Boutros is a graduate of Baylor University, Harvard University, Oxford University, and the University of Chicago Law School.

INTERNATIONAL JUSTICE MISSION

International Justice Mission is a human rights agency that seeks to rescue thousands, protect millions and prove that justice for the poor is possible.

IJM's local teams of lawyers, social workers, investigators and community activists—the world's largest international corps of indigenous advocates providing direct service to victims of violence in the developing world—work within their own communities to protect the poor from violence by rescuing victims from the hand of abuse, bringing the criminals to justice, restoring survivors to safety and strength, and helping local law enforcement build a safe future that lasts.

Since the organization's founding in 1997, IJM's local teams have worked alongside local criminal justice systems to rescue thousands of victims of trafficking, slavery, abusive police, illegal property seizure and sexual violence, secure the conviction of hundreds of criminals for their abuse of the poor, and demonstrate groundbreaking transformations in "broken" criminal justice systems.

Inspired by a Christian conviction to love all people and to seek justice for victims of oppression, IJM serves all, without regard to race, religion or any other factor, and seeks to partner with all of good will. IJM has been featured by *The New York Times, The Times of India, The Washington Post, The Guardian, Foreign Affairs, Forbes Magazine, U.S. News & World Report, The New Yorker, Christianity Today,* NPR, BBC *World News,* and CNN, among many other outlets.

Learn more at IJM.org.

"WHAT DO I DO RIGHT NOW?"

Now that you've read *The Locust Effect*, if you can do just *one* thing today to combat the plague of violence, **share.**

The world has not yet woken up to the plague of violence that is engulfing the lives of our poorest neighbors around the world—or the desperate need that millions like Yuri, Laura and Mariamma have for effective law enforcement to protect them.

You can change that. Wake the world up.

Who is the most influential person you know? Who do you know who is passionate about poverty in our world? Tell that person about *The Locust Effect*. Pass along your copy of this book or encourage them to buy a copy (all author royalties go to protect those suffering from abuse), point them to TheLocustEffect.com or tell them about what you've read.

And when you've shared the message, let us know you did—and get resources and more action steps—at TheLocustEffect.com.

It's going to take a sustained struggle to finally address the terror of poverty in the developing world. But it is worth it. Thank you for taking this first, simple step with us.

Gary Haugen and Victor Boutros

INDEX